The Regulation of Medical Products

This book develops a theoretical framework for examining and assessing the regulatory arrangements for medical products.

Since the first half of the 20th century, the regulation of pharmaceuticals, medical devices and, more recently, biologicals have been controlled in many jurisdictions by specific regulatory regimes and agencies. Their regulatory mandates are similar – to ensure the quality, safety and efficacy of medical products. This book provides a timely and relevant assessment of the complexities of medical regulatory regimes, by drawing on a particular theory of political legitimacy. In this respect, the book adopts a 'dialogic' approach – according to which a shared set of normative beliefs and values are formulated – as a theoretical 'tool' to identify deficiencies in the regulatory arrangements for medical products. Drawing on several Australian cases studies, characterised by divergent normative perspectives, the book develops its dialogic approach in order to challenge the usual legitimation of regulatory regimes from the perspective of science alone. Specifically, it maintains that such regimes need to embrace a normative pluralism that admits a diversity of types and sources of knowledge.

This evaluation of the increasingly influential domain of medical regulation will appeal to a range of scholars and practitioners working in law, public health, politics and science and technology studies.

Penny Gleeson is Lecturer at Deakin Law School, Melbourne, Australia.

Part of the
LAW, SCIENCE AND SOCIETY
series

series editors

John Paterson, *University of Aberdeen, UK*
Julian Webb, *University of Melbourne, Australia*

for information about the series and details of previous and forthcoming titles, see https://www.routledge.com/Law-Science-and-Society/book-series/CAV16

A GlassHouse book

The Regulation of Medical Products

Dope, Drugs and Devices

Penny Gleeson

Routledge
Taylor & Francis Group
a GlassHouse Book

First published 2025
by Routledge
4 Park Square, Milton Park, Abingdon, Oxon OX14 4RN

and by Routledge
605 Third Avenue, New York, NY 10158

Routledge is an imprint of the Taylor & Francis Group, an informa business

A GlassHouse book

British Library Cataloguing-in-Publication Data
A catalogue record for this book is available from the British Library

Library of Congress Cataloging-in-Publication Data
Names: Gleeson, Penny, 1976- author.
Title: The regulation of medical products : dope, drugs, and devices / Penny Gleeson.
Description: Abingdon, Oxon [UK] ; New York, NY : Routledge, 2025. | Series: Law, science, and society | Includes bibliographical references and index.
Identifiers: LCCN 2024037696 (print) | LCCN 2024037697 (ebook) | ISBN 9781032277127 (hardback) | ISBN 9781032277172 (paperback) | ISBN 9781003293811 (ebook)
Subjects: LCSH: Medical instruments and apparatus industry–Law and legislation–Australia. | Medical supplies industry–Law and legislation–Australia. | Abortion–Law and legislation–Australia. | Drugs–Law and legislation–Australia. | Cannabis–Therapeutic use–Australia.
Classification: LCC KU1529.M43 G54 2025 (print) | LCC KU1529.M43 (ebook) | DDC 344.9404/2–dc23/eng/20240814
LC record available at https://lccn.loc.gov/2024037696
LC ebook record available at https://lccn.loc.gov/2024037697

ISBN: 978-1-032-27712-7 (hbk)
ISBN: 978-1-032-27717-2 (pbk)
ISBN: 978-1-003-29381-1 (ebk)

DOI: 10.4324/9781003293811

Typeset in Sabon
by Deanta Global Publishing Services, Chennai, India

Contents

Acknowledgements

This book began as a PhD thesis at Melbourne Law School and I am grateful to its academic and professional staff for facilitating my return to academia. I also thank those who contributed to formally overseeing my progress as a PhD candidate: Professors Kirsty Gover, Shaun McVeigh and Julian Webb; and the examiners of my thesis. Thank you also to the group of exceptional PhD and Masters candidates at Melbourne Law School. I am also grateful for the hospitality and support extended to me by the team at the Centre for Health, Law and Emerging Technologies (HeLEX) in Oxford.

Throughout the writing of this book I met many outstanding academics and individuals. I thank in particular Professors Marie Bismark, Lyle Gurrin, Clara Gaff, Graeme Hodge, Sheila Jasanoff, Jane Kaye, Louise Keogh, Megan Munsie, Jon Pierre, Alan Petersen; Associate Professor Marco Rizzi and Dr Peter Collins. I add to this list the generous mentorship and friendship of Professor Ingrid Winship.

The book was finished while I was an academic at Deakin Law School. I am grateful to the scholars, colleagues and friends there who have supported me.

My final words of thanks are for my friends and family. I include amongst these my PhD supervisors Professor Christine Parker and Associate Professor Michelle Taylor-Sands. I also owe particular thanks to Professor Sunita Jogarajan who was an exceptional and generous friend, colleague and mentor. I am immensely grateful for the friendship of Kathryn Anderson; Dr Jessica Bell and family; Annalise and Aurelia Bamford; Dr Anne Carter and family; Dr Elena Cirkovic; Dr Kathryn Greenman; Laura, Robert and Charlie Jericevich; Lucy Kirwan; Kellie Knowles, Associate Professor Yee-Fui Ng, Chantelle Renn, Dr Harriet Teare, Daniel Tynan, and Associate Professor Ntina Tzouvala.

My late mother, Helen Just, my stepmother Denise Whelan and my father Jim Gleeson enveloped me with a love of learning and the joy of knowledge. I thank them for their enduring love, faith and encouragement. Thank you also to my siblings: Michael, Jasmine, Adam, and their partners Suzanne, Tom and Maggie. Thank you also to my nephews, Roy and Charlie, Henry and Leo. My thanks reach to my extended family, including that of my partner.

My final words are for my partner, David: thank you, for teaching me the only thing that I ever truly needed to know.

Abbreviations

ACCS	Advisory Committee on Chemicals Scheduling
ACMS	Advisory Committee on Medicines Scheduling
ACMD	Advisory Committee on Medical Devices
ACSQHC	Australian Commission on Safety and Quality in Health Care
ACT	Australian Capital Territory
ADEC	Australian Drug Evaluation Committee
AHMAC	Australian Health Ministers' Advisory Council
Ahpra	Australian Health Practitioner Regulation Agency
AMA	Australian Medical Association
ARTG	Australian Register of Therapeutic Goods
AusPAR	Australian Public Assessment Reports
Cth	Commonwealth
DEA	United States Drug Enforcement Agency
EMA	European Medicines Agency
EU	European Union
FDA	United States Food and Drug Administration
ICH	International Council for Harmonisation of Technical Requirements for Pharmaceuticals for Human Use
ICMRA	International Coalition of Medicines Regulatory Authorities
IMDRF	International Medical Device Regulators Forum
IRIS	TGA Incident Reporting and Investigation Scheme
MTAA	Medical Technology Association of Australia
MOU	Memorandum of Understanding
NSW	New South Wales
NT	Northern Territory
POP	Pelvic Organ Prolapse
Qld	Queensland
RACGP	The Royal Australian College of General Practitioners
RANZCOG	The Royal Australian and New Zealand College of Obstetricians and Gynaecologists
SA	South Australia
SUI	Stress Urinary Incontinence
Tas	Tasmania
TGA	Therapeutic Goods Administration
UMDs	Urogynaecological Mesh Devices
Vic	Victoria
WA	Western Australia

Chapter 1

Introduction

Introduction

On 3 December 2020 an extraordinary press conference took place at Australia's Parliament House in Canberra. The topic was the COVID-19 pandemic, but this was not why it was extraordinary. Nor was it because the then Prime Minister and Health Minister were fronting the nation's media on the virus that had stopped the world. Across the globe it had become commonplace for a nation's political leaders to address their citizens about the pandemic declared by the World Health Organization in March of that year.[1] What made this press conference extraordinary was that alongside the country's leaders was the then head of the nation's regulator for medical products, the Therapeutic Goods Administration, or 'TGA'. There, in the nation's democratic home and alongside its political leaders, a regulator was addressing the people.[2]

A key focus of that press conference was when vaccines would be approved by the TGA to combat the Coronavirus-19 disease, and a reassurance by the TGA's head that 'safety, as well as performance, efficacy and the quality of these vaccines is front of mind'.[3] To achieve that, the TGA was sharing information with 'global groups of regulators' to 'see how these vaccines work … in tens or hundreds of millions of people'.[4]

In August 2020, the head of the United States Food and Drug Administration (the FDA) found himself in a similarly odd position. He flanked President Donald Trump in front of the White House press corps as the President advocated treatment of COVID-19 using the plasma of patients who had

1 'Coronovirus Disease (COVID-19) Pandemic', *World Health Organization* (Web Page, 2023) https://www.who.int/europe/emergencies/situations/covid-19.

2 'Press Conference – Australian Parliament House, ACT' *PM Transcripts: Transcripts from the Prime Ministers of Australia*, Department of the Prime Minister and Cabinet, 3 December 2020, <https://pmtranscripts.pmc.gov.au/release/transcript-43163>.

3 Ibid.

4 Ibid.

DOI: 10.4324/9781003293811-1

recovered from the virus, and which had received emergency approval by the FDA.[5] Four months later US media reported that the FDA Commissioner had been 'summoned to the White House' for a lengthy meeting with the President's Chief of Staff to discuss President Trump's impatience that the FDA had not yet approved a COVID-19 vaccine.[6]

In Europe, the United Kingdom's Medicines and Healthcare products Regulatory Agency (MHRA) inadvertently assumed the role of a political life-raft for Prime Minister Boris Johnson's government when the regulator approved a vaccine against COVID-19 prior to its international counterparts.[7] In less favourable terms, leaders of EU member states pushed the European Medicines Agency (EMA) into the spotlight by criticising the length of time that it took to approve a vaccine[8] and later publicly appealed to its guidance about rare side effects arising from the AstraZeneca vaccine.[9]

The public is not used to seeing the regulators of medical products in the spotlight. And the regulators themselves are not accustomed to addressing a national audience with a country's political leaders or to being the focus of controversy as is so commonly associated with the daily machinations of politics and the news cycle. Far more often regulators are relatively unknown, applying their expertise to the control of medicines and medical devices in the

5 Sasha Pezenik and Elizabeth Thomas, 'Trump, FDA Tout Covid-19 Convalescent Plasma Treatment, But Some Experts Express Concerns', *ABC News* (24 August 2020) https://abcnews.go.com/Health/fda-issue-emergency-authorization-convalescent-plasma-treatment-hospitalized/story?id=72556828. The FDA Commissioner was later widely criticised for his advocacy of the treatment in that press conference: see, eg, Katherine Eban, '"A Tsunami of Randoms": How Trump's COVID Chaos Drowned the FDA in Junk Science' *Vanity Fair* (19 January 2021) https://www.vanityfair.com/news/2021/01/how-trumps-covid-chaos-drowned-the-fda-in-junk-science.

6 Ben Gittleson, Katherine Faulders and Jordyn Phelps, 'FDA Chief Summoned to White House Amid Pressure to Authorize Vaccine Emergency Use', *ABC News* (2 December 2020) https://abcnews.go.com/Politics/fda-chief-summoned-white-house-amid-pressure-authorize/story?id=74480021; Jonathan Swan, 'Scoop: FDA Chief Called to West Wing', *Axios* (30 November 2020) https://www.axios.com/2020/12/01/fda-chief-called-to-west-wing.

7 Hans van Leeuwen, '"No Corners Have Been Cut" in Pfizer Approval: UK Vaccine Body', *Financial Review* (online, 3 December 2020) https://www.afr.com/world/europe/no-corners-have-been-cut-uk-vaccine-body-reassures-on-pfizer-jab-20201202-p56k2q.

8 Jillian Deutsch and Ashleigh Furlong, 'Pressure Mounts on EU Regulator to Approve Coronavirus Vaccine – and Fast', *Politico* (online, 12 December 2020) https://www.politico.eu/article/pressure-mounts-on-eu-regulator-to-approve-coronavirus-vaccine-quickly/; 'EMA Ought to Approve Coronavirus Vaccine Soon, Says Poland's PM', *Reuters* (online, 11 December 2020) https://www.reuters.com/article/eu-summit-vaccine-poland/ema-ought-to-approve-coronavirus-vaccine-soon-says-polands-pm-idINW8N2ID004/.

9 'France to Suspend AstraZeneca COVID Vaccine Pending EMA Guidance', *Reuters* (online, 16 March 2021) https://www.reuters.com/article/france-spain-vaccine-astrazeneca-idINL8N2LD54D/; 'French PM Castex Receives AstraZeneca Shot in Bid to "Restore Public Confidence"', *France24* (online, 19 March 2021) https://www.france24.com/en/france/20210319-french-pm-castex-to-get-astrazeneca-shot-in-bid-to-restore-public-confidence.

bureaucratic shadows. Yet the COVID-19 pandemic put these entities – and their leaders – front and centre of the health, policy and political fight against the virus. The public were told that they were essential in the front line battle to prevent, treat and cure COVID-19. Vaccines, face masks and hand sanitisers became part of our day-to-day routine. And medical regulators were at the vanguard of whether such products were approved as safe and effective to protect the nation. The COVID-19 pandemic made regulators of medical products part of our daily lives in a far more visible and compelling way than ever before.

This book is about those regulators, and more specifically about their political legitimacy. In particular, it is about why the political legitimacy of regulators of medical products is important, how and why it is challenged and what should be done in light of those challenges. The COVID-19 pandemic brought regulators of medical products into the spotlight to an extent that they had not previously experienced. But it was not the first time that these regulators were the focus of instances of public controversy. This book will focus on such examples to examine and highlight the importance of political legitimacy to the regulation of medical products.

Like pharmaceuticals and medical devices themselves, the regulatory environment for these products is itself global in nature, the significance of which was highlighted and enhanced during the COVID-19 pandemic.[10] It is beyond the scope of this work to examine such regulation by reference to all regulators of medical products worldwide. This book will therefore do so by primarily examining the Australian regulator of medical products, the Therapeutic Goods Administration. While the Australian market for medical products is relatively small,[11] I will highlight shortly why the TGA is a highly appropriate focus for such analysis.

This introductory chapter begins by outlining key aspects of the regulation of medical products worldwide before summarising the interrelationship between national regulators that regulatory harmonisation has encouraged. It highlights the spotlight the COVID-19 pandemic has shone on the regulation of medical products and the consequent importance of the regulation

10 Therapeutic Goods Administration ('TGA'), *International Engagement Strategy 2021–2025: Advancing Australia's Health through International Regulatory Engagement* (2021) 6, https://www.tga.gov.au/resources/publication/publications/tga-international-engagement-strategy-2021-2025; Wendy Elizabeth Bonython and Bruce Baer Arnold, 'Transitioning Up to Best Practice, or Down to the Bare Minimum? Global Harmonisation of Regulation of Therapeutic Goods' in Umair Ghori, Mary Hiscock, Louise Parsons et al (eds) *Globalisation in Transition: Human and Economic Perspectives* (2023, Springer) 45.

11 Parliament of Australia, House of Representatives Standing Committee on Health, Aged Care and Sport, *The New Frontier – Delivering Better Health for All Australians: Inquiry into Approval Processes for New Drugs and Novel Medical Technologies in Australia* (Final Report, November 2021) 85.

of medical products and its investigation. The chapter then introduces the Australian regulatory regime for medical products as the focus of this book and the concept of political legitimacy as a tool for its investigation. It introduces the three case studies that will be examined in this book and how their failings in political legitimacy point to challenges to be addressed. Finally, it provides an outline of the book's structure.

The Global Regulation of Medical Products

The Role of Regulatory Regimes for Medical Products

Medical products in today's Global North are as common to many of us as milk and bread. They include pharmaceuticals or medicines (such as paracetamol and vaccines), medical devices (like bandages and syringes) and biological material (that is, tissue or cell-based products). Yet, until the COVID-19 pandemic, we rarely considered whether and how such products are approved and monitored by the state. In Australia, such medical products are referred to as 'therapeutic goods' under the regulatory regime overseen by the TGA.[12] The US FDA similarly oversees the regulation of pharmaceuticals, medical devices and biological materials, as well as food, cosmetics and tobacco products.[13] In Europe, the European Medicines Agency's ('EMA') role is largely focussed on the regulatory oversight of 'medicinal products'.[14] With some important exceptions, the EMA's role does not include medical devices. These are instead primarily regulated by individual member states.[15]

In broad terms, these regulatory regimes are all concerned with applying a risk-based framework to ensure the safety, efficacy and quality of medical products.[16] A key means by which this is achieved is the role of regulatory regimes for medical products as, in effect, 'approval schemes' for such products. That is, the regulator must approve the product in one of a number of ways before it can be made available to the public. For this reason the regulators of medical products have often been described as 'gatekeepers'.[17] For example, in Australia medical products can only be supplied, sold, imported or exported according to the federal *Therapeutic Goods Act 1989* ('the TGA

12 *Therapeutic Goods Act 1989* (Cth) s 3 (definitions of 'therapeutic goods', 'therapeutic use', 'medical device', 'biological') ss 41BD, 32A.

13 *Federal Food, Drug and Cosmetic Act*, 21 USC (1938); 'What Does FDA Regulate', *FDA: US Food & Drug Administration* (Web Page, 18 January 2022) <https://www.fda.gov/about-fda/fda-basics/what-does-fda-regulate>.

14 Sabrina Rottger-Wirtz, *The Interplay of Global Standards and EU Pharmaceutical Regulation: The International Council for Harmonisation*' (Hart Publishing, 2021) 11.

15 'Medical Devices', *European Medicines Agency* (Web Page) <https://www.ema.europa.eu/en/human-regulatory-overview/medical-devices>.

16 See, eg, Bonython and Arnold (n 10) 46.

17 See, eg, ibid 56.

Act'), associated subsidiary legislation and other instruments.[18] Similar provisions apply under the US regulatory regime.[19] In Europe, the EMA regulatory regime provides a centralised means for authorisation of medicines, biologicals and certain veterinary medicines for supply and sale in the European Union (EU) and certain member states of the European Economic Area.[20] Each regulatory regime also plays an important role in the regulatory compliance of medical products after they are approved for supply. This is often referred to as 'pharmacovigilance' and in the Australian context as 'post-market monitoring', which is examined further in Chapter 6.[21]

The objectives of these regulatory regimes are analogous: a primary goal of the TGA Act, and therefore of the TGA itself, is the 'quality, safety, efficacy and timely availability' of therapeutic goods that are used in or exported from Australia.[22] The FDA describes its mission as including responsibility 'for protecting the public health by ensuring the safety, efficacy and security of human and veterinary drugs, biological products, and medical devices; and by ensuring the safety of our nation's food supply, cosmetics and products that emit radiation'.[23]

Similarly, the EMA's role is neatly summarised as 'central' to 'the marketing authorisation procedure'[24] of medicinal products and 'the coordination of the scientific evaluation of the quality, safety and efficacy of medicinal products which are subject to Community marketing authorisation procedures'.[25] The EMA operates within the unique context of the European Union (EU).[26] It undertakes its regulatory responsibilities, including recommendations for the approval of medicines, through committees which include individuals

18 See, eg, 'Overview of Supplying Therapeutic Goods in Australia' *Therapeutic Goods Administration*, (Web Page, 28 August 2020) https://www.tga.gov.au/overview-supplying-therapeutic-goods-australia.

19 See, eg, *Federal Food, Drug and Cosmetic Act*, 21 USC (1938) §355, §360c.

20 European Medicines Agency, *The European Regulatory System for Medicines: Bringing New Safe and Effective Medicines to Patients Across the European Union* (2023); Fabian Grunwald and Tom Stargardt, 'Harmonizing Regulatory Market Approval of Products with High Safety Requirements: Evidence from the European Pharmaceutical Market' (2024) *Health Economics* 1.

21 See, eg, *Therapeutic Goods Act 1989* ss 41MP, 41MPA; *Regulation (EC) No 726/2004 of the European Parliament and of the Council of 31 March 2004 Laying Down Community Procedures for the Authorisation and Supervision of Medicinal Products for Human and Veterinary Use and Establishing a European Medicines Agency* ('*Regulation (EC) No 726/2004*') [2004] OJ L 136, art 1; *Food and Drug Administration*, 21 CFR 314.80 (2024).

22 *Therapeutic Goods Act 1989* (Cth) s 4(1).

23 'What We Do' *FDA: US Food & Drug Administration* (Web Page, 21 November 2023) <https://www.fda.gov/about-fda/what-we-do>.

24 Rottger-Wirtz, *The Interplay of Global Standards and EU Pharmaceutical Regulation* (n 14) 21.

25 Ibid 21, citing *Regulation (EC) No 726/2004* (n 21) art 57.

26 Ibid 12.

from member states.[27] Ultimately, however, it is the European Commission that receives the EMA's recommendation as to whether a medicine should be approved and determines whether it can be supplied throughout the EU.[28] Typically, manufacturers of pharmaceuticals will seek the centralised EMA process to obtain approval for the marketing of their product.[29] It is, however, possible for approval to also be obtained directly from the relevant regulatory authority in a member state and via mutual recognition of such authorisations.[30]

In the view of the National Academy of Sciences, therefore,

> [t]he standards for ... safety efficacy, and quality judgments among the major well-resourced regulators (the U.S. Food and Drug Administration [FDA]; the European Medicines Agency; the Pharmaceuticals and Medical Devices Agency, Japan; Health Canada; the Medicines & Healthcare products Regulatory Agency, UK; Swissmedic; and the Therapeutic Goods Administration, Australia) are well known and similar, if not identical.[31]

(It goes on to state, however, that the ultimate decision about the approval of a medical product is 'an important sovereign decision for each national regulator to make, based on what is appropriate' and the relevant 'level of risk tolerance'.[32])

What further links all of these regulatory regimes are consistent and evolving challenges in their operation.[33] How should they approach the regulation

27 European Medicines Agency, *From Laboratory to Patient: The Journey of a Medicine Assessed by EMA* (2019) 7, 12–13, 15, 17–21. For an overview of the role of 'regulatory cooperation' in the EU in relation to medical products see Rottger-Wirtz, *The Interplay of Global Standards and EU Pharmaceutical Regulation* (n 14) 14–17.

28 European Medicines Agency, *From Laboratory to Patient* (n 27); *Regulation (EC) No 726/2004* (n 21) 311. Note that the European Commission has proposed a new Regulation and Directive to replace the above: 'Reform of the EU Pharmaceutical Legislation', *European Commission* (Web Page, 26 April 2023) <https://health.ec.europa.eu/medicinal-products/pharmaceutical-strategy-europe/reform-eu-pharmaceutical-legislation_en>.

29 European Medicines Agency, *From Laboratory to Patient* (n 27) 2. See also Grunwald and Stargardt (n 20).

30 'Authorisation Procedures – National Authorisation Procedures', *European Commission* (Web Page) https://health.ec.europa.eu/medicinal-products/legal-framework-governing-medicinal-products-human-use-eu/authorisation-procedures-national-authorisation-procedures_en; European Medicines Agency, *From Laboratory to Patient* (n 27) 2.

31 National Academies, *Regulating Medicines in a Globalized World: The Need for Increased Reliance Among Regulators (2020)* (National Academies Press, 2020) http://nap.nationalacademies.org/25594 xi–xii.

32 Ibid xii.

33 Holly Fernandez Lynch and I Glenn Cohen, 'Introduction' in Holly Fernandez Lynch and I Glenn Cohen (eds) *FDA in the Twenty-First Century: The Challenges of Regulating Drugs and New Technologies* (Columbia University Press, 2015) 1, 15–16.

of new medical products such as genetic and mobile health technologies,[34] or the re-emergence of substances such as medical cannabis and psychedelics?[35] What is the appropriate regulatory balance between ensuring the safety and efficacy of medical products and the timeliness of their availability to the public?[36] To what extent, and how, should such regulators engage with industry, different parts of government and the public without compromising their responsibilities?[37] Should they be funded on a cost-recovery basis from commercial entities seeking medical product approval or would the regulator's independence be better protected if funds were raised from public taxes?[38] What role should medical product regulators have in relation to the liability of manufacturers of medical products that cause illness and injury?[39] While the answers to many of these questions may differ between jurisdictions, regulators of medical products in Europe, the United States, Australia and elsewhere all grapple with similar issues. And while the focus of this book is Australia and the Global North, it is acknowledged that a further array of complex issues face regulators of medical products in the Global South.[40] It is therefore vital that research such as this assess the role of regulatory regimes for medical products.

Regulatory Harmonisation

Regulators of medical products have, in part, sought to meet these similar challenges through enhanced international harmonisation of their respective regulatory regimes.[41] The following brief description of these efforts further

34 Ibid 1; Christopher Rudge, Sara Attinger and Ian Kerridge et al 'A New Priority Pathway for Biologicals in Australia: Contextualising and Evaluating the Proposed Reforms' (2022) 29 *Journal of Law and Medicine* 677.

35 Jennifer H Martin, Wayne Hall and Mary-Ann Fitzcharles et al, 'Ensuring Access to Safe, Effective, and Affordable Cannabis Based Medicines' (2020) 86 *British Journal of Clinical Pharmacology* 630; Amy L McGuire, Holly Fernandez Lynch and Lewis A Grossman et al, 'Pressing Regulatory Challenges for Psychedelic Medicine' (2023) 380 *Science* 347.

36 Fernandez Lynch and Cohen (n 33) 1–2.

37 National Academies of Science, *Stronger Food and Drug Regulatory Systems Abroad* (The National Academies Press, 2020) 4-3–4-6.

38 Ibid 4-6–4-10.

39 See, eg, Catherine M Sharkey, 'The Opiod Litigation: The FDA is MIA' (2020) 124 *Dickinson Law Review* 669; Esme Shirlow and Thomas Faunce, 'Recent Legal Developments and the Authority of the Australian Therapeutic Goods Administration' (2009) 16 *Journal of Law and Medicine* 764; *Gill v Ethicon Sarl* [2018] FCA 470 [75]–[76], [79]; *Therapeutic Goods Act 1989* (Cth) s 61A.

40 See, eg, National Academies of Science (n 37) 3-1, 3-23; Dinesh S Thakur and Prashant Reddy T, *The Truth Pill: The Myth of Drug Regulation in India* (Simon & Schuster, 2022).

41 The term 'harmonisation' here is used broadly to encompass both practices towards alignment of technical requirements and more generally informal and formal collaborative arrangements. See Bonython and Arnold (n 10) 45–6.

fills in the picture of the operation of regulatory regimes for medical products globally. Significantly, it also highlights that what affects one regime may affect another, and that the focus on one jurisdiction in this book likely points to similar challenges faced by other regulatory regimes for medical products.

The objective of international harmonisation of the regulation of medical products is for such products to be more quickly approved in multiple jurisdictions and to make use, in effect, of shared resources between regulators as part of that process.[42] This does not suggest, however, that there are not diverse perspectives and interests at play in the global regulatory context, nor that such harmonisation is not difficult to achieve or is without criticism.[43] But the move towards regulatory harmonisation continues apace. The TGA, EMA and FDA all publicly promote their extensive programs for engagement in international harmonisation activities and in international partnerships and support.[44] In recent years this has encompassed a recognition of the significance that the COVID-19 pandemic has played in increasing jurisdictions' need and desire to work collaboratively and to 'accelerate' the approval and availability of medical products relevant to that, and future, health emergencies.[45]

To an extent the EMA is an obvious example of such harmonisation across Europe. Attempts to align the regulatory regimes also cross continents. This can be seen in the establishment and operation of cooperative regulatory entities, the reliance by individual regulatory regimes on commonly applied regulatory arrangements and on mutual recognition agreements and memoranda of understanding (MOUs).[46]

The International Council for Harmonisation of Technical Requirements for Pharmaceuticals for Human Use (ICH) is a primary example of cooperation between regulatory regimes.[47] Its membership also includes pharmaceutical industry representatives.[48] First established as the International Conference on Harmonisation in 1990 between the USA, European

42 See, eg, ibid 56–7.

43 See, eg, ibid 48–9, 52, 57–9.

44 See, eg, 'International Programs', *FDA*, (Web Page) <https://www.fda.gov/international-programs>; 'International', *Therapeutic Goods Administration* (Web Page, 2017) https://www.tga.gov.au/about-tga/international; 'International Activities' *European Medicines Agency* (Web Page, 2024) <https://www.ema.europa.eu/en/partners-networks/international-activities>.

45 TGA, *International Engagement Strategy 2021–2025*, (n 10) 6. See also at 8–11.

46 National Academies, *Regulating Medicines in a Globalized World* (n 31) xi–xii.

47 See, eg, Sabrina Rottger-Wirtz, *The Interplay of Global Standards and EU Pharmaceutical Regulation* (n 14) ; Ashley Boam and Theresa Mullin, 'FDA Voices: Harmonization – Convergence in the Global Regulatory Village' (2023) *Pharmaceutical Technology* 30.

48 'Welcome to the ICH Official Website', *ICH* (Web Page) https://www.ich.org/.

Community and Japan,[49] the ICH is a non-profit body whose mission is to 'achieve greater harmonisation worldwide to ensure that safe, effective and high quality medicines are developed, and registered and maintained in the most resource efficient manner whilst meeting high standards'.[50] To this end it produces a series of guidelines in the areas of quality, safety, efficacy and in other 'multidisciplinary' areas such as gene therapy[51] through consultation with its twenty-one members.[52] While Australia's TGA is not a member of the ICH, its regulatory requirements are 'closely aligned' with relevant ICH guidelines.[53]

The TGA, along with the EMA and FDA, is a member of the International Coalition of Medicines Regulatory Authorities (ICMRA).[54] In broad terms, the ICMRA aims to enhance dialogue and the exchange of information to support the safety, efficacy and quality of medicines, and 'other health products as appropriate'.[55] The ICMRA's role was most recently notable during the COVID-19 pandemic. With the World Health Organization it committed to cooperation between its members to ensure speedy access to medical products related to COVID-19 while also maintaining standards for safety and efficacy.[56] This included the sharing of relevant data between regulators of medical products 'in real time to facilitate multi-country approvals'.[57] More specifically, the Pharmaceutical Inspection Cooperation Scheme seeks to establish harmonised standards between national regulators in relation to 'Good Manufacturing Practice' of medical products.[58]

The International Medical Device Regulators Forum (IMDRF) plays a key role in the harmonisation of medical device regulation to 'strategically

49 'History', *ICH* (Web Page) https://www.ich.org/page/history; Bonython and Arnold (n 10) 52.

50 'Welcome to the ICH Official Website' (n 48).

51 'ICH Guidelines', *ICH* (Web Papge) https://www.ich.org/page/ich-guidelines.

52 'Process of Harmonisation', *ICH* (Web Page) https://www.ich.org/page/process-harmonisation.

53 'International Scientific Guidelines Adopted in Australia', *Therapeutic Goods Administration* (Web Page) <https://www.tga.gov.au/resources/resource/international-scientific-guidelines>.

54 'ICMRA Membership Country/Region and Regulatory Authority's Website', *ICMRA* (Web Page, 2024) <https://www.icmra.info/drupal/en/aboutus/participatingregulatoryauthorities>.

55 'History of ICMRA', *ICMRA* (Web Page, 2024) https://www.icmra.info/drupal/aboutus/history; ICMRA, *International Coalition of Medicines Regulatory Authorities: Terms of Reference and Rules of Procedure* (15 November 2023) https://www.icmra.info/drupal/sites/default/files/2024-01/icmra_terms_of_reference_15november2023.pdf 3, n 1.

56 'WHO-ICMRA Joint Statement on the Need for Improved Global Regulatory Alignment on COVID-19 Medicines and Vaccines', *ICMRA* (Web Page, 6 November 2020) https://icmra.info/drupal/covid-19/who_icmra_statement.

57 Ibid.

58 'Introduction', *PIC/S* (Web Page) https://picscheme.org/en/about.

accelerate medical device regulatory convergence'.[59] Its members comprise representatives of national regulators, including from Australia, the USA and the EU.[60] An additional entity that sought regulatory cooperation during the COVID-19 pandemic was the 'Access Consortium'.[61] 'Access' referred to its members: Australia, Canada, Singapore, Switzerland and the United Kingdom. Its goals include 'opportunities for information and work-sharing' in relation to the approval of new medicines and post-approval safety monitoring.[62] In the TGA's view, this means that medical products can be 'simultaneously' evaluated for approval 'with reduced evaluation times'.[63] More regionally focussed entities driving regulatory harmonisation include the Asia-Pacific Economic Cooperation forum's Regulatory Harmonization Steering Committee; the Pan American Network for Drug Regulatory Harmonization;[64] and, more recently, the anticipated establishment of the African Medicines Agency.[65]

In addition to the institutional arrangements for regulatory harmonisation, regulators increasingly rely on Mutual Recognition Agreements, MOUs and other arrangements to facilitate the exchange of information about medical products between jurisdictions. Such arrangements may include the recognition of certain regulatory analysis and decisions by another regulator.[66] Parties to such agreements include the TGA, EMA, FDA and the relevant regulatory agencies for Japan, Canada and Switzerland.[67] They have been observed to 'inform and build trust among regulators facing the same

59 International Medical Device Regulators Forum, *Final Document: IMDRF Terms of Reference* (18 January 2024) https://www.imdrf.org/documents/imdrf-terms-reference 5.

60 Ibid 7.

61 'COVID-19 Vaccine: International Collaboration' *Therapeutic Goods Administration* (Web Page, 16 September 2021) https://www.tga.gov.au/products/covid-19/covid-19-vaccines/covid-19-vaccine-international-collaboration.

62 'Australia-Canada-Singapore-Switzerland-United Kingdom (Access) Consortium' *Therapeutic Goods Administration* (Web Page, 2 November 2023) <https://www.tga.gov.au/international-activities/australia-canada-singapore-switzerland-united-kingdom-access-consortium>.

63 COVID-19 Vaccine: International Collaboration' (n 61).

64 Orin Chisolm and Helen Critchley, 'Future Directions in Regulatory Affairs' (2023) 9 *Frontiers in Medicine* 1, 6.

65 'African Medicines Agency (AMA)' *AUDA-NEPAD: African Union Development Agency* (Web Page, 2022) <https://www.nepad.org/microsite/african-medicines-agency-ama>; see also Nancy Ngum, Margareth Ndomondo-Sigonda, Stuart Walker et al 'Regional Regulatory Harmonisation Initiatives: Their Potential Contribution to the Newly Established African Medicines Agency' (2023) 145 *Regulatory Toxicology and Pharmacology* 1.

66 Boam and Mullin (n 47) 31; Tania Teixeira, Sandra L Kweder and Agnes Saint-Raymond, 'Are the European Medicines Agency, US Food and Drug Administration, and Other International Regulators Talking to Each Other? (2020) 107 *Clinical Pharmacology & Therapeutics* 507; Chisolm and Critchley (n 64) 6.

67 Teixeira et al (n 66) 508–10.

challenges'.[68] Better resourced and established regulators further seek to enhance the capacity of regulators in their region through a range of training and other assistance programs.[69]

While this book will largely focus on the Australian regulatory regime for medical products, the context of the significant harmonisation of such regulatory regimes means that its examination inevitably highlights other regulatory regimes. This is most notably illustrated in Chapter 6 on urogynaecological mesh and the Australian regulatory regime's reliance on European device approvals. And it is clear that there is international enthusiasm for harmonisation between the regulators of medical products to continue and increase.[70] It has been anticipated that the future of regulatory harmonisation will see '"a single regulatory position worldwide' as part of a global approach to quality".[71] While clearly this is an ambitious goal, it indicates the force with which the medical product sector is moving towards enhanced globalisation and therefore the strength of the push for regulatory harmonisation. What happens in any one jurisdiction will almost inevitably play out in some way in another. To this end, I will shortly turn to look at Australia as the focus of this book.

An Unwavering Spotlight on Medical Products Regulation: The COVID-19 Pandemic

The above description plainly distils the vital importance of regulating medical products and the role of regulators in doing so. As already mentioned, the COVID-19 pandemic brought this into sharp and constant focus for the broader public. While the examples identified at the start of this chapter highlight this, a more definitive search of media sources show that the TGA, EMA and FDA were cited in the media many more times during the pandemic than in the years that preceded it.[72] This is consistent with surveys

68 Ibid 508.

69 See, eg, TGA, *International Engagement Strategy 2021–2025*, (n 10) 11; 'Training Opportunities for Non-EU Regulators', *European Medicines Agency* (Web Page, 2024) https://www.ema.europa.eu/en/partners-networks/international-activities/training-opportunities-non-eu-regulators; 'Fellowships', *European Medicines Agency* (Web Page, 2024) https://www.ema.europa.eu/en/partners-networks/international-activities/fellowships; 'Partnerships and Collaboration', *FDA* (Web Page, 2023) <https://www.fda.gov/international-programs/partnerships-and-collaboration>.

70 See, eg, National Academies, *Regulating Medicines in a Globalized World* (n 31).

71 Boam and Mullin (n 47) 30, quoting FDA Principal Deputy Commissioner, Janet Woodcock.

72 A search of the media database Factiva shows that between 30 January 2019 and 5 May 2023 the Food and Drug Administration was cited in English-language publications 450,638 times, compared with between 30 January 2016 and 30 December 2019 when it was cited 323,943 times. For the same dates the European Medicines Agency was cited 97,081 times and 49,688 respectively and the Therapeutic Goods Administration 23,585 times and 8281

by the regulatory agencies themselves, which indicated, for example, a 17% rise in awareness of the TGA during the years of the pandemic from 2020 to 2022.[73]

The far-reaching health, social and economic impact of the virus rendered those regulatory regimes pivotal. They became the means by which medical products to treat COVID-19 could be approved, and therefore the lives of those infected saved.[74] And the means by which the virus spread could be contained through the approval of tests, vaccines, masks and certain sanitisation products.[75] In the midst of crisis and widespread misinformation about COVID-19,[76] media, public health officials and politicians frequently pointed to the regulators of medical products as the source of decisions and accurate information on which the public should rely.[77] Most relevantly, analysis of

times respectively: 'Factiva', *Dow Jones* (Online Database, 2024) <https://www.dowjones.com/professional/factiva/>.

73 'TGA Stakeholder Survey Report 2023', *Therapeutic Goods Administration* (Web Page, 1 December 2023) https://www.tga.gov.au/resources/publication/publications/tga-stakeholder-survey-report-2023. See also, European Medicines Agency, *Annual Report 2022* (Report, 2023) 106 <https://www.ema.europa.eu/en/documents/annual-report/2022-annual-report-european-medicines-agency_en.pdf>; European Medicines Agency, *Annual Report 2021* (Report, 2022) 133 https://www.ema.europa.eu/en/documents/annual-report/2021-annual-report-european-medicines-agency_en.pdf.

74 See eg, 'COVID-19 Treatments', *Therapeutic Goods Administration* (Web Page, 20 August 2021) https://www.tga.gov.au/products/covid-19/covid-19-treatments; 'COVID-19 Medicines', *European Medicines Agency* (Web Page, 2024) https://www.ema.europa.eu/en/human-regulatory-overview/public-health-threats/coronavirus-disease-covid-19/covid-19-medicines; 'Know Your Treatment Options for COVID-19', *FDA: US Food and Drug Administration* (Web Page, 19 December 2023) https://www.fda.gov/consumers/consumer-updates/know-your-treatment-options-covid-19.

75 See eg, 'COVID-19 Tests', *Therapeutic Goods Administration* (Web Page, 16 May 2024) https://www.tga.gov.au/products/covid-19/covid-19-tests; 'COVID-19 Vaccines', *Therapeutic Goods Administration* (Web Page) https://www.tga.gov.au/products/covid-19/covid-19-vaccines; 'COVID-19 Personal Protective Equipment', *Therapeutic Goods Administration* (Web Page) https://www.tga.gov.au/products/covid-19/covid-19-personal-protective-equipment-ppe; 'COVID-19 Medicines', *European Medicines Agency* (Web Page, 2024) https://www.ema.europa.eu/en/human-regulatory-overview/public-health-threats/coronavirus-disease-covid-19/covid-19-medicines; 'COVID-19 Vaccines', *FDA: US Food and Drug Administration* (Web Page, 30 August 2024) https://www.fda.gov/emergency-preparedness-and-response/coronavirus-disease-2019-covid-19/covid-19-vaccines; 'Safely Using Hand Sanitizer', *FDA, US Food and Drug Administration* (Web Page, 12 April 2023) https://www.fda.gov/consumers/consumer-updates/safely-using-hand-sanitizer.

76 See, eg, Sooyoung Kim, Ariadna Capasso and Shahmir H Ali et al, 'What Predicts People's Belief in COVID-19 Misinformation? A Retrospective Study Using a Nationwide Online Survey Among Adults Residing in the United States' (2022) 22 *BMC Public Health* 2114; Darren M Roberts and Alexandra Bennett, 'COVID-19 and the Quality Use of Medicines: Evidence, Risks and Fads' (2020) 43 *Australian Prescriber* 78.

77 See, eg, 'France to Suspend AstraZeneca COVID Vaccine Pending EMA Guidance', *Reuters* (online, 16 March 2021) https://www.reuters.com/article/france-spain-vaccine-astrazeneca

public health misinformation also highlighted the importance of 'the legitimacy of the information as well as the source' in effectively engaging citizens in health messages at a time of 'scientific uncertainty'.[78]

While the COVID-19 pandemic has for many been consigned relievedly to history, the threat of future pandemics and their widespread disruption continues.[79] So too, does the pivotal role that the regulatory regimes for medical products will play, including the need for regulators worldwide to cooperate across borders.[80] In reflecting on its role during the pandemic, the TGA has also observed that its role has changed 'to provide greater education and support, including to the public, which has been highlighted during the COVID-19 response'.[81] As we will see, this has not always been the perspective held by that regulator.

Australia's Regulatory Regime for 'Therapeutic Goods' in the Global Context

In examining the regulation of medical products this book will focus on Australia and what its political legitimacy can tell us about the regulation of such products more broadly. Australia is an appropriate jurisdiction for such an examination. While a smaller player in the global pharmaceutical market, it has a solid international regulatory presence and influence. It has, for example, been a consistent and leading member in the global community of regulators of medical products, including the International Coalition of Medicines Regulatory Authorities, the International Medical Device Regulators Forum and the ICH.[82] It is focussed on 'convergence of regulatory approaches for

-idINL8N2LD54D/; Scott Gottlieb and Mark McClellan, 'You Can trust the FDA's Vaccine Process', *Wall Street Journal* (online, 20 September 2020) https://www.wsj.com/articles/you-can-trust-the-fdas-vaccine-process-11600633351; Jack Snape, 'Pfizer COVID-19 Vaccine Approved for Use by TGA in Australia Ahead of Rollout', *ABC News* (online, 25 January 2021) https://www.abc.net.au/news/2021-01-25/pfizer-covid-19-vaccine-approved-australia-tga/13087990; Jessica Yun, Supratim Adhikari and Paul Sakkal, 'Push for "Gold Standard PCR" Leaves Gaping Hole in Rapid Test Supply', *The Sydney Morning Herald* (online, 31 December 2021) https://www.smh.com.au/business/consumer-affairs/gold-standard-pcr-push-leaves-a-gaping-hole-in-rapid-test-supply-20211229-p59knx.html.

78 Judith Green, Edward F Fischer and Des Fitzgerald et al, 'The Publics of Public Health: Learning from COVID-19' (2022) 32 *Critical Public Health* 592, 593–4.

79 See, eg, World Health Organization, 'WHO Launches New Initiative to Improve Pandemic Preparedness' (News Release, 26 April 2023) https://www.who.int/news/item/26-04-2023-who-launches-new-initiative-to-improve-pandemic-preparedness.

80 TGA, *International Engagement Strategy 2021–2025* (n 10) 6.

81 Ibid 5.

82 Therapeutic Goods Administration, *TGA International Engagement Strategy 2016–2020: Highlights and Achievements Report* (9 September 2021) https://www.tga.gov.au/resources/publication/publications/tga-international-engagement-strategy-2016-2020-highlights-and-achievements-report; TGA, *International Engagement Strategy 2021–2025* (n 10) 5–6.

pharmaceutical approvals and monitoring',[83] including through alignment with the US Food and Drug Administration and its counterparts in Europe.[84] And it plays a leading role in enhancing the capabilities of smaller and developing regulators of medical products in Southeast Asia and the western Pacific.[85] The TGA has also been a 'first mover' in approving certain medical products, notably psilocybin and MDMA for the limited treatment of certain psychiatric disorders,[86] and international regulators have taken note of this.[87]

In focusing on the Australian context, this book is the first major critical work on the regulation of therapeutic goods in Australia and its regulator, the TGA. The home of the TGA is in Symonston on the outskirts of Canberra. It sits next to the former Brucella Building, once a Commonwealth government complex built in the mid-1970s[88] to house a program of Australia's National Biological Standards Laboratory, a precursor of the TGA Laboratories.[89] That program was the elimination of Brucellosis, a disease caused by the bacterial organism *Brucella* and contracted by humans from pigs and cattle.[90] Due to the transmissible nature of its namesake, the building was in many respects fortress-like.[91] Black-and-white photos reveal a laboratory adorned with enclosed safety benches and fume hoods. Shots of the exterior present a brutalist-inspired design, purpose-driven and compact, jarring with the surrounding Australian landscape.[92] The official history of the TGA only briefly discusses the Brucella Building,[93] yet its proximity to the current home of the TGA is a reminder of the enduring scientific traditions and principles at the heart of the control of therapeutic goods. These principles have fortified

83 Ibid 5.
84 Ibid 5–6; 'TGA Supports MHRA's New International Recognition Framework for Medicines', *Therapeutic Goods Administration* (Web Page, 2 June 2023) < https://www.tga.gov.au/news/news/tga-supports-mhras-new-international-recognition-framework-medicines>.
85 TGA, *International Engagement Strategy 2021–2025* (n 10) 11.
86 Rich Haridy, 'Australia to Prescribe MDMA and Psyilocybin for PTSD and Depression in World First' (2023) 619 *Nature* 227.
87 McGuire et al (n 35) 348.
88 John McEwen, *A History of Therapeutic Goods Regulation in Australia* (2007) 70; Han Nguyen, 'Site of Former Federal Government IT Provider Up for Auction', *The Canberra Times* (online, 2 March 2018) <https://www.canberratimes.com.au/story/6022269/site-of-former-federal-government-it-provider-up-for-auction/>; National Archives of Australia, B6295, 3652F, *Canberra Brucella Vaccine Testing Laboratory* (7 June 1974) 1.
89 McEwen (n 88) 70–1. The building appears to have later been transferred to the private sector: Nguyen (n 88).
90 McEwen (n 88) 70; 'Brucellosis Laboratory Case Definition (LCD)', *Department of Health* (Web Page) <https://www.health.gov.au/resources/publications/brucellosis-laboratory-case-definition?language=en>.
91 McEwen (n 88) 80.
92 National Archives of Australia, B6295, 4034A, *Brucella Vaccine Test Laboratories* (18 April 1975) 1; National Archives of Australia (n 88) 1.
93 McEwen (n 88) 70–1, 76, 80, 83.

the frequently expressed view that the regulation of therapeutic goods in Australia is effective, credible, reliable and uncontroversial.[94]

Almost 300 kilometres northeast of Symonston is the Sydney Registry of the Federal Court of Australia. There, on 21 November 2019, Justice Katzmann found in favour of a group of women injured by urogynaecological mesh medical devices. The devices were manufactured and supplied by companies forming part of the Johnson & Johnson corporate family.[95] The Court later ordered the companies to pay the women compensation for chronic and aggravating pain; infection; extrusion and erosion of the devices into their organs; reduced quality of life; and psychiatric and other injuries.[96] In reaching her findings, Katzmann J concluded that 'the scheme governing medical devices was largely self-regulating'.[97] Women injured by the mesh devices were present in the courtroom to hear the decision, some standing because of pain and others assisted by mobility aids.[98] Outside, an advocate for the women told the media that they 'have been placated, ignored and this needs to be immediately addressed by the Government'.[99] The enduring scientific foundations of an ostensibly meritorious regulatory regime were of little meaning or comfort to these women or the Court.

These contrasting vignettes highlight the paradox of the regulatory regime for therapeutic goods – that it is at once widely well-regarded and marked by public controversy. The therapeutic goods regulatory regime is considered to be well-functioning, credible and uncontentious by a range of institutions and individual commentators within Australia and internationally. However, the longstanding and generally unchallenged operation of the regulatory regime sits uneasily with intermittent instances of public discord and controversy in which it has been involved. These examples can be described as 'difficult' or 'hard' cases, characterised by conflicts that have shone a spotlight on the traditionally demure regulator, the TGA, and its regulatory regime.

This paradox leads to the question that is central to this book: what do instances of public controversy tell us about the regulatory regime for therapeutic goods in Australia and, consequently, for medical products in other

94 See, eg, Lloyd Sansom, Will Delaat and John Horvath, *Review of Medicines and Medical Device Regulation: Report on the Regulatory Framework for Medicines and Medical Devices* (Department of Health, March 2015) vii.

95 *Gill v Ethicon Sàrl (No 5)* [2019] FCA 1905.

96 *Gill v Ethicon Sàrl (No 6)* [2020] FCA 279; *Gill v Ethicon Sàrl (No 5)* [2019] FCA 1905; Liv Casben, 'Johnson & Johnson to Pay $2.6m to Women with Faulty Pelvic Mesh Implants', *ABC News* (online, 4 March 2020) <https://www.abc.net.au/news/2020-03-03/johnson-and-johnson-damages-for-vaginal-mesh-implants/12021908>.

97 *Gill v Ethicon Sàrl (No 5)* [2019] FCA 1905, [3687]. See also at [1408].

98 Casben (n 96).

99 Ibid.

jurisdictions? This is answered by investigating three contentious case studies involving the regulatory regime through the conceptual lens of political legitimacy: the regulation of medicinal cannabis; the control of the abortion drug RU486; and, as mentioned, the events surrounding urogynaecological mesh devices. What emerges from this analysis is a picture of a regulatory regime whose political legitimacy has been challenged and undermined. This has occurred because of the continued dominance over the regulatory regime of the influential ideologies of scientism and technocracy. An evolution in the ideological foundations of the regulatory regime, underpinned by the notion of regulatory 'courage',[100] is proposed to address deficiencies in political legitimacy and to better enable the regime, and others, to engage with future issues of public discord. In particular, it is argued that the therapeutic goods regulatory regime should embrace a new ethos, including a normatively pluralist perspective on regulatory knowledge and a facilitative approach to expertise.

It is useful at this point to provide definitions of three key terms and phrases referred to throughout the book. First, Julia Black's expansive definition of 'regulation' is adopted:

> [b]y regulation is meant sustained and focused attempts to change the behavior of others in order to address a collective problem or attain an identified end or ends, usually through a combination of rules or norms and some means for their implementation and enforcement, which can be legal or non-legal.[101]

A simpler, and equally broad, definition of regulation is 'influencing the flow of events'.[102] Second, the phrase 'therapeutic goods regulatory regime' encompasses all legal and non-legal instruments, policies, practices, decisions and actors that surround the control of therapeutic goods in Australia. This includes the role and actions of the TGA as regulator, its officers, and the Minister for Health as the responsible Minister. Third, the phrase 'regulatory power' describes the exercise of power by, and via, this regulatory regime.[103]

This book does not contend that the conclusions reached about the Australian regulatory regime for medical products can or should be applied identically to other jurisdictions. It does, however, claim that such conclusions

100 Oren Perez, 'Courage, Regulatory Responsibility, and the Challenge of Higher-Order Reflexivity' (2014) 8 *Regulation & Governance* 203.

101 Julia Black, 'Constructing and Contesting Legitimacy and Accountability in Polycentric Regulatory Regimes' (2008) 2 *Regulation & Governance* 137, 139.

102 Christine Parker and John Braithwaite 'Regulation' in Mark Tushnet and Peter Cane (eds) *The Oxford Handbook of Legal Studies* (Oxford University Press, 2005) 119, 119.

103 See generally Mark Thatcher and Alec Stone Sweet, 'Theory and Practice of Delegation to Non-majoritarian Institutions' (2002) 25(1) *West European Politics* 1.

are indicative of challenges facing other regulatory regimes for medical products, and that this examination is therefore instructive for those regulatory regimes, in relation to both analogous case studies in those regimes and more broadly.

Political Legitimacy as a Tool of Investigation

The concept of political legitimacy is applied in this book to investigate the paradoxical perspectives of the therapeutic goods regulatory regime. Broadly, theories of political legitimacy seek to explain the 'justification of political authority'[104] and, in relation to regulatory schemes, the 'right to govern in the manner in which they are governing'.[105] Commentary relevant to regulatory studies frequently invokes political legitimacy as a basis on which to evaluate regulatory arrangements. This includes research on international and regional institutions, healthcare, essential services (e.g., telecommunications) and the financial and justice systems.[106] In particular, political legitimacy has been used to analyse regulatory arrangements similar to the Australian therapeutic goods regulatory regime in other jurisdictions.[107] Commentators typically emphasise that political legitimacy is an important indicator of compliance with, and the effectiveness, stability and durability of, a regulatory

104 Steffen Schneider et al, *Democracy's Deep Roots: Why the Nation State Remains Legitimate* (Palgrave Macmillan, 2010) 2.

105 Julia Black, 'Legitimacy and the Competition for Regulatory Share' (LSE Law, Society and Economy Working Papers No 14/2009, London School of Economics and Political Science, Law Department, 2009) 9.

106 See, eg, David Beetham and Christopher Lord, *Legitimacy and the European Union* (Longman, 1998); David Beetham, 'Revisiting Legitimacy, Twenty Years On' in Justice Tankebe and Alison Liebling (eds), *Legitimacy and Criminal Justice: An International Exploration* (Oxford University Press, 2013) 19 ('Revisiting Legitimacy'); Lisa Maria Dellmuth, Jan Aart Scholte and Jonas Tallberg, 'Institutional Sources of Legitimacy for International Organisations: Beyond Procedure Versus Performance' (2019) 45(4) *Review of International Studies* 627; Pedro A Villarreal, 'Pandemic Declarations of the World Health Organization as an Exercise of International Public Authority: The Possible Legal Answers to Frictions between Legitimacies' (2016) 7(1) *Goettingen Journal of International Law* 95; Keith Syrett, *Law, Legitimacy and the Rationing of Health Care* (Cambridge University Press, 2007); Camilla Pondel, 'Legitimacy in Australia's Financial System External Dispute Resolution Framework: New and Improved or Simply New?' (2019) 42(1) *University of New South Wales Law Journal* 335; Karen Lee, *The Legitimacy and Responsiveness of Industry Rule-Making* (Hart, 2018); Justice Tankebe, 'Legitimacy and Regulatory Compliance' in Maria Krambia-Kapardis (ed), *Financial Compliance: Issues, Concerns and Future Directions* (Palgrave Macmillan, 2019) 47; Tom Tyler, 'Trust and Legitimacy: Policing in the USA and Europe' (2011) 8 *European Journal of Criminology* 254.

107 Syrett (n 106); Keith Syrett, 'Courts, Expertise and Resource Allocation: Is There a Judicial "Legitimacy Problem"'? (2014) 7(2) *Public Health Ethics* 112.

regime.[108] Legitimacy is consequently indicative of the ultimate achievement of a regulatory regime's goals.[109] Casey and Scott, for example, contend that 'legitimacy is of crucial important[ce] to the processes of the crystallization' through which regulatory norms successfully direct behaviour.[110]

In examining what constitutes 'good regulation', commentators have identified diverse criteria they consider essential to the attainment of political legitimacy.[111] A different approach is adopted in this book. The concept of political legitimacy is applied as a theoretical 'tool' to three case studies, described below. In relation to each case study the question considered is, 'What does this case study tell us about the political legitimacy of the regulatory regime?' Through this analysis, deficiencies in the political legitimacy of the regulatory regime are identified. Common themes are drawn from across the case studies and challenges for the therapeutic goods regulatory regime are described. The resulting analysis provides broader insights about the challenges confronting the regulatory regime and, ultimately, an enhanced understanding of the paradoxically opposed perspectives on its legitimacy.

Political legitimacy and its diverse interpretations have long been a topic of debate among philosophers, political scientists and sociologists.[112] Chapter 3 outlines these views and proposes an approach to political legitimacy, which this book labels the 'constant dialogic approach'. This approach reformulates the dialogic approach to political legitimacy developed by criminologists Anthony Bottoms and Justice Tankebe.[113] Bottoms and Tankebe drew on the foundational work of political and social scientist David Beetham, as explained in Chapter 3.[114] The constant dialogic approach developed requires

108 See, eg, David Beetham, *The Legitimation of Power* (MacMillan Education, 2013) xi–xii, 33–4; Donal Casey and Colin Scott, 'The Crystallization of Regulatory Norms' (2011) 38(1) *Journal of Law and Society* 76, 88–9.

109 See, eg, Robert Baldwin, Martin Cave and Martin Lodge, *Understanding Regulation: Theory, Strategy, and Practice* (Oxford University Press, 2011) 26–7. See also Bronwen Morgan and Karen Yeung, *An Introduction to Law and Regulation: Text and Materials* (Cambridge University Press, 2007) 221–3, 237–79.

110 Casey and Scott (n 108) 89.

111 See, eg, Black, 'Constructing and Contesting Legitimacy and Accountability' (n 101) 145–6; Morgan and Yeung (n 109) 238–53.

112 See, eg, Black, 'Constructing and Contesting Legitimacy and Accountability (n 101) 144–5; Beetham, 'Revisiting Legitimacy' (n 106) 19–20; Tom R Tyler and Yuen J Huo, *Trust in the Law: Encouraging Public Cooperation with the Police and Courts* (Russell Sage Foundation, 2002); Melissa Schwartzberg, 'Introduction' in Jack Knight and Melissa Schwartzberg (eds), *Political Legitimacy* (NYU Press, 2019) 1; Chris Thornhill, 'Political Legitimacy: A Theoretical Approach between Facts and Norms' (2011) 18(2) *Constellations: An International Journal of Critical and Democratic Theory* 135, 135–6.

113 See, eg, Anthony Bottoms and Justice Tankebe, 'Beyond Procedural Justice: A Dialogic Approach to Legitimacy in Criminal Justice' (2012) 102(1) *Journal of Criminal Law and Criminology* 119.

114 See, eg, Beetham *The Legitimation of Power* (n 108).

that political legitimacy should be analysed as three elements: (a) a constant dialogue, (b) through which a set of shared normative beliefs and values are formulated (c) between all parties to a power relationship. The constant dialogic approach therefore reflects the relational and dialogical nature of political legitimacy advocated by Bottoms and Tankebe. It provides a readily applicable framework for the analysis of the legitimacy of the therapeutic goods regulatory regime which also mitigates the limitations of Beetham's, and Bottoms's and Tankebe's, approaches.

The terms 'political legitimacy' and 'legitimacy' will be used interchangeably throughout this book. Certain commentators have distinguished between 'legitimacy', as the outcome of the rightful justification of power, and 'legitimation' as the 'process' of attaining such a justification.[115] For simplicity, this approach will not be adopted as both the process and outcome of the legitimacy of the therapeutic goods regulatory regime will be analysed simultaneously.

Failings in Political Legitimacy and Addressing the Challenges

The rationale for this book lies in two broadly inconsistent accounts of the therapeutic goods regulatory regime. As stated, the orthodox perspective of the regulatory regime is that it is uncontroversial, meritorious and well-regarded.[116] An alternative perspective arises episodically around instances of public contest and controversy in relation to the regulation of particular therapeutic goods. This is a contrasting account of the regulatory regime that portrays it as marked by conflict and unable to provide a stable regulatory basis for the control of therapeutic goods. Such cases are frequently characterised by divergent ethical or social views or otherwise conflicting normative perspectives.

The three case studies examined in this book concern the regulation of medicinal cannabis, RU486 and urogynaecological mesh devices. Chapters 4 to 6 investigate what these case studies tell us about the political legitimacy of the therapeutic goods regulatory regime according to the constant dialogic approach. The cases are characterised by public controversy and conflict and are therefore examples of the alternative account of the therapeutic goods regulatory regime that this book seeks to investigate. The exploration of these three difficult or hard cases reflects an established approach in regulatory studies. Julia Black states that such case studies provide insights

115 See, eg, Tankebe (n 106) 52; Beetham *The Legitimation of Power* (n 108).
116 See, eg, Sansom et al (n 94) 3.

about regulatory regimes that more 'typical' or non-controversial examples may not.[117] As examples of divergent normative positions, they are sites of contestation, and consequently 'vehicle[s] for change' in which 'new meanings develop ... and different systems of knowledge and configurations of power come in to prominence'.[118] Similarly, Parker et al. describe contentious decisions in relation to the regulation of food as 'flashpoints" for policy contestation'.[119] At least one of the selected cases – that of urogynaecological mesh devices – arguably contains elements of what Hutter and Lloyd-Bostock refer to as a 'regulatory crisis'.[120] However, the selected case studies are not necessarily preceded by the 'disaster' or 'wider crisis' that characterises their concept.[121] The cases considered here are therefore better described as difficult cases for the regulatory regime.

The first case study concerns the regulation of medicinal cannabis in Australia between 2014 and 2018. Prior to this, medicinal cannabis was effectively prohibited and unavailable under the therapeutic goods regulatory regime. Individual patients, carers, parts of the media and the Victorian state government successfully advocated for greater access to the drug.[122] The regulatory regime was consequently subject to direct and indirect criticism by patients, the media and through alternative regulatory proposals, including replacing the TGA as the responsible regulator of the drug.[123]

The second case study is the medical abortion drug RU486. RU486 was the subject of intense political and public contest in Australia between 1996 and 2012. Amendments to legislation passed in 1996 significantly recast and

117 See, eg, Black, 'Constructing and Contesting Legitimacy and Accountability (n 101) 138. See also Bent Flyvbjerg, 'Five Misunderstandings About Case-Study Research' (2006) 12(2) *Qualitative Inquiry* 219, 229–30.

118 Julia Black, 'Regulatory Conversations' (2002) 29(1) *Journal of Law and Society* 163.

119 Christine Parker et al, 'Can the Hidden Hand of the Market Be an Effective and Legitimate Regulator? The Case of Animal Welfare under a Labeling for Consumer Choice Policy Approach' (2017) 11 *Regulation & Governance* 368, 369, 372.

120 Bridget M Hutter and Sally Lloyd-Bostock, *Regulatory Crisis: Negotiating the Consequences of Risk, Disasters and Crises* (Cambridge University Press, 2017) 4.

121 The authors considered case studies including the experience of bovine spongiform encephalopathy (BSE) in the United Kingdom, the 2007 to 2009 financial crisis and the 2010 Icelandic volcanic eruption. Notably, however, they conclude that the nature of 'recognizing or defining a disaster or crisis' involves 'socially constructed events': ibid 4–9, 28–9, 225, 230–1. See also Julia Black, 'Learning from Regulatory Disasters' (LSE Law, Society and Economy Working Papers 24/2014, London School of Economics and Political Science, Law Department, 2014).

122 See, eg, Victorian Law Reform Commission, *Medicinal Cannabis* (Report, August 2015).

123 See, eg, Michelle Ainsworth, 'Labor to Seek to Overturn "Outdated" Laws Banning Medical Marijana [sic]', *The Herald Sun* (online, 24 August 2014) <https://www.heraldsun.com.au/news/victoria-state-election-2014/labor-to-seek-to-overturn-outdated-laws-banning-medical marijana/newsstory/beed551eb3fa33278061e5e2e9edf8d5>; Regulator of Medicinal Cannabis Bill 2014 (Cth).

diminished the role of the therapeutic goods regulatory regime in relation to this drug.[124] The amendments also effectively prevented Australian women from accessing medical abortion for a decade.

The third and final case study concerns medical devices, specifically the controversy surrounding the regulation of urogynaecological mesh between 2006 and 2021. These devices caused extensive, and in many cases irreversible, harm to a minority of female patients in which the devices were implanted. Strong and sustained advocacy by patients, carers, public health advocates, the media and politicians led to civil litigation against the manufacturers and suppliers of the devices, and a parliamentary review of their use and regulation in Australia.[125] The therapeutic goods regulatory regime was criticised for its role in the harm the devices caused, including the protracted period over which they remained available.[126]

As stated, each case study is investigated through the lens of the constant dialogical approach to political legitimacy (and elements of other legitimacy frameworks on which it is based). This analysis reveals that the political legitimacy of the therapeutic goods regulatory regime was challenged or undermined in each instance. The failure by the regulatory regime to adopt a constant dialogic approach to legitimacy is identified as the reason for these challenges. However, each case study divulges different reasons for these failings in political legitimacy.

In light of the analysis of the case studies, two broad or 'meta' challenges are identified to explain the failings in the political legitimacy of the therapeutic goods regulatory regime. The first challenge is the regulatory regime's technocratic *approach* to expertise. In particular, this approach is both directive (professing certainty and neutrality) and unilateral (excluding other voices and knowledge). The second challenge is the dominance of scientism in relation to the *content* of the knowledge and expertise on which the regulatory regime relies. The content of this expertise is almost exclusively grounded in the sciences. This second challenge leads to certain obstacles for the regulatory regime, specifically 'epistemic arrogance' (an overconfidence in the ability of science to provide solutions for the regulatory regime) and 'epistemic scarcity' (limiting the types of knowledge on which the regulatory regime relies).[127] The identification of these challenges enables a better understanding of the paradoxical accounts of the regulatory regime.

124 Caroline de Costa, *RU-486: The Abortion Pill* (Boolarong Press, 2007).

125 See, eg, *Gill v Ethicon Sàrl (No 5)* [2019] FCA 1905; Senate Community Affairs References Committee, Parliament of Australia, *Number of Women in Australia Who Have Had Transvaginal Mesh Implants and Related Matters* (Report, March 2018).

126 See, eg, Senate Community Affairs References Committee (n 125).

127 See, eg, Michael Patrick Lynch, 'Arrogrance, Truth and Public Discourse' (2018) 15(3) *Episteme* 283; Perez (n 100).

Oren Perez's notion of 'regulatory courage' is drawn on as a starting point from which to address these challenges.[128] Regulatory courage can be interpreted as meaning confidence and open-mindedness by a regulatory regime to new values, beliefs and norms beyond, and contrary to, those inherent in its historical foundations. Regulatory courage may be particularly relevant to a regulatory regime in the midst of public controversy, competing norms and without clear and certain guidance as to a path forward.

Regulatory courage should be embraced by the therapeutic goods regulatory regime to address the challenges it faces through two bold ideological changes. First, the regulatory regime should embrace an approach to regulatory knowledge and expertise that considers a diversity of types and sources of knowledge. This is described as normative pluralism. Second, the regulatory regime should adopt the concept of facilitative regulation and expertise advocated by Black.[129] Each of these changes has the potential to address multiple aspects of the challenges facing the regulatory regime. These proposals are fundamentally ideological in nature. They therefore differ from the more pragmatic responses of many regulatory commentators to circumstances where political legitimacy is found to be lacking.[130] Instead, the suggested approach requires an evolution in the foundational ideas of the regulatory regime which directly challenges its scientific and technocratic nature. This is necessary before a more 'practical' program of regulatory reform can be initiated.

Outline of the Book

The following summary sets out how the key contentions of this book are presented in the subsequent chapters.

Chapter 2 begins by describing the ideologies of scientism and technocracy. It outlines the historical development of the American and European regulatory regimes for medical products and then turns to the history and current operation of the Australian regulatory regime. The chapter argues that the history and contemporary operation of these regulatory regimes reflect the dominant influence of the ideologies of scientism and technocracy.

Chapter 3 sets out the approach to the theoretical concept of political legitimacy that is adopted to analyse the regulation of medical products – here, particularly in relation to the controversial case studies involving the Australian therapeutic goods regulatory regime. The foundational framework

128 Perez (n 100).

129 Julia Black, 'Regulation as Facilitation: Negotiating the Genetic Revolution' in Roger Brownsword, WR Cornish and Margaret Llewelyn (eds), *Law and Human Genetics: Regulating a Revolution* (Hart Publishing, 1998) 29.

130 See, eg, Tankebe (n 106). Cf Black, 'Legitimacy and the Competition for Regulatory Share' (n 105) 31.

of political legitimacy developed by Beetham and the dialogic approach of Bottoms and Tankebe are discussed. The chapter proposes that the legitimacy of regulatory arrangements for medical products should be analysed by applying a 'constant dialogic approach' to political legitimacy. This approach is a reformulation of Bottoms's and Tankebe's dialogic approach.[131] The three elements of the constant dialogic approach are described as a readably applicable means of investigating regulatory regimes for medical products.

Chapters 4 to 6 consider three controversial or difficult case studies involving the Australian therapeutic goods regulatory regime. Each case study is analysed using the constant dialogic approach to political legitimacy in order to identify what the case indicates about the political legitimacy of that regulatory regime and consequential insights for its international counterparts.

Chapter 4 examines the reforms to the regulation of medicinal cannabis in Australia between 2014 and 2018. It begins by outlining the contemporary regulation of the drug in Australia and describes the 2014 to 2018 reforms. It identifies three distinct 'voices' that emerged during the regulatory reform period. Each voice expressed different views about reform, the nature of the drug and reflected different types of knowledge about medicinal cannabis and historical approaches to its regulation. Voices that diverged from the status quo of the therapeutic goods regulatory regime, such as those expressed by patients and carers, challenged the regime's political legitimacy. The regulatory regime's failure to adopt a constant dialogic approach to political legitimacy explains this challenge. Its absence is evident in two respects. First, the regulatory regime did not engage in a constant dialogue with all parties to the regulatory relationship, and consequently with their respective perspectives. Second, the regulatory regime emphasised traditional scientific expertise over discourse with alternative sources of knowledge. The chapter concludes by describing relevant developments in the regulation of medicinal cannabis since 2018.

Chapter 5 considers the events surrounding the regulation of the medical abortion drug RU486 in Australia between 1996 and 2012 and what they indicate about the political legitimacy of the therapeutic goods regulatory regime. The history of the law of abortion in Australia and the regulation of RU486 is outlined. This includes legislative reform in 1996 that effectively removed the drug from the ambit of the regulatory regime for a decade. The chapter argues that distinct conceptualisations of abortion are co-produced with surrounding social and ethical issues. It contends that the 1996 amendments, and related events, constituted a challenge to the political legitimacy of the therapeutic goods regulatory regime. This challenge was facilitated by the regulatory regime's failure to act consistently with the constant dialogic approach to political legitimacy in two key respects. First, the regulatory

131 See, eg, Bottoms and Tankebe (n 113).

regime did not identify or engage with the social and ethical issues surrounding RU486. This effectively camouflaged highly relevant normative questions and deterred any possible congruence in the values held by the regulatory parties. Second, the regulatory regime failed to engage in an ongoing and relational dialogue with all regulatory parties, further inhibiting political legitimacy. The chapter concludes by describing recent reforms to the regulation of RU486.

Chapter 6 analyses the case study of the regulation of urogynaecological mesh devices in Australia between 2006 and 2021. The regulation of urogynaecological medical devices and key regulatory actors are outlined. The polycentric nature of the regulatory regime is then described. Crucial to these regulatory arrangements is a 'loop' of information generation and exchange between these regulatory actors, including the TGA. The public, political and judicial criticism of the regulatory regime in relation to urogynaecological mesh devices is identified as constituting a challenge to the regime's political legitimacy. Contributing to this challenge was the absence of a constant dialogic approach to legitimacy. This is illustrated by the divergence in values and beliefs held by the relevant regulatory parties about what constituted an acceptable risk of harm in relation to the devices, and an adverse event resulting from their use. Failings in the polycentric information loop are argued to have contributed significantly to the absence of a constant dialogic approach to political legitimacy.

The final two chapters discuss how the challenges to the legitimacy of the regulation of medical products can be addressed. These chapters draw together insights from the analysis of the case studies and draw conclusions for the regulation of medical products.

Chapter 7 brings together the insights from the case studies that constitute 'teachable moments' for the regulation of medical products. It concludes that the application of the constant dialogic approach to political legitimacy highlights significant deficiencies in the political legitimacy of Australia's therapeutic goods regulatory regime. The reasons for these failings lie in two 'meta' challenges related to the nature and foundations of the regulatory regime. The first is the technocratic characteristics of the regulatory regime, in particular its directive and unilateral approach to expertise. The second challenge is the regulatory regime's almost exclusive reliance on scientific expertise and the epistemic constraints this imposes on the regime. These two challenges are arguably inherent to the regulatory regime, stemming from the dominant influence of scientism and technocracy as discussed in Chapter 2.

There are two significant implications of this analysis. These implications are generalisable beyond the Australian regulatory regime for medical products to its international counterparts. First, the legitimacy of such regulatory regimes should not be assessed purely from the perspective of their founding ideologies in scientism and technocracy. Second, an evolution in the ideologies that shape these regulatory regimes is required. Drawing on the concept of regulatory 'courage',[132] the chapter argues that regulatory schemes for medical products should embrace normative pluralism and an approach to expertise that is fundamentally facilitative.

Chapter 8 concludes this book and revisits its primary rationale – to understand what can be learned about the regulation of medical products from the theoretical perspective of political legitimacy. It anticipates some of the expectations, challenges and opportunities for the regulation of medical products that will follow in the wake of the COVID-19 pandemic. It argues, for example, that in this 'post-pandemic' environment, the general public and media will be more informed and vocal about issues affecting individual and public health. Regulatory decisions and actions in relation to medical products will therefore be subject to higher levels of scrutiny than prior to the start of the pandemic. The chapter discusses new opportunities for regulatory regimes to embrace regulatory courage and ideological evolution. It concludes that the theoretical lens of political legitimacy will continue to provide meaningful insights for regulatory regimes for medical products and a sound basis for necessary and urgent change.

132 Perez (n 100).

Chapter 2

The Foundations of the Regulation of Medical Products

Introduction

This chapter begins by outlining the historical development of the regulation of medical products. Its focus is on the ideological foundations of the evolution of those regulatory regimes – namely scientism (the belief that scientific knowledge can provide comprehensive answers to all societal problems) and technocracy (broadly, government by experts). It begins with a description of these ideologies and their role in the foundations of the regulation of medical products in the United States, the European Union and Australia. While this part of the chapter loosely adopts a chronological perspective on the development of the regulatory regime, it does not provide a definitive historical description.[1] The discussion then outlines the current operation of the Australian regulatory regime, providing the basis for the exploration of case studies in the chapters to follow. The chapter concludes by explaining how the ideologies of scientism and technocracy dominate the regulatory power exercised by the Australian regime for medical products. More specifically it will be argued that scientific-based expertise is a both a *mandatory* and *a dominant* condition of the regulatory regime's power and *the primary conduit* of that power.

The importance of these contentions regarding the nature of the therapeutic goods regulatory regime will be revisited in Chapter 7. It will be argued that the deficiencies in the political legitimacy of the regulatory regime, identified in the three case studies, can be explained by the continued influence of scientism and technocracy. The ongoing dominance of these ideologies contributes to significant challenges for the Australian regulatory regime and, arguably, its international counterparts also.

1 See, eg, a monograph commissioned by the TGA: John McEwen, *A History of Therapeutic Goods Regulation in Australia* (2007).

DOI: 10.4324/9781003293811-2

Scientism and Technocracy: The Ideas That Shaped the Regulation of Medical Products

The two ideologies that fundamentally underpin the regulatory regimes for medical products are scientism and technocracy. Broadly, scientism advances 'a supreme confidence that the practices and attitudes associated with natural sciences could be effectively used to solve a virtually unlimited range of social problems'.[2] While clearly related, scientism is distinguishable from science itself. The latter term encapsulates the 'gathering and reporting of empirical findings' according to an established methodology,[3] while the former proclaims that science is the pinnacle of human knowledge and thought.[4] What scientism requires is an exhaustive commitment to scientific thought, knowledge and exploration: '[s]cientism entails a zealous metaphysical commitment and a requisite orthodoxy in method and in thought regarding the nature of the world and how understanding of the world is to be approached'.[5]

Scientism purports that alternative modes of knowledge – typically those grounded in the humanities – are incapable of providing answers to fundamental questions or addressing social problems. In essence, 'science is the only way to gain reliable knowledge about the world'.[6] Alternative sources of knowledge, such as most strands of philosophy and sociology, are perceived as subjective, irrational, uncertain and therefore of limited use.[7] Scientism consequently devalues questions about, or discussion of, morality, ethics and values.[8] Accordingly, it encourages a 'hierarchical' approach to knowledge that distinguishes between the value of different 'disciplines or discourses'.[9]

Scientism's perspective on, and approach to, knowledge finds its origins in the Scientific Revolution of the 17th century and in the Enlightenment's advocacy of human rationalism and reason.[10] The extensive influence of, and

2 Richard Olson, *Scientism and Technocracy in the Twentieth Century: The Legacy of Scientific Management* (Lexington Publications, 2016) 2. A variety of other consistent definitions of scientism exist, including, for example, those that focus on academic methodology.

3 Richard N Williams, 'Introduction' in Richard N Williams and Daniel N Robinson (eds), *Scientism: The New Orthodoxy* (Bloomsbury, 2015) 1, 4.

4 Tom Sorell, *Scientism: Philosophy and the Infatuation with Science* (Routledge, 1991) 1. See also Jeroen de Ridder, Rik Peels and Rene van Woudenberg, *Scientism: Prospects and Problems* (Oxford University Press, 2018) 29–31; Erikki Vesa Rope Kojonen, *The Intelligent Design Debate and the Temptation of Scientism* (Routledge, 2016) 4.

5 Williams (n 3) 2.

6 Kojonen (n 4) 2.

7 Ibid 2, 4.

8 See, eg, Brent Dean Robbins, *The Medicalized Body and Anesthetic Culture: The Cadaver, the Memorial Body, and the Recovery of Lived Experience* (Palgrave Macmillan, 2018) 58.

9 Nico Stehr and Reiner Grundmann, *Experts: The Knowledge and Power of Expertise* (Routledge, 2011) 65, discussing Raphael Sassower, *Knowledge without Expertise: On the Status of Scientists* (SUNY Press, 1993) 54.

10 Williams (n 3) 8–10.

diverse approaches to, scientism can be found in the work of Auguste Comte, Saint-Simon, Karl Popper and Karl Marx,[11] and its practical exposition in the writings of Frederick W Taylor, among many others.[12] Scientism has come to dominate most, if not all, private and public expressions of power in modern society, government and industry.[13] It is, for example, the dominant ideology of modern medicine and[14] is expressed in the spheres of contemporary politics and management as quantifiable measures of 'efficiency'.[15]

A significant expression of scientism's influence and reach has been in the domains of public administration and policy.[16] In that context, scientism 'lay embedded within movements associated with the terms "technocracy" and "technocratic"' – that is, in 'government by experts'.[17] 'Technocrats', as they have consequently become known, are 'those who exercise power by virtue of their technical knowledge'.[18] In essence the 'technocratic' approach to management generally, and public administration more specifically, promotes the application of neutral or apolitical expertise to advance 'administrative rather than political solutions to problems' in the public sphere.[19] Beetham and Lord note that advocates of technocracy 'claim that the public good is better realised through having professionals in charge, who are not subject to the vagaries, biases and distortions of democratic and especially electoral politics'.[20]

Underpinning this perspective is a reliance on the 'scientific foundations of ... expertise'.[21] Technocrats advocate that their expertise is the highly

11 See, eg, Lawrence M Principe, 'Scientism and the Religion of Science' in Richard N Williams and Daniel N Robinson (eds), *Scientism: The New Orthodoxy* (Bloomsbury, 2015) 41, 43; Daniel N Robinson, 'Science, Scientism and Explanation' at 23, 35; John Paterson, 'Trans-Science, Trans-Law and Proceduralization' (2003) 12(4) *Social & Legal Studies* 525, 529–30; Lee-Anne Broadhead and Sean Howard, 'Nanotechnology and the Developing Critique of Scientism' (2010) 74(4) *Science & Society* 553, 553–5.
12 See, eg, Olson (n 2).
13 Ibid xvi.
14 Robbins (n 8) 11.
15 See, eg, ibid 58.
16 See, eg, Anders Esmark, 'Maybe It Is Time to Rediscover Technocracy? An Old Framework for a New Analysis of Administrative Reforms in the Governance Era' (2017) 27(3) *Journal of Public Administration Research and Theory* 501.
17 Olson (n 2) ix; Paterson (n 11) 529.
18 Olson (n 2) ix, quoting Robert Putnam 'Elite Transformation in Advanced Industrial Societies' (1977) 10 *Comparative Political Studies* 383, 383.
19 Ibid xi (quoting Putnam, ibid, at 385–7). While the emphasis of this book is on the modern expressions of 'government by experts', its ancient origins can be located in Plato's discussion of 'philosopher kings': Plato, *Republic*, tr Robin Waterfield (Oxford University Press, 1993) 190–226.
20 David Beetham and Christopher Lord, *Legitimacy and the European Union* (Longman, 1998) 16–17.
21 Olson (n 2) xii. See also Beetham and Lord (n 20) 17.

preferable path to solving contemporary public policy and administrative challenges and that 'public opinion, sufficiently well informed, would accord with their views'.[22] Accordingly, technocracy has typically been viewed as a potential threat to democracy, particularly as its exercise and influence has grown in burgeoning state bureaucracies.[23]

An understanding of the nature of technocracy naturally requires some insight into what constitutes 'expertise' and who are 'experts'. While aspects of the nature of expertise will be discussed further in Chapter 7, it is useful at this point to briefly explore these terms. As Stehr and Grundmann state, '[t]he assertion that the carriers of expert knowledge ... are advancing into the centre of political decision-making power ... is dependent upon how the role of experts is defined and generally accepted'.[24] Expertise can be defined as 'specialised knowledge' and an expert as 'those who deal with *transferring* and *applying knowledge*'.[25] According to Stehr and Grundmann, contemporary experts '*pass on* access to specialized knowledge' to those who need it.[26] Experts are thus 'mediators between producers of knowledge and users of knowledge ... between those who create the capacity to take action and those whose task it is to act'. They emphasise that experts are not, however, 'passive' receivers and providers of knowledge. Instead, the 'work' of an expert 'alters the knowledge that they operate with', changing as the expert engages with it.[27] The regulatory regimes for medical products can be viewed as supporting this receipt, handling and passing on of specialised knowledge – in particular, scientific knowledge – as part of controlling the approval and supply of medical products in relevant jurisdictions.[28]

The History of the Regulation of Medical Products

Safety, quality and efficacy. These are the regulatory tenets reflected in the regimes for medical products of the United States, European Union, Australia and many other jurisdictions. Yet it took some time before all of these requirements were included as explicit values of these respective regulatory regimes. The following brief overview of the history of the regulation of

22 Olson (n 2) 40.
23 Paterson (n 11) 530; Olson (n 2) xiv, xvi–xvii.
24 Stehr and Grundmann (n 9) 86.
25 Ibid 8–9,12 (emphasis in the original).
26 Ibid 40 (emphasis in the original).
27 Ibid 41–2.
28 Jasanoff contends that 'regulatory science' – the use of 'science' in the formulation of policy – includes 'knowledge production', 'knowledge synthesis' and the 'prediction' of risk: Sheila Jasanoff, *The Fifth Branch: Science Advisers as Policymakers* (Harvard University Press, 1998) 77.

medical products in the United States, European Union and Australia highlights the key steps on this journey and how those regulatory regimes were imbued with and influenced by the principles of scientism and technocracy.

An Overview of the United States and European Union

Carpenter, writing extensively on the United States's FDA and its regulatory arrangements, considers that it has been the most emulated by international counterparts seeking to implement robust oversight of medical products.[29] It is therefore logical to briefly describe the history of this regulatory regime first, before moving on to discuss the trajectory that led to that of the European Union.

The United States

The birth of the United States regulation of medical products in the late 19th century lies with regulation at a state and local government level.[30] Federally, the passage of the *Biologics Act* 1902 and the *Pure Food and Drugs Act* 1906 marked the beginning of national regulation of medical products, driven by concerns about the adulteration of food and medicines.[31] These concerns were spearheaded by Harvey Washington Wiley, Head of the US Department of Agriculture's Bureau of Chemistry (later to be named the Food and Drug Administration[32]), and by consumer and women's groups.[33] Wiley was pivotal to achieving the passage of the 1906 Act. He was one of the motivated 'scientists and specialists' whose influence was clear during these early years of the regulatory regime for medical products.[34] So too, was the significant role of scientific evidence in supporting his position.[35] The political and economic context of the United States at that time also meant its lawmakers

29 John Carpenter, *Reputation and Power: Organizational Image and Pharmaceutical Regulation at the FDA* (Princeton University Press, 2010) 726.

30 Ibid 75.

31 Marc T Law, 'History of Food and Drug Regulation in the United States' in Robert Whaples (ed) (2004) *Economic History Association: Encyclopedia* https://eh.net/encyclopedia/history-of-food-and-drug-regulation-in-the-united-states/.

32 Food and Drug Administration (FDA), *A History of the FDA and Drug Regulation in the United States* (2006).

33 Carpenter (n 29) 75; Law (n 31).

34 E Pendleton Herring, 'The Balance of Social Forces in the Administration of the Pure Food and Drug Act' (1935) 13 *Social Forces* 358, 358.

35 Jillian London, 'Tragedy, Transformation, and Triumph: Comparing the Factors and Forces That Led to the Adoption of the 1860 Adulteration Act in England and the 1906 Pure Food and Drug Act in the United States' (2014) 69 *Food and Drug Law Journal* 315, 322–4.

were receptive to the new laws. Progressivism[36] laid sound ideological foundations for the reforms, including an enhanced appreciation of the role of the state in protecting the health of its citizens.[37] In doing so, it also advanced the ideology of scientism.[38]

As was often the case in the history of medical product regulation, wide coverage of deaths and illness associated with adulterated medicines and vaccines caused public outcry and also assisted in the passage of the early laws.[39] Their main achievement was enabling the confiscation of adulterated and fraudulently advertised food and medicines.[40] Led by key bureaucrats, the FDA pushed for stronger regulation in the 1930s.[41] It was not achieved, however, until 1938 when the *Federal Food, Drug and Cosmetic Act* 1938 was passed to replace the 1906 Act.[42] This required manufacturers of medical products to demonstrate the safety of their product before placing it on the market.[43] These pivotal reforms were achieved following the determination and widely publicised zeal of the FDA in responding to more than a hundred deaths from adulterated elixir sulfanilamide. It acted with almost the same determination in seeking to influence a report on the matter by the Secretary of the Department of Agriculture, which, reflecting the FDA's appeals, called for the introduction of a pre-market approval process for medical drugs and the requirement that drugs disclose their ingredients.[44] 'A few simple and inexpensive tests on experimental animals' would have revealed the danger of the sulfanamide product, the report stated.[45] Science was presented as *the*

36 The American Progressive movement advocated a range of government-led reforms in American politics and society including to combat inequality and poverty and to advance suffrage, labour rights, public education and health. Its presence was arguably dominant from the late 1800s to the early 1920s: Walter Nugent, *Progressivism: A Very Short Introduction* (Oxford University Press, 2010) 1–4. See also David B Woolner and John M Thompson (eds), *Progressivism in America: Past, Present and Future* (Oxford University Press, 2016) 6–7.

37 London (n 35) 337–8.

38 Scientism was one of the key features underpinning the Progressive ideology in America, reflecting, for example, one of the main tenants of 'scientific management' as espoused by Frederick Winslow Taylor in *The Principles of Scientific Management*, first published in 1911: Olson (n 2) 2, 14, citing Frederick Winslow Taylor, *The Principles of Scientific Management* (The Floating Press, 2012)

39 London (n 35) 327–8, 331–2.

40 Carpenter (n 29) 80–2; Mikkael A Sekeres, *Drugs and the FDA: Safety, Efficacy, and the Public's Trust* (MIT Press, 2022) 6.

41 Carpenter (n 29) 80–2.

42 Law (n 31).

43 FDA, *A History of the FDA and Drug Regulation in the United States* (2006).

44 Carpenter (n 29) 85–95, 98–100.

45 US Department of Agriculture, *Report of the Secretary of Agriculture on Deaths Due to Elixir Sulfanilamide-Massengill, Submitted in Response to Senate Resolution 194 of November 16, 1937*, Senate Document No 124, 75th Congress, quoted in Carpenter (n 29) 96–7.

solution to the scourge of adulterated medicines, and the men of the FDA as providing the bureaucratic capability to implement its power. Carpenter describes the Secretary's Report as follows:

> It proceeded, not unlike a court brief, from facts to conclusions in a near deductive manner. The ... report started on its strongest footing, dealing first with those facts of a scientific character, then the facts of historical and legal ones. It then proceeded methodically to limitations of the 1906 statute and suggestions for reform.[46]

The significance of the reforms cannot be overstated: they gave the FDA powers to determine what a new drug was, and in relation to medical devices and cosmetics. It further paved the way for the regulation of medical products not only in the United States but in other jurisdictions that have sought to replicate it.[47] Notably, the reforms required the implementation of new 'processes and standards'[48] to test new drugs to be brought to market. Science, and, in particular, pharmacology, therefore dominated, and manufacturers followed suit.[49]

The exercise of this expanded power continued into the 1950s, including new regulations that mandated aspects of clinical experiments, and the publication of the proforma 'New Drug Application' form. The changes anticipated many aspects of the legislative reform to follow.[50] Notable also was the birth of the first advisory committee in the FDA's history. A '"representative citizens" advisory group' established in 1954 was not, however, true to its name; members were drawn from corporate groups subject to the FDA's regulation, women's groups and academics.[51] Jasanoff, in her examination of the FDA's use of advisory committees, portrays how the FDA has 'experimented' with different forms of technocratic regulation throughout its history. In all cases, deference to scientism in relation to the regulation of medicines is a constant, including, for example, the FDA's engagement with 'the independent scientific community [as] indispensable to the success of its regulatory programs'.[52]

The FDA's powers were enhanced by amendments in 1962, and for the first time medical drugs were required to be not only safe but also effective.[53] FDA bureaucrats were again involved extensively in pushing for these

46 Carpenter (n 29) 97.
47 Ibid 99–101; Law (n 31).
48 Carpenter (n 29) 112.
49 Ibid 113–4.
50 Ibid 157–9.
51 Ibid 167.
52 Sheila Jasanoff, *The Fifth Branch* (Harvard University Press, 1994) 153.
53 *Drug Amendments of 1962* Pub L No 87-781, 76 Stat 80; Sharon B Jacobs, 'Crises, Congress, and Cognitive Biases: A Critical Examination of Food and Drug Legislation in the United States' (2009) 64 *Food and Drug Law Journal* 599, 607–8.

amendments,[54] which were spurred on by the thalidomide crisis (although the drug had not been approved in the United States thanks to the efforts of the FDA and, in particular, the celebrated Dr Frances Kelsey).[55] Carpenter, however, observes that FDA bureaucrats had informally adopted requirements for efficacy during the late 1940s and early 1950s as part of their assessment of drug safety.[56] The 1962 amendments also gave the FDA power over advertising of prescription drugs and responsibility for the regulation of good manufacturing practices in the pharmaceutical industry.[57] The result was a victory for technocracy and scientism:

> FDA officials began to shape almost every facet of the ethical drug industry and much of medicine – clinical experimentation, manufacturing, labelling, promotion and prescribing behavior – through the new drug approval process.[58]

Standardisation was one way in which the FDA exercised its power over industry, including in relation to establishing a drug's efficacy.[59] The modern era of pharmaceutical standardisation had begun in the 19th century, alongside the scientific developments of that time.[60] Commonly referred to as 'pharmacopoeia', pharmaceutical standards were, and are, 'work[s] of reference providing specifications for the preparation and testing of individual drugs'.[61] More broadly, standardisation reflected growth in the 'pre-eminent role' of science, the result of which was, and is, increasing 'fields of society … treated as sciences and then subjected to standardization'.[62] Standardisation developed as an essential limb of the scientific endeavour, reflecting a desire

54 Carpenter (n 29) 236–8.
55 Jacobs (n 53) 608–12.
56 Carpenter (n 29) 120.
57 Law (n 31).
58 Carpenter (n 29) 121. See also at 125–32.
59 Ibid 49–50; Boris Hauray, 'From Regulatory Knowledge to Regulatory Decisions: The European Evaluation of Medicines' (2017) 55 *Minerva: A Review of Science, Learning & Policy* 187.
60 Lembit Rago and Budiono Santoso, 'Drug Regulation: History, Present and Future' in CJ van Boxte, B Santoso and IR Edwards, *Drug Benefits and Risks: International Textbook of Clinical Pharmacology* (2nd ed, 2008, IOS Press) 65, 65.
61 Frederick M Abbott and Graham Dukes, *Global Pharmaceutical Policy: Ensuring Medicines for Tomorrow's World* (Edward Elgar, 2009) 90.
62 Nils Brunsson and Bengt Jacobsson, *A World of Standards* (Oxford University Press, 2002) 43. See also Mike Michael, 'Sticking Plasters and the Standardizations of Everyday Life' in Vaughan Higgins and Wendy Larner (eds), *Calculating the Social: Standards and the Reconfiguring of Governing* (Palgrave Macmillan, 2010) 131.

to measure items, actions and even persons objectively and precisely.[63] Commonly encountered examples of standardisation included statistical analysis, instruments employed for the conduct and replication of experiments, methods for conducting those investigations and even the laboratory rats subject to such trials:[64] '[t]he history of modern science is the history of the creation of ever more precise, ever more standardized, ever more predictable experiments, machines and experiments that require machines'.[65] The centrality of pharmaceutical standards to the purpose of the early FDA (and, as we will see, its counterparts in other countries) reflected the ideology of scientism – science was not just a means to an end, but was an end in itself.

By the late 1960s the FDA had established itself as both 'protectorate and gatekeeper', ensuring that the public was protected 'through pharmaceutical gatekeeping', primarily through the approval of new drugs.[66] This was strengthened by subsequent amendments in 1976 to give the FDA additional powers in relation to the growing class of medical devices.[67] The ideological foundations of the FDA's identity consequently reflected the 'heroic vision' of public health described by Porter in her history of the concept.[68] This vision comprised 'grand narratives of progress, arising from the technological advance of science and medicine and its capacities to combat endemic and epidemic disease', and, further, as 'a great achievement of Enlightenment rationalism'.[69] This partnership of 'community health' and 'efficiency' was an international ideological phenomenon, to be achieved through 'administrative and scientific expertise'.[70] In doing so both it and the role of the FDA

63 Lawrence Busch, *Standards: Recipes for Reality* (MIT Press, 2011) 83–5. The extensive science and technology studies literature on standardisation is acknowledged but will not be explored here: See, eg, Sheila Jasanoff, 'The Idiom of Co-Production' in Sheila Jasanoff (ed), *States of Knowledge: The Co-production of Science and Social Order* (Routledge, 2004) 1, 5; Sheila Jasanoff, 'Ordering Knowledge, Ordering Society' in Sheila Jasanoff (ed), *States of Knowledge: The Co-production of Science and the Social Order* (Routledge, 2004) 13, 26–7.

64 Busch (n 63) 85–90.

65 Ibid 86.

66 Carpenter (n 29) 172–3, 192.

67 Law (n 31).

68 Dorothy Porter, *Health, Civilization and the State: A History of Public Health from Ancient to Modern Times* (Routledge, 1999) 1. See also Patricia J Zettler, Margaret Foster Riley and Aaron S Kesselheim, 'Implementing a Public Health Perspective in FDA Drug Regulation' (2018) 73 *Food and Drug Law Journal* 221, 224.

69 Porter (n 68) 1, 3.

70 Michael Roe, 'The Establishment of the Australian Department of Health: Its Background and Significance' (1976) 17(67) *Australian Historical Studies* 176, 184. Roe observes that this ideology 'crystallised in the eugenics movement'. It was further evident in early manifestations of the Australian health bureaucracy, including the Australian Quarantine service and the interest in tropical medicine in Australia and throughout the Asia-Pacific: at 184–5, 188–9.

in implementing it fundamentally reflected the ideologies of scientism and technocracy.[71]

European Union

The European Union (EU) regulation and recognition of medical products occupies a distinct space in the regulatory landscape for these goods, and while the United States may have led the way in the regulation of medical products, the EU has been the leader in pushing for the harmonisation of such regulation.[72] The first steps towards the EU regulation of medical products were taken in 1965 with an European Economic Community directive encapsulating the principles of pre-market approval and safety, efficacy and quality.[73] Key jurisdictions (Great Britain, Germany and France) implemented approval systems to meet these requirements in the late 1960s and 1970s,[74] although these countries and others had a significant history of regulating medicines, including their standards via respective pharmacopeia.[75] In Hauray's view, '[t]he rise of the scientific disciplines played a crucial role in these developments', in particular that of pharmacology.[76] A subsequent directive in 1975 further instilled the importance of key clinical evidence to support approval of medical products, including the randomised clinical trial.[77] As was the case with the FDA, this scientistic approach to regulation '"shaped" (or by some accounts gave birth to) the modern clinical trial industry'.[78] The EU further agreed in 1975 to mutual recognition of approvals of medical products.[79] Subsequent developments paved the way for harmonisation of the regulation of medical products across the EU. They included the introduction in 1987 of the EU centralised procedure for the regulation of medical products[80] and, in 1992, harmonised rules

71 See, eg, Carpenter (n 29) 192.

72 John Abraham and Graham Lewis, *Regulating Medicines in Europe* (2000, Routledge) 2–3.

73 Boris Hauray and Philipe Urfalino, 'Mutual Transformation and the Development of European Policy Spaces. The Case of Medicines Licensing' (2009) 16 *Journal of European Public Policy* 431, 435.

74 Hauray (n 59) 190.

75 Rago and Santoso (n 60) 65.

76 Hauray (n 59) 191.

77 Ibid 191; *Council Directive 75/318/EEC of 20 May 1975 on the Approximation of the Laws of Member States Relating to Analytical, Pharmaco-toxicological and Clinical Standards and Protocols in Respect of the Testing of Proprietary Medicinal Products* [1975] OJ L 147/1.

78 Hauray (n 59) 191.

79 Rago and Santoso (n 60) 66 citing *Council Directive 75/319/EEC of 20 May 1975 on the Approximation of Provisions Laid Down by Law, Regulation or Administrative Action Relating to Proprietary Medicinal Products* [1975] OJ L 147/13.

80 Ibid.

on the 'labelling, advertising, prescriptions and distribution of medicines'.[81] Ultimately the European Medicines Evaluation Agency (later the EMA) was established under resolution EEC/2309/93 in 1993 as the coordinating body for the evaluation and recognition of medical products across 28 EU member states, plus Norway, Iceland and Liechtenstein.[82]

Hauray argues that the 'Europeanisation' of the regulatory regime for medical products sought to erase the differences between countries and, in doing so, any potential differences of opinion on whether a product was safe and/or effective. It did so through the promulgation, similar to the FDA, of a plethora of standards against which these assessments were to be conducted[83] and to the exclusion of evidence other than that relevant to the 'objective scientific criteria of quality, safety and efficacy'.[84] Further, he concludes that the key committee of the EMA – the Committee for Medicinal Products for Human Use – was dominated by a perspective that there exists 'objective' evidence [of] safety and efficacy'.[85] Scientism therefore prevails as the dominant ideology – as one member of the Committee states '[r]egarding the other issues, issues of a political nature, the impact of decisions ... that isn't science so it has no place here'.[86] Abraham and Lewis, in their seminal work on the European regulation of medicines, argue that the 'Europeanisation of medicines regulation' is fundamentally technocratic, with efficiency (the speed and cost at which drugs are approved) becoming the key goal of the regulatory system.[87]

The influence of the ideologies of scientism and technocracy is seen also in the regulatory dominance across the EC regime for medical products of 'risk versus benefit' as a means of evaluating quality, safety and efficacy. This approach is akin to that adopted in other jurisdictions. This 'impersonal' method of measurement is, in Hauray's view of the operation of the EMA, a 'fiction': 'no single measurement aggregating the risks and benefits of a product is calculated during its evaluation'.[88] Such an approach to risk assessment is further evidence of a technocratic approach to the regulation of medical

81 Peter Feldschreiber, *The Law and Regulation of Medicines and Medical Devices* (2nd ed, 2021) 6.

82 Hauray (n 59) 193; Sabine Haubenreisser and Martin Harvey-Allchurch, 'The European Medicines Agency and the Regulation of Medicines in the European Union' in SF Halabi (ed) *Food and Drug Regulation in an Era of Globalized Markets* (Elsevier, 2015); Rago and Santoso (n 60) 66 citing *Council Regulation (EEC) No 2309/93 of 22 July 1993 Laying Down Community Procedures for the Authorization and Supervision of Medicinal Products for Human and Veterinary Use and Establishing a European Agency for the Evaluation of Medicinal Products* [1993] OJ L 214/1.

83 Hauray (n 59) 193–4.

84 Ibid 195.

85 Ibid 190.

86 Ibid 195.

87 Abraham and Lewis (n 72) 209–10.

88 Hauray (n 59) 196.

products[89] and an extension of the ideology of scientism itself. Scientism and its technocratic applications have established a deep foothold in the modern day operations of government and regulation through their convergence on risk.[90] The development of risk analysis from scientism is described as follows by Jasanoff: '[i]n the world of regulatory risk assessment, causation generally is viewed as a linear and mechanistic phenomenon' and 'quantitative risk assessment ... is founded on the untenable premise that a perfectly objective, god's-eye view can be attained through scientific inquiry'.[91] In contrast, what such an assessment actually involves is also the interpretation of 'ambiguous' data, various perspectives on different applicant companies, the trustworthiness of the data presented to the EMA, the needs of patients and differing views about the interpretation of relevant rules and procedures.[92]

Australia in Focus

Australia's therapeutic goods regulatory regime was established as one of a number of population-focussed health policies and programmes during the first half of the 20th century. As in the United States, the development of the arrangements for therapeutic goods did not occur as a single act of policy or legislative reform. It was instead characterised by the incremental development and application of the legislative framework. Nevertheless, a consistent theme was an almost unquestioning faith in the scientific advances that characterised the late 19th and early 20th centuries. Successive Australian governments relied increasingly on scientific knowledge, and its underpinning practices, to support a range of policies and reforms associated with planning for the emerging nation. In describing the influence of the ideology of scientism on the establishment of the first Commonwealth Department of Health, Roe comments that 'Australia marched in step with world trends ... in terms of bureaucracy, ideas, and sentiment'. [93] This statement arguably applies equally to the development of the therapeutic goods regulatory regime. This section will examine the significant influence of the ideologies of scientism and technocracy on the establishment of the Australian regulatory regime.

89 Ibid 202.

90 See, eg, David Demortain, *Scientists and the Regulation of Risk: Standardising Control* (Edward Elgar, 2011); Stuart Shapiro, *Analysis and Public Policy: Successes, Failures and Directions for Reform* (Edward Elgar, 2016) 57–81.

91 Sheila Jasanoff, 'The Songlines of Risk' in Sheila Jasanoff (ed), *Science and Public Reason* (Routledge, 2012) 133, 139, 141. The role and foundations of risk assessment have been extensively addressed elsewhere: see, eg, Ulrich Beck, *Risk Society: Towards a New Modernity* (SAGE Publications, 1992).

92 Hauray (n 59) 196–200. See also Abraham and Lewis (n 72).

93 Roe (n 70) 181.

The 1907 Royal Commission

The earliest evidence of the influence of the ideology of scientism in the development of the therapeutic goods regulatory regime is found in the 1907 Commonwealth Royal Commission on Secret Drugs, Cures and Foods. The Commission represented the new Commonwealth's 'first action about medicines'.[94] Its report anticipated, in many respects, the extensive influence that scientism and technocracy were to have on therapeutic goods regulation in Australia. The Commission was tasked with investigating the sale of patented medicines and of disreputable products, promoted by salespeople ('quacks') as curing illness and promoting health. The sole, and highly motivated, Commissioner interpreted his remit broadly.[95] He concluded that there was 'sufficient evidence ... as to the universality of the social injury and of racial deterioration' associated with the promotion and use of 'secret alleged cures' and the 'manipulation of medicaments and foods'.[96] 'Quackery', according to the Commissioner, offended the pursuit by the new nation of its 'racial interests'.[97] The Commissioner's primary focus was the supply and use of contraception and products used to induce abortion,[98] thereby depriving Australia of a thriving birth rate amongst the Anglo-Saxon population.[99] While the racial dimension and implication of the history of health policy

94 McEwen (n 1) 1.

95 The Commissioner, Octavius Beale, had also served as a Commissioner on the 1903 New South Wales Royal Commission into the Decline of the Birthrate and the Mortality amongst Children. He considered that the Commonwealth Royal Commission should continue the work of the NSW Royal Commission. Specifically, he advocated that it should consider 'agents which, in chief, bring about the decline in fertility, and those which affect in a high degree the mortality of children' and 'the whole range of life with the alleged and accepted, though secret, curation of every kind of disease that afflicts mankind from birth to death': *Royal Commission on Secret Drugs, Cures and Foods* (Report, 1907) vol 1, 1–2 ('*Royal Commission on Secret Drugs Report*').

96 Ibid 426. The *Royal Commission on Secret Drugs Report* provides significant indications that the Commissioner was at the very least a pronatalist, and most likely also a eugenicist: see, eg, at 9–10, 26–7, 31, 42–4, 372–3. See also Stephen Garton, 'Eugenics in Australia and New Zealand: Laboratories of Racial Science' in Alison Bashford and Philippa Levine (eds), *The Oxford Handbook of the History of Eugenics* (Oxford University Press, 2010) 243, 253. The Commissioner's views mirrored that of segments of the Australian medical profession that a 'white infant life was indeed viewed as a resource for the nation' during a time in which the development of medicine and its practice converged with the subjugation of Aboriginal and 'other non-white' peoples: Lisa Featherstone, 'The Value of the Victorian Infant: Whiteness and the Emergence of Paediatrics in Late Colonial Australia' (Conference Paper, Historicising Whiteness: Transnational Perspectives on the Construction of an Identity Conference, University of Melbourne, 22–24 November 2006) 445–6.

97 *Royal Commission on Secret Drugs Report* (n 95) 426.

98 Ibid.

99 See, eg, ibid 40–1.

and therapeutic goods regulation in Australia is not a focus of this book, these observations raise important issues for future analysis and reflection.

The Commissioner was concerned that certain therapeutic products were being sold without 'preliminary examination, license, and inspection'.[100] Consequently, among a range of recommendations, he urged the Commonwealth Government to coordinate uniform legislative and administrative efforts across the states and the Commonwealth 'to control the handling and the sale of drugs ... apart from patent or proprietary drugs'.[101] Such reforms, he insisted, should be modelled on those of Germany and its 'scientific experience'.[102] Notable also was his recommendation that the Government establish a 'Bureau of Chemistry',[103] similar to that of the United States, for the 'examination and control of articles for human consumption'.[104] Despite the apparently strong influence of the Commissioner and his supporters,[105] the recommendations were not acted on at a national level.[106] Indeed, no significant national reform followed from the successive meetings between the Commonwealth and state governments between 1900 and 1942 in relation to 'foods and drugs'.[107]

The First Commonwealth Department of Health

The Royal Commission's ethos was, however, reflected in some respects in the establishment of the first Commonwealth Department of Health in 1921. The Department's establishment articulated the beliefs of its founders that the free market was unable to adequately support the health of the nation.[108] These beliefs reflected the conclusions of the Royal Commission that therapeutic products were often produced and sold in Australia to promote the financial interests of their sellers rather than delivering promised health

100 Ibid 427.
101 Ibid 430.
102 Ibid 429–30. See also at 372.
103 Ibid 430–1.
104 Ibid 3.
105 Lynette Finch, 'Soothing Syrups and Teething Powders: Regulating Proprietary Drugs in Australia, 1860–1910' (1999) 43 *Medical History* 74, 88–9.
106 They were implemented in part and to different degrees by the states: McEwen (n 1) 3; Finch (n 105) 90.
107 McEwen (n 1) 4–5. This was unsurprising given that the Constitution at the time did not provide the Commonwealth with powers in relation to health (which was left to the states), except in relation to quarantine: Karen Wheelwright, 'Commonwealth and State Powers in Health a Constitutional Diagnosis' (1995) 21(1) *Monash University Law Review* 53, 56–8. Regulatory uniformity was, however, achieved to an extent in relation 'the purity of food and drugs' between the states: *Royal Commission on Health* (Report, 1925) 29.
108 Roe (n 70) 181–3.

benefits.[109] The founders of the new Department of Health embraced an alternative ideological perspective that science should be applied to achieve broader social objectives.[110] In his analysis of the Department's establishment, Roe describes that part of its driving philosophy was that '[l]aissez-faire must be replaced by organisation of every aspect of life, giving the individual a sense of fellowship and commitment ... [i]n every way society would become taut, determined, effective'.[111] This reflected the influence, Roe argues, of American Progressivism and British Fabianism.[112] These two philosophical and social movements extolled 'faith in the power of an expert bureaucracy to apply technological and scientific skills for the betterment of all society'.[113]

The new Department's ideological foundations also reflected the 'heroic vision' of public health described earlier.[114] It was embedded as such in the foundations of the new Department of Health.[115] Consequently, so too was the significant international reach of scientism and technocracy in public administration and policy.[116] It was the new Department's key personnel who, from at least the early 1930s, actively pursued the establishment of a uniform, national regulatory regime for therapeutic goods. From 1950, they were also motivated by the introduction of pharmaceutical benefits and the Government's focus on not only the population's health needs, but also control over the quality of now state-subsidised therapeutic goods.[117]

Commonwealth Legislation on Therapeutic Goods

Two pieces of legislation to establish a regulatory regime for therapeutic goods were passed by the Commonwealth Parliament in 1937 ('the 1937 Act') and 1938 ('the 1938 Act'), respectively. However, neither Act was proclaimed,

109 Ibid 181–2; *Royal Commission on Secret Drugs Report* (n 99) 426.
110 Roe (n 70) 183–5.
111 Ibid 183.
112 Ibid 183–4. The American Progressive movement advocated a range of government-led reforms in American politics and society, including to combat inequality and poverty and to advance suffrage, labour rights, public education and health. Its presence was arguably dominant from the late 1800s to the early 1920s: Nugent (n 36) 1–4. See also Woolner and Thompson (n 36)6–7. The British Fabian Society advocated an evolutionary, rather than revolutionary, socialist approach to societal and economic challenges. Described as an 'intellectual elite ... the early Fabians sought to educate both themselves and the wider society': Anthony Wright, 'A Century of Fabianism 1884–1984' (1984) 34(5) *History Today* 50, 50. There were arguably close ties between the British and American movements: Melvyn Stokes, 'American Progressives and the European Left' (1983) 17(1) *Journal of American Studies* 5, 14–5, 26.
113 Roe (n 70) 184.
114 Porter (n 68) 1.
115 Including the Department's key personnel: ibid 184–5.
116 Olson (n 2) xvii.
117 McEwen (n 1) 5–6, 19–20.

apparently because of the interruption of the Second World War.[118] Even at this preliminary stage the dominance of science and the significant reliance on scientific expertise in the formulation of the therapeutic goods regulatory regime was evident.

Particularly prominent in this early regulatory attempt (and its successors) was a focus on standardisation as the primary regulatory goal. The purpose of the 1937 and 1938 Acts was to ensure that certain medical remedies were 'true to a determined standard, that standard having an official and legal status'.[119] The standards in this instance were established under the auspices of the League of Nations.[120]

In addition, the reliance on scientific, and indeed technocratic, expertise to facilitate the passage of the Acts was evident in the statements of the opposition Australian Labor Party in supporting the 1937 Act:

> This bill deals with a subject with which lay members cannot hope to make themselves familiar in the short time at our disposal. The Minister for Health ... was good enough to explain to me before the House met what the bill is intended to do. He was *supported by the advice of the medical officers of his department, men in whom we have the greatest confidence.*[121]

The *Therapeutic Substances Act 1953* ('the 1953 Act') was the first piece of the therapeutic goods regulatory regime to become law.[122] Again, the centrality of scientific standards was clearly evident. Similar to the 1937 and 1938

118 The Bills were the Therapeutic Substances Bill 1937 (Cth) and the Therapeutic Substances Bill 1938 (Cth): ibid 9.

119 Commonwealth, *Parliamentary Debates*, Senate, 23 June 1937, 241 (Senator Brennan).

120 Ibid; see also W Chas Cockburn, 'The International Contribution to the Standardization of Biological Substances. I. Biological Standards and the League of Nations 1921–1946' (1991) 19(1) *Biologicals* 161. It is important to note that the 1937 Act was drafted to reflect UK legislation passed for the same purposes. It was also intended to work in harmony with the regulatory arrangements of countries that had adopted the standards produced by the League of Nations, in particular the United States: ibid; McEwen (n 1) 10.

121 McEwen (n 1) 11, quoting Commonwealth, *Parliamentary Debates*, House of Representatives, 15 September 1937, 1134 (Francis Forde) (emphasis added).

122 *Therapeutic Substances Act 1953* (Cth). It was supported, in part, by the 1946 'welfare' amendments to the Commonwealth Constitution and was soon followed by complementary legislation in the Australian states. The amendments gave the Commonwealth an additional constitutional head of legislative power in relation to '[t]he provision of maternity allowances, widow's pensions, child endowment, unemployment, *pharmaceutical, sickness and hospital benefits, medical and dental services (but not so as to authorize any form of civil conscription)*, benefits to students and family allowances: *Australian Constitution* s 51 (xxiiiA) (emphasis added); McEwen (n 1) 29–33. It is important to note, however, the lack of clarity that existed at the time regarding whether the constitutional powers of the Commonwealth were sufficient to support the 1953 Act: McEwen (n 1) 37–8, 42–3.

Acts, the primary purpose of the 1953 Act was 'to provide standards for certain Therapeutic Substances'.[123] The standards were specified as including the British Pharmacopoeia and the British Pharmaceutical Codex.[124]

The subsequent *Therapeutic Goods Act 1966* ('the 1966 Act') was passed in the wake of the thalidomide tragedy.[125] It was similarly focussed on providing for 'standards for goods for therapeutic use'.[126] Notably, the Minister for Health emphasised the centrality of standards in the second reading speech:

> The rapid introduction of many potent agents of diverse characteristics, such as antibiotics, and the advances of science and technology, have made the question of their standards a scientifically sophisticated field requiring much work and careful evaluation.[127]

Significantly the 1966 Act enabled the Minister to alone determine an applicable standard, rather than doing so by regulation approved by the Governor-General in Council.[128] Cabinet minutes approving the 1966 Bill noted that this proposed new Ministerial declaration could be justified 'on the grounds of *technical complexity* and the *eminence of specialist advice* under the procedures for arriving at the standards'.[129] This highlighted the centrality of experts or technocrats to the developing regulatory regime. Their importance was also evident in the establishment of the Australian Drug Evaluation Committee ('ADEC') in the lead up to the 1966 Act. The primary role of the ADEC was 'to make medical and scientific evaluations' of therapeutic substances and advise the Minister if the ADEC thought necessary.[130] The

123 McEwen (n 1) 29–31; *Therapeutic Substances Act 1953* (Cth) ss 4, 10, 11, 15.

124 *Therapeutic Substances Act 1953* (Cth) s 4 (definitions of 'the British Pharmaceutical Codex', 'the British Pharmacopoeia', 'the standard'). It appears that any other relevant standards were to be the subject of advice to the relevant Minister by Committees established under the Act and Regulations: at s 19; *Therapeutic Substances Regulations 1956* (Cth) regs 20(3), 21(4).

125 McEwen (n 1) 43–9. Thalidomide was prescribed to women in a number of countries, including Australia, during the 1950s and 1960s, primarily to treat morning sickness. The drug caused thousands of infants to be born with a range of disabilities: see, eg, James H Kim and Anthony R Scialli, 'Thalidomide: The Tragedy of Birth Defects and the Effective Treatment of Disease' (2011) 122(1) *Toxicological Sciences* 1, 1.

126 *Therapeutic Goods Act 1966* (Cth) as enacted.

127 Commonwealth, *Parliamentary Debates*, House of Representatives, 28 April 1966, 1310 (Alexander Forbes, Minister for Health).

128 *Therapeutic Goods Act 1966* (Cth) ss 11, 13, as enacted. The Minister's declaration was required to be notified in the Government Gazette: at s 18.

129 McEwen (n 1) 48. The National Biological Standards Laboratory focussed on the creation of 'Australian-specific' standards under these new Ministerial powers. Further, the Minister was supported by advice from the Therapeutic Goods Standards Committee from the early 1970s: at 64–6.

130 Ibid 46–7, 105.

commissioned history of the TGA notes that, through such advice, the ADEC exercised 'considerable influence'.[131]

The year 1989 was important in the life of the therapeutic goods regulatory regime. In that year a new principal Act was passed ('the 1989 Act') and existing units in the Commonwealth Department of Health reorganised to form the 'Therapeutic Goods Administration'.[132] Significantly, the 1989 Act explicitly broadened the goals of the regulatory regime beyond standardisation for the first time.[133] While preceding Acts had focussed on compliance with pharmaceutical standards, the object of the 1989 Act was to provide for a 'national system of controls relating to the *quality, safety and efficacy* of therapeutic goods'.[134] In doing so, the 1989 Act reflected the regulatory regimes of the UK and the United States.[135]

Despite the expanded purpose of the regulatory regime from 1989, the influence of scientism remained strong. Commenting on the attribution of meaning to terms such as 'quality, safety and efficacy' in the American context, Carpenter states that '[m]any terms were the co-creation of pharmacologists, industry-based clinicians, academic physicians, and others in a process of therapeutic reform that extended through the twentieth century'.[136] In relation to the development of the concept of 'efficacy', he emphasises the pivotal role of the FDA in developing the meaning of the term in relation to the acceptance or rejection of new drugs. Similarly in the Australian context, the broader goals were described by the Minister for Health in terms that recall the foundations and applications of scientism:

> *[Q]uality* which refers to aspects such as its proper manufacture, the trueness of the contents to the label and its compliance with any relevant product standards ... *safety*, that is its lack of toxicity or hazard ... [t]his aspect is often demonstrated from animal experiments.[137]

The role of standards as a means of assessing these objectives also remained paramount in provisions of the 1989 Act as it was introduced.[138] The current version of the Act maintains their centrality: the registration and listing

131 Ibid 111.

132 Ibid 138. The 1989 Act and the *Therapeutic Goods Regulations 1990* (Cth) ('the 1990 Regulations') came into effect in early 1991: at 62.

133 *Therapeutic Goods Act 1989* (Cth) s 4 as enacted.

134 Ibid.

135 Commonwealth, *Parliamentary Debates*, House of Representatives, 5 October 1989, 1613–4 (Peter Staples, Minister for Housing and Aged Care).

136 Carpenter (n 29) 270.

137 Commonwealth, *Parliamentary Debates*, House of Representatives, 5 October 1989, 1613 (Peter Staples, Minister for Housing and Aged Care) (emphasis added).

138 *Therapeutic Goods Act 1989* (Cth) pt 2, s 25(1)(f) as enacted.

of medicines is subject to the decision-maker's consideration of compliance with the applicable standard,[139] and 'compliance with applicable medical device standards ... is one way to establish compliance with essential principles'.[140] Ascertaining how the broader objectives introduced by the 1989 Act are met is therefore exclusively dominated by scientific principles and methodology. This is further evidenced by the requirement that, in relation to medical devices, 'clinical evidence' is necessary to demonstrate compliance with the essential principles.[141] Such evidence is required to 'provide ... a current and accurate picture of both the state of scientific knowledge in relation to the treatment modality to which a device relates, and in relation to the particular device specifically'.[142]

The 1989 Act also included a more contemporary expression of scientism: a risk-based regulatory approach in which higher risk goods were subjected to a higher level of scrutiny (and the requirement that all non-exempt goods be included in the Australian Register of Therapeutic Goods (ARTG), as explained later in this chapter).[143] The continued dominance of scientism is evident also in the Advisory Committees established by the 1989 Act and the 1990 Regulations. The overwhelming emphasis on the importance of scientific expertise – particularly and unsurprisingly in the fields of pharmacology, chemistry and medical specialities – remains pivotal.[144] For example, the current regulatory regime establishes an Advisory Committee on Medicines to provide advice and recommendations to the Minister or Secretary about the safety, quality and efficacy of medicines.[145] Committee members can only be appointed if they have expertise in general or specialist medical practice, a range of medical or scientific specialities, or the manufacture of medicines or medical ethics.[146] A further provision provides that 'one member of the committee may have expertise in consumer health issues'. The discretionary nature of this provision indicates the relative lack of importance attributed to expertise beyond the traditional scientific domain.[147] While the 1989 Act

139 Ibid ss 25(1)(f), 26(f).
140 Ibid ss 41C, 41D.
141 *Therapeutic Goods (Medical Devices) Regulations 2002* (Cth) sch 1, cl 14.
142 Therapeutic Goods Administration, Department of Health (Cth), *Clinical Evidence Guidelines for Medical Devices* (Guidelines, November 2023) 17.
143 McEwen (n 1) 137–8.
144 *Therapeutic Goods Act 1989* (Cth) s 63(2)(a); *Therapeutic Goods Regulations 1990* (Cth) regs 35B, 38B, 39B, 39E, 39H, 42ZCC, 42ZCS. See also McEwen (n 1) 36–7.
145 *Therapeutic Goods Regulations 1990* (Cth) reg 35A.
146 Ibid reg 35B(1A), (2). Analogous provisions provide for the expertise of members of the Advisory Committee on Medical Devices: at regs 38B(2), (4), (5).
147 Ibid reg 35B(1B). A similar provision is included in relation to the Advisory Committee on Medical Devices: at reg 38(B)(3).

has been subject to numerous reviews and amendments,[148] its fundamental structure and foundational ideas remain the backbone of the current regulatory regime for therapeutic goods in Australia.[149]

A Brief Outline of the Therapeutic Goods Regulatory Regime[150]

Australia's therapeutic goods regulatory regime is a complex mix of regulatory tools applying to the manufacture, import, export and supply of therapeutic goods in and from Australia. The most significant of these instruments is the *Therapeutic Goods Act 1989* ('the Act'). In addition to the Act, a range of secondary legislation, guidelines and standards, and the decisions and practices of the executive branch of government, also form part of the regulatory framework.[151] The Act establishes a cooperative Commonwealth–State regulatory scheme which reflects the respective constitutional powers of the two tiers of government.[152] These regulatory arrangements are complemented by schemes for the subsidisation of medicines and medical services via the Pharmaceutical Benefits Scheme and the Medicare Benefits Scheme, respectively.[153]

At the centre of the regulatory regime for therapeutic goods is the definition of the term 'therapeutic goods' and the Act's two objects. 'Therapeutic

148 See, eg, McEwen (n 1) 141–63; Lloyd Sansom, Will Delaat and John Horvath, *Review of Medicines and Medical Device Regulation: Report on the Regulatory Framework for Medicines and Medical Devices* (March 2015).

149 For example, the Minister may still determine applicable standards: *Therapeutic Goods Act 1989* (Cth) s 10. For the purposes of this book, the most significant amendments to the 1989 Act were those introduced in 2002 to provide for more comprehensive regulation of medical devices: *Therapeutic Goods Amendment (Medical Devices) Act 2002* (Cth). See also McEwen (n 1) 161–3. Chapter 6 expands on the regulation of medical devices.

150 A significant part of this section is drawn from the author's previously published article: Penny Gleeson, 'The Challenge of Medicinal Cannabis to the Political Legitimacy of Therapeutic Goods Regulation in Australia' (2019) 43(2) *Melbourne University Law Review* 558.

151 See, eg, *Therapeutic Goods Regulations 1990* (Cth); *Therapeutic Goods (Poisons Standard - June 2024) Instrument 2024*; *Therapeutic Goods (Medical Devices) Regulations 2002* (Cth); *Therapeutic Goods (Medical Devices - Specified Articles) Instrument 2020* (Cth); *Therapeutic Goods (Guidelines for Multi-Site Licences) Instrument 2020* (Cth).

152 See, eg, Victorian Law Reform Commission, *Medicinal Cannabis* (Issues Paper, March 2015) 56–7, 59–60; McEwen (n 1) 57–8.

153 See, eg, 'What Is Not Regulated by the TGA', *Therapeutic Goods Administration* (Web Page, 2 August 2012) <https://www.tga.gov.au/about-tga/what-we-do/what-not-regulated-tga>; 'MBS Online', *MBS Online: Medicare Benefits Schedule* (Web Page) <http://www.mbsonline.gov.au/internet/mbsonline/publishing.nsf/Content/Home>; 'Pharmaceutical Benefits Scheme', *PBS: The Pharmaceutical Benefits Scheme* (Web Page) <http://www.pbs.gov.au/pbs/home;jsessionid=cr0heafq4if2nwi8rvl1yxad>; Westlaw AU, *The Laws of Australia* (online at 17 May 2024) [20.11].

goods' is defined and applied broadly.[154] Medicines (e.g., headache tablets),[155] medical devices (e.g., bandages, gloves)[156] and biologicals (e.g., stem cells or skin)[157] all fall under its definition. The first object of the Act is to establish and maintain 'a national system of controls relating to the quality, safety, efficacy and timely availability' of therapeutic goods that are used in, or exported from, Australia.[158] If the therapeutic good is a medical device (instead of, for example, a medicine), then the term 'efficacy' is replaced by 'performance ... as the manufacturer intended'.[159] The second object of the Act is to provide a 'framework' for a uniform national approach in relation to 'poisons', which is defined as including ingredients or preparations which may cause death, illness or injury.[160] This second object will be discussed shortly. In relation to the first object of the Act, the regulatory regime adopts a risk–benefit approach to determine whether a proposed therapeutic good

154 '[T]herapeutic goods' are defined to include goods 'that are represented in any way to be, or that are ... likely to be taken to be: (i) for therapeutic use; or (ii) for use as an ingredient or component in the manufacture of therapeutic goods; or (iii) for use as a container ... for [therapeutic] goods'. '[T]herapeutic use' is defined to include 'use in or in connection with: (a) preventing, diagnosing, curing or alleviating a disease, ailment, defect or injury in persons; or (b) influencing, inhibiting or modifying a physiological process in persons; or (c) testing the susceptibility of persons to a disease or ailment': *Therapeutic Goods Act 1989* (Cth) s 3 (definitions of 'therapeutic goods'; 'therapeutic use'). See also 'What Are Therapeutic Goods', *Therapeutic Goods Administration* (Web Page) <http://www.tga.gov.au/what-are-therapeutic-goods>.

155 'Medicine' is defined as 'therapeutic goods (other than biologicals) that are represented to achieve, or are likely to achieve, their principal intended action by pharmacological, chemical, immunological or metabolic means in or on the body of a human': *Therapeutic Goods Act 1989* (Cth) s 3 (definition of 'medicine').

156 A 'medical device' is defined to include 'any instrument, apparatus, appliance, material or other article ... intended ... to be used for human beings for the purpose of ... (i) diagnosis, prevention, monitoring, treatment or alleviation of disease; (ii) diagnosis, monitoring, treatment, alleviation of or compensation for an injury or disability; (iii) investigation, replacement or modification of the anatomy or of a physiological process; (iv) control of conception; and that does not achieve its principal intended action ... by pharmacological, immunological or metabolic means': ibid ss 3, 41BD.

157 A 'biological' is defined as including something that 'comprises, contains or is derived from human cells or human tissues' and is '(i) for use in the treatment or prevention of a disease, ailment, defect or injury affecting persons; or (ii) for use in making a medical diagnosis of the condition of a person; or (iii) for use in influencing, inhibiting or modifying a physiological process in persons; or (iv) for use in testing the susceptibility of persons to a disease or ailment; or (v) for use in the replacement or modification of parts of the anatomy in persons': ibid ss 3, 32A. See also Lisa Eckstein and Dianne Nicol, 'Gene Editing Clinical Trials Could Slip through Australian Regulatory Cracks' (2019) 27 *Journal of Law and Medicine* 274, 279.

158 *Therapeutic Goods Act 1989* (Cth) s 4(1)(a).

159 Ibid s 4(1A).

160 Ibid ss 3, 4(1).

should be made available to the public.[161] In simple terms, a higher degree of regulatory scrutiny is imposed on higher risk goods. Generally, before medicines can be made available to the public, the Secretary of the Department of Health (or, typically, her or his delegate) must evaluate the proposed goods, 'having regard to ... whether the *quality, safety and efficacy* of the goods for the purpose for which they are to be used have been satisfactorily established'.[162] In determining whether this is the case, the decision-maker must consider whether medicines 'conform to any standard applicable' and the acceptability of the applicable manufacturing and quality control procedures.[163] Analogous requirements apply to biologicals.[164] In relation to medical devices, the decision-maker must be satisfied that the device complies with 'essential principles' relating to the 'safety and performance characteristics' of the device.[165] The device must also meet certain 'conformity assessment procedures' relating to 'quality management systems'.[166] The regulation of medical devices will be examined further in Chapter 6 in relation to urogynaecological mesh devices.

If a particular therapeutic good has been subject to, and passed, the applicable level of regulatory scrutiny it is included on the ARTG. The ARTG is separated into five parts: (1) 'registered' and (2) 'provisionally registered' goods, which are considered to pose a higher level of risk to human safety; (3) 'listed' goods, which are deemed to have a lower risk profile; and finally (4) 'biologicals' and (5) 'medical devices'.[167] Biologicals and medical devices are subject to analogous, but not identical, risk–benefit scrutiny.[168] Medical devices are classified into specific classes according to the 'intended purpose' of the device or, if the device is an 'in vitro diagnostic' medical device (e.g., pathology tests), according to the public health or personal risk posed by the device.[169] A higher level of classification indicates a higher level of risk associated with the device.[170] Medical devices are applied for, and included on, the

161 There are, however, regulatory differences between the frameworks for medicine and medical devices: Sansom et al (n 148) 6, 13, 62.

162 *Therapeutic Goods Act 1989* (Cth) ss 25(1)(c) (in relation to registration of medicines), 32DA, 32DE (in relation to biologicals) (emphasis added). See also s 26 in relation to the listing of medicines.

163 Ibid s 25(1)(f), (g), (h). There are a range of additional matters that the Secretary must also consider: at ss 25(1)(e), (fa), (j), (ja), (k), (2), (2E), (2G).

164 Ibid pt 3-2A div 4.

165 Ibid ss 41BA(a), 41BH, pt 4-2.

166 Ibid s 41BA(b), pt 4-3.

167 Ibid s 9A(3). See also, Therapeutic Goods Administration, Department of Health (Cth) 'Educational Materials: The Regulation of Medicines in Australia' 5 .

168 *Therapeutic Goods Act 1989* (Cth) pts 4–5 (medical devices), 3-2A div 4 (biologicals).

169 Ibid s 41DB; *Therapeutic Goods (Medical Devices) Regulations 2002* (Cth) div 3.1, schs 2, 2A, Dictionary (definitions of 'intended purpose'; 'IVD medical device').

170 *Therapeutic Goods (Medical Devices) Regulations 2002* (Cth) reg 3.1(2).

ARTG as 'kinds' of medical devices.[171] Accordingly the ARTG 'may cover a range of products that are of the same kind rather than individual devices'.[172] Certain exceptions apply in relation to the normal regulatory scrutiny of therapeutic goods if a good or class of goods has been determined as 'exempt' under the Act.[173]

The Act imposes criminal penalties for the import, export, manufacture or supply of therapeutic goods not approved for inclusion on the ARTG.[174] As will be explained further in Chapter 4, the Act provides that therapeutic goods may, however, be made available when they are not on the ARTG, 'in response to the needs of particular people or circumstances'.[175]

It is the 'sponsor' of the medicine or medical device who is responsible for applying for it to be included on the ARTG. In broad terms, the sponsor provides information to the TGA in support of the application for inclusion of their product on the ARTG, in accordance with the requirements of the Act and subordinate legislation.[176] The sponsor may be a person or company who exports or imports the goods to or from Australia, or the Australian manufacturer of the goods, or a party who arranges for someone else to manufacture the goods (either in Australia or overseas).[177] Many of the obligations under the Act and subordinate legislation, and the penalties for failing to meet those obligations, fall on the sponsor of the therapeutic good. There are also obligations imposed on the manufacturers of a therapeutic good (which may be a different entity from the sponsor).[178]

In relation to the second object of the Act – to facilitate the uniform regulation of poisons throughout Australia – the Act enables the making and amendment of the *Standard for the Uniform Scheduling of Medicines and*

171 *Therapeutic Goods Act 1989* (Cth) s 41BE.

172 Therapeutic Goods Administration, Department of Health and Ageing (Cth), *Including IVD Medical Devices in the ARTG* (Version 1.1, May 2021) 10.

173 *Therapeutic Goods Act 1989* (Cth) ss 3 (definition of 'exempt goods'), 18-19A (therapeutic goods), 32C-32CO (biologicals), 41GR-41HD (medical devices).

174 Or otherwise deemed exempt or subject to other specified approvals: ibid ss 19B(4), (4A). More serious criminal penalties apply where the use of the goods has, will, or would be likely to, result in 'harm or injury to any person': s 19(1). See also, at ss 32BA–32BJ for criminal offences in relation to biologicals.

175 'Australian Register of Therapeutic Goods', *Therapeutic Goods Administration, Department of Health (Cth)*, (Web Page, 29 October 2019) <https://www.tga.gov.au/artg>. The availability of goods in these circumstances is explained further in Chapter 4 in relation to medicinal cannabis.

176 See, eg, *Therapeutic Goods Act 1989* (Cth) ss 23B, 24, 41FD.

177 *Therapeutic Goods Act 1989* (Cth) s 3 (definition of 'sponsor').

178 See, eg, *Therapeutic Goods Act 1989* (Cth) pt 3-3. 'Manufacture' is defined differently for medicines and biologicals, on the one hand, and medical devices on the other. In relation to medical devices, a separate definition of 'manufacturer' is also provided by the Act: at ss 3 (definition of 'manufacture' in relation to therapeutic goods that are not medical devices), (definition of 'manufacturer', of a medical device), 41BG.

Poisons ('the Poisons Standard').[179] The Poisons Standard classifies poisons in one of ten schedules according to their level of risk to public health. It imposes a range of requirements and restrictions on the sale and supply, storage, labelling, advertisement, and disposal of poisons in accordance with that level of risk.[180] The Poisons Standard is therefore central to the control of public access to drugs in Australia. It will be examined further in Chapter 4 in relation to the case study of medicinal cannabis. The regulatory regime for therapeutic goods in Australia is overseen by the TGA, which forms part of the Commonwealth Government's Department of Health.[181] The Act specifies that the key regulatory decision-makers are the relevant Minister and the Secretary of the Department of Health and Aged Care (or, typically, their delegates).[182] They are supported in relation to parts of their functions by certain advisory committees, including the Advisory Committee on Medicines Scheduling.[183] Aspects of this brief overview of the therapeutic goods regulatory regime will be expanded on in subsequent chapters, as relevant to each case study.

Scientific Expertise and Regulatory Power

This final section describes the nature of the regulatory power established and exercised by the therapeutic goods regime in light of the preceding ideas that have shaped it. It contends that the significant influence of scientism and technocracy means that scientific-based expertise is both a *mandatory* and a *dominant* condition of the regulatory regime's power and *the primary conduit* of that power. The essential nature of the regulatory regime is, therefore, both that of a 'scientist' and an 'expert': scientific-based knowledge is the core of the regulatory regime's power, and that power is exercised through

179 Ibid s 4(1)(b).

180 Australian Health Ministers' Advisory Council, *Scheduling Policy Framework for Medicines and Chemicals* (January 2018) 5–7; *Poisons Standard June 2024 (Cth).*

181 The TGA is not established by legislation. However, the *Therapeutic Goods Act 1989* (Cth) confirms the 'continued ... existence' of the 'Therapeutic Goods Administration Account' for the purpose of public finance administration: *Therapeutic Goods Act 1989* (Cth) s 45(1); and the *Therapeutic Goods Regulations 1990* (Cth) state that the TGA is 'part of the Department': reg 2 Various proposals to enhance the actual or perceived independence of the TGA by formally separating it from the Department have been considered but not implemented. The question of the TGA's independence is not part of the scope of this book: See, eg, Panel to Review the Transparency of the Therapeutic Goods Administration, *Review to Improve the Transparency of the Therapeutic Goods Administration: Final Report* (Report, June 2011) 52.

182 See, eg, *Therapeutic Goods Act 1989* (Cth) ss 3, 7A, 7AA, 9A(1), 9D, 10.

183 Ibid ss 52B (establishing the Advisory Committee on Medicines Scheduling), 52C (establishing the Advisory Committee on Chemicals Scheduling), 63(2)(a) (enabling the Governor-General to make regulations to establish such committees).

a technocratic approach to expertise. As will emerge from the analysis of the three case studies and the conclusions drawn in Chapter 7, these characteristics pose a significant threat to the political legitimacy of the regulatory regime.

The above outline of the operation of the therapeutic goods regulatory regime was an exposition of the key objects and obligations under the regime. According to Doris Fuchs's 'three-dimensional approach to power', these elements constitute the 'structural' dimension of power.[184] The structuralist dimension is composed of the 'material structures that allocate direct and indirect decision-making power', [185] such as the therapeutic goods regulatory regime's functions and responsibilities under its legislative framework. While the object of Fuchs' analysis is largely the power of corporations, her approach provides a useful lens through which to consider the regulatory power of the therapeutic goods regulatory regime. A further dimension of power is described by Fuchs as 'instrumentalist' – the 'direct influence of one actor over another' that is typically seen through, for example, the lobbying and financing of politicians or political parties.[186] A regulator informally threatening a regulated entity with enforcement action is an example of instrumentalist power in a regulatory context. The main argument of this book concerns Fuchs's third, 'discursive', dimension of power. Discursive power 'recogni[s]es that power is also a function of norms and ideas and is reflected in discourse, communicative practices, and cultural values and institutions'.[187] It is this third dimension of power that acknowledges the *nature* of the therapeutic goods regulatory regime. An examination of discursive power provides greater insight into the 'mind set' – the values, philosophy and assumptions – of the regulatory power that is exercised by the regime.

As discussed, the ideology of scientism pervades the establishment and objectives of the therapeutic goods regulatory regime. Scientific principles and methodology are embedded in the rationale and intention of the regime. This is fundamentally illustrated by the objects of 'quality, safety and efficacy'. Scientific principles and methodology define the very nature of these attributes and the broader regime. They are the precedent condition of the regulatory power and are therefore inherent in the regulatory power itself. This recalls a statement in relation to scientism 'that the science precedes the question, and is used to redefine it as a question that the science can

184 Jennifer Clapp and Doris Fuchs, 'Agrifood Corporations, Global Governance, and Sustainability' in Jennifer Clapp and Doris Fuchs (eds), *Corporate Power in Global Agrifood Governance* (MIT Press, 2009) 1, 8, 11–12. See also Doris Fuchs, *Business Power in Global Governance* (Lynne Rienner, 2007).

185 Clapp and Fuchs (n 184) 8.

186 Ibid.

187 Ibid 9–10.

solve'.[188] In relation to the therapeutic goods regulatory regime, the goals and mechanisms of regulatory power were, and are, determined by the scientific ideology that preceded and produced the regulatory regime itself.[189] A similar observation can be made about the regulation of therapeutic products in the United States and EU.[190] As will be expanded on in Chapter 7, this defining characteristic of the regulatory regime precludes a consideration of other types of knowledge, such as humanities-based disciplines, to provide additional and critical perspectives on the complex and controversial challenges it faces. Further, it is a characteristic that supports the fallible assumption that science can provide an objective or neutral answer to such challenges.[191] This will be illustrated by the analysis of the case studies, and again in Chapter 7.

Further, the use of that regulatory power relies on the exercise and application of scientific expertise. Scientific methodology and principles dictate how the goals of the regulatory regime are to be met and assessed for compliance. For example, in order to understand, interpret and apply the requirements of 'quality, safety and efficacy', those exercising regulatory power must possess the scientific expertise that enables them to do so. Indeed, such expertise is typically the 'primary criterion for appointment, as is typical for bureaucracies exercising regulatory power'.[192] It is only through the possession of this knowledge that those who exercise the regulatory power can access and exercise regulatory power.[193] This illustrates the observation by Paterson regarding the relationship between law and science in the context of risk that 'regulators are exercising a legal function and ultimately issuing an instrument that respects legal requirements, but they are working *with information that has been generated by science*'.[194]

Scientific expertise is therefore the primary, and arguably sole, conduit of regulatory power for the therapeutic goods regulatory regime.[195] Such power

188 Roger Scruton, 'Scientism and the Humanities' in Richard N Williams and Daniel N Robinson (eds), *Scientism: The New Orthodoxy* (Bloomsbury, 2015) 131, 136.

189 To a degree this reflects aspects of Foucault's foundational work on knowledge and power, for example that '[k]nowledge does not "reflect" power relations ... it is immanent in them': Alan Sheridan, *Michael Foucault: The Will to Truth* (Tavistock Publications, 1980) 220.

190 Hauray (n 59) 188.

191 See, eg, ibid 188.

192 Olson (n 2) xiii–xiv.

193 See, eg, Carpenter (n 29) 33, 139, 688. Similarly, writing in the broader context of world politics and economy, Kennedy states that '[e]xpert rule mobilizes knowledge as power': David Kennedy, *A World of Struggle: How Power, Law and Expertise Shape Global Political Economy* (Princeton University Press, 2016) 7.

194 Paterson (n 11) 526 (emphasis added).

195 See generally David Demortain, 'Expertise, Regulatory Science and the Evaluation of Technology and Risk: Introduction to the Special Issue' (2017) 55 *Minerva: A Review of Science, Learning & Policy* 139, 140.

is inevitably exercised by technocrats – the Minister, the TGA and its officers – as 'those who exercise power by virtue of their technical knowledge'.[196] In this respect, the officers of the TGA have authority because of the expertise they possess and the position they hold, although it is logical to assume that the former precedes the latter.[197] In turn, the use of scientific expertise and knowledge to exercise regulatory power contributes to the dominance of scientism embedded in the regulatory regime.[198] The TGA is therefore a 'stable repositor[y] of knowledge and power', and through the exercise of regulatory power imbued with scientism 'make[s] life-and-death decisions for society' in relation to access to therapeutic goods.[199] This constitutes a unilateral and directional use of regulatory power, which undermines the regulatory regime's political legitimacy. This challenge will be explored through the case studies in Chapters 4 to 6, and in Chapter 7. An alternative, facilitative, approach to regulatory power will also be examined in Chapter 7.

Conclusion

This chapter has outlined the history of the regulatory regime for medical products in the United States, European Union and Australia, and the contemporary operation of the Australian regulatory regime. It highlighted the dominant role of scientism and technocracy in those historical and current regulatory schemes. Scientific-based expertise is a mandatory and central condition of the regulatory power at the centre of regulatory regimes for medical products, and the primary conduit of that power. This will be subsequently shown to pose significant challenges for the Australian regulatory regime. In light of this description of the nature of the regulatory regimes for medical products, attention can now turn to determine how to best investigate their political legitimacy.

196 Olson (n 2) ix, quoting Robert Putnam, 'Elite Transformation in Advanced Industrial Societies' (1977) 10 *Comparative Political Studies* 383, 383.

197 See, eg, David Beetham, *Bureaucracy* (Open University Press, 1996) 15.

198 Recalling the concept of 'co-production': Jasanoff, *States of Knowledge* (n 63) 39–40.

199 Ibid. On the role of institutions in creating 'stability' in a political and policy context see, eg, B Guy Peters, 'Institutionalism and Public Policy' in B Guy Peters and Philippe Zittoun (eds), *Contemporary Approaches to Public Policy: Theories, Controversies and Perspectives* (Palgrave Macmillan, 2016) 57, 63. Similarly, Carpenter describes 'expertise' as one attribute of the FDA which enables it 'to define basic terms of debate, essential concepts of thought, learning and activity.': Carpenter (n 29) 33. See also at 64–5.

Chapter 3

A Constant Dialogic Approach to Political Legitimacy

Introduction

The previous chapter outlined the nature of the power exercised by the therapeutic goods regulatory regime. The question now addressed is how that power can be analysed by applying the concept of political legitimacy. This chapter elaborates on how political legitimacy will be applied to the case studies in Chapters 4 to 6 to examine the regulatory regime for therapeutic goods. It proposes an approach to political legitimacy – the 'constant dialogic approach' – and outlines how it will be applied to the case studies.[1] The constant dialogic approach reformulates the dialogic model of political legitimacy developed by criminologists Anthony Bottoms and Justice Tankebe. In turn, their model builds on the foundational theory of political legitimacy offered by political and social scientist David Beetham.[2] The constant dialogic approach contends that political legitimacy should be analysed as three elements: a *constant dialogue*; through which a set of *shared normative beliefs and values* is formulated; between *all parties* to a power relationship. At the core of the constant dialogic approach is the *relational* nature of legitimacy and the *dialogue* between parties to that relationship to establish the legitimacy of power.[3]

The constant dialogic approach reveals key insights about the political legitimacy of the Australian therapeutic goods regulatory regime. First, the approach brings to light the perspectives of multiple parties to a regulatory power relationship. It therefore recognises the layered and complex interactions that frequently characterise regulatory arrangements, including that of

1 Portions of this chapter are drawn from the author's previously published article: Penny Gleeson, 'The Challenge of Medicinal Cannabis to the Political Legitimacy of Therapeutic Goods Regulation in Australia' (2019) 43(2) *Melbourne University Law Review* 558.

2 Anthony Bottoms and Justice Tankebe, 'Beyond Procedural Justice: A Dialogic Approach to Legitimacy in Criminal Justice' (2012) 102(1) *Journal of Criminal Law and Criminology* 119; David Beetham, *The Legitimation of Power* (MacMillan Education, 2nd ed, 2013).

3 Bottoms and Tankebe, 'Beyond Procedural Justice' (n 2) 129.

DOI: 10.4324/9781003293811-3

the therapeutic goods regime. Second, it recognises that the nature of these relationships 'is in large part a communicative process' in which 'understandings and definitions of problems ... and acceptable and appropriate solutions' are constructed between those parties.[4] Finally, the approach emphasises the ongoing or perpetual nature of the dialogue between parties. This is particularly relevant for regulatory relationships that are enduring in nature, such as the regulation of essential services and therapeutic goods.

The chapter begins by summarising the diverse meanings of, and approaches to, political legitimacy. It then examines the work of Beetham and discusses its limitations before outlining the expansion of Beetham's framework in Bottoms's and Tankebe's dialogic approach to political legitimacy. Finally, the three fundamental elements of the constant dialogic approach developed are outlined, along with how this approach will be used to analyse the political legitimacy of the therapeutic goods regulatory regime in the chapters that follow.

The Diverse Meanings of Political Legitimacy

In broad terms, the question of political legitimacy has been described as one which asks 'whether a power-holder is justified in claiming the right to hold power over other citizens' or those otherwise subject to such power.[5] An analysis of political legitimacy therefore seeks to explain whether there is a 'recognition of the right to govern',[6] or why those subject to government authority should, and do, obey such authority.[7] Such general descriptions, however, reveal as many questions about the nature of political legitimacy as they do answers. Is political legitimacy achieved through the mere existence of a belief in the legitimacy of those exercising power? Or should there also be satisfactory reasons for holding such a belief?

Despite the significance of the concept of political legitimacy for regulatory schemes (as described in Chapter 1), there is no widely accepted meaning of the concept in academia, regulatory practice or public administration.[8] The aim is not to meet this, arguably insurmountable, challenge. The constant

4 Julia Black, 'Regulatory Conversations' (2002) 29(1) *Journal of Law and Society* 163, 164–5. See also Alanna Linn, 'Raw Milk Is Always Risky: Stabilising the Danger of Raw Milk in Australia Food Safety Regulation' (2019) 21 *Journal of Health, Risk & Society* 304.

5 Bottoms and Tankebe, 'Beyond Procedural Justice' (n 2) 124–5. It is acknowledged, however, that any attempt to define political legitimacy carries with it the weight of its particular and contested perspective.

6 Ibid 125, quoting Jean-Marc Coicaud, *Legitimacy and Politics: A Contribution to the Study of Political Right and Political Responsibility*, tr David Ames Curtis (Cambridge University Press, 2002) 10.

7 See, eg, Rodney Barker, *Political Legitimacy and the State* (Clarendon Press, 1990) 7–8.

8 See, eg, Melissa Schwartzberg, 'Introduction' in Jack Knight and Melissa Schwartzberg (eds), *Political Legitimacy* (NYU Press, 2019) 1.

dialogic approach to political legitimacy proposed in this chapter, and applied to the subsequent case studies, provides important insights about the therapeutic goods regulatory regime. Other perspectives on political legitimacy also provide important context for the constant dialogic approach and may contribute to future analysis of the regulatory regime. Certain notable interpretations of political legitimacy are therefore outlined in the following discussion. Generally, these have been described as either normative or descriptive in nature, or as a combination of both.[9]

There are similarities and overlap between political legitimacy and commonly associated concepts, such as trust in government, integrity of those exercising power and accountability and reputation of powerholders.[10] However, each of these concepts is narrower than that of political legitimacy. Accountability, for example, has been described as 'one avenue for securing legitimacy'.[11] Similarly, 'trustworthy government' has been considered a necessary, but not sufficient, condition for the political legitimacy of that government.[12] The concept of political legitimacy therefore offers richer analytical insight with which to investigate the therapeutic goods regulatory regime.

Normative Approaches to Political Legitimacy

Normative approaches to political legitimacy advocate that politically legitimate power is 'rightful according to rationally defensible standards or principles'.[13] Power is legitimate 'if it meets "objective [normative] criteria of

9 Increasingly, commentary on political legitimacy has also attempted to grasp the interaction between the normative and descriptive perspectives: see, eg, Chris Thornhill, 'Political Legitimacy: A Theoretical Approach between Facts and Norms' (2011) 18(2) *Constellations: An International Journal of Critical and Democratic Theory* 135.

10 See, eg, Margaret Levi, 'Trustworthy Government and Legitimating Beliefs' in Jack Knight and Melissa Schwartzberg (eds), *Political Legitimacy* (NYU Press, 2019) 361; Julia Black, 'Legitimacy and the Competition for Regulatory Share' (LSE Law, Society and Economy Working Papers No 14/2009, London School of Economics and Political Science, Law Department, 2009) 8–9; Martino Maggetti, 'Legitimacy and Accountability of Independent Regulatory Agencies: A Critical Review' (2010) 2 *Living Reviews in Democracy* 1; Daniel Carpenter, *Reputation and Power: Organizational Image and Phamaceutical Regulation at the FDA* (Princeton University Press, 2010).

11 Brownwen Morgan and Karen Yeung, *An Introduction to Law and Regulation: Text and Materials* (Cambridge University Press, 2007) 228.

12 Levi (n 10) 373. Others have distinguished trust from legitimacy: see, eg, Sanford C Gordon and Gregory A Huber, 'The Empirical Study of Legitimate Authority: Normative Guidance for Positive Analysis' in Jack Knight and Melissa Schwartzberg (eds) *Political Legitimacy* (New York University Press, 2019) 328, 339–40.

13 David Beetham, 'Revisiting Legitimacy, Twenty Years On' in Justice Tankebe and Alison Liebling (eds), *Legitimacy and Criminal Justice: An International Exploration* (Oxford University Press, 2013) 19, 19 (emphasis altered).

legitimacy"'.[14] The relevant question is, therefore, whether a regulator, for example, '*should* be regarded as legitimate' according to such criteria and not, as the alternative, descriptive approach contends, whether the regulator '*is* regarded as legitimate'.[15] Scholars applying normative approaches to political legitimacy are therefore concerned with whether there exists a 'right to rule' or justification for the exercise of power from both the perspective of those subject to power, and those exercising power.[16] Such commentary typically emanates from the disciplines of philosophy, law and political sciences.[17]

Commentators diverge, however, on the normative criteria according to which political legitimacy should be determined.[18] Commonly, such criteria include concepts of constitutionality, accountability, effectiveness and a reliance on expertise and substantive and procedural justice.[19] Further, modern conceptualisations of the normative strand of political legitimacy include, for example, those intertwined with social contract theory as developed by Hobbes, Locke and Rousseau. According to these perspectives, voluntary consent to state power is also pivotal to, although not necessarily determinative of, political legitimacy.[20]

Descriptive Approaches to Political Legitimacy

The second broad approach to political legitimacy is descriptive or empirical. It is commonly formulated by sociological commentators through the question 'when is an actor regarded as legitimate, and why?'[21] According to the descriptive approach, politically legitimate power is '*acknowledged* as

14 Anthony Bottoms and Justice Tankebe, 'Police Legitimacy and the Authority of the State' in Antje du Bois-Pedain, Magnus Ulvang and Petter Asp (eds), *Criminal Law and the Authority of the State* (Hart Publishing, 2017) 47, 49 quoting Wilfried Hinsch, 'Justice, Legitimacy, and Constitutional Rights' (2010) 13(1) *Critical Review of International Social and Political Philosophy* 39, 40. Peter draws a distinction between 'normative' and 'meta-normative' political legitimacy to arrive at a hybrid model: Fabienne Peter, *The Grounds of Political Legitimacy* (Oxford University Press, 2023) 3–4, 8.

15 Julia Black, 'Constructing and Contesting Legitimacy and Accountability in Polycentric Regulatory Regimes' (2008) 2 *Regulation and Governance* 137, 145 (emphasis altered).

16 Bottoms and Tankebe, 'Beyond Procedural Justice' (n 2) 124–5.

17 See, eg, Black, 'Constructing and Contesting Legitimacy' (n 15) 145; Schwartzberg (n 8); Beetham, 'Revisiting Legitimacy' (n 13) 19–20; Thornhill (n 9) 135–6.

18 See, eg, Black, 'Constructing and Contesting Legitimacy' (n 15) 145.

19 See, eg, ibid 145–6; Morgan and Yeung (n 11) 238–53.

20 See, eg, Alex Levitov, 'Normative Legitimacy and the State' in *Oxford Handbooks OnLine* (Oxford University Press, 2016) 5–7; Peter Fabienne, 'Political Legitimacy', *The Stanford Encyclopedia of Philosophy* (Web Page, 24 April 2017) <https://plato.stanford.edu/archives/sum2017/entries/legitimacy/>.

21 Black, 'Constructing and Contesting Legitimacy' (n 15) 144. See also Beetham, 'Revisiting Legitimacy' (n 13) 19–20; Schwartzberg (n 8).

rightful' by those who are subject to such power.[22] That is, political legitimacy is 'a matter of fact'.[23] Max Weber's influential conceptualisation of political legitimacy can be characterised as descriptive or empirical in nature.[24] In his view, 'power ... relations are legitimate where those engaged in them perceive or believe them to be so'.[25] From this perspective, legitimacy is determined according to the particular social context in which power is exercised, and at the specific point in time at which power is used. Unlike normative approaches, political legitimacy is therefore not determined according to generalisable principles across different societies and time periods.[26] It is, instead, determined by examining only the views held by those who are subject to the exercise of power.[27]

Combined Normative and Descriptive Approaches to Political Legitimacy

Objections to both the normative and the descriptive perspectives on political legitimacy have led to the development of alternative approaches. These alternatives seek to capture the interaction between normative and descriptive perspectives. For example, the descriptive approach has been criticised for failing to consider the interests of minority populations where state power is unjustifiably exercised (e.g., arbitrary detention).[28] Bottoms and Tankebe argue, however, that while this is a sound argument against '*exclusively* empirical' notions of legitimacy, the value of the empirical or descriptive approach should not be dismissed in its entirety.[29]

Most notably, Habermas has criticised the strict categorisation of political legitimacy as either descriptive or normative in nature. He further considers that the abstract nature of the normative approach is too divorced from the historical context it seeks to analyse. He views the descriptive approach as equally inadequate because it fails to recognise broader, principle-based

22 Black, 'Constructing and Contesting Legitimacy' (n 15) 144, quoting Mark C Suchman, 'Managing Legitimacy: Strategic and Institutional Approaches' (1995) 30(3) *The Academy of Management Review* 571, 574; Beetham, 'Revisiting Legitimacy' (n 13) 19–20.

23 Bottoms and Tankebe, 'Police Legitimacy and the Authority of the State' (n 14) 48 quoting Hinsch (n 14) 40.

24 Camilla Pondel, 'Legitimacy in Australia's Financial System External Dispute Resolution Framework: New and Improved or Simply New?' (2019) 42(1) *University of New South Wales Law Journal* 335, 351.

25 Black, 'Constructing and Contesting Legitimacy' (n 15) 144 quoting Max Weber, 'Bureaucracy' in Hans Heinrich Gerth and Charles Wright Mills (eds), *Max Weber: Essays in Sociology* (Routledge, 1948) 196, 213.

26 Beetham, *The Legitimation of Power* (n 2) 5–6.

27 See, eg, Bottoms and Tankebe, 'Beyond Procedural Justice' (n 2) 124.

28 See, eg, Bottoms and Tankebe, 'Police Legitimacy and the Authority of the State' (n 14) 49.

29 Ibid (emphasis in the original).

standards relevant to political legitimacy.[30] He therefore advocates an alternative approach to legitimacy which is grounded in deliberative democracy and discourse.[31]

Beetham similarly develops a combined perspective of political legitimacy in his foundational work on the concept. He rejects the descriptive account of Weber and argues that 'a given power relationship is not legitimate because people believe in its legitimacy, but because it can be *justified in terms of* their beliefs'.[32] He therefore advocates for both a consideration of the beliefs that *are* held by a particular society at a point in time (a descriptive question) along with the particular *justifications* for such beliefs (a normative question).[33] Bottoms and Tankebe build on Beetham's framework in the criminal justice context to develop their dialogic perspective on political legitimacy, as discussed below.[34]

A Foundation for Legitimacy: David Beetham's Framework of Legitimacy

Beetham presents his framework for political legitimacy in *The Legitimation of Power*.[35] At the core of his concept of political legitimacy are *the societal values and beliefs that constitute a shared normative justification for power for a specific society at a particular point in time*. Using Beetham's approach to analyse legitimacy therefore requires determining 'the degree of congruence, or lack of it, between a given system of power and the beliefs, values and expectations that provide its justification'.[36] As will be described shortly, his legitimacy framework comprises three key elements, called here the 'legality', 'normative' and 'consent or acknowledgement' elements. His approach focuses on the question of political legitimacy from the perspective of those subject to power – the subordinate 'audience'.[37] In developing this framework, Beetham adopts a multi-disciplinary approach, drawing on politics, law and philosophy. Notably, Bottoms and Tankebe observe that in

30 See, eg, Beetham, *The Legitimation of Power* (n 2) 15–16; Arie Brand, *The Force of Reason: An Introduction to Habermas' Theory of Communicative Action* (Allen & Unwin, 1990) 93.
31 See, eg, Fabienne (n 20); Brand (n 30) 63, 93.
32 Bottoms and Tankebe, 'Police Legitimacy and the Authority of the State' (n 14) 52 quoting David Beetham, *The Legitimation of Power* (Macmillan, 1st ed, 1991) 12. Cf Frederick Barnard, *Democratic Legitimacy: Plural Values and Political Power* (McGill-Queens University Press, 2001) 31–3.
33 Beetham, *The Legitimation of Power* (n 2) 11.
34 Bottoms and Tankebe, 'Police Legitimacy and the Authority of the State' (n 14) 51.
35 Beetham, *The Legitimation of Power* (n 2). See also Beetham, 'Revisiting Legitimacy' (n 13); David Beetham and Christopher Lord, *Legitimacy and the European Union* (Longman, 1998).
36 Beetham, *The Legitimation of Power* (n 2) 11.
37 Ibid 256.

a number of respects Beetham's approach to legitimacy is analogous to that developed by another social scientist, Jean-Marc Coicaud. Beetham's and Coicaud's legitimacy frameworks both adopt a multi-disciplinary perspective and comprise three elements.[38] However, as will be noted shortly, their focus differs in relation to these elements.

As already noted, Beetham's approach to political legitimacy is distinct from both the traditional empirical and normative approaches described earlier. While his framework is grounded in the social sciences he is at pains to distinguish it from his social scientist contemporaries.[39] He argues that they adopt Weber's flawed understanding of legitimacy as constituting a '*belief in legitimacy*'.[40] Beetham considers that this view manifests as an assessment of the ability of those in power to superficially convince others of their legitimacy.[41] Further, Beetham does not adopt a comprehensively normative perspective on political legitimacy. He considers that such traditional philosophical approaches to legitimacy fail to account for particular social contexts and power relations – that is, 'legitimacy-in-context'.[42]

Beetham's Three Elements of Legitimacy

Beetham's framework outlines three elements or dimensions that are necessary for power to be considered politically legitimate.[43] The first is the 'legality' element, which concerns obtaining and using power according to existing rules.[44] The second element relates to beliefs that justify these rules. Beetham has termed this 'normative justifiability', but for ease of reference it is referred to here as the 'normative' element.[45] The third dimension of Beetham's framework is the 'consent or acknowledgement' element.[46] The absence or dilution of any one of these three dimensions constitutes a deviation from legitimacy. Each of these elements will now be discussed in turn.

38 Bottoms and Tankebe therefore refer to the framework as 'the Beetham-Coicaud conceptual scheme': Bottoms and Tankebe, 'Beyond Procedural Justice' (n 2) 132-3. For ease of reference I will refer to it as 'Beetham's framework or approach'. See also Coicaud (n 6).
39 Beetham, *The Legitimation of Power* (n 2) 7.
40 Ibid 6 (emphasis in the original), 13.
41 Ibid 6–9, 13–4.
42 Ibid 6–7, 13–4.
43 Ibid 64; Beetham and Lord (n 35) 3.
44 Beetham, *The Legitimation of Power* (n 2) 64–9.
45 Beetham and Lord (n 35) 3.
46 Beetham, *The Legitimation of Power* (n 2) 64.

The Legality Element

Beetham's first requirement for legitimate power is that it is 'acquired and exercised in accordance with established rules'.[47] Rules that determine whether power has been 'acquired and exercised' in a legally valid manner include constitutions, legislation, the common law and unwritten conventions.[48] Power that is acquired or exercised contrary to such rules is 'illegitimate' to the extent that it deviates from those rules.[49] The legality element broadly aligns with the conventional perspective of legal commentators and, in particular, those who adopt a positivist view of the law.[50] For example, an application of this element to the therapeutic goods regulatory regime would require an assessment of whether the *Therapeutic Goods Act 1989* (Cth) ('the Act') is constitutionally valid, or whether decisions made and actions taken by the regulator comply with relevant legislation and principles of Australian public law. Historically, it is the legality element of legitimacy against which the therapeutic goods regulatory regime has been most publicly and formally scrutinised.[51]

In Beetham's view, those who hold and exercise power frequently appeal to the law and 'legality' as the 'ultimate' basis for the legitimacy of their power. This is, he considers, characteristic of a society in which the law and its institutions are inaccessible, inclined to affirm and protect the status quo, and are largely unchanging.[52] Beetham is clear, however, that legal validity is not enough to determine that power is legitimate:

> [A]ppeal to the law can never provide more than a primary, and therefore provisional, ground for legitimacy ... rules cannot justify themselves simply by being rules, but require justification by reference to considerations which lie beyond them.[53]

47 Ibid.
48 Ibid 16.
49 Ibid.
50 Ibid 4.
51 See eg 'Pan Founder Wins $55m from Taxpayers'', *The World Today* (ABC Local Radio, 14 August 2008) <https://www.abc.net.au/listen/programs/worldtoday/pan-founder-wins-55m-from-taxpayers/477036>; Esme Shirlow and Thomas Faunce, 'Recent Legal Developments and the Authority of the Australian Therapeutic Goods Administration' (2009) 16 *Journal of Law and Medicine* 764.
52 Beetham, *The Legitimation of Power* (n 2) 67–8.
53 Ibid 69.

The Normative Element

Beetham considers that the second, normative, element of his three-part framework 'may indeed form the core of legitimacy'.[54] The normative element requires that rules of power and their exercise must be justified 'by reference to beliefs shared by both dominant and subordinate' parties to a relationship of power.[55] Therefore, rules that ostensibly support a position of power of a 'dominant' over a 'subordinate', and the exercise of that power, must be justified according to normative considerations.[56] In formulating the normative element Beetham shifts his focus from what a rule 'is' (the legality element) to what a rule 'ought' to be (the normative element) – that is, from the realism of power to its justifiability. The legitimacy of power is therefore to be determined by 'assessing how far it can be justified in terms of people's beliefs, how far it conforms to their values or standards, how far it satisfies the normative expectations they have of it'.[57]

Beetham thus contends that power must be considered legitimate in the eyes of the party that is subject to that power – the subordinate. It is the existence of shared legitimising beliefs between the dominant and the subordinate that creates the normative obligation on the subordinate to follow the power arrangements.[58] Notably, Bottoms's and Tankebe's dialogic approach advocates an expanded understanding about whose beliefs and values are relevant for the formulation of a shared normative justification for power.[59] This will be discussed shortly.

There are further aspects of the normative element that are worth elaborating. In simplified form, Beetham argues that a society's beliefs determine the normative criteria against which legitimacy is assessed. This can occur in two ways.[60] First, societal beliefs provide an ultimate 'source of legitimacy' for power – that is, an authorising base from which power is drawn.[61] Sources of legitimacy may be 'external' to a society (e.g., religion, secular natural law, scientific theories) or 'internal' to a society (e.g., societal traditions such as hereditary power or present-day decisions by a society's governing representatives).[62] The case study of the abortifacient RU486 illustrates the application of Beetham's observations about sources of legitimacy. As will be discussed in Chapter 5, key legislative changes in that case represented a shift in the source of legitimacy for the therapeutic goods regulatory regime.

54 Ibid 293.
55 Ibid 16; Beetham, 'Revisiting Legitimacy' (n 13) 20. Cf Barnard (n 32) 33–4.
56 Beetham, *The Legitimation of Power* (n 2) 4.
57 Ibid 11.
58 Ibid.
59 Bottoms and Tankebe, 'Beyond Procedural Justice' (n 2) 132–54.
60 Ibid 69.
61 Ibid 70.
62 Ibid 71–5.

This shift was from the *external* authorising source of science to that of religion and natural law; and from the *internal* source of decision-makers under the therapeutic goods regulatory regime to Parliament. This shift reflected a change in societal beliefs away from a traditional reverence for science and technocratic-based decision-making, and therefore reflected a change in the legitimating normative criteria for the regulatory regime.

Beetham contends that there is a second way in which society's beliefs determine the normative criteria against which legitimacy is assessed. Societal beliefs, he argues, determine the legitimate 'content' of power – that is the substantive norms or values that constitute that power.[63] Beetham argues that for power to be legitimate it must contain a shared or 'common interest' between dominant and subordinate parties.[64] It would be difficult, for example, to justify a power to quarantine people if it protected only those in a dominant position of power from the outbreak of an infectious disease such as SARS-CoV-2 (the virus which causes COVID-19).[65]

The Consent or Acknowledgement Element

The third and final dimension of Beetham's legitimacy framework is established by 'evidence of consent by the subordinate to the particular power relation' and according to that society's conventions.[66] In both the 1991 and 2013 editions of *The Legitimation of Power*, Beetham considers that express 'actions' provide evidence of consent. They assist in the conferral of legitimacy through the moral commitment to, and public expression of, the legitimate power relation.[67] In the contemporary liberal democratic context, consent typically involves the act of deciding between eligible candidates in an election or, to a lesser degree, participating in a community consultation process.[68] In the 2013 edition of his book and in a further publication that year, Beetham revised his original description of this element. He states that the emphasis on 'consent' should be replaced by 'acts of recognition, acknowledgement or engagement, from which authorities can derive legitimacy to a greater or lesser extent'. Further, he clarifies that legitimacy may be 'constituted by actions *as well as beliefs*'.[69] Beetham describes this third

63 Ibid 76.
64 Ibid 82.
65 See, eg, Lawrence O Gostin, Eric A Friedman and Sarah A Wetter, 'Responding to Covid-19: How to Navigate a Public Health Emergency Legally and Ethically' (2020) 50(2) *Hastings Center Report* 8.
66 Beetham, *The Legitimation of Power* (n 2) 14.
67 Ibid 18, 91; David Beetham, *The Legitimation of Power* (Palgrave Macmillan, 1st ed, 1991) 12.
68 Beetham, *The Legitimation of Power* (n 2) 92–3.
69 Ibid 267–8 (emphasis added).

element as the 'legitimation' element.[70] Delegitimation occurs where there are 'public acts of protest, disobedience and withdrawal of endorsement or recognition'.[71] The stronger the action, and the greater the number of those acting, the greater the impact on legitimacy.[72] Notably, while Beetham considered 'consent' as the final element in his framework, his contemporary Coicaud considered that it was the primary element.[73] Coicaud's perspective has been reflected by others who consider that 'consent' is 'constitutive of legitimacy'.[74]

The Limitations of Beetham's Framework

Beetham's legitimacy framework provides an approach to begin to navigate the regulatory contours of the therapeutic goods regime. Its benefits include the capacity to capture and consider the diverse views of the pluralistic society in which the regulatory regime operates.[75] The multi-disciplinary basis of Beetham's framework also presents a broad lens with which to analyse the range of therapeutic goods that are subject to regulation and the changing social and political environment in which this occurs.[76] Most relevantly, Beetham's framework provides a practical 'heuristic framework' of three elements against which political legitimacy can be considered.[77] For these reasons, aspects of Beetham's framework will be used to identify challenges to the political legitimacy of the therapeutic goods regulatory regime as they arise in relation to each of the selected case studies. However, Beetham's framework also presents certain limitations, summarised below. In part in order to overcome, or at least mitigate, these challenges, I now turn to the constant dialogic approach to political legitimacy to enhance the investigation of the political legitimacy of the therapeutic goods regulatory regime.

The Application Problem

Beetham's approach to political legitimacy is arguably frustrated by the challenge of application. One example is the difficulty of determining the strands

70 Beetham, 'Revisiting Legitimacy' (n 13) 20. For ease of reference this third element will be called the 'consent/ acknowledgement element' or 'third element'.
71 Ibid 26.
72 Beetham, *The Legitimation of Power* (n 2) 19.
73 Coicaud (n 6) 10–14. Coicaud's perspective has been reflected by others who consider that 'consent' is 'constitutive of legitimacy.': Bottoms and Tankebe, 'Beyond Procedural Justice' (n 2) 134.
74 Bottoms and Tankebe, 'Beyond Procedural Justice' (n 2) 134.
75 See, eg, ibid 133.
76 Beetham and Lord (n 35) 5.
77 Ibid.

of Beetham's second element of legitimacy – the source and content of shared normative beliefs – in any given situation. This is acknowledged by Beetham himself, who describes the framework as 'general or abstract' and requiring that the 'specific content' be determined in relation to the social and political context in question.[78] However, it is not clear from Beetham's analysis precisely how this is to be achieved. It is possible that Beetham does not consider that there is a need to address this challenge in light of his discussion of empirical studies in which theories of political legitimacy are applied and analysed by others.[79]

A second potential application challenge is whether Beetham's framework can be used at a level below the overarching power arrangements of the nation-state. The question is whether it can provide useful insights about a nation-state's various regulatory arrangements, such as the therapeutic goods regime? The bulk of Beetham's commentary on the application of his framework focuses on the nation-state or international governance.[80] He has, however, described approvingly the application of his framework to research at the sub-state level, specifically in criminal law enforcement.[81]

The Circularity Problem

Beetham's approach has been criticised for the circularity present in the second 'normative' element of his framework.[82] It is arguable that, in seeking to identify shared values and beliefs between subordinate and dominant parties, Beetham's approach will inevitably identify the values and beliefs of the existing and dominant political system and its underlying norms. For example, one of the objects of the Act is the safety of therapeutic goods.[83] This arguably constitutes evidence of a shared value between those subject to power and those exercising power about the importance of safety in the regulation of therapeutic goods. However, it is the Act itself, via the safety provision, that provides the evidence for its own legitimacy. Nevertheless, it could also be argued that the problem of circularity is almost unavoidable in a stable political and social context.[84]

It is perhaps in anticipation of this criticism that Beetham requires that the third 'consent/acknowledgement element' of his framework be satisfied in order to establish legitimacy.[85] A dilution of the political legitimacy of the

78 Ibid 4, 10–11.
79 Beetham, *The Legitimation of Power* (n 2) 256–65.
80 See, eg, ibid 259–92; Beetham and Lord (n 35).
81 Beetham and Lord (n 35) 254, 256.
82 Rosemary O'Kane, 'Against Legitimacy' (1993) XLI *Political Studies* 471, 475.
83 *Therapeutic Goods Act 1989* (Cth) s 4(1)(a).
84 O'Kane (n 82) 475.
85 Ibid 476.

therapeutic goods regulatory regime would therefore be indicated by public dissent about the importance of safety itself or about what the term 'safety' means. This can be illustrated by the case study of urogynaecological mesh devices in Chapter 6. As will be argued, the political legitimacy of the regulatory regime was challenged in that case by public dissent about, among other things, the interpretation of what constituted an 'adverse event' arising from the use of the devices. This reflects the argument of Black that difficult or controversial cases often highlight points of weakness in otherwise stable regulatory schemes.[86]

The Multiple Players Problem

Beetham's approach to legitimacy is largely presented in the context of a power relationship between two parties – the dominant and the subordinate. A simple dyadic relationship of this kind is, however, rarely the case in reality, particularly in the regulatory context in which multiple parties are typically involved. Many different groups and sub-groups are likely to constitute subordinate parties to a power relationship. Reflecting on legitimacy research in criminal policy and law enforcement, Beetham acknowledges that 'different audiences may be concerned with different dimensions of legitimacy and assign differential importance to them'.[87]

Beetham's notion of the 'dominant' party is, in many circumstances, also likely to constitute multiple actors. At the level of the nation-state the dominant party consists of those who hold power at the highest levels of the executive, legislative and judicial arms of government. But even within those arms – and most obviously in the executive and legislature – there will be different and conflicting values. At the sub-state level there will be a cascade of formal institutions, party-political groups, non-government organisations and individuals exercising power. An analysis of legitimacy must therefore be capable of capturing a dynamic and complex exchange between these multiple dominant and subordinate parties.

The Subordinate Focus Problem

As described earlier, Beetham is concerned primarily with political legitimacy as it is viewed by those subject to power.[88] He considers that 'the key question for the study of legitimacy … is how to ascertain empirically what the beliefs of those subject to authority may be, and how consistent they are

86 Black, 'Constructing and Contesting Legitimacy' (n 15) 138.
87 Beetham, *The Legitimation of Power* (n 2) 258.
88 Ibid 256.

with the legitimacy claims of the powerful'.[89] For Beetham, it is the views of subordinate parties about the legitimacy of those in power that produce an obligation on the subordinate to 'support and cooperate' with the dominant party.[90] As will be explained shortly, Beetham's perspective largely omits the role played by the dominant party's view of their *own* legitimacy.[91] Arguably a powerholder's understanding of their legitimacy is closely linked with notions of self-identity or self-confidence and with their use of authority.[92] Consequently a focus on the legitimacy of power solely from the perspective of the subordinate parties misses a crucial element in the analysis of legitimacy.

The Time Problem

A final limitation with Beetham's political legitimacy framework is its predominant focus on determining legitimacy at a particular point in time, rather than over the course of time. On the one hand, Beetham is clear that the degree of legitimacy in a relationship of power changes over time and that 'the study of power relations and their legitimation' is therefore 'an ongoing process'.[93] On the other hand, his preferred approach to investigating legitimacy appears to focus on the collection of evidence at a particular moment in order 'to assess the legitimacy of power *in its context*, i.e. against the norms and values of *a given society*'.[94] However, such 'snapshots' of legitimacy do not necessarily provide guidance for the continuous nature of regulatory relationships. What is required, therefore, is an approach to legitimacy that is able to capture the perpetual nature of the relevant regulatory power arrangements and to better reflect Beetham's own position that 'legitimacy involves a *relationship*'.[95] In light of the preceding discussion of Beetham's foundational approach, such an approach to legitimacy can now be discussed.

89 Ibid.
90 Ibid 13.
91 Anthony Bottoms and Justice Tankebe, '"A Voice Within": Power-Holders' Perspectives on Authority and Legitimacy' in Justice Tankebe and Alison Liebling (eds), *Legitimacy and Criminal Justice: An International Exploration* (Oxford University Press, 2013) 60, 60 (emphasis added).
92 Ibid 60, 68, 73.
93 Beetham, *The Legitimation of Power* (n 2) 22–3, 103.
94 Ibid 21 (emphasis added).
95 Ibid 259.

Building on Beetham: A Constant Dialogic Approach to Political Legitimacy

This part turns to an alternative and enhanced approach to investigating the political legitimacy of the therapeutic goods regulatory regime. It begins by outlining Bottoms's and Tankebe's dialogic approach to political legitimacy and provides an example of its use in criminal justice research. Their approach is then reformulated to enable it to be applied to the therapeutic goods regulatory regime. The reformulation developed is a three-element, applied approach to political legitimacy called the 'constant dialogic approach'. The chapter describes the three elements of the constant dialogic approach and how they will be applied to the case studies that follow to investigate the political legitimacy of the therapeutic goods regulatory regime.

Key Characteristics of a Dialogic Approach to Political Legitimacy

Bottoms's and Tankebe's dialogic approach to legitimacy conceives of legitimacy as a relational concept developed over the course of a dialogue between those exercising power (referred to earlier as the dominant party) and those subject to power (the subordinate party).[96] There are three key characteristics of the dialogic model: the distinction between dominant and subordinate perspectives on legitimacy; the existence of multiple subordinate and dominant parties; and the relational nature of dialogic legitimacy. Each characteristic will now be discussed, including, where relevant, the extent to which it addresses the limitations of Beetham's legitimacy framework.

Dominant and Subordinate Parties' Different Perspectives about Legitimacy

Bottoms's and Tankebe's dialogic approach explicitly distinguishes between political legitimacy as perceived by different parties to a power relationship. It identifies that legitimacy is perceived both by those who hold and exercise power ('power-holder legitimacy', referred to hereafter as 'dominant legitimacy') and by those subject to power ('audience legitimacy', hereafter 'subordinate legitimacy').[97] In this respect their dialogic approach addresses Beetham's predominant and limiting focus on subordinate views of legitimacy discussed above.

Bottoms and Tankebe describe dominant legitimacy as the 'inner beliefs and feelings in relation to the power that has been assigned to them'.[98] Such

96 Bottoms and Tankebe, 'Beyond Procedural Justice' (n 2) 129.
97 Ibid 132–54.
98 Bottoms and Tankebe, 'A Voice Within' (n 91) 63.

beliefs and feelings differ, they argue, between dominant powerholders.[99] But, ultimately, for all dominant parties such beliefs are intimately connected with notions of self-identity.[100] Bottoms and Tankebe highlight that 'symbols and rituals' may serve as a means of communicating legitimacy not only to those subject to power, but also to the powerholder themselves.[101] For example, as will be argued in the chapters to follow, the therapeutic goods regulatory regime's sense of its own legitimacy has been dominated by the paradigms of scientism and technocracy discussed in Chapter 2.

Multiple Subordinate and Dominant Parties

The dialogic approach acknowledges that there may be multiple subordinate parties with distinct views about the legitimacy of power to which they are subject.[102] Bottoms and Tankebe build on observations by Weber and Raz that dominant parties 'claim' to hold and exercise power that is legitimate by addressing different subordinate audiences.[103] Bottoms and Tankebe also consider that the dialogic approach makes room for multiple dominant parties or powerholders. Consequently, between diverse groups of both subordinate and dominant parties 'there can be many different dialogues happening simultaneously'.[104]

The recognition by the dialogic approach of multiple subordinate and dominant parties and their respective views about legitimacy addresses two limitations of Beetham's framework identified earlier. First, it responds to 'the multiple players problem'. For example, Beetham acknowledges but does not explore the different conceptions of legitimacy experienced and perceived by distinct subordinate audiences.[105] A second criticism of Beetham's framework is that notions of political legitimacy inevitably reflect dominant values. This is described earlier as 'the circularity problem'. The dialogic approach, however, recognises that each subordinate party – including those who constitute a minority group – can ask a dominant party to justify their power and contest a claim to political legitimacy. The dialogic approach therefore provides 'a partial normative brake' on the majority's dominance regarding what beliefs and values constitute political legitimacy.[106]

99 Ibid.
100 Ibid 68, discussing Rodney Barker, *Legitimating Identities: The Self-Presentation of Rulers and Subjects* (Cambridge University Press, 2001).
101 Ibid 69.
102 Bottoms and Tankebe, 'Beyond Procedural Justice' (n 2) 128.
103 Ibid 128–9.
104 Bottoms and Tankebe, 'Police Legitimacy and the Authority of the State' (n 14) 73–4.
105 Beetham, *The Legitimation of Power* (n 2) 256–8.
106 Bottoms and Tankebe, 'Police Legitimacy and the Authority of the State' (n 14) 60.

The Relational Nature of Political Legitimacy

At the core of the dialogic model of legitimacy is its relational nature. To establish legitimacy, a dominant party must 'cultivate' an ongoing relationship with subordinate audiences.[107] It is this characteristic of the dialogic approach that distinguishes Bottoms's and Tankebe's view of legitimacy from that of their predecessors, including Beetham. Bottoms and Tankebe explain that

> [l]egitimacy needs to be perceived as always *dialogic* and *relational* in character. That is to say, those in power (or seeking power) in a given context make a claim to be the legitimate ruler(s); then members of the audience respond to this claim; the power-holder might adjust the nature of the claim in light of the audience's response; and this process repeats itself.[108]

In engaging in such a dialogue, the dominant party develops a 'narrative' justifying why they should and do hold power.[109] The aim of such a narrative is to cultivate a view amongst the subordinate audience that the dominant party is normatively justified to hold power and therefore represents social stability and order. A failure to achieve this aim signifies instability and disorder and that the dominant party, in exercising power, is no better than a 'hostage-taker' of her or his subordinate audience.[110]

Consistent with this relational conception of legitimacy are observations that a dominant party's 'understanding of their own legitimacy may evolve' in response to the subordinate party.[111] In an acknowledgement of the dialogic approach Beetham states that it

> serves to highlight sites or moments of intervention which may bring about changes in power holders' perceptions of their own legitimacy … The legitimacy of authorities, in sum, is not something given or unalterable but can be enhanced where they show themselves prepared to listen and respond to experiences and challenges from below.[112]

107 Bottoms and Tankebe, 'Beyond Procedural Justice' (n 2) 128–9.
108 Ibid 129.
109 Referred to as 'narratives of legitimation': Bottoms and Tankebe, 'Police Legitimacy and the Authority of the State' (n 14) 50.
110 Ibid 48–50.
111 Belén V Lowrey-Kinberg and Grace Sullivan Buker, '"I'm Giving You a Lawful Order": Dialogic Legitimacy in Sandra Bland's Traffic Stop' (2017) 51(2) *Law & Society Review* 379, 385.
112 Beetham, *The Legitimation of Power* (n 2) 258, citing Bottoms and Tankebe, 'Beyond Procedural Justice' (n 2) 119.

Bottoms and Tankebe stress the importance of each exchange between parties to a power relationship because every interaction can affect the legitimacy of that relationship. Each exchange between the parties potentially alters the subordinate party's perception of the dominant's legitimacy. Further, such instances can serve as 'teachable moments' for the dominant party to better understand whether and why they are perceived as legitimate, and their own perceptions of their legitimacy.[113]

An example of the relational nature of the dialogic approach to legitimacy is found in research in the criminal justice context by Lowrey-Kinberg and Sullivan Buker.[114] Their work highlights the significance of an exchange between parties to a power relationship and how it can constitute a 'teachable moment'.[115] The authors apply Bottoms's and Tankebe's dialogic approach to the events that ultimately led to the tragic death in police custody of an African American woman, Sandra Bland, in 2015. Ms Bland was arrested after a Texan police officer asked her to pull over because she allegedly changed lanes without signalling. The authors analysed the escalating exchange between Ms Bland and the police officer which was recorded on the police officer's dashboard camera.[116]

The authors outline how the dialogic approach demonstrates that legitimacy is 'negotiated' and evolves between police officers and members of the public. Typically, they contend, a police officer will make a claim to legitimacy through words or actions, such as by pulling over a car and explaining why to the driver. The driver will then consider the police officer's claim to legitimacy and their response will reflect their assessment of that claim. In turn, the police officer may alter their claim to legitimacy in light of the driver's reaction.[117]

The authors describe how questions posed by Ms Bland such as 'When are you going to let me go?', 'Why am I being arrested?' and 'Why do I have to put out my cigarette?' were 'a tool to challenge [the police officer's] legitimacy'.[118] The authors argue that Ms Bland's questions constituted a 'basic legitimation demand' – a request 'that the power-holder should offer normatively appropriate reasons why the citizen must obey the command'.[119]

113 Bottoms and Tankebe, 'A Voice Within' (n 91) 62–3, quoting Tom Tyler, 'Trust and Legitimacy: Policing in the USA and Europe' (2011) 8 *European Journal of Criminology* 254, 257.

114 Lowrey-Kinberg and Sullivan Buker (n 111).

115 Bottoms and Tankebe, 'A Voice Within' (n 91) 62.

116 Lowrey-Kinberg and Sullivan Buker (n 111) 386–9.

117 Ibid 385.

118 Ibid 391.

119 Ibid. See also Bottoms and Tankebe, 'Police Legitimacy and the Authority of the State' (n 14) 73.

In describing how the concept of a basic legitimation demand aligns with their dialogic approach to political legitimacy, Bottoms and Tankebe state:[120]

> It enhances our original conception of the 'dialogue' by pointing out that audiences may make reasonable demands on power-holders as to the kinds of legitimations that they (the power-holders) might justifiably offer within the dialogue.[121]

Legitimate power therefore requires that each subordinate party be able to make a basic legitimation demand of the dominant party to justify power and to do so in normative terms.[122] Logically, those subject to power are arguably also entitled to receive a clear and reasoned response from the dominant party. The authors of the 'traffic stop' study considered that the police officer failed to adequately respond to Ms Bland's basic legitimation demand, as illustrated in the following exchange:

Q: Bland: When are you going to let me go?
A: [police officer]: I don't know
Q: Bland: Why will you not tell me what's going on?
A: [police officer]: You are not complying.[123]

It is likely that from Ms Bland's perspective her questions were not answered in a considered and reasoned way that justified the power that was being exercised against her. The police officer's responses resulted in Ms Bland feeling a strong sense of 'procedural injustice' and an absence of legitimacy about the power being exercised.[124]

The authors' conclusions support Beetham's and Bottoms's and Tankebe's views that shared normative beliefs and values are central to political legitimacy:

> [T]he acute escalation of the encounter was due in large part to each speaker's steadfast adherence to their respective beliefs about [the police officer's] legitimacy. The events of Bland's traffic stop therefore exemplify

120 The concept of a 'basic legitimation demand' was developed by Bernard Williams in his work on legitimacy and was subsequently adopted by Bottoms and Tankebe: ibid 73, discussing Bernard Williams (selected and edited by Geoffrey Hawthorn), *In the Beginning Was the Deed: Realism and Moralism in Political Argument* (Princeton University Press, 2005).

121 Bottoms and Tankebe, 'Police Legitimacy and the Authority of the State' (n 14) 73.

122 Ibid 57, 60, quoting Williams (n 120).

123 Lowrey-Kinberg and Sullivan Buker (n 111) 392.

124 Ibid 392–3.

the consequences of audience legitimacy and power-holder legitimacy *incongruence*.[125]

A further insight gained from this study is that both the police officer and Ms Bland use 'law enforcement jargon and epistemics ... to strengthen their respective [legitimacy] claims'.[126] Examples include the police officer's use of the phrase 'lawful order' to communicate that he had the support of the state.[127] This recalls Bottoms and Tankebe's observation that 'symbols and/or rituals' are often used by those who hold power to assert legitimacy to subordinate parties and to themselves.[128] As will be discussed, the use of such mechanisms to support claims of political legitimacy is also evident in the case studies involving the therapeutic goods regulatory regime.[129] Ms Bland asserted her own legal rights to redress by stating 'let's take this to court' and challenging the officer's request that she stop using her mobile phone by responding '[t]his is my property'.[130] These statements highlight Bottoms's and Tankebe's view that dialogue in the context of political legitimacy need not be verbal and may include symbols, rituals and effective performance.[131]

The escalating exchange between Ms Bland and the police officer culminated in Ms Bland's arrest for 'assaulting a public servant'.[132] She was taken to a county jail. Three days later she was found dead in a police cell. Her cause of death was determined to be 'suicide by hanging', a finding that was questioned by activists and Ms Bland's family.[133] The death of Ms Bland is a confronting indictment of the treatment of African Americans by law enforcement officials in the United States. It also highlights the significant

125 Ibid 403 (emphasis added). There are similarities between the basic legitimation demand in the formation, maintenance and challenging of legitimacy and Black's observation about the role of accountability mechanisms in the regulatory context: Black, 'Constructing and Contesting Legitimacy' (n 15) 149.

126 Lowrey-Kinberg and Sullivan Buker (n 111) 402. Note that the authors define 'epistemics' as 'knowledge in interaction': at 398.

127 Ibid 402.

128 Bottoms and Tankebe, 'A Voice Within' (n 91) 69.

129 See Chapters 4 (medicinal cannabis), 5 (medical abortion) and 6 (urogynaecological mesh devices).

130 Lowrey-Kinberg and Sullivan Buker (n 111) 400.

131 Bottoms and Tankebe, 'A Voice Within' (n 91) 69–71.

132 David Montgomery, 'The Death of Sandra Bland: Is There Anything Left to Investigate?', *New York Times* (online, 8 May 2019) <https://www.nytimes.com/2019/05/08/us/sandra-bland-texas-death.html?auth=login-google>.

133 Tom Dart, 'Independent Committee to Investigate Sandra Bland Death and Traffic Stop', *The Guardian* (online, 28 July 2015) <https://www.theguardian.com/us-news/2015/jul/27/sandra-bland-attorney-committee-death-traffic-stop>; Tom Dart and Jon Swaine, 'Sandra Bland: Suspicion and Mistrust Flourish Amid Official Inconsistencies' *The Guardian* (online 26 July 2015) <https://www.theguardian.com/us-news/2015/jul/25/sandra-bland-suspicion-mistrust-official-inconsistencies>.

importance of political legitimacy, and the profound consequences of its failure.

A Concluding Word on the Dialogic Approach

Bottoms's and Tankebe's dialogic approach constitutes a significant contribution to the literature on political legitimacy. In particular, and as described above, it requires the consideration of previously unrecognised aspects of legitimacy. These aspects include the significance of a dominant party's own perspective of their legitimacy; the existence of multiple subordinate and dominant parties to a power relationship; and their respective views on legitimacy. Above all, Bottoms and Tankebe contend that legitimacy is relational in nature and is constructed through the interactions or dialogue of dominant and subordinate parties. The dialogic approach therefore builds constructively on the work of legitimacy scholars such as Beetham and addresses the limitations identified in his framework.

Analysing the Therapeutic Goods Regulatory Regime: The Constant Dialogic Approach to Political Legitimacy

Having outlined the dialogic approach, the question remains whether and how it can be applied to analyse the political legitimacy of the therapeutic goods regulatory regime? Bottoms and Tankebe developed and applied their dialogic approach in the context of research on criminal justice. As the above 'traffic stop' example highlights, the limited literature on the consideration of dialogic legitimacy is predominantly confined to criminal justice research.[134] Further, many of the rich insights arising from the application of the dialogic approach are strengthened by broader research in the field of criminal law enforcement, such as in relation to procedural justice.[135]

The dialogic approach to legitimacy has not been widely applied to other contexts, including regulatory arrangements and actors like those of the therapeutic goods regime. This section therefore reformulates Bottoms's and Tankebe's dialogic approach as a three-element approach to political

134 Lowrey-Kinberg and Sullivan Buker (n 111); Jonathan Jackson et al, 'Empirical Legitimacy as Two Connected Psychological States' in Gorazd Mesko and Justice Tankebe (eds), *Trust and Legitimacy in Criminal Justice: European Perspectives* (Springer, 2015) 137; Joseph A Hamm et al '(Re)Organizing Legitimacy Theory' (2022) 27 *Legal and Criminological Psychology* 129.

135 See, eg, Bottoms and Tankebe, 'Police Legitimacy and the Authority of the State' (n 14) 73, 75–6; Jackson (n 134) 138–44; Lowrey-Kinberg and Sullivan Buker (n 111) 380, 382–3, 389–93; Anthony Bottoms and Justice Tankebe, 'Procedural Justice, Legitimacy and Social Contexts' in Denise Meyerson, Catriona Mackenzie and Therese MacDermott (eds) *Procedural Justice and Relational Theory: Empirical, Philosophical, and Legal Perspectives* (Routledge, 2020) 85.

legitimacy which can be readily applied beyond the realm of criminal justice. For this purpose, it will be called the 'constant dialogic approach'. This title emphasises the significance of the ongoing, relational nature of the regulatory arrangements which are to be investigated.

The three elements of the constant dialogic approach require that *legitimacy be analysed as a constant dialogue; through which a set of shared normative beliefs and values are formulated; between all parties to a power relationship*. Each of the three elements of the constant dialogic approach is drawn from Bottoms's and Tankebe's work and, in turn, that of Beetham. However, they do not represent that work in their entirety. Each element will now be discussed in turn.

Legitimacy Should Be Analysed as Constant Dialogue

The first element of the constant dialogic approach requires that legitimacy be analysed as a constant dialogue. This element reflects the pivotal role of dialogue between parties to a power relationship found in Bottoms's and Tankebe's approach. In turn, it captures Bottoms's and Tankebe's view that political legitimacy is fundamentally relational. Further, the first element of the constant dialogic approach emphasises the ongoing nature of such dialogue.[136] It requires that political legitimacy should not be conceived as occurring, as Beetham arguably considered, at a 'snapshot' of a moment in time (described earlier as 'the time problem' of Beetham's framework). Instead, the constant dialogic approach contends that legitimacy should be analysed as 'a *perpetual* discussion, in which the content of powerholders' later claims will be affected by the nature of the audience response'.[137] Consequently, legitimacy should be seen and analysed as 'an ongoing process of claim and response' that may not only 'repeat itself several times'[138] but perpetually. Such dialogue should never be 'understood as episodic transactions'.[139]

This concept of continuous dialogue is, as stated above, coherent with the nature of modern regulatory relationships between the state, institutions and officials, on the one hand, and the community and individuals, on the other. Regulatory arrangements are woven into the fabric of everyday life in a multitude of aspects: health, telecommunications, water and electricity.[140] This is particularly true in relation to the therapeutic goods regulatory regime,

136 See, eg, Hamm et al '(Re)Organizing Legitimacy Theory' (n 134) 131–2.

137 Bottoms and Tankebe, 'Beyond Procedural Justice' (n 2) 129 (emphasis added).

138 Lowrey-Kinberg and Sullivan Buker (n 111) 384.

139 Justice Tankebe, 'Legitimacy and Regulatory Compliance' in Maria Krambia-Kapardis (ed), *Financial Compliance: Issues, Concerns and Future Directions* (Palgrave Macmillan, 2019) 47.

140 See, eg, Karen Lee, *The Legitimacy and Responsiveness of Industry Rule-Making* (Hart, 2018).

which influences the individual's and the community's access to pharmaceuticals and medical devices. Such arrangements have a significant and consistent impact on the lives of subordinate parties. Their activity is ceaseless. Accordingly, the political legitimacy of such regulatory schemes should be conceived as *ongoing* or *constant* and as 'a *relationship* between authorities and those subject to them'.[141]

Through Which a Set of Shared Normative Beliefs and Values Are Formulated

The second element of the constant dialogic approach requires that the legitimacy of a power relationship should be analysed by reference to the extent to which the parties are able to develop shared normative beliefs and values. This element adopts a fundamental aspect of both Beetham's and Bottoms's and Tankebe's legitimacy frameworks. The second 'normative' element of Beetham's approach requires that for power to be legitimate it must be justified 'by reference to beliefs *shared* by both dominant and subordinate' parties. The approach advanced by Bottoms and Tankebe depicts dialogue as the central means by which this congruence in values and beliefs is achieved. Their position is made explicit in this second element of the constant dialogic approach: that dialogue between the dominant and subordinate parties is the basis for the formulation of shared normative beliefs and values. This dialogue can also be analysed to identify what constitutes the parties' values and the source of those values. The constant dialogic approach therefore addresses the 'application problem' of Beetham's framework discussed earlier – that is, how to determine shared normative beliefs in a power relationship.

An example of this second aspect of the constant dialogic approach is the work of Lowrey-Kinberg and Sullivan Buker in relation to the 'traffic stop' incident discussed above. Their analysis illustrates the significant role of dialogue between dominant and subordinate parties in the formation of different (and conceivably shared) normative beliefs and values which are determinative of political legitimacy. In a further example, Bottoms and Tankebe apply the dialogic approach to identify shared normative values (e.g., procedural justice) for legitimate police activity. They consider that these values arise from 'legitimation discussion[s]' and 'real-world debates'.[142]

These examples illustrate a further point. Inherent to a dialogue between parties are elements that may enhance or diminish the formation or maintenance of a congruence in beliefs and values, and therefore political

141 BeethamP, *The Legitimation of Power* (n 2) 259. See also at 255–6.
142 Bottoms and Tankebe, 'Police Legitimacy and the Authority of the State' (n 14) 84–5.

legitimacy.[143] This may include, for example, a commitment by all parties to fully participate in such a dialogue and to enable all other parties to freely do the same; a predisposition to reaching a congruence in values and beliefs;[144] sufficiently well-reasoned contributions to the dialogue (including how a dominant party responds to a subordinate's basic legitimation demand); and, as mentioned, the reliance on jargon and epistemic traditions.[145] Again, Lowrey-Kinberg's and Sullivan Buker's commentary illustrates the potential significance of these dialogic features to the formation and maintenance of political legitimacy.

Between All Parties to a Power Relationship

The third element of the constant dialogic approach is that all parties to a power relationship should be engaged in the dialogue through which shared normative beliefs and values are formulated. This reflects two of the key distinguishing features of Bottoms's and Tankebe's approach. First, different parties may have divergent perspectives about what constitutes political legitimacy.[146] Those who hold and exercise power will have a view about their own legitimacy that relates to their notion of self-identity.[147] This view may differ from that held by those who are subject to such power. Second, this element of the constant dialogic approach explicitly embraces the possibility of multiple dominant and subordinate parties to a power relationship with their respective normative values and beliefs.[148] Consequently a dominant party may need to interact with a range of subordinate audiences and with other dominant parties who hold a variety of beliefs and values. Furthermore, subordinate perspectives on the legitimacy of a dominant party may be as diverse as those who are involved in the power relationship with that dominant party. By embracing both of these elements of Bottoms's and Tankebe's

143 Tal Jonathan-Zamir and Amikam Harpaz, 'Police Understanding of the Foundations of Their Legitimacy in the Eyes of the Public: The Case of Commanding Officers in the Israel National Police' (2014) 54(3) *British Journal of Criminology* 469.

144 See, eg, Tankebe (n 139) 50, discussing Kimberley Brownlee, 'The Offender's Part in the Dialogue' in Rowan Cruft, Matthew H Kramer and Mark R Reiff (eds), *Crime, Punishment, & Responsibility: The Jurisprudence of Antony Duff* (Oxford University Press, 2011) 54.

145 Lowrey-Kinberg and Sullivan Buker (n 111) 483.

146 Bottoms and Tankebe, 'Beyond Procedural Justice' (n 2) 132–54.

147 Bottoms and Tankebe, 'A Voice Within' (n 91) 63, 68–9.

148 Bottoms and Tankebe, 'Beyond Procedural Justice' (n 2) 128; Bottoms and Tankebe, 'Police Legitimacy and the Authority of the State' (n 14) 73–4; Richard Martin and Ben Bradford, 'The Anatomy of Police Legitimacy: Dialogue, Power and Procedural Justice' (2021) 25 *Theoretical Criminology* 559, 562–69.

approach to political legitimacy, the constant dialogic approach similarly seeks to rectify their comparative absence from Beetham's framework.[149]

The recognition of multiple parties or actors and their respective beliefs and values is particularly relevant to the complex regulatory environment for therapeutic goods. In this context there are both multiple dominant and subordinate parties. Subordinate parties include patients, carers and the wider public. Dominant parties typically include the Therapeutic Goods Administration, the broader executive government and state and Commonwealth parliaments. An analysis of political legitimacy in this context requires a consideration of the extent to which the beliefs and values of all subordinate parties to the power relationship are congruent with the numerous dominant parties exercising power.

Conclusion

This chapter has outlined the diverse meanings of, and approaches to, political legitimacy. It traced a path from the broad body of work on political legitimacy to Beetham's and Bottoms's and Tankebe's respective approaches. The constant dialogic approach to political legitimacy builds on and reformulates the frameworks of Beetham and of Bottoms and Tankebe. The three elements of the constant dialogic approach provide a readily applicable framework to a regulatory environment characterised by ongoing relationships between multiple actors. The approach enables the interrogation of the difficult case studies presented in the chapters which follow whilst also mitigating the limitations of the frameworks of Beetham and of Bottoms and Tankebe, respectively.

149 See, eg, Bottoms and Tankebe, 'Beyond Procedural Justice' (n 2) 150; Beetham, *The Legitimation of Power* (n 2) 256–8; Bottoms and Tankebe, 'Police Legitimacy and the Authority of the State' (n 14) 60.

Chapter 4

Voices of Change

Regulatory Reform of Medicinal Cannabis in Australia

Introduction

The years 2014 to 2018 were a watershed in the regulation of medicinal cannabis in Australia.[1] It was a period of public controversy regarding the medicinal use of cannabis that engaged individual patients and their families, advocacy groups, state and Commonwealth governments and the media. At the centre of this controversy was the question of whether those suffering from an illness or disorder should be allowed access to a drug traditionally regulated in a highly restrictive manner. This chapter considers what the contentious case of medicinal cannabis reform indicates about the political legitimacy of the therapeutic goods regulatory regime. This same question will, in turn, be asked of each of the case studies to follow.

The chapter begins by outlining the contemporary regulation of medicinal cannabis in Australia and the reforms of 2014 to 2018. It identifies three key 'voices' that emerged during public debate, each expressing a different conception of what constituted medicinal cannabis and, therefore, a different view about regulatory reform. Each of these voices was also influenced by different types of knowledge about medicinal cannabis and reflected divergent historical approaches to the regulation of the drug. The chapter then applies the constant dialogic approach to political legitimacy to investigate what the reforms to the regulation of medicinal cannabis indicate about the political legitimacy of the therapeutic goods regulatory regime.

I argue that alternative voices to the regulatory status quo expressed values and beliefs that were incongruent with the regulatory status quo, or dominant voice. This amounted to a challenge to the political legitimacy of the therapeutic goods regulatory regime. This challenge was the result of the regulatory regime's failure to adopt a constant dialogic approach to political legitimacy in two key respects. First, the regulatory regime did not engage in a

1 A significant part of this chapter is drawn from the author's previously published article: Penny Gleeson, 'The Challenge of Medicinal Cannabis to the Political Legitimacy of Therapeutic Goods Regulation in Australia' (2019) 43(2) *Melbourne University Law Review* 558.

DOI: 10.4324/9781003293811-4

dialogue with all relevant parties to the regulatory relationship and therefore did not embrace their respective voices and, consequently, their different values and beliefs. Second, the regulatory regime prioritised traditional sources of expertise over discourse in order to meet its regulatory objects. This blinkered the regulatory regime from considering alternative or additional sources of knowledge and contributed to its failings in relation to political legitimacy.

While this chapter discusses events in Australia, the case study has clear relevance for other regulatory regimes for medical products. At the time of writing, 38 US states allowed medicinal cannabis for certain illnesses.[2] In August 2023 the United States FDA recommended to the US Drug Enforcement Agency ('DEA') that restrictions around the use of cannabis be relaxed through rescheduling the drug from prohibited to controlled under the *Controlled Substances Act*,[3] including on the basis that it had 'a currently accepted medical use in treatment in the US'.[4] This followed a request by President Biden that a review be undertaken into the scheduling of cannabis.[5] At the time of writing, it was reported that the DEA was intending to follow the FDA's recommendation, potentially requiring additional states to similarly relax controls on cannabis.[6] In Europe, while numerous countries allow for individual use of medicinal cannabis products,[7] there are few relevant drugs yet approved under the EMA's harmonised pathway.[8] Australia is one of the 'first movers' internationally to allow medicinal cannabis as a medical product via its therapeutic goods regulatory arrangements.[9]

2 Larry K Houck, 'DEA Concurs: Marijuana Meets Schedule III Criteria', *FDA Law Blog* (6 May 2024) https://www.thefdalawblog.com/2024/05/dea-concurs-marijuana-meets-schedule-iii-criteria/?utm_source=rss&utm_medium=rss&utm_campaign=dea-concurs-marijuana-meets-schedule-iii-criteria.

3 Alicia Ault, 'FDA Recommends DEA Move Cannabis from Schedule I to III', *Medscape* (online, 19 May 2024) https://www.medscape.com/viewarticle/fda-recommends-dea-move-cannabis-schedule-iii-2024a100010v?form=fpf citing correspondence from Rachel L Levine, Assistant Secretary for Health, US Department of Health and Human Services to Anne Milgram, Administrator, Drug Enforcement Administration, US Department of Justice (29 August 2023).

4 Houck (n 2).

5 Ault (n 3).

6 Houck (n 2).

7 Toby Seddon and William Floodgate, *Regulating Cannabis: A Global Review and Future Directions* (Palgrave Macmillan, 2020) 43–52.

8 Markus Veit, 'Quality Requirements for Medicinal Cannabis and Respective Products in the European Union – Status Quo' (2023) 89 *Planta Medica* 808; Ricardo Ferriera de Oliveira e Silva and Emilio Nabas Figueiredo, 'Current Legislation on Medical Cannabis in the European Union: Historical Background, Movements, Trends, and Counter-Trends Lessons for Brazil' (2023) 6(2) *Brazilian Journal of Pain* 90.

9 Katherine Cheng, Joanna Harnett, Sharon Davis et al 'Conversations about Cannabis: The Supply Process in Australia' (2023) 10 *Advances in Integrative Medicine* 190, 191; Myfanwy

At the outset it is useful to briefly describe the substance with which this case study is concerned. Cannabis is the generic name given to three species of plants.[10] It can be used for a variety of purposes – as a fibre (known as hemp), an oil for fuel, varnish and soap and, most relevantly, as a drug.[11] In biological terms, it is the nature and level of cannabinoids, the active components of the cannabis plant, that determine the medical impact of cannabis and its psychoactive effect. The cannabinoid delta-9-tetrahydrocannbinol (THC) primarily provides the euphoric effect of the drug.[12] THC and the non-psychoactive cannabidiol (CBD) are the key cannabinoids with medicinal properties.[13]

Cannabis is commonly dried and smoked, but it may also be administered as a resin, oil or raw as food.[14] Claims about the medicinal potential of the cannabis plant appear in texts on folk medicine from around the 3rd to 8th centuries BCE.[15] While the debate regarding what constitutes 'medicinal cannabis' and 'cannabis' will be discussed shortly, it is necessary to clarify the use of these terms for present purposes. Therefore, this chapter defines medicinal cannabis as cannabis that is 'used for a medicinal objective' to achieve 'a curative or remedial effect', rather than for 'recreational' use.[16] The term 'cannabis' will be used to describe both recreational and medicinal cannabis.

The Contemporary Regulation of Medicinal Cannabis

Cannabis has traditionally been dealt with strictly by Australian law at both the Commonwealth and the state level, including under the therapeutic goods regulatory regime. This section describes the regulation of medicinal cannabis, with a focus on the therapeutic goods regulatory regime, prior to the reform period of 2014 to 2018. It then summarises the constraints these arrangements had on access to medicinal cannabis up until the regulatory reforms.

Graham, Vivian Chiu, Daniel Stjepanovic et al 'A Provisional Evaluation of Australia's Medical Cannabis Program' (2023) 122 *International Journal of Drug Policy* 1, 1.

10 Martin Booth, *Cannabis: A History* (Doubleday, 2003) 2.

11 Ibid 4–5.

12 Mahmoud A ElSohly and Waseem Gul, 'Constituents of Cannabis Sativa' in Roger G Pertwee (ed), *Handbook of Cannabis* (Oxford University Press, 2014) 3, 4; Victorian Law Reform Commission, *Medicinal Cannabis,* (Report, August 2015) 20.

13 Victorian Law Reform Commission (n 12) xvi–xvii.

14 Ibid 21–2.

15 Ethan Russo, 'Cannabis in India: Ancient Lore and Modern Medicine' in Raphael Mechoulam (ed), *Cannabinoids as Therapeutics* (Birkhauser Verlag, 2005) 1, 2.

16 Victorian Law Reform Commission (n 12) 21, citing Jonathan P Caulkins, Beau Kilmer and Mark AR Kleiman, *Marijuana Legalization: What Everyone Needs to Know* (Oxford University Press, 2012) 14.

Commonwealth Regulation

The *Narcotic Drugs Act 1967* (Cth) is one of the primary legislative mechanisms through which drugs are controlled in Australia. It has generally reflected a highly restrictive approach to the regulation of the drugs subject to it, including cannabis. It provides, for example, that such drugs can be produced in Australia only if a licence is granted by the Commonwealth government.[17] In doing so, the Act gives effect to Australia's obligations under the international regime for the control of 'narcotic drugs'. This regime is largely established under the 1961 United Nations Single Convention on Narcotic Drugs ('Single Convention'),[18] which limits the production and cultivation of narcotic drugs, including cannabis, and requires signatories such as Australia to impose domestic licensing and reporting requirements.[19]

The Single Convention seeks to strike a balance between a high degree of state control to combat drug abuse and addiction and the legitimate availability of drugs for therapeutic purposes.[20] Accordingly, Australia's therapeutic goods regulatory regime provides a basis for scheduling certain drugs to enable 'restrictions to be placed on their supply to the public, in the interests of public health and safety'.[21] As described briefly in Chapter 2, this is achieved in Australia via the *Standard for the Uniform Scheduling of Medicines and Poisons* ('the Poisons Standard'), which classifies poisons in one of ten schedules according to their respective level of risk to public

17 Victorian Law Reform Commission (n 12) 105.

18 *Single Convention on Narcotic Drugs*, signed 30 March 1961, 520 UNTS 204 (entered into force 13 December 1964). Subsequent UN conventions in 1971 and 1988 reinforced the Single Convention's regime. This is despite recent reform by some signatories to facilitate domestic access to the drug, for example, Canada: Roojin Habibi and Steven J Hoffman, 'Legalizing Cannabis Violates the UN Drug Control Treaties, but Progressive Countries Like Canada Have Options' (2018) 49 *Ottawa Law Review* 427. There are some indications of the possibility of reform to relax the international regime. For example, at the end of 2018, the World Health Organization Expert Committee on Drug Dependence recommended changes to the international control of certain cannabis and cannabis-related substances: 'WHO Endorses Decisions of Expert Committee on Cannabis and Other Substances', *World Health Organization* (Web Page, 2019) <https://www.who.int/news/item/03-04-2019-WHO-endorses-decisions-Expert-Committee-on-cannabis-and-other-substances>. In early December 2020 the UN Commission on Narcotic Drugs accepted some of these recommendations by amending the classification of cannabis to recognise 'its medical value': 'UN Commission on Narcotic Drugs Reclassifies Cannabis to Recognize Its Therapeutic Uses', *World Health Organization* (Web Page, 4 December 2020) <https://www.who.int/news/item/04-12-2020-un-commission-on-narcotic-drugs-reclassifies-cannabis-to-recognize-its-therapeutic-uses>.

19 Alice Mead, 'International Control of Cannabis' in Roger Pertwee (ed), *Handbook of Cannabis* (Oxford University Press, 2014) 44, 47–8; *Single Convention on Narcotic Drugs* (n 18).

20 Mead (n 19) 47; *Single Convention on Narcotic Drugs* (n 18).

21 *Therapeutic Goods Act 1989* (Cth) s 52AA.

health.[22] A higher scheduling classification indicates 'an increasing level of professional healthcare intervention combined with increasingly stricter restrictions on availability'.[23]

Prior to the reforms, cannabis was listed as a 'prohibited substance' under Schedule 9 of the Poisons Standard.[24] Schedule 9 is the second highest level of classification. It recognises that the drugs contained within it 'may be abused or misused' and therefore that their 'manufacture, possession, sale or use ... should be prohibited by law' except for the purposes of particular medical or scientific research or teaching.[25] However, certain cannabinoid substances used for specific therapeutic purposes, were (and still are) included in other schedules to indicate a lower level of risk associated with these products.[26]

The Australian Health Ministers' Advisory Council ('AHMAC') determines the policy framework according to which the Poisons Standard is made and amended.[27] However, it is the Secretary of the Commonwealth Department of Health who makes and amends the Poisons Standard.[28] In doing so, the Secretary or delegate must have regard to several matters under the *Therapeutic Goods Act 1989* (Cth) ('the Act'), its Regulations, AHMAC's

22 See Chapter 2; *Therapeutic Goods Act 1989* (Cth) s 4(1)(b); *Therapeutic Goods (Poisons Standard - June 2024) Instrument 2024*. Further, the Poisons Standard imposes certain constraints and requirements on the sale, supply, storage, labelling, advertisement and disposal of poisons in accordance with their level of risk: Australian Health Ministers' Advisory Council, *Scheduling Policy Framework for Medicines and* Chemicals (January 2018) 5–7; Poisons Standard pt 2.

23 Therapeutic Goods Administration, Department of Health (Cth), *Scheduling Handbook: Guidance for Amending the Poisons Standard* (Guidance v 1.1, July 2019) 7.

24 *Poisons Standard February 2016* (Cth) sch 9.

25 Ibid iii–iv. In contrast, Schedule 10 contains 'substances of such danger to health as to warrant prohibition of supply and use'. The less restrictive Schedule 8 is for 'controlled drugs' which are described as '[s]ubstances which should be available for use but require restriction of manufacture, supply, distribution, possession and use to reduce abuse, misuse and physical or psychological dependence'. This description of the classification of poisons is reflected in the *Poisons Standard* (Cth) ix–x.

26 Therapeutic Goods Administration, Department of Health (Cth), *Final Decisions and Reasons for Decisions by a Delegate of the Secretary to the Department of Health* (31 August 2016) 8 ('*Final Decisions and Reasons for Decisions*'). Included amongst these products is Nabiximol, better known by its brand name Sativex, which is intended for use by multiple sclerosis patients. Sativex was the only biological (non-synthetic) cannabis drug approved for medicinal use in Australia under the therapeutic goods regulatory regime prior to the reform period: Therapeutic Goods Administration, Department of Health (Cth), *Australian Public Assessment Report for Nabiximols* (Report, 27 September 2013) 189.

27 The Australian Health Ministers' Advisory Council (as at May 2024 the 'Health Ministers' Meeting') consists of '[s]tate and territory government ministers responsible for health portfolios, along with the Australian Government Minister for Health and Aged Care': *Health Ministers' Meeting* (Web Page, 2024) https://www.health.gov.au/committees-and-groups/health-ministers-meeting-hmm#members.

28 *Therapeutic Goods Act 1989* (Cth) s 52D.

policy framework, any advice of the Advisory Committee on Medicines Scheduling ('ACMS') or the Advisory Committee on Chemicals Scheduling and public submissions.[29] Further, the Poisons Standard is enforceable only in the states and territories that incorporate it in their statutes.[30] Thus, while the regulatory framework is intended to, and largely does, achieve the uniform regulation of poisons across Australia, this is not necessarily the case. Ultimately, uniformity depends on each state's position regarding any amendment to the Poisons Standard.[31]

Restricted Access to Medicinal Cannabis in Australia

This restrictive regulatory regime meant that medicinal cannabis was effectively prohibited and unavailable in Australia. It is important to appreciate this highly controlled environment in order to understand the drive for reform that arose from it. To access medicinal cannabis patients were left, broadly, with two main exceptional pathways under the therapeutic goods regulatory regime, which remain in place today.[32] The remaining alternative was the illegal market.

Under one option, patients could obtain access to medicinal cannabis via the therapeutic goods 'special access' regulatory arrangements.[33] This enables a patient to seek, through a clinician, the approval of the Secretary of the

29 Ibid ss 52B(4), 52C(4), 52D(2), 52E; *Therapeutic Goods Regulations 1990* (Cth) pt 6 divs 3A–3B, 3D.

30 Australian Health Ministers' Advisory Council (n 22) 6.

31 See, eg, 'Australian State & Territory Variations from Part 4 of the Poisons Standard', *Therapeutic Goods Administration, Department of Health and Aged Care (Cth)* (Web Page, 11 October 2021) <https://www.tga.gov.au/how-we-regulate/ingredients-and-scheduling-medicines-and-chemicals/poisons-standard-and-scheduling-medicines-and-chemicals/scheduling/australian-state-territory-variations-part-4-poisons-standard>.

32 Therapeutic Goods Administration, Department of Health and Aged Care (Cth), 'Access Unapproved Products (Consumers)' (Web Page) <https://www.tga.gov.au/products/unapproved-therapeutic-goods/access-unapproved-products-consumers>; *Therapeutic Goods Act 1989* (Cth) ss 19, 31B. If patients or prescribers use one of these two pathways, they must also meet certain conditions to import the drug: Therapeutic Goods Administration, Department of Health and Aged Care (Cth), 'Import' <https://www.tga.gov.au/how-we-regulate/import-and-export/import>. Access may also be obtained through participation in a clinical trial: *Therapeutic Goods Act 1989* (Cth) s 19(1)(b).

33 While there are three categories of special access available, commonly it is 'special access' category B which is used in relation to medicinal cannabis: Senate Community Affairs References Committee, Parliament of Australia, *Current Barriers to Patient Access to Medicinal Cannabis in Australia* (Report, March 2020) 24–6; Therapeutic Goods Administration, Department of Health and Aged Care (Cth), *Special Access Scheme (SAS): Guidance for Health Practitioners Accessing Unapproved Therapeutic Goods* (March 2024)); 'Accessing Medicinal Cannabis for a Patient', *Therapeutic Goods Administration* (Web Page, 27 March 2024) <https://www.tga.gov.au/accessing-medicinal-cannabis-patient>.

Commonwealth Department of Health to obtain a cannabis product that is not listed on the ARTG, commonly through importation.[34] Applications under these arrangements are assessed against specific criteria.[35] This pathway is typically considered an exceptional basis on which to obtain access to otherwise unapproved therapeutic goods.[36] It has been perceived to be a complex process and, following the reforms, initial application numbers were low.[37] It is important to note that the TGA 'does not vouch for the quality, safety and effectiveness' of drugs obtained via the 'special access' regulatory pathway.[38] A second way in which medicinal cannabis may be legally accessed by patients is if their clinician applies to become an 'authorised prescriber' 'for a specified unapproved medicinal cannabis product for a particular indication (usage) for a class of patients in their immediate care'.[39]

Anecdotally it appeared that prior to the reforms, it was far more common for patients to access medicinal cannabis illegally than to use the special access or authorised prescriber regulatory routes to import the drug.[40] The Victorian Law Reform Commission concluded in its 2015 Inquiry on medicinal cannabis (discussed further below) that 'cannabis is currently being used illegally by a wide range of Victorians to attempt to alleviate a broad array of health conditions' and that '[o]thers informed the Commission that they

34 Victorian Law Reform Commission (n 12) 112.

35 Ibid 112; 'Accessing Medicinal Cannabis for a Patient', Therapeutic Goods Administration (Web Page, 27 March 2024) <https://www.tga.gov.au/accessing-medicinal-cannabis-patient>.

36 Ibid 113; Therapeutic Goods Administration, Department of Health and Aged Care (Cth), *Special Access Scheme (SAS): Guidance for Health Practitioners Accessing Unapproved Therapeutic Goods* (March 2024).

37 Ibid 112–13; 'Medicinal Cannabis "Red-Tape" Pushing Doctors and Patients Back to Illegal Products', *Lateline* (ABC, 2017) <https://www.abc.net.au/news/2017-08-16/medicinal-cannabis-red-tape-government-doctors-black-market/8813962>. The TGA responded that it was the absence of evidence in relation to the therapeutic use of medicinal cannabis that explained the low levels of prescription under the special access scheme: 'Responding to Lateline – Accessing Medicinal Cannabis Products', *Therapeutic Goods Administration* (17 August 2017). However, the head of the TGA stated in August 2016 that imported cannabis products 'have proven difficult for Australian patients to access': John Skerritt, 'Medicinal Cannabis – What's Happening?' (Conference Presentation, Association of Regulatory and Clinical Scientists, August 2016) 8. Over time, application numbers have increased significantly: 'Medicinal Cannabis: Access Pathways and Usage Data', *Therapeutic Goods Administration* (Web Page, 1 May 2024) <https://www.tga.gov.au/products/unapproved-therapeutic-goods/medicinal-cannabis-hub/medicinal-cannabis-access-pathways-and-usage-data>.

38 Medicinal Cannabis: Access Pathways and Usage Data' (n 37).

39 Ibid.

40 Victorian Law Reform Commission (n 12) xvii–xviii; Ian Freckleton, 'Medicinal Cannabis Law Reform in Australia' (2016) 23 *Journal of Law and Medicine* 497, 499. The TGA has acknowledged patient access of illegal products: 'Responding to Lateline – Accessing Medicinal Cannabis Products' (n 37).

would use it but are deterred by its current unlawful status'.[41] However, little empirical data has historically been available on the extent and method by which patients access and use medicinal cannabis.[42] Data that does exist indicates that the illicit nature of the drug in Australia discouraged, or was a concern for, those using or wanting to use medicinal cannabis.[43]

The Regulatory Reform Period of 2014 to 2018

Given the apparent demand for medicinal cannabis and its prohibitive regulatory treatment in Australia, it is not surprising that numerous attempts have been made to reform laws around its access and use.[44] It was not until 2014, however, that genuine momentum built for change. The resulting reforms, driven by the state of Victoria, are consequently significant.[45] The circumstances that made reform possible were multifactorial. Anecdotal accounts of seriously ill patients and their families who accessed medicinal cannabis illegally played a considerable role.[46] So, too, did the media, providing widespread coverage of such stories and supporting enhanced access to the drug. Included amongst the media supporters were outlets with a traditionally conservative perspective on 'law and order' issues, which, unsurprisingly, caveated their position by objecting to 'indiscriminate' recreational use.[47] Further,

41 Victorian Law Reform Commission (n 12) 23.

42 See, eg, Peter Gates, Stephanie Todd and Jan Copeland, 'Survey of Australian's Knowledge, Perception and Use of Cannabis for Medicinal Purposes' (2017) 5(1) *Journal of Addiction and Prevention* 10. Following the reforms, research conducted by the Australian Institute of Health and Welfare found that 2.7% of the Australian population used cannabis for medical purposes. Only 3.9% of those who used it for medical purposes obtained the drug via a medical professional. Others obtained it from a 'friend', 'dealer' or 'grew it themselves'. However a high sampling error was associated with these results: Australian Institute of Health and Welfare, *National Drug Strategy Household Survey 2019* (Survey, 2020) 50–3.

43 A study exploring patterns of medicinal cannabis use prior to the reforms concluded that '[i]llicitly sourced cannabis is used to treat a broad range of medical conditions in Australia'. Over 90% of respondents believed that 'medicinal cannabis should be integrated into mainstream health care' and reported concerns about 'legal and employment problems' as a result of medicinal cannabis use: Nicholas Lintzeris et al, 'Medicinal Cannabis in Australia, 2016: the Cannabis as Medicine Survey (Cams-16)' (2018) 209(5) *The Medical Journal of Australia* 211, 211, 215–16. A study of epilepsy patients reported that 14% of respondents used or had previously used cannabis products in relation to their condition. Of those participants that did not use cannabis, a large proportion said that access to the drug, including its illegality, was the key reason for not doing so: Anastasia S Suraev et al, 'An Australian Nationwide Survey on Medicinal Cannabis Use for Epilepsy: History of Antiepileptic Drug Treatment Predicts Medicinal Cannabis Use' (2017) 70 *Epilepsy and Behavior* 334.

44 Freckleton, 'Medicinal Cannabis Law Reform in Australia' (n 40) 498.

45 Ibid.

46 Ibid 498–500.

47 See, eg, Annika Smethurst, 'Desperate Parents Turn to Medical Marijuana in Last-Ditch Effort to Improve Their Children's Lives', *Herald Sun* (online, 12 January 2014)

by 2013 more than two-thirds of the Australian population supported legislative change to enable the therapeutic use of cannabis.[48] This reflected a similar evolution in the USA of greater legislative and de facto support for both medicinal and recreational cannabis.[49] It is important to also note the relevant party-political and constitutional factors that influenced reform in Australia, some of which will be identified shortly.

The State of Victoria

In Victoria, the relevant legislation is the *Drugs, Poisons and Controlled Substances Act 1981* and its associated regulations.[50] Historically the Victorian legislation reflected the approach of the Commonwealth and treated cannabis as a 'drug of dependence' and a 'poison'.[51] The cultivation, possession or use of cannabis was therefore prohibited in Victoria unless a person was licensed or authorised to do so.[52] The legislation prior to reform allowed for a registered medical practitioner to apply to the Secretary of the Victorian Department of Health and Human Services for a permit to prescribe Schedule 9 drugs, including cannabis, for a specified person. In its 2015 report, the Victorian Law Reform Commission noted that '[i]n practice, applications to prescribe are not made'. [53]

It was against this background that the then Victorian Labor opposition party committed, during the 2014 state election campaign, to 'seek advice from the Victorian Law Reform Commission on medical cannabis, so it can

<http://www.heraldsun.com.au/news/victoria/desperate-parents-turn-to-medical-marijuana-in-lastditch-effort-to-improve-their-childrens-lives/news-story/11d70cfbec24e37668d8dd53378d33eb>; Grant McArthur and Andrea Hamblin, 'Medical Benefits of Cannabis Must Be Examined, Say Health Experts', *Herald Sun* (online, 25 August 2014).

48 Gates et al (n 42) 10, citing the Australian Institute of Health and Welfare, *National Drug Strategy Household Survey: Detailed Report: 2013* (Report, 2014). Subsequent studies with lower numbers of participants reported similar or higher levels of support for legalisation of medicinal cannabis: Freckleton, 'Medicinal Cannabis Law Reform in Australia' (n 40) 503–4.

49 See, eg, Peter Homel and Rick Brown, 'Marijuana Legalisation in the United States: An Australian Perspective' (2017) (535) *Trends & Issues in Crime & Criminal Justice* 1.

50 *Drugs, Poisons and Controlled Substances Regulations 2017* (Vic).

51 *Drugs, Poisons and Controlled Substances Act 1981* (Vic) s 4(1), sch 8, as enacted. Nevertheless, it has been observed that this 'thoroughly modern drug law' was 'equivocal' in relation to cannabis because certain offences relating to it were subject to lesser penalties than for other drugs: Desmond Manderson, *From Mr Sin to Mr Big: A History of Australian Drug Laws* (Oxford University Press, 1993) 185–6.

52 Typically, a licence to cultivate, possess and use cannabis was issued only to those who needed the drug in relation to their profession or in performing duties under the Act: Victorian Law Reform Commission (n 12) 107.

53 Ibid.

be used to treat people in exceptional circumstances'.[54] Its promise largely mirrored the campaign by sections of the media, described above, which had preceded the announcement. Notably, the Labor opposition rejected legalisation of recreational cannabis.[55] In contrast, the position of the then conservative Victorian Coalition government was that the effective prohibition of medicinal cannabis was not an issue for it, as a state government, to determine.[56] Its view was that this was instead a matter for the Commonwealth government, and the TGA, to determine according to 'the best medical advice and science'.[57] The Victorian Coalition government committed instead to facilitate clinical trials with a view to potentially allowing therapeutic use in the future.[58] This position in relation to medicinal cannabis reflected that of the existing Commonwealth Coalition government, and that of the TGA.[59] What the Victorian Labor opposition had achieved politically was to effectively adopt a popular media campaign supporting enhanced access to medicinal cannabis as its own policy. In doing so, the Victorian Labor opposition distinguished itself from both the state and the Commonwealth governments. Labor was then able to portray the incumbents as 'out of touch' with the community.[60]

It was the election of the Victorian Labor government in November 2014 and its fulfilment of its election promise that proved to be the 'tipping point' for medicinal cannabis reform in Australia. The new Labor Attorney-General issued terms of reference to the Victorian Law Reform Commission to report 'on options to allow people to be treated with medicinal cannabis in exceptional circumstances'.[61] In early October 2015 the new state Labor government accepted the vast majority of the Victorian Law Reform Commission's recommendations to 'legalise access to locally manufactured

54 Victorian Labor, 'Labor: Medical Cannabis Should Be Legal' (2014).

55 Ibid.

56 Michelle Ainsworth, 'Labor to Seek to Overturn "Outdated" Laws Banning Medical Marijana [sic]', *Herald Sun* (online, 24 August 2014) <http://www.heraldsun.com.au/news/victoria-state-election-2014/labor-to-seek-to-overturn-outdated-laws-banning-medical-marijana/news-story/beed551eb3fa33278061e5e2e9edf8d5>.

57 Ibid.

58 Ibid; Melissa Davey, 'Medical Marijuana to Undergo Clinical Trials in Victoria', *The Guardian* (online, 28 August 2014) <https://www.theguardian.com/society/2014/aug/28/medical-marijuana-undergo-clinical-trials-victoria>.

59 Smethurst (n 47); Matthew Knott, 'Medical Cannabis Closer to Federal Approval', *Sydney Morning Herald* (online, 29 September 2014) <https://www.smh.com.au/politics/federal/medical-cannabis-closer-to-federal-approval-20140928-10n5rd.html>.

60 Davey (n 58).

61 Significantly, the VLRC noted that the Government was 'committed' to this policy and that the VLRC could not, therefore, provide its views on the policy or on broader legalisation: Victorian Law Reform Commission (n 12) 2.

medicinal cannabis products for use in exceptional circumstances'.[62] The *Access to Medicinal Cannabis Act 2016* (Vic) was passed with the intention of providing access to medicinal cannabis to Victorians with specific conditions.[63] The Victorian Labor government had therefore quickly signalled its intention to implement reform in Victoria, irrespective of the position of the Commonwealth.[64] This marked a significant departure from the entrenched cooperative regulatory arrangements that had characterised the regulation of drugs, including medicinal cannabis, up to this point.

The Commonwealth

On 2 December 2015, the Commonwealth Coalition government acted to keep pace with Victoria. The Minister for Health announced amendments to the *Narcotics Drugs Act 1967* (Cth) to introduce a 'nationally consistent licensing scheme regulating the controlled cultivation of cannabis for medicinal or scientific purposes'.[65] The scheme was to be administered by the Commonwealth Office for Drug Control and would ensure that Australia continued to meet its international obligations under the Single Convention.[66] The aim of the amendments was to facilitate the availability of medicinal cannabis for patients as determined by each state and territory.[67]

Despite claims that the Commonwealth government was delivering the 'missing piece' in making medicinal cannabis available,[68] it was apparent that access to the drug remained dependent on its status under the therapeu-

62 Daniel Andrews, 'Medicinal Cannabis to Be Legalised in Victoria' (Media Release, Premier of Victoria, 6 October 2015).

63 *Access to Medicinal Cannabis Act 2016* (Vic) ss 1(a)(i), 3 (definition of 'eligible patient'). The Victorian government ultimately announced that it would not proceed with the 'stand-alone' scheme established by the Act in light of the Commonwealth reforms that followed: 'Medicinal Cannabis', *Health Vic: Victoria's Hub for Health Services & Business* (Web Page), archived at <https://perma.cc/9RBK-83P3>.

64 The *Access to Medicinal Cannabis Act 2016* (Vic) was introduced and first read in the Legislative Assembly on 8 December 2015: Victoria, *Parliamentary Debates*, Legislative Assembly, 8 December 2015, 5340 (Jill Hennessy, Minister for Health).

65 Sussan Ley, 'Medicinal Cannabis to Be Cultivated through Single National Scheme' (Media Release, 2 December 2015) <http://sussanley.com/medicinal-cannabis-to-be-cultivated-through-single-national-scheme/>; Narcotics Drugs Amendment Bill 2016 (Cth).

66 Explanatory Memorandum, Narcotic Drugs Amendment Bill 2016 (Cth) 17.

67 Freckleton, 'Medicinal Cannabis Law Reform in Australia' (n 40). Note the subsequent 2019 review of the *Narcotic Drugs Act 1967* (Cth) and the Commonwealth government's agreement in principle with the review's recommendations: John McMillan, *Review of the Narcotic Drugs Act 1967: Final Report* (Report, July 2019); Greg Hunt, 'Boosting Australia's Medicinal Cannabis Industry' (Media Release, 2 August 2019) <https://www.health.gov.au/ministers/the-hon-greg-hunt-mp/media/boosting-australias-medicinal-cannabis-industry>.

68 Sussan Ley, 'Turnbull Govt Delivers Medicinal Cannabis "Missing Piece"' (Media Release, 17 October 2015) archived at <https://perma.cc/7E5D-2EHD>.

tic goods regulatory regime. In describing the amendments to the *Narcotics Drugs Act 1967*, the Commonwealth Health Minister affirmed that the *Therapeutic Goods Act 1989* and the TGA would continue to regulate the registration of new medicinal cannabis products (on the ARTG) and the supply of unregistered medicinal cannabis products to 'specific patients' (under the special access and authorised prescriber schemes described above).[69] The Commonwealth was therefore placing the 'Therapeutic Goods Administrator, our drug regulator, at the centre' of the legal regime for medicinal cannabis in Australia.[70] Regulation under the therapeutic goods regulatory regime was the basis on which the Commonwealth government committed to 'maintain the same high safety standards for cannabis derived products that we apply to any other medicine'.[71] The key role of the TGA and its regime was further reflected in the amendments to the *Narcotics Drugs Act 1967* that required a decision-maker to refuse an application for a licence to manufacture a medicinal cannabis product where they were not satisfied that the drug would be used in accordance with the *Therapeutic Goods Act 1989*, or that the drug was already registered on the ARTG.[72]

It was therefore almost inevitable that reforms to the therapeutic goods regime would need to follow. In January 2016 the TGA announced a proposal to amend the Poisons Standard to reschedule cannabis from a 'prohibited substance' under Schedule 9 to a 'controlled drug' under Schedule 8.[73] In explaining the proposal, the TGA stated that it 'complements' the (at that stage) intended reforms to the *Narcotic Drugs Act 1967* and 'aims to simplify access for those qualified for such access'.[74] Despite this, and amidst the momentum of the respective Commonwealth and state government reforms, the TGA emphasised that any decision to down-schedule cannabis was still to be made by the delegate of the Secretary of the Department of Health and according to established processes, including the receipt of public comments

69 Commonwealth, *Parliamentary Debates*, House of Representatives, 10 February 2016, 1166 (Sussan Ley, Minister for Health, Sport and Aged Care). Applications under these schemes are decided on an individual basis. However, the TGA has subsequently provided a list of medical indications for which applications for medicinal cannabis have been approved: 'Authorised Prescriber Established History of Use Lists', *Therapeutic Goods Administration* (Web Page, 15 January 2024) <https://www.tga.gov.au/products/unapproved-therapeutic-goods/prescribe-unapproved-therapeutic-good-health-practitioners/lists-products-established-history-use/authorised-prescriber-established-history-use-lists>.

70 Commonwealth, *Parliamentary Debates*, House of Representatives, 10 February 2016, 1167 (Sussan Ley, Minister for Health, Sport and Aged Care).

71 Ibid.

72 *Narcotic Drugs Amendment Act 2016* (Cth) s 11K.

73 'Cannabis Re-scheduling Proposal - Questions and Answers', *Therapeutic Goods Administration* (20 January 2016).

74 Ibid.

and a recommendation by the ACMS. It therefore invited public submissions on the proposal.[75]

On 31 August 2016 a delegate of the Secretary of the Department of Health decided to downgrade cannabis from Schedule 9 to Schedule 8 of the Poisons Standard, where the substance was for therapeutic use and prescribed by an authorised medical practitioner.[76] The decision was consistent with ACMS advice to the delegate that Schedule 8 'provid[ed] a suitable level of oversight ... and safety'.[77] On the issue of the drug's efficacy, the ACMS concluded that 'moderate-quality evidence' was available to support the use of cannabis for 'chronic pain and spasticity' and that 'low-quality evidence of benefit' existed for a range of other conditions.[78] It advised that there was a 'low risk of dependence' particularly in relation to other opioids but noted that cannabis was a potential 'pathway' drug.[79]

The effect of this decision was to amend the Poisons Standard so that patients could access medicinal cannabis where it was approved and included on the ARTG or, as had existed previously, as an unapproved drug under the 'special access' scheme or for an approved 'authorised provider'.[80] Despite the reforms to the Poisons Standard, few new cannabis products have been approved by the TGA for entry on the ARTG.[81] For the most part, therefore, patients remain reliant on the 'special access' or 'authorised prescriber' schemes to obtain medicinal cannabis products that have not been approved for use in Australia, generally by importing those products from overseas markets. At the time of writing, the Special Access Scheme Pathway B is the main way that patients obtain access to medicinal cannabis products.[82]

75 Ibid.

76 *Final Decisions and Reasons for Decisions* (n 26) 12–14. Low-dose THC and CBD formulations were re-scheduled under the Poisons Standard to the lower Schedule 4 or 'Prescription' medicine: Christine Mary Hallinan and Yvonne Ann Bonomo, 'The Rise and Rise of Medicinal Cannabis, What Now? Medicinal Cannabis Prescribing in Australia 2017–2022' (2022) 19 *International Journal of Environmental Research and Public Health* 1, 1.

77 Ibid 9.

78 Ibid.

79 Ibid. The decision further stated that the drug must be for use in products produced, imported or supplied in accordance with the *Narcotic Drugs Act 1967* (Cth) and the *Therapeutic Goods Act 1989* (Cth): at 14–16.

80 Note that for a medicinal cannabis product to be imported into Australia and supplied or manufacturered there, it must meet the requirements of the relevant Order: see, eg, Delegate of the Minister for Health (Cth), *Therapeutic Goods (Standard for Medicinal Cannabis) (TGO 93) 2017*.

81 Graham et al 'A Provisional Evaluation of Australia's Medical Cannabis Program' (n 9) 1; Cheng et al (n 9) 191.

82 Olivia Dobson et al '"The Wild West of Medicine": A Qualitative Investigation of the Factors Influencing Australian Health-Care Practitioners' Delivery of Medicinal Cannabis' (2024) *Drug and Alcohol Review* 1, 2.

The Different Voices of Medicinal Cannabis Regulatory Change

Three competing, and at times overlapping, 'voices' dominated the medicinal cannabis reform debate in Australia from 2014 to 2018.[83] Each of these voices expressed a different conception of what constitutes 'medicinal cannabis' and, indeed, what cannabis itself is. The 'dominant' voice asserted the position of the regulatory status quo to exercise a high degree of social and legal control over cannabis as an illicit substance. A more 'moderate', middle-ground voice sought to embrace cannabis as both a therapeutic substance and a mechanism of delivering compassion to patients. A third, 'radical' voice conceived of cannabis as a mainstream substance for consumption that should be normalised and legalised. These perspectives in turn emphasised different epistemological[84] traditions to justify their respective views on the regulation of medicinal cannabis.[85] Further, each voice reflected the divergent historical approaches that had been adopted to control medicinal cannabis in Australia and internationally.

The Dominant Voice

The dominant voice shaping the concept and regulation of medicinal cannabis was predominantly expressed by the TGA, established medical professional bodies and political conservatives. This was the voice of the regulatory status quo. Cannabis from this perspective was an illicit substance, with little therapeutic value and posing risks to public health. According to this view, cannabis production and use should be prohibited or at least subject to strict regulatory control, including in circumstances where it was to be used medicinally. This view was steeped in the national regulatory background, outlined earlier, in which cannabis is conceived of as a drug that is unsafe and without therapeutic merit.

83 Freckleton contends that there is an additional, fourth voice – that of child patients: Ian Freckleton, 'Children as Voices and Images for Medicinal Cannabis Law Reform' (2021) 39 *Monash Bioethics Review* S4, 9.

84 The term 'epistemological' is used broadly here to refer to assertions of knowledge that are typically grounded in a particular disciplinary tradition. For an overview of the philosophy of epistemology, see, eg, Mattias Steup, 'Epistemology', *The Stanford Encyclopedia of Philosophy* (Web Page, 14 December 2005) <https://plato.stanford.edu/archives/win2018/entries/epistemology/>.

85 This contention is supported by a 2019 empirical study regarding medicinal cannabis and health policy in Israel. The authors observed that different 'stakeholders presented different views on what types of knowledge should be considered as valid and objective, what may be considered "evidence," and how knowledge should be acquired and acted upon': Darna Zarhin et al, '"Medical Cannabis" as a Contested Medicine: Fighting over Epistemology and Morality' (2019) 45(3) *Science, Technology & Human Values* 488, 495.

The regulatory status quo that was embodied by the dominant voice reflected the historical approach to medicinal cannabis in influential overseas jurisdictions, under international law and, ultimately, in Australia.[86] In Britain, for example, domestic drug control was the subject of regulation and bureaucratisation from the early 1900s.[87] The supply of cannabis in particular was restricted by amendments in 1925 to the country's *Dangerous Drugs Act 1920*. That Act ratified the *International Opium Convention* ('Opium Convention'), which will be described shortly.[88] This restrictive regulatory approach continued throughout the remainder of that century and assumed greater prominence into the 1960s, with the introduction of additional controls and penalties and an enhanced focus on drug addiction.[89] It was an approach that reflected the position of the UK government that cannabis had no therapeutic worth.[90] Similarly, in the United States cannabis was transformed from a common therapeutic substance to an illicit one, as federal and state legislators and bureaucrats sought to control the growth, sale and use of cannabis by the 1930s.[91] This prohibitive approach continued throughout the counter-culture movement of the 1960s and merged with the country's infamous 'war on drugs' of the 1970s and 1980s. Despite a renewal of medicinal support for the drug, it was not until the early 1990s that certain

86 More extensive accounts of the regulation and control of cannabis in the United Kingdom, the USA and under international law can be found in James H Mills, *Cannabis Britannica: Empire, Trade, and Prohibition* (Oxford University Press, 2003) ('*Cannabis Britannica*'); James H Mills, *Cannabis Nation: Control and Consumption in Britain, 1928–2008* (Oxford University Press, 2012) ('*Cannabis Nation*'); Nancy E Marion, *The Medical Marijuana Maze: Policy and Politics* (Carolina Academic Press, 2014); Booth (n 10); Mead (n 19).

87 Virginia Berridge, 'Drugs and Social Policy: The Establishment of Drug Control in Britain 1900–30' (1984) 79(4) *Addiction* 17, 21–3.

88 *Dangerous Drugs Act 1925*, 15 & 16 Geo 5, c 74; *International Opium Convention,* signed 19 February 1925, 81 LNTS 319 (entered into force 25 September 1928) arts 4–11.

89 See, eg, *Dangerous Drugs Act 1965* (UK); *Misuse of Drugs Act 1971* (UK); John Lawrence Jiggens, 'Marijuana Australiana: Cannabis Use, Popular Culture, and the Americanisation of Drugs Policy in Australia, 1938–1988' (PhD Thesis, Queensland University of Technology, 2004) 28; Mills, *Cannabis Nation* (n 86) 6, 82, 91–5, 133; Booth (n 10) 269–70. See also Berridge (n 87) 28.

90 Booth (n 10) 274; *Misuse of Drugs Act 1971* (UK); *Misuse of Drugs Regulations 2001* (UK). This is a perspective that changed relatively recently in relation to particular medicinal cannabis products: see, eg, Tim Wyatt, 'Cannabis Products Available for Prescription within Weeks, Government Announces', *The Independent* (online, 11 October 2018) <https://www.independent.co.uk/news/uk/home-news/cannabis-prescription-doctors-nhs-home-office-medical-marijuana-sajid-javid-a8579256.html>; Letter from Sally C Davies, Stephen Powis and Keith Ridge, 31 October 2018, archived at <https://perma.cc/3RJW-CWZA>; *The Misuse of Drugs (Amendments) (Cannabis and Licence Fees) (England, Wales and Scotland) Regulations 2018* (UK) SI 2018/1055.

91 See, eg, *Marijuana Transfer Tax Act* 1937 (US); Marion (n 86) 21–6; Troy Duster, *The Legislation of Morality: Law, Drugs and Moral Judgment* (The Free Press, 1970) 44.

state governments took steps to facilitate access to medicinal cannabis in their jurisdictions.[92]

On the international stage, the 1925 Opium Convention was the first significant step by the international community in relation to drug control. While its proposed intention was to regulate the opium trade,[93] cannabis was ultimately included at the urging of Egypt.[94] It was, however, the 1961 Single Convention that established what is now recognised as the international regime for the control of illegal drugs.[95] The Single Convention provides that only a 'rational' medical or scientific use of controlled substances such as cannabis can be considered justifiable.[96] This highly controlled approach to cannabis remained the status quo at international law until relatively recently.[97]

The first significant legal regulation of cannabis in Australia was introduced as an amendment to Victoria's *Poisons Act* in 1927 to make it an offence to possess cannabis, coca leaves and cocaine.[98] The same set of amendments provided for the regulation of the production, possession and sale of those substances.[99] Other states adopted a similar approach.[100] It appears that cannabis was included amongst the emerging nation's prohibited drugs

92 Marion (n 86) 26–38. As of 2023, medicinal cannabis was legal in 38 American states and recreational use legal in 24. At the federal level of government, both medicinal and recreational use of cannabis remains prohibited and highly controlled: 'State Medical Marijuana Laws', *National Conference of State Legislatures* (Web Page, 22 June 2023) <https://www.ncsl.org/research/health/state-medical-marijuana-laws.aspx>; Daniel J Mallinson and Lee Hannah, 'Marijuana Expands into 3 More States, but Nationwide Legalization Still Unlikely', *The Conversation* (online, 8 November 2018) <https://theconversation.com/marijuana-expands-into-3-more-states-but-nationwide-legalization-still-unlikely-106512>.

93 *International Opium Convention* (n 88).

94 The Egyptian delegation was concerned about the extent of the use of cannabis in its country and urged that the drug should be included in the Convention: Booth (n 10) 117–8. In 1931 and 1936 additional treaties were developed in response to the illicit drug trade and concern about drug addiction: *Convention for Limiting the Manufacture and Regulating the Distribution of Narcotic Drugs*, opened for signature 13 July 1931, 139 LNTS 303 (entered into force 9 July 1933); *Convention of 1936 for the Suppression of the Illicit Traffic in Dangerous Drugs*, opened for signature 26 June 1936, 198 LNTS 301 (entered into force 26 October 1939).

95 *Single Convention on Narcotic Drugs* (n 18).

96 Mead (n 19) 48–9.

97 Subsequent UN conventions in 1971 and 1988 reinforced the Single Convention's regime: ibid.; *World Health Organization* (n 18).

98 *Poisons Act 1927* (Vic) s 24(3).

99 Terry Carney, 'The History of Australian Drug Laws' (1981) 7(3) *Monash University Law Review* 165, 196. Less significant, but noteworthy provisions were enacted earlier to regulate the control of a variety of drugs, including cannabis via food, customs and housing legislation: at 168, 175–6.

100 Ibid 196 n 226.

at this point to fulfil its obligations under the Opium Convention.[101] The reforms were also influenced by the British Parliament's amendments to its *Dangerous Drugs Act 1925* to restrict the sale of cannabis.[102] By 1956 the Commonwealth government had declared cannabis a prohibited import, and in mid-1960 it broadened the legislative definition of the drug in its customs' regulations.[103] In the early 1960s, the Commonwealth pressured all states to rewrite or introduce their respective *Poisons Acts*.[104] The aim was to ensure that each state adopted a uniform schedule of drugs, thereby enabling the Commonwealth to meet its obligations under the Single Convention.[105] It also resulted in the classification of cannabis as a prohibited and highly controlled substance.[106] These regulatory arrangements established the basis of the cooperative legislative scheme between the Commonwealth and the states for drug control outlined earlier. Despite this prohibitive legislative approach, recreational use of cannabis increased from the second half of the 1960s.[107] Its use symbolised an emerging 'counter-culture' to existing social and political mores.[108] Cannabis was soon labelled by the police and popular press as a precursor to heroin use and it became a key target of strict social control.[109]

The dominant voice echoed this historically restrictive approach to medicinal cannabis and reflected the regulatory status quo in which medicinal cannabis was defined as a 'prohibited substance' under the Poisons Standard. As stated, this voice was largely used by the TGA. The dominant voice reflected the TGA's legislative responsibilities to ensure the quality, safety and efficacy of therapeutic goods and fundamental standards dictated by the scientific method.[110] Accordingly, medicinal cannabis was conceptualised by the TGA as an appropriately classified Schedule 9 drug with 'no currently established therapeutic value and [as] likely to present a high risk of dependency, abuse, misuse or illicit use'.[111] Even in the midst of the process to consider the rescheduling of cannabis under the Poisons Standard, the head of the TGA

101 *International Opium Convention* (n 88).

102 See, eg, Victoria, *Parliamentary Debates*, Legislative Council, 28 September 1927, 1529 (WJ Beckett, Minister of Public Health); Manderson (n 51) 9; *Dangerous Drugs Act 1925*, 15 & 16 Geo 5, c 74.

103 Carney (n 99) 198–9.

104 Manderson (n 51) 141–3.

105 Ibid.

106 Ibid.

107 Predominantly amongst older teenagers and young adults: see, eg, ibid 144.

108 Jiggens (n 89) 38–44; Manderson (n 51) 145–7.

109 Jiggens (n 89) 39, 56.

110 *Therapeutic Goods Act 1989* (Cth) s 4(1).

111 Australian Health Ministers' Advisory Council, *Scheduling Policy Framework for Medicines and Chemicals* (February 2015) 27.

stated that '[e]vidence for efficacy [of cannabis] is mixed, and incomplete'.[112] The then Victorian Coalition government was reluctant to consider any alternatives to the voice of the TGA, arguing that it was the official source of expertise on the nature of medicinal cannabis.[113] Following the regulatory reforms, the TGA Standard for Medicinal Cannabis required that any medicinal cannabis products comply with the exacting scientific requirements of the European Pharmacopeia.[114]

This dominant voice was also echoed by the medical professional associations. The Victorian branch of the Australian Medical Association ('AMA') told the Victorian Law Reform Commission that it supported limited law reform 'only where *evidence, safety* and law reform are key considerations'.[115] The AMA called on the newly elected Victorian Labor government to seek further evidence from clinical trials.[116] It considered that the 'state of clinical knowledge' was 'the primary consideration to ensure that no harm comes to patients as a result of using a substance, the efficacy of which is currently not evidence-based'.[117] In its view, 'there should be no exceptional circumstances or "compassionate considerations" where medicinal cannabis is used to treat a patient until such use is evidence-based'.[118] The AMA subsequently expressed concern that the Victorian government was reforming the availability of medicinal cannabis in the absence of further results from clinical trials: '[t]his deviates from the *usual process of how medications are approved for use* in Australia, where there is either thorough international evidence and / or Australian evidence'.[119] Other medical professional bodies publicly expressed similar sentiments, including that the existing therapeutic

112 Skerritt (n 37) 5. Subsequent statements on the 'patient information' section of the TGA's website include that 'there is limited evidence about the effectiveness of medicinal cannabis' for use in different medical conditions. There is also little known about the most suitable doses': 'Guidance for the Use of Medicinal Cannabis in Australia: Patient Information', *Therapeutic Goods Administration* (Web Page, December 2017) <https://www.tga.gov.au/resources/resource/guidance/guidance-use-medicinal-cannabis-australia-patient-information>.

113 Ainsworth (n 56).

114 Delegate of the Minister for Health (Cth), *Therapeutic Goods (Standard for Medicinal Cannabis) (TGO 93) Order 2017*, (6 December 2022) s 7; Therapeutic Goods Administration, Department of Health (Cth), *Conforming with Therapeutic Goods (Standard for Medicinal Cannabis) (TGO 93) Order 2017* (26 September 2022) 6, 9–10.

115 Australian Medical Association Victoria, Submission No 38 to Victorian Law Reform Commission, *Medicinal Cannabis Issues Paper* (2015) 1 (emphasis added).

116 Ibid.

117 Ibid.

118 Ibid.

119 Australian Medical Association Victoria, 'AMA Victoria's Response to the VLRC's Recommendation to Legalise Medicinal Cannabis' (Media Release, 6 October 2015) (emphasis added).

goods regulatory regime should constitute the way in which any medicinal cannabis products were regulated.[120]

The dominant perspective held by the status quo, and its construction of medicinal cannabis, reflects an epistemological background embedded in the scientific tradition and its associated, and almost irrefutable, claims to objectivity.[121] According to the dominant voice, what medicinal cannabis 'is' is determined by evidence as to its quality, safety and efficacy as dictated by the scientific method. This alone was perceived to determine the societal value of medicinal cannabis and, consequently, how it should be viewed by the therapeutic goods regulatory regime.[122] As outlined in Chapter 2, the influence of scientism on the voice of the TGA and its regulatory regime is clearly evident here. Consequently, the dominant view provided by the TGA established a sharp dichotomy. Either a drug such as cannabis is determined to constitute a credible 'therapeutic' substance according to established regulatory and scientific criteria or it is a drug without therapeutic merit and constitutes an illicit 'recreational' drug subject to a highly restrictive and often criminal law-based regime.[123] The voice offered by the TGA and its regulatory regime offered no middle ground.

The Moderate Voice

This middle ground was instead initiated and developed by the Victorian Labor government and the Victorian Law Reform Commission's 2015 Inquiry. What is called here the 'moderate' voice adopted aspects of the dominant position but emphasised strong elements of the need to act

120 See, eg, The Royal Australasian College of Physicians, Submission No 52 to the Victorian Law Review [sic] Commission, (April 2015); Clinical Oncology Society of Australia and Cancer Council Australia, Submission No 37 to Senate Legal and Constitutional Affairs Legislation Committee, Parliament of Australia, *Regulator of Medicinal Cannabis Bill 2014* (March 2015).

121 See, eg, Julia Black, 'Regulation as Facilitation: Negotiating the Genetic Revolution' in Roger Brownsword, WR Cornish and Margaret Llewelyn (eds), *Law and Human Genetics: Regulating a Revolution* (Hart Publishing, 1998) 29, 63.

122 See, eg, Sheila Jasanoff's rejection of the expertise of 'technocracy', including the scientific method, as the sole mechanism through which decisions for contemporary society are made: Sheila Jasanoff, *The Ethics of Invention: Technology and the Human Future* (WW Norton and Company, 2016) 19–21, 28–9.

123 See eg, Lancaster, Seear and Ritter who argue that, in the context of the VLRC Inquiry, 'medicinal cannabis' is 'constituted as unique and fundamentally different from … recreational cannabis' but that medicinal cannabis depends on the concept of 'recreational cannabis' for its own definition: Kari Lancaster, Kate Seear and Alison Ritter, 'Making Medicine; Producing Pleasure: A Critical Examination of Medicinal Cannabis Policy and Law in Victoria, Australia' (2017) 49 *International Journal of Drug Policy* 117, 118; See also Manderson, who notes that the increase in 'recreational' cannabis use by a younger cohort in the 1960s 'challenged medico-legal drug control': Manderson (n 51) 145.

compassionately towards seriously ill patients and their carers.[124] The moderate voice constructed its own conception of cannabis as a beneficial therapeutic substance by looking partly to anecdotal individual experience and the medicinal *potential* of the drug. This was despite the acknowledged paucity of clinical evidence in support of medicinal cannabis and contrasted starkly with the reliance by the dominant voice on the gold standard of the scientific method.[125] In some respects the moderate perspective's recognition of the therapeutic possibilities of medicinal cannabis reflected the first recognition of the drug by Western medical commentators in the early 1800s, and its pre-prohibition use in Britain, Europe and North America.[126]

Patient experience and need was a key element in constructing the moderate perspective on medicinal cannabis during the reform period.[127] The Victorian Labor government was motivated by a patient and media campaign that focussed on anecdotal experiences of patients and carers using medicinal cannabis to alleviate the symptoms of serious illnesses, including childhood epilepsy.[128] The credibility attributed to individual patient experiences was inherent in the Victorian Labor government's request that the Victorian Law Reform Commission consider how medicinal cannabis should be made available in 'exceptional circumstances'.[129] It was strengthened by submissions made throughout the Inquiry by patient advocacy groups and specific professional associations.[130] This necessitated that the Victorian Law Reform Commission identify a means of determining 'who is eligible and who is not' for medicinal cannabis and 'to take certain products *outside of the conventional, evidence-driven* approval and treatment framework'.[131]

124 See, eg, Freckleton, 'Medicinal Cannabis Law Reform in Australia' (n 40) 507–8.
125 Lancaster et al (n 123) 122.
126 Russo (n 15) 6; Andrew D Hathaway and Kate Rossiter, 'Medical Marijuana, Community Building, and Canada's Compassionate Societies' (2007) 10(3) *Contemporary Justice Review* 283, 284; Booth (n 10) 89–94. Cf the alternative conclusion reached by one commentator in relation to Britain, that 'there was very little use of preparations of the plant in the UK in the period of 1800–1928'. The author describes extensively, however, the experimental use of cannabis by the British medical establishment: Mills, *Cannabis Britannica* (n 86) 208–10.
127 See, eg, Freckleton, 'Medicinal Cannabis Law Reform in Australia' (n 40) 498–9.
128 See, eg, Victorian Labor (n 54); Victoria, *Parliamentary Debates*, Legislative Assembly, 10 December 2015, 5528 (Jill Hennessy, Minister for Health); Andrea Hamblin, 'Parents Face Questions over Marijuana Oil Treatment for Sick Child', *Herald Sun* (online, 18 August 2014) <http://www.heraldsun.com.au/news/victoria/parents-face-questions-over-marijuana-oil-treatment-for-sick-child/news-story/815a8dc2a3075a0885eee16017980648>.
129 Victorian Law Reform Commission (n 12) vii.
130 Australian Nursing and Midwifery Federation (Victorian Branch), Submission No 75 to Victorian Law Reform Commission, *Medicinal Cannabis Issues Paper* (4 June 2015) 1; Cancer Action Victoria, Submission No 54 to Victorian Law Reform Commission, *Medicinal Cannabis Issues Paper* 1.
131 Victorian Law Reform Commission (n 12) 52–3 (emphasis added).

The Victorian Law Reform Commission therefore sought to 'cater to the present-day suffering of patients that is not being adequately alleviated by *conventional forms of relief*'.[132] Illustrative of the advocacy for an alternative to the dominant voice was the submission of the Australian Nursing and Midwifery Federation, which argued for 'a scheme that is driven by compassionate grounds and which provides treatment options that are not wholly established by orthodox double blind, placebo controlled trials'.[133]

The concept of compassion provided the Victorian Law Reform Commission with an explicit basis on which it could move beyond the dominant and conventional construction of medicinal cannabis and its regulation.[134] Described as 'empathy and an authentic desire to address another person's suffering', compassion provided the basis on which the Victorian Law Reform Commission could 'mitigate the harshness of a wholly evidence-based approach'.[135] The emphasis on compassion reflected the philosophy of international and domestic 'compassion clubs'.[136] Compassion clubs first appeared in Canada and the USA as part of the advocacy movement for medicinal cannabis.[137] The clubs were traditionally operated as cooperatives, producing and supplying cannabis and extensive cannabis-related health information to a membership of largely seriously ill individuals. Additional services such as hospice care were commonly a part of the cooperative's purpose and the communities provided support, acceptance, empathy and a sense of 'belonging' to members.[138]

Further, the moderate voice adopted by the Victorian Law Reform Commission emphasised the therapeutic potential of medicinal cannabis and, therefore, the hope it generated for patients. The Commission recommended that the Victorian government establish an independent medical advisory committee to provide advice about the '*potential* efficacy' of medicinal cannabis for conditions and symptoms on which eligibility for the drug would be determined.[139] This again represented a departure from the dominant voice of orthodox scientific methodology and an endorsement of anecdotal patient

132 Ibid 54 (emphasis added).
133 Australian Nursing and Midwifery Federation (Victorian Branch) (n 130) 2.
134 Victorian Law Reform Commission (n 12) 54–5.
135 Ibid 54.
136 Ibid 55.
137 See generally Hathaway and Rossiter (n 126).
138 On compassion societies in the USA and Canada, respectively, see, eg, Wendy Chapkis, 'Legalization and Medicalization in the Marijuana Reform Movement' (Conference Paper, American Sociological Association Annual Meeting, 2013) 2–3. In Australia, see, eg, United in Compassion, an organisation which advocates for access to medicinal cannabis and whose 'philosophy' is 'the dignified relief of suffering with compassion [and] empathy': 'About Us', *United in Compassion* (Web Page, 2019) <https://unitedincompassion.com.au/about-uic/>.
139 Victorian Law Reform Commission (n 12) 75 recommendation 5 (emphasis added).

stories about the drug's efficacy.[140] In many respects, the Victorian Law Reform Commission's perspective recalls the work by Alan Petersen on the sociopolitical dimension of 'hope'.[141] Petersen argues that hope has assumed a powerful place in a healthcare environment that increasingly emphasises the role and responsibility of the individual.[142] In this respect, the moderate voice expresses the same 'rhetoric of hope' articulated by advocates for new biomedical treatments, including genetic and stem cell medicines.[143]

However, the Victorian Law Reform Commission and the Labor government also drew on clinical evidence and medical expertise to construct their notion of medicinal cannabis and its regulation. The Commission stated that '[c]ompassion demands that individual suffering be taken into account, but not that clinical efficacy be ignored'.[144] It accepted significant and orthodox aspects of the dominant voice and that of its advocates, including the AMA, which argued that 'compassion should not constitute a licence for undue latitude' in determining risks to patients.[145] Medicinal cannabis was therefore only to be provided to patients on the prescription of a medical practitioner and clinicians were to 'act as "gatekeepers" to the scheme'.[146] As a result, the moderate voice constructed its own dichotomy around medicinal cannabis. To the Victorian Labor government and the Victorian Law Reform Commission, cannabis was, on the one hand, a 'thoroughly *medical* object',[147] imbued with hope for desperate patients, posing comparatively little risk to those with a recognised serious illness and serving as a means by which government and society could act compassionately. On the other hand, the drug also had the potential to be used by healthy individuals for recreational pleasure which could not be endorsed and should therefore remain prohibited and controlled.[148] It has been argued that this position 'silenced' alternative voices on the interaction between the medicinal benefit of cannabis and the pleasure obtained from its use.[149] Such a dichotomy arguably restricts more expansive considerations of what 'therapeutic benefit' means in this context

140 See, eg, ibid 54–5.
141 Alan Petersen, *Hope in Health: The Socio-Politics of Optimism* (Palgrave MacMillan, 2015).
142 Ibid 5. Advocates of medicinal cannabis may contend that they '[expect]' or '[predict]' the drug to provide a health benefit based on past individual experience. Petersen acknowledges that such an 'expectation' can be distinguished from a mere 'feeling' or 'desire' that a positive outcome will result: at 11–12.
143 Ibid 10–11.
144 Victorian Law Reform Commission (n 12) 52.
145 Freckleton, 'Medicinal Cannabis Law Reform in Australia' (n 40) 508.
146 Victorian Law Reform Commission (n 12) 52.
147 Lancaster et al (n 123) 120 (emphasis in the original).
148 See, eg, Victoria, *Parliamentary Debates*, Legislative Assembly, 10 December 2015, 5529 (Jill Hennessy, Minister for Health).
149 Lancaster et al (n 123) 118.

and, indeed, how medicinal cannabis is itself constructed as an object of regulation.[150]

The Radical Voice

The 'radical' voice is the third conceptualisation of medicinal cannabis which was evident during the regulatory reforms of 2014 to 2018. Elements of this voice were present in a range of submissions to the Victorian Law Reform Commission during its Inquiry and to the TGA.[151] There are three key elements to the notion of medicinal cannabis constructed by the radical voice: first, the rejection of the notion of cannabis as a substance with a standalone therapeutic identity; second, the notion of cannabis as a 'natural' object of human consumption that should be normalised in a social and regulatory context; and, finally, the making of cannabis into a political symbol. As will be highlighted, the elements of the radical voice of medicinal cannabis regulatory reform are not new. However, the term 'radical' is nevertheless apt to describe this particular conceptualisation of reform in contrast to the dominant and moderate positions set out above.

The radical voice constructs cannabis as a substance that is harmless, naturally derived and a source of pleasure for the user.[152] This understanding of cannabis merges the notion of cannabis as a 'recreational' and 'therapeutic' substance.[153] According to this perspective, cannabis is a source of relief or 'solace' from suffering in all forms[154] – not just from those conditions and symptoms that traditional scientific and medical methods recognise.[155] The radical voice views the dichotomy established by the dominant and moderate

150 Ibid 120. Further, such a dichotomy fails to recognise research indicating that users of medicinal cannabis often also use the drug for 'recreational' purposes and that they initially discover the drug's medicinal qualities through recreational use: Gates et al (n 42) 10.

151 See, eg, Michelle O'Dea and a Working Group of the Cannabis Community of Victoria, Submission No 95 to Victorian Law Reform Commission, *Medicinal Cannabis Issues Paper* (2015); The Australian Lawful Use of Cannabis Alliance, Submission No 35 to Victorian Law Reform Commission, *Medicinal Cannabis Issues Paper* (18 April 2015); Cannabis Social Club Australia, Submission No 15 to the Victorian Law Reform Commission, *Medicinal Cannabis Issues Paper* (27 March 2015).

152 See generally Lancaster et al (n 123).

153 O'Dea and a Working Group of the Cannabis Community of Victoria (n 151) 16. See also the suggestion that 'it may also be that distinctions between "medicinal" and so-called "recreational" cannabis become unstable and difficult to sustain once discourses of pleasure are made visible': ibid 124.

154 The Australian Lawful Use of Cannabis Alliance (n 151) 6–7, 11. For a broader analysis of the role of drugs as objects of 'desire' for 'transformation and connection with the imperceptible', see also John L Fitzgerald, *Framing Drug Use: Bodies, Space, Economy and Crime* (Palgrave Macmillan, 2015) 9–12.

155 Lancaster, Seear and Ritter argue that the VLRC alludes to the broader benefits of medicinal cannabis for 'wellbeing' and 'quality of life' in its discussion of anecdotal evidence of

voices of cannabis as either a 'recreational' drug, on the one hand, or a 'therapeutic' drug, on the other, as inimical to the fundamental nature of the drug. Even the moderate voice's attempt to temper the dichotomy with the notion of human compassion is insufficient to embrace the radical view of cannabis as a potential source of human enjoyment. The radical conception of medicinal cannabis blurs the line between 'therapeutic' and 'recreational'.[156] It renders these terms, and therefore the very notion of '*medicinal* cannabis', irrelevant. In constructing cannabis in this way, the radical voice, perhaps inadvertently, challenges the very scientific and medical expertise, and underlying epistemology, that determines and defines the line between 'recreational' and 'therapeutic'.

The radical voice refers frequently to cannabis as 'natural' – that is, unprocessed and unrefined in comparison to modern 'man-made' pharmaceuticals.[157] This leads to an often-expressed conclusion that cannabis supports human health and wellbeing, is of inherent therapeutic value and is safe for human consumption. Frequently, such views are supported by anecdotal evidence and appeals to the long history of human cannabis use.[158] The approach to cannabis in Australia up until the start of the 20th century, for example, suggests that the drug was accepted as part of every-day consumption for therapeutic purposes.[159] Cannabis is similarly rendered by the radical voice as a normal, everyday object of human consumption. This contrasts with the highly marginalised status assigned to it by the dominant voice. The radical position therefore advocates various degrees of legalisation and deregulation. This reflects the contemporary reality of parts of the United States in

the drug's impact. Consequently, this may enhance how the capacity of 'medicine' is understood: Lancaster et al (n 123) 122–3.

156 '[A]ll use of cannabis provides therapeutic benefits, irrespective of the user's intent. Relaxation and stress relief are legitimate therapeutic needs.': O'Dea and a Working Group of the Cannabis Community of Victoria (n 151) 20; Lancaster, Seear and Ritter argue that aspects of the VRLC's discussion of 'medicinal cannabis' results in its 'co-constitution' with 'recreational cannabis': Lancaster et al (n 123) 121.

157 See, eg, Delegate of the Secretary to the Department of Health (Cth), *Public Consultation on the Proposed Amendments to the Poisons Standard* (March 2016) pt 2, 4, 12; Emeritus Professor David Penington anticipated that medicinal cannabis would 'end [up] being designated as a regulated "herbal" product rather than registered under the Therapeutic Goods Act': David Penington, Submission No 24 to Victorian Law Reform Commission, *Medicinal Cannabis Issues Paper* (14 April 2015) 1.

158 See, eg, O'Dea and a Working Group of the Cannabis Community of Victoria (n 151) 14–17; The Australian Lawful Use of Cannabis Alliance (n 151) 5.

159 According to one commentator, for example, cannabis was an ingredient in the popular, and over-the-counter, pain relief preparation Chlorodyne – 'the country's favourite panacea' – and of cigarettes used widely for asthmatic conditions: Jiggens (n 89) 25–8.

which cannabis has been legalised and where cannabis production and sale are increasingly commercialised and marketed as a 'lifestyle brand'.[160]

Finally, we see the radical voice remain, to some extent, true to its namesake. Many of the submissions to the Victorian Law Reform Commission Inquiry, and to the TGA on the rescheduling of medicinal cannabis under the Poisons Schedule, raised political concerns. These included criticism of the historical reasons for the prohibition of cannabis,[161] arguments that access to cannabis was a human right[162] and that restrictions on the drug constituted discrimination,[163] and objections to the power exercised by the pharmaceutical industry.[164] In this respect, the use of cannabis as a symbol of political protest reflected 1960s and 1970s Australia (and elsewhere), in which the drug was 'a "revolutionary" symbol' of anti-establishment culture – and a challenge to the legal and medical status quo.[165]

The above analysis examines how the dominant, moderate and radical voices of the medicinal cannabis regulatory reform period offered distinct but interrelated conceptualisations about the nature of the drug itself. These voices consequently directed debate, recommendations and conclusions about the reforms required in the context of the broader therapeutic goods regulatory regime. I now turn to this broader regulatory context.

What Does This Case Study Indicate about the Political Legitimacy of Therapeutic Goods Regulation?

This section addresses what the reforms to the regulation of medicinal cannabis between 2014 and 2018 indicate about the political legitimacy of the therapeutic goods regulatory regime according to the constant dialogic approach. First, it contends that the debate regarding, and the reforms to,

160 See, eg, *Oil & Gold Los Angeles: The American Dream* (Web Page) <http://oilandgold.la/>; *Bloom* (Web Page, 2019) <https://thebloombrands.com/>; Chapkis (n 138) 8.

161 For example, that '[t]he "War on Drugs" is an internationally acknowledged failure': O'Dea and a Working Group of the Cannabis Community of Victoria (n 151) 16; and that '[cannabis'] proscription was ... propagated throughout the world in furtherance of American national security objectives': The Australian Lawful Use of Cannabis Alliance (n 151) 4.

162 See, eg, Delegate of the Secretary to the Department of Health (Cth), *Public Consultation on the Proposed Amendments to the Poisons Standard* (March 2016) pt 3, 20, 28. See also O'Dea and a Working Group of the Cannabis Community of Victoria (n 151) 17.

163 '[T]o prosecute and punish people who are DISABLED by their conditions, for seeking relief from their ailments': Delegate of the Secretary to the Department of Health (Cth), *Public Consultation on the Proposed Amendments to the Poisons Standard* (March 2016) pt 3, 28 (emphasis in original). See also O'Dea and a Working Group of the Cannabis Community of Victoria (n 151) 17.

164 See, eg, Delegate of the Secretary to the Department of Health (Cth), *Public Consultation on the Proposed Amendments to the Poisons Standard* (March 2016) pt 3, 32.

165 Jiggens (n 89) 38–9; Manderson (n 51) 145–7.

medicinal cannabis regulation constituted a challenge to the political legitimacy of the regulation of therapeutic goods in Australia. It explains how this challenge is evident from the public presence of alternative voices to that of the dominant regulatory status quo. It contends that these alternative voices challenged the legitimacy of the therapeutic goods regulatory regime because it did not engage with all relevant parties and their respective voices, as advocated by the constant dialogic approach. The result was a lack of congruence, to varying degrees, between the normative beliefs and values expressed by the dominant voice, on the one hand, and those expressed by the moderate and radical voices, on the other.

The Challenge of the 'Moderate' and 'Radical' Voices to the Political Legitimacy of Therapeutic Goods Regulation

This chapter has described the competing voices present throughout the 2014 to 2018 medicinal cannabis regulatory reforms. The alternatives to the dominant voice were the moderate and radical voices with their respective conceptualisations of medicinal cannabis and views on its regulation. The alternative voices generated considerable media coverage and political comment. They were a source of strong community interest and engagement in the policy and law reform process of that period. In addition, these alternative perspectives contributed significantly to reformist regulatory positions adopted by the Victorian Labor government and ultimately accepted by the Commonwealth. But what did the presence and impact of these alternative voices mean for the political legitimacy of the dominant therapeutic goods regulatory regime and the TGA? The constant dialogic approach, and the work of Beetham on which it builds, provides an insightful perspective on this question.

The constant dialogic approach advocates that political legitimacy should be analysed and assessed by reference to the extent to which regulatory parties are able to develop shared normative beliefs and values. As explained in Chapter 3, this element of the constant dialogic approach reflects the central normative element of Beetham's framework – that an exercise of power should be justified 'by reference to beliefs shared by both dominant and subordinate' parties to a relationship of power.[166] The alternative voices of medicinal cannabis regulation were indicative of an absence of shared beliefs between the dominant regulatory position, on the one hand, and those who held the moderate or radical perspective, on the other. According to the constant dialogic approach, the moderate and radical voices embodied an incongruence in values around the regulation of medicinal cannabis and,

166 See Chapter 3; David Beetham, *The Legitimation of Power* (MacMillan Education, 2013) 16.

consequently, a challenge to, or even a lack of, political legitimacy in relation to the regulatory status quo.[167]

Further, these alternative voices were evidence of an absence of Beetham's third element of political legitimacy – that of consent to a relationship of power. According to Beetham, acts of consent to, or acknowledgement of, the exercise of power provide a public expression of a legitimate power relationship.[168] In relation to medicinal cannabis, however, the Victorian Labor government, non-government organisations and individuals expressed alternative voices through public statements, election commitments, law reform initiatives, draft legislation, consultation submissions, media comment and admissions of growing, supplying, accessing and using cannabis illegally. These were 'public acts of protest, disobedience and withdrawal of endorsement or recognition' of the therapeutic goods regulation of medicinal cannabis at that time.[169] In Beetham's words, such acts constituted a 'withdrawal' of consent.

The vulnerability of the therapeutic goods regulatory regime to this challenge to its political legitimacy is further reflected in frequent references to its legal status and mandate by the TGA, Commonwealth government and their supporters.[170] The reliance on 'legality' (notably the first element of Beetham's framework) as an attempt to sustain legitimacy recalls the following observation: '[t]he much readier access of the powerful to the law, and the fact that it provides both the source and protection of their power, makes appeal to the law as the ground of legitimacy a particularly favoured strategy for dominant groups'.[171] As Beetham makes clear, however, the legality of the status quo is not a sufficient basis to establish and preserve its legitimacy.[172] Further, the TGA's (and others') reliance on this basis for its legitimacy was short-sighted. What the medicinal cannabis regulatory reform debate highlighted was that sites of power, and therefore potential sources of legality, are diverse. This is particularly the case in Australia's federal constitutional system and the cooperative Commonwealth–state regulatory arrangements for therapeutic goods. Consequently, the Victorian government was able to present a possible alternative legal regime for regulation of medicinal cannabis that challenged the role of the TGA.[173] Similarly, in 2014, a cross-party

167 David Beetham, 'Revisiting Legitimacy, Twenty Years On' in Justice Tankebe and Alison Liebling (eds), *Legitimacy and Criminal Justice: An International Exploration* (Oxford University Press, 2013) 19, 19–20; 205–6, 209–10.

168 Beetham, *The Legitimation of Power* (n 166) 18, 91.

169 Beetham, 'Revisiting Legitimacy, Twenty Years On' (n 167) 26.

170 See, eg, Ainsworth (n 56); Smethurst (n 47).

171 Beetham, *The Legitimation of Power* (n 166) 67.

172 Ibid 68.

173 However, it is important to acknowledge the potential limitations of this alternative legal regime: see, eg, Victorian Law Reform Commission (n 12) 114–17, recommendation 17.

group of Commonwealth Senators, led by the Australian Greens, proposed a Bill to establish new regulatory arrangements for medicinal cannabis that sought to provide an alternative to the TGA.[174] The introduction of this Bill further highlighted the competition between state and Commonwealth governments and political parties

> for the political kudos of being seen as the first to champion the therapeutic benefits of medicinal cannabis and to promulgate schemes which circumvent the processes of the TGA and enable access to Australian-grown forms of the [medicinal cannabis] product.[175]

The regulatory reforms proposed by Victorian Labor and the Commonwealth Greens embraced alternative voices. Further, they highlighted the short-sightedness of the TGA and others to anticipate alternative sites and sources of legality as a basis for regulatory legitimacy.

The reform debate of 2014 to 2018 exposed the incongruence between the values and beliefs of the regulatory status quo and the moderate and radical voices that sought reform. It also indicated that the legal basis on which the dominant parties relied to justify the existing regulatory arrangements was replaceable in relation to medicinal cannabis. At the very least, this amounted to a challenge to the political legitimacy of the TGA and its regulatory regime.

The Failure of Therapeutic Goods Regulation to Embrace the Constant Dialogic Approach to Political Legitimacy

This challenge to the legitimacy of the therapeutic goods regulatory regime can be largely explained by the absence of a constant dialogic approach to political legitimacy. As described in Chapter 3, this approach advocates that regulators and their regimes facilitate a *relational* approach to legitimacy. It requires a *constant dialogue, through which a set of shared normative beliefs and values are formulated, between all parties to a power relationship*. The challenge to the legitimacy of the therapeutic goods regulatory regime makes apparent that neither the TGA nor its regulatory framework facilitated such a dialogue. There are two factors that contributed to this situation.

The Absence of a Constant Dialogue with All Relevant Parties

First, it appears that the TGA and its supporters did not facilitate or engage in a dialogue over time with all relevant parties to the regulatory relationship,

174 Regulator of Medicinal Cannabis Bill 2014 (Cth).
175 Freckleton, 'Medicinal Cannabis Law Reform in Australia' (n 40) 512.

including patients, carers and cannabis societies. For example, in an August 2016 presentation, the head of the TGA described consultations 'within [the] Commonwealth, states and territories' (presumably with those governments) and with 'interested growers and manufacturers'.[176] Patients, their families and advocates seem absent. Further, only partial consultation appears to have occurred as part of the process to reschedule medicinal cannabis under the Poisons Standard. This process required that the decision-maker consider submissions made by the public. A total of 35 submissions were received.[177] In comparison, the Victorian Law Reform Commission received 99 submissions and conducted 32 consultations as part of its Inquiry.[178] Further, the reasons for the decision to reschedule medicinal cannabis make no substantive reference to the contents of the public submissions.[179] The format and predominant tone of the reasons is legalistic and markedly different from the more conversational style of the Victorian Law Reform Commission Inquiry report.[180] The absence of a dialogue between the therapeutic goods regulator and all relevant parties to the regulatory relationship appears to extend to before the reform period. Despite the long historical antecedents of alternative voices, there is no indication that a discourse had previously existed. There was arguably, therefore, no opportunity for the TGA to build on existing relationships for dialogue as pressure for reform arose in Victoria.

The apparent absence of an ongoing, relationship-based discourse with all relevant parties to the regulatory scheme effectively blinkered the TGA and other supporters of the dominant voice. It arguably obscured the alternative moderate and radical voices from consideration as part of regulatory reforms to medicinal cannabis. Also obscured, therefore, was the existence of incongruent values and beliefs to those of the regulatory status quo. It is consequently unsurprising that the TGA and its supporters relied on legality to advocate for the legitimacy of the regulatory regime. The TGA's view was that it and its regulatory responsibilities were validly established by enabling legislation and were therefore legitimate. The significance of Beetham's 'normative' and 'consent' elements of legitimacy simply did not appear relevant

176 Skerritt (n 37) 10.

177 *Final Decisions and Reasons for Decisions* (n 26) 8.

178 Victorian Law Reform Commission (n 12) 214–17 apps B–C. Although the VLRC Inquiry was broader than that of the TGA's rescheduling process, it was limited to one Australian state.

179 *Final Decisions and Reasons for Decisions* (n 26) 10–11.

180 For example, the VLRC summarised the views of experts, patients and their families about a mooted 'grow your own' medicinal cannabis scheme and stated that it 'shares their concerns': Victorian Law Reform Commission (n 12) xxvi. The VLRC further suggested that a list of clinical indications for medicinal cannabis should be 'a basis for further discussion between the government, the medical community and patients' and that future consultation between government and patients should ensure a means of communication is adopted that is best suited to 'this disparate and widespread group of people': at xxi, 13.

to the dominant parties in reflecting on the political legitimacy of the existing regulatory regime. For example, in announcing the amendments to the *Narcotic Drugs Act 1967* to regulate the cultivation of medicinal cannabis, the Commonwealth Department of Health explained that '[t]here are already mechanisms in place to enable access to unregistered medicinal cannabis products through the *Therapeutic Goods Act 1989*'.[181] This statement appeared to defend the legitimacy of the existing regulatory arrangements, rather than support the then Commonwealth Health Minister's attempt to extend sympathy to patient's with 'debilitating illnesses' and to 'enable access to the most effective medical treatments available'.[182]

The View That Expertise Trumps Discourse

A second factor which contributed to the absence of a constant dialogic approach to legitimacy was inherent in the TGA's regulatory aims. These aims require it to prioritise expertise over discourse and therefore discourage it from acting consistently with the constant dialogic approach to legitimacy. The objects of the *Therapeutic Goods Act 1989* are to control the quality, safety, efficacy and timely availability of therapeutic goods in Australia.[183] As discussed in Chapter 2, the inherent nature of these aims requires the TGA to engage largely with established, technical sources of scientific and medical expertise to the exclusion of additional or alternative sources of relevant information. Expertise is therefore perceived to trump discourse.[184]

I noted above that epistemological traditions associated with quality, safety and efficacy shaped the TGA's conceptualisation of medicinal cannabis. Contrary to the expansive approach of dialogical legitimacy, these traditions arguably dictated a narrow perspective on who and what information should contribute to the TGA's role in regulating medicinal cannabis. The TGA therefore approached the reforms by engaging almost solely in a dialogue with established forms and sources of scientific and medical expertise. This can be seen again in the process to reschedule medicinal cannabis under the Poisons Standard. The decision-maker for the rescheduling proposal was required to consider the advice of the ACMS, the members of which are largely required to have medical or scientific expertise.[185] It is therefore unsurprising that the advice of ACMS focussed on evidence obtained from clinical

181 Department of Health (Cth), *Medicinal Cannabis* (Fact Sheet) 1, archived at <https://perma.cc/MWP8-STCY>.
182 Ley (n 65) 1.
183 *Therapeutic Goods Act 1989* (Cth) s 4(1)(a).
184 See also Black (n 121) 30.
185 One member '*may* have expertise in consumer health issues' and it is possible for members to hold expertise in medical ethics: *Therapeutic Goods Regulations 1990* (Cth) regs 35B(1A)–(1B), (2)(w) (emphasis added).

trials and the need to support research through rescheduling. Supporters of the TGA, including the then (Coalition) Premier of Victoria,[186] also advocated the TGA's reliance on 'the best medical advice and science' as the basis for its legitimacy.[187]

In contrast, a broader group of stakeholders, including patients, carers and cannabis societies, viewed their own experience and knowledge as also constituting a form of expertise.[188] In their view, this expertise was as valid as that offered by recognised clinicians and scientists. Their stories were embraced by the Victorian Law Reform Commission Inquiry as valid and credible sources of information.[189] This phenomenon – in which 'the boundaries between lay knowledge and expertise are ... increasingly blurred' – has been described as emanating from the 'reflexive society'.[190] Kennedy explores this society and its members in the context of complementary and alternative medicines:

> The 'reflexive individual' relies less on the traditional authority ... and is more reliant on her own judgment about health matters ... medicine must be interrogated: trust must be earned and medicine must learn to accept the relevance of lay and alternative voices ... Consequently, the belief that 'the doctor knows best' is increasingly challenged.[191]

Viewed from this perspective, the TGA was not able to adequately justify its power by relying solely on traditional medical and scientific expertise. Such expertise was considered an insufficient basis for the TGA to differentiate itself from those expressing alternative perspectives on medicinal cannabis and, therefore, for it to exercise legitimate power over those parties.[192] In the context of medicinal cannabis regulatory reform, the TGA arguably employed traditional expertise to *speak to* the community over which it exercised power rather than to use that expertise as one basis on which to facilitate a *dialogue with* the community. Expertise was, therefore, elevated above

186 Prior to the election of the Labor state government and Labor Premier.

187 Smethurst (n 47).

188 See, eg, Victorian Law Reform Commission (n 12) 214–17 apps B-C.

189 Lancaster et al. (n 123) 123: 'These "patients" (along with their families, carers and advocates) were positioned as legitimate and essential voices to be heard within the Commission's review process ... these "cannabis users" become legitimate stakeholders in the policy debate, in possession of valuable expertise and knowledge based on experience.'

190 Peter Kennedy, 'Habermas and the Self-Regulation of Complementary and Alternative Medicine (CAM)' in Mark Murphy (ed), *Habermas and Social Research: Between Theory and Method* (Routledge, 2017) 56, 60 (citations omitted).

191 Ibid 60–1.

192 Beetham, *The Legitimation of Power* (n 166) 77–82.

discourse, and the opportunity to establish and maintain legitimacy through a relationship based on constant dialogue was lost.

Developments since 2018

Since the reforms over 450,000 Special Access Scheme Category B approvals have been granted for patients to access medicinal cannabis products in Australia[193] and, as of August 2024, over 2900 medical practitioners have been approved under the Authorised Prescriber Scheme to prescribe medicinal cannabis.[194] This represents the peak of a steady increase since 2016.[195] There remain few products currently registered on the ARTG.[196] Clinicians must therefore rely on the special access pathways when prescribing medicinal cannabis. This raises a crucial question for the TGA: whether access paths 'designed for exceptional use' should continue to be the main means by which patients and consumers access medicinal cannabis.[197] Many who use cannabis for medical purposes continue to obtain it illicitly.[198] Inevitably, commercial interest in medicinal cannabis products has also grown, including focussed cannabis-prescribing clinics.[199]

Further reforms have followed since 2018. Products with low amounts of CBD were rescheduled to Schedule 3 'Pharmacist Only Medicine', consistent with the approach in parts of the United States and Europe.[200] The key mechanisms by which the TGA regulates the quality of medicinal cannabis products have also been revised,[201] including to now require that medicinal cannabis

193 Dobson et al 'The Wild West of Medicine' (n 82) 2. Note that this figure is not equivalent to the number of individuals but instead to the number of approvals. There may therefore be multiple approvals for an individual: Graham et al, 'A Provisional Evaluation of Australia's Medical Cannabis Program' (n 9) 5; 'Medicinal Cannabis Special Access Scheme Data', *Therapeutic Goods Administration*, (Web Page, 1 May 2024) <https://www.tga.gov.au/products/unapproved-therapeutic-goods/medicinal-cannabis-hub/medicinal-cannabis-access-pathways-and-usage-data/medicinal-cannabis-special-access-scheme-data>.

194 'Medicinal Cannabis Authorised Prescriber Scheme Data', *Therapeutic Goods Administration*, (Web Page, 1 May 2024) https://www.tga.gov.au/products/unapproved-therapeutic-goods/medicinal-cannabis-hub/medicinal-cannabis-access-pathways-and-usage-data/medicinal-cannabis-authorised-prescriber-scheme-data.

195 Hallinan and Bonomo (n 76) 4.

196 Graham et al, 'A Provisional Evaluation of Australia's Medical Cannabis program' (n 9) 1.

197 Penington Institute, *Cannabis in Australia* (Report, 2022) 8.

198 Ibid 11.

199 Freckleton, 'Children as Voices and Images for Medicinal Cannabis Law Reform' (n 83) S7, S9–10.

200 Cheng et al (n 9) 191.

201 *Therapeutic Goods (Standard for Medicinal Cannabis) (TGO 93) Order 2017.*

products that are imported must comply with the 'Good Manufacturing Practice' requirements set by the TGA.[202]

In response to concerns that the 'supply process (including the special access schemes) is fragmented, complex and underdeveloped',[203] the TGA has attempted to streamline relevant processes.[204] Commentators, however, continue to note that access is challenging for certain medical practitioners.[205] They also note that it is difficult to obtain prescriptions because of lack of clinical training, information and support about the product and the relative lack of evidence available for its safety and efficacy.[206] Ultimately '[h]ealthcare professionals at the coal face of [medicinal cannabis] supply are in a tug of war between a lack of clinical trail data and the pressure from patients seeking ... products'.[207] This raises further questions of whether and how the TGA should provide assistance as a key regulator in relation to medicinal cannabis,[208] and whether a failure to do so contributes to an ongoing challenge to its political legitimacy. To a certain extent it has sought to do so by making information about medicinal cannabis relatively easy to access via an online 'Medicinal Cannabis Hub'.[209]

As additional evidence relating to efficacy and safety of medicinal cannabis becomes available and as demand for these products increase the TGA will continue to need to grapple with how it regulates such products into the future. Further, it is clear that the path of medical cannabis has inspired a push for other, traditionally illicit, drugs to seek similar approval pathways. Most notably, this includes psychedelics in both Australia and the United States.[210]

202 Graham et al, 'A Provisional Evaluation of Australia's Medical Cannabis Program' (n 9) 4; 'Medicinal Cannabis: Information for Sponsors' *Therapeutic Goods Administration* (Web Page, 11 January 2024) https://www.tga.gov.au/products/unapproved-therapeutic-goods/medicinal-cannabis-hub/medicinal-cannabis-information-sponsors#manuf-standards.

203 Cheng et al (n 9)195.

204 Graham et al, 'A Provisional Evaluation of Australia's Medical Cannabis Program' (n 9) 3.

205 Cheng et al (n 9) 192.

206 Ibid 193–5.

207 Ibid 195.

208 For example, by collecting and analysing more data associated with the use of products obtained via the special access schemes: ibid 195–6.

209 'Medicinal Cannabis Hub', *Therapeutic Goods Administration,* (Web Page) https://www.tga.gov.au/products/unapproved-therapeutic-goods/medicinal-cannabis-hub.

210 Graham et al 'A Provisional Evaluation of Australia's Medical Cannabis Program' (n 9) 8; Matt Lamkin, 'Prescription Psychedelics: The Road from FDA Approval to Clinical Practice' (2022) 135 *The American Journal of Medicine* 15.

Conclusion

The regulatory reforms to medicinal cannabis between 2014 and 2018 constituted a watershed moment in Australian drug law and policy. The reform period was also significant because of the insight it provided about the nation's therapeutic goods regulatory framework. Medicinal cannabis ultimately constituted a challenge to the political legitimacy of the therapeutic goods regulatory regime. This was because the moderate and radical voices that emerged during the reform period expressed values and beliefs incongruent with the dominant views of the regulatory status quo. This incongruence can be explained by the absence of a constant dialogic approach to political legitimacy on the part of the therapeutic goods regulatory regime and its supporters. The failure to embrace a constant dialogue with all relevant parties to the regulatory power relationship blinkered the TGA and others to alternative normative positions. Further, an exclusive focus on established claims to legality and on scientific expertise instead of discourse rendered the regulatory status quo vulnerable to alternative sites of power and, ultimately, to reform. The TGA will continue to face challenges associated with the regulation of medical cannabis products and analogous goods that have previously been regarded as illicit and without therapeutic value.

Chapter 5

A Normative Void

The Regulation of Medical Abortion in Australia

Introduction

Abortion is the 'intentional termination of pregnancy' through 'artificial means'.[1] Commonly understood as a surgical procedure, the advent of medical abortion in the early 1980s marked a turning point for women's reproductive freedom. Medical abortion meant that women could rely on pharmaceuticals – known as abortifacients[2] – rather than surgery to end a pregnancy. For many women, medical abortion therefore offered the prospect of access to termination services otherwise impeded by physical distance from an abortion provider or the direct and indirect costs of surgical abortion.[3] However, abortion, by whichever means, has historically been steeped in social, ethical and political controversy. The arrival of medical abortion posed particular challenges for Australia's therapeutic goods regulatory regime.[4] In this chapter I consider the case study of the abortifacient commonly known as RU486, and the political and regulatory events that surrounded it between 1996 and 2012.[5] Australian Senator Brian Harradine, a pro-life independent politician from Tasmania, plays a prominent role in this account. In 1996, the Senator

1 Sheila Jasanoff, 'In the Democracies of DNA: Ontological Uncertainty and Political Order in Three States' (2005) 24(2) *New Genetics and Society* 139, 143.

2 Defined as 'a drug that induces abortion or miscarriage': Elizabeth Martin, *Concise Medical Dictionary* (Oxford University Press, 9th ed, 2015).

3 See, eg, Barbara Baird, 'Medical Abortion in Australia: A Short History' (2015) 23(46) *Reproductive Health Matters* 169, 171.

4 Drugs used for medical abortion have historically engaged social conflict: see, eg, R Alta Charo (with Commentary by Paul Berg and Ernest R May), 'A Political History of RU-486' in Kathi E Hanna (ed), *Biomedical Politics: Institute of Medicine (US) Committee to Study Decision Making* (National Academies Press, 1991) 43. On the 'ethical and legal problems' confronting the pharmaceutical industry in relation to the production and supply of abortifacients: see, eg, Graham Dukes, *The Law and Ethics of the Pharmaceutical Industry* (Elsevier BV, 2006) 347, 350–1.

5 See, eg, Rosalyn Diprose, 'The Political Technology of RU486: Time for the Body and Democracy' in Bruce Braun and Sarah J Whatmore (eds), *Political Matter: Technoscience, Democracy, and Public Life* (University of Minnesota Press, 2010) 211.

DOI: 10.4324/9781003293811-5

initiated amendments to the therapeutic goods regulatory regime to effectively restrict the availability of RU486 to Australian women. These reforms are referred to as the 'Harradine Amendments'.

This chapter examines the challenge posed by RU486 to the political legitimacy of the therapeutic goods regulatory regime. I begin with a brief description of the drug, then outline the history of the law of abortion and the regulation of RU486 in Australia, with a focus on the therapeutic goods regulatory regime. Despite this focus, the significant role of the criminal law and other legal doctrine in constructing and reflecting the social and ethical norms surrounding abortion is recognised.[6] I examine the social and ethical context surrounding abortion through the identification and description of two distinct conceptualisations of abortion that are shaped by, and with, relevant social and ethical norms. While there are a range of conceptualisations of abortion,[7] these two conceptualisations have traditionally dominated the public debate around abortion. Drawing on the science and technology studies' concept of 'co-production', I argue that the way in which the act of abortion is understood is socially and politically constructed and contestable.[8]

The chapter then analyses what the case study of RU486 reveals about the political legitimacy of the therapeutic goods regulatory regime. The Harradine Amendments constituted a challenge to the regulatory regime's political legitimacy. This challenge was unintentionally assisted by the regulatory regime's failure to act consistently with the constant dialogic approach to political legitimacy. There were deficiencies in relation to two key aspects of the constant dialogic framework. First, the therapeutic goods regulatory regime did not identify or engage with the social and ethical issues surrounding RU486, which co-produced distinct conceptualisations of abortion. Instead, the regulatory regime staunchly asserted that the scientific and technical objectives and principles of the regime, and their purported objectivity, were the only means to determine regulatory control of the drug. This was despite the significant normative issues surrounding medical abortion and RU486. This blinkered perspective made it impossible for the regulatory regime to engage with the social and ethical values held by the parties to the regulatory relationship in relation to RU486 and to potentially facilitate a congruence regarding those values. Further, according to Beetham's legitimacy framework, this left the therapeutic goods regulatory regime vulnerable to a destabilising change in the source of authority from which the regulatory

6 See, eg, Regina Graycar and Jenny Morgan, *The Hidden Gender of Law* (Federation Press, 2002) 200–7.

7 See, eg, Kristin Savell, 'Life and Death before Birth: 4D Ultrasound and the Shifting Frontiers of the Abortion Debate' (2007) 15 *Journal of Law and Medicine* 103.

8 See, eg, Sheila Jasanoff, 'The Idiom of Co-production' in Sheila Jasanoff (ed), *States of Knowledge: The Co-production of Science and Social Order* (Routledge, 2004) 1.

regime drew its normative legitimacy. Second, the regulatory regime failed to engage in an ongoing dialogue with all parties to the regulatory relationship, including responding adequately to basic legitimation demands to justify the power it exercised. This relational dimension of political legitimacy is pivotal to enabling the formulation of a shared set of normative beliefs and values according to the constant dialogic approach but, as I will discuss, was absent in relation to RU486.

Like others in this book, this case study largely focuses on Australia. Developments in other jurisdictions, however – most notably the United States following the reversal of *Roe v Wade* by the Supreme Court – mean that the focus on medical abortion is extremely relevant.[9] Commentators on the situation in the United States have described 'abortion pills and their attendant controversies' as 'transforming the abortion debate' there.[10] Medical abortion has 'radically changed' how abortion is provided (e.g., via telehealth and the postage of medical abortion drugs) and poses a range of new questions and challenges.[11] A key example is the legal challenge to the FDA's power to approve drugs for medical abortion,[12] in relation to which the Supreme Court determined that the plaintiffs did not have standing.[13]

Medical Abortion and RU486

It is estimated that between 65,000 and 89,000 abortions occur in Australia each year.[14] Women rely on a variety of surgical and medical methods to induce the termination of a pregnancy. Until the 1980s, however, the most commonly available method of abortion was surgical – typically via vacuum

9 See, eg, David S Cohen, Greer Donley and Rachel Rebouche, 'Abortion Pills' (2024) 76 *Stanford Law Review* 317.
10 Ibid 317.
11 Ibid 321, 329.
12 Ibid 333–7.
13 *Food and Drug Administration v Alliance for Hippocratic Medicine*, 602 US 1 (2024). See also Holly Fernandez Lynch and Aaron S Kesselheim, 'The FDA in the Crosshairs – Science, Politics and Abortion' (2024)331 *JAMA* 1269.
14 There is some debate regarding the precise numbers: see, eg, Louise A Keogh, Lyle C Gurrin and Patricia Moore, 'Estimating the Abortion Rate in Australia from National Hospital Morbidity and Pharmaceutical Benefits Scheme Data' (2021) 215 *Medical Journal of Australia* 375; LA Keogh et al, 'Intended and Unintended Consequences of Abortion Law Reform: Perspectives of Abortion Experts in Victoria, Australia' (2016) 43 *Journal of Family Planning and Reproductive Health Care* 18; Victorian Law Reform Commission, *Law of Abortion* (Final Report, March 2008) 32–3; Alison Branley and Sophie Scott, 'The Rate of Abortion in Australia Is Lower Than You Think', *ABC News* (online, 13 December 2017) <https://www.abc.net.au/news/2017-12-13/the-rate-of-abortion-in-australia-is-lower-than-you-think/9250122>.

aspiration, dilatation and curettage or dilatation and evacuation.[15] The term 'medical abortion' is typically used to refer to any non-surgical abortion procedure. Medical abortion was introduced following the development of mifepristone – better known in Australia as RU486[16] – a synthetic steroid that inhibits the role of progesterone and the continuation of pregnancy. While RU486 can be effective for other purposes (e.g., metastatic breast cancer)[17], it is most commonly used in conjunction with the drug misoprostol to induce an abortion. Misoprostol causes uterine contractions and the evacuation of the contents of the uterus.[18] RU486 was first developed by the French pharmaceutical company Roussel Uclaf.[19] The lengthy and contentious history of the drug's development, including opposition from within the company and its corporate iterations, has been detailed extensively elsewhere.[20]

The development of RU486 is considered a significant development in reproductive health medicine.[21] When used to terminate an early-stage pregnancy a woman can take RU486 and misoprostol and have the abortion in her home.[22] This compares starkly with the clinical nature of surgical abortion. Empirical research indicates that some women feel that medical abortion is 'less medicalised ... less invasive'.[23] Further, women may feel that medical abortion is emotionally easier because it is similar to experiencing a miscarriage and provides a greater sense of control and privacy.[24] Medical abortion also offers a safe option for women living in more remote locations

15 World Health Organization, *Safe Abortion: Technical and Policy Guidance for Health Systems* (2nd ed, 2012) 40–3. Non-surgical methods of abortion were, however, historically made and administered by women and 'amateur apothecaries': Gideon Haigh, *The Racket: How Abortion Became Legal in Australia* (Melbourne University Press, 2008) 12–23. See also Graycar and Morgan (n 6) 201.

16 The unusual initials by which the drug became known reflected its laboratory name (RU38486): Caroline de Costa, *RU-486: The Abortion Pill* (Boolarong Press, 2007) 6.

17 Therapeutic Goods Administration (TGA), Department of Health and Ageing (Cth), *Australian Public Assessment Report for Mifepristone (RU486) (Abortifacient)* (October 2012) 25.

18 de Costa, *RU-486: The Abortion Pill* (n 16) 7. RU486 is not the same as the so-called morning after or emergency contraceptive pill. The latter prevents a pregnancy from occurring whereas RU486 is used to terminate a pregnancy after it has been established: at 23.

19 Ibid 6.

20 See, eg, ibid 25–34.

21 Anne O'Rourke, Suzanne Belton and Ea Mulligan, 'Medical Abortion in Australia: What Are the Clinical and Legal Risks? Is Medical Abortion Over-Regulated?' (2016) 24 *Journal of Law and Medicine* 221, 229; Barbara Baird, *Abortion Care is Health Care* (Melbourne University Press, 2023) 145–46.

22 World Health Organization, *Clinical Practice Handbook for Safe Abortion* (2014) 28.

23 Danielle Newton et al, 'How Do Women Seeking Abortion Choose between Surgical and Medical Abortion? Perspectives from Abortion Service Providers' (2016) 56 *Australian and New Zealand Journal of Obstetrics and Gynaecology* 523, 527.

24 Ibid 523, 527.

with no or limited access to adequate surgical abortion services.[25] This is particularly relevant in the Australian context, where women living in rural areas have significant difficulty accessing surgical abortion clinics that are typically located in the capital cities of each state and in larger regional centres.[26] RU486 therefore represents a response to the various needs of different women seeking abortion.[27] Since 2005, the drug has been part of the World Health Organization's list of 'essential medicines'.[28]

The Regulatory History of RU486

The regulatory story of RU486 in Australia is one of controversy and disruption. This is, in part, because RU486 was a new drug which offered the promise of enhancing Australian women's reproductive freedom. But it is also because it is a story infused by a range of social and ethical issues, detailed below. To appreciate these issues, and the test that RU486 posed for the therapeutic goods regulatory regime, it is important to first outline the law relating to abortion in Australia. The path taken by RU486 through the therapeutic goods regulatory regime over a ten-year period is then discussed.

The Law of Abortion in Australia

The law relating to abortion in Australia has been described as complex and ambivalent, combining criminal and health law, common law, legislation and their pragmatic application.[29] Generally, Australian state and territory criminal laws dictate the lawfulness, or otherwise, of abortion and these laws can vary to different degrees between each state and territory. Historically, the 1861 English statutory prohibition of abortion was reflected in each state and territory's criminal statutes.[30] These legislative provisions made it unlawful for a woman 'with intent to procure her own miscarriage' to use 'any

25 O'Rourke et al (n 21) 222.
26 de Costa, *RU-486: The Abortion Pill* (n 16) 14–19.
27 O'Rourke et al (n 21) 238. See also Bushra Alam, Amy Kaler and Zubia Mumtaz, 'Women's Voices and Medical Abortions: A Review of the Literature' (2020) 249 *European Journal of Obstetrics & Gynecology and Reproductive Biology* 21.
28 Liza Gibson, 'WHO Puts Abortifacients on Essential Drug List' (9 July 2005) 331(7508) *British Medical Journal* 68.
29 O'Rourke et al (n 21) 232, citing Mark J Rankin 'Contemporary Australian Abortion Law: The Description of a Crime and the Negation of a Woman's Right to Abortion' (2001) 27 *Monash Law Review* 229, 231.
30 See, eg, *Crimes Act 1890* (Vic) ss 55, 56, as enacted; Joanne Howe and Suzanne Le Mire, 'Medical Referral for Abortion and Freedom of Conscience in Australian Law' (2019) 34(1) *Journal of Law and Religion* 85, 87–8; Graycar and Morgan (n 6) 200, 205; Rankin, 'Contemporary Australian Abortion Law' (n 29) 230.

poison or other noxious thing or ... any instrument or other means'.[31] It was also unlawful for another person to do so, or to supply or procure the poison or instrument.[32]

The illegality of abortion in Australia did not appear to diminish the demand for the procedure.[33] In his historical narrative of the practice and law of abortion in the state of Victoria, Gideon Haigh details the illegal procurement of abortion from the mid-1800s; the relative tolerance of the practice following the First World War; and the furtive relationships between abortionists and corrupt police throughout the 1950s and 1960s. The push for law reform around abortion gathered pace in the mid-1960s along with a resurgence of interest in pursuing prosecutions for its occurrence.[34] Ultimately, the 'draconian' abortion provisions of the criminal law statutes were interpreted more liberally by the courts.[35] By the 1970s, surgical abortion was, in practice, widely available.[36] The procedure was subsidised under the Medical Benefits Scheme[37] and opinion polls broadly reflected its acceptance by Australian society.[38] Yet the combination of restrictive statutes and their interpretation by judges sitting alone meant that the legal basis of abortion remained uncertain.[39] This tension continued to pose an unresolved challenge for state and territory law makers as Australia headed into the late 20th and early 21st century. Consequently, parliaments in Western Australia, Tasmania, the Australian Capital Territory, Victoria and, eventually, Queensland and New South Wales removed abortion as a crime from their statute books.[40] These reforms restricted the circumstances in which

31 Jenny Morgan, 'Abortion Law Reform: The Importance of Democratic Change' (2012) 35(1) *UNSW Law Journal* 142, 144–5, quoting the *Crimes Act 1958* (Vic) s 65, as at 2012.

32 Ibid, quoting the *Crimes Act 1958* (Vic) s 66, as at 2012.

33 Ibid 145.

34 Haigh (n 15) 111–13; Morgan (n 31) 146.

35 Morgan (n 31) 142, 146, discussing *R v Davidson* [1969] VR 667, known more commonly as the 'Menhennitt' ruling. The presiding judge directed the jury that abortion was not unlawful according to the Victorian statute if the accused 'honestly believed on reasonable grounds' that the abortion was 'necessary to preserve the woman from a serious danger to her life or her physical or mental health' and that the abortion was 'in the circumstances not out of proportion to the danger to be averted'.

36 Baird, 'Medical Abortion in Australia' (n 3) 169. However, the availability of the procedure has been a long-standing issue for women in regional and remote areas of Australia: see, eg, de Costa, *RU-486: The Abortion Pill* (n 16) 14-19.

37 Morgan (n 31) 143.

38 See, eg, ibid 148.

39 Ibid 142–3, 147. Greycar and Morgan describe the status of the judicial precedents on which the legality of abortion rested at that time as 'flimsy': Graycar and Morgan (n 6) 202.

40 Baird (n 21) 175–80; *Acts Amendment (Abortion) Act 1998* (WA); *Criminal Code Act Compilation Act 1913* (WA); *Health (Miscellaneous Provisions) Act 1911* (WA); *Crimes (Abolition of Offence of Abortion Act 2002)* (ACT); *Health (Improving Abortion Access) Amendment Act 2018* (ACT); *Abortion Law Reform Act 2008* (Vic); *Reproductive Health*

abortion was to be considered a crime, or introduced certain conditions about which clinicians had to be satisfied before performing the procedure, or did both.[41] Additional reforms were passed in Western Australia, South Australia and the Northern Territory in the early 2020s.[42]

RU486 and the Therapeutic Goods Regulatory Regime

The advent of modern medical abortion occurred in the midst of these attempts to reform Australia's criminal laws on abortion. However, as will be described, it was events surrounding the therapeutic goods regulatory regime, rather than the criminal law per se, which meant that RU486 was largely inaccessible to Australian women until the late 2000s. This contrasted sharply with the approval and availability of the drug in numerous countries in Western Europe, the United States, the United Kingdom, Russia, Israel, New Zealand and parts of Asia.[43]

What became a decade-long restriction on RU486 coincided with a new era of conservative politics in Australia following the 1996 election of the Howard Commonwealth Government. At best, this period has been described as reflecting an 'ambivalence that characterised the cultural politics of abortion'.[44] Not unusually, the Howard Government did not have a majority in the Senate. It relied on the vote of the independent Senator Brian Harradine to secure, amongst other things, a significant election commitment to privatise part of the national telecommunications provider.[45] Senator Harradine was a former trade union official first elected to the Senate in 1975.[46] His views aligned closely with the position of the Catholic Church on policy issues regarding birth control, assisted reproduction, censorship,

(Access to Terminations) Act 2013 (Tas); *Termination of Pregnancy Act 2018* (Qld); *Abortion Law Reform Act 2019* (NSW).

41 O'Rourke et al (n 21) 232.

42 Baird (n 21) 183–84; *Termination of Pregnancy Act 2021* (SA); *Termination of Pregnancy Law Reform Legislation Amendment Act 2021* (NT); *Abortion Legislation Reform Act 2023* (WA).

43 de Costa, *RU-486: The Abortion Pill* (n 16) 68–73; Luke Buckmaster, 'RU486 for Australia?' (Research Note, Parliamentary Library, Parliament of Australia, 28 November 2005) 1.

44 Barbara Baird, 'Abortion Politics during the Howard Years: Beyond Liberalisation' (2013) 44(2) *Australian Historical Studies* 245, 248.

45 de Costa, *RU-486: The Abortion Pill* (n 16) 89–90. The reforms to partially privatise the national communications provider – Telstra – were a fundamental and controversial part of the mandate for the reelected Coalition Government led by Prime Minister John Howard: see, eg, Murray Goot, 'Public Opinion, Privatisation and the Electoral Politics of Telstra' (1999) 45(2) *Australian Journal of Politics and History* 214.

46 Senator Harradine retired in 2004: 'Former Senator Brian Harradine', *Parliament of Australia* (Web Page) <https://www.aph.gov.au/Senators_and_Members/Parliamentarian?MPID=6H4>.

euthanasia and stem cell research.[47] It was not surprising, therefore, that, in return for his vote the government supported amendments proposed by the senator to the therapeutic goods regulatory regime that significantly restricted abortifacients.[48]

The Harradine Amendments

The Harradine Amendments were contained in the *Therapeutic Goods Amendment Act 1996* (Cth), an Act originally intended to enhance the operation of the therapeutic goods regulatory regime.[49] The Harradine Amendments added a new category of goods to the *Therapeutic Goods Act 1989* (Cth) ('the Act'). 'Restricted goods' was defined to mean drugs 'intended for use in women as abortifacients'.[50] Further, section 25 of the Harradine Amendments provided that

> (1) restricted goods must not be evaluated or registered or listed without the written approval of the Minister [for Health].
> (2) A written approval shall be laid before each House of the Parliament by the Minister [for Health] within 5 sitting days of being given.[51]

In contrast, the minister was not required to notify parliament where he or she had *not* given written approval under s 25(1).[52] The Harradine Amendments added that restricted goods must not be imported into Australia unless approved by the Minister for Health. This written approval could be conditional and had to be laid before each house of parliament within five sitting days.[53] The provisions relating to importation of abortifacients appeared

47 David Marr, 'Balancing Acts: How Senator Brian Harradine Straddles Heaven and Earth', *Sydney Morning Herald* (Sydney, 1 February 1997). See also, Commonwealth, *Parliamentary Debates*, Senate, 15 May 2003, (Brian Harradine) 11222–3.

48 Nicola Bodor, 'Regulation of the Abortion Drug RU 486: The Collision of Politics, Ethics and Morals in Australia' (2020) 27 *Journal of Law and Medicine* 928, 930.

49 de Costa, *RU-486: The Abortion Pill* (n 16) 90.

50 *Therapeutic Goods Amendment Act 1996* (Cth) s 3. The section provided that '*restricted goods* means drugs within regulation 2 of the Therapeutic Goods Regulations (including progesterone antagonists and vaccines against human chorionic gonadotrophin) intended for use in women as abortifacients' (emphasis in original). RU486 is a progesterone antagonist. Human chorionic gonadotrophin (hCG) is a hormone produced in the early stages of pregnancy: see, eg, N Terakawa et al, 'RU486, a Progestin Antagonist, Binds to Progesterone Receptors in a Human Endometrial Cancer Cell Line and Reverses the Growth Inhibition by Progestins' (1988) 31(2) *Journal of Steroid Biochemistry* 161.

51 *Therapeutic Goods Amendment Act 1996* (Cth) s 25.

52 Buckmaster (n 43) 3.

53 The Harradine Amendments also provided that restricted goods were 'prohibited imports' under the *Customs Act 1901* (Cth) unless the Minister for Health had approved, in writing,

intended to address the senator's dismay at the commencement of clinical trials of RU486 in Australia in the early 1990s.[54]

The Harradine Amendments passed with the support of the Coalition Government and the Labor opposition. Only the Australian Democrats and some members of the Greens, both minor parties in the Senate, voted against the reforms.[55] During the parliamentary debates on the amendments, Senator Harradine and his supporters attempted to portray the reforms as not implementing a prohibition on RU486. They insisted that the purpose of the amendments was to enhance the accountability of the approval process for RU486 via parliamentary checks.[56] But the effect of the Harradine Amendments was to carve out abortifacients for special treatment under the therapeutic goods regulatory regime. Abortifacients were made an exception. They became the only drugs that could not be evaluated, listed or registered by the Secretary of the Department of Health (or their delegate) according to the criteria of quality, safety and efficacy without first receiving the Minister of Health's approval to do so.[57] Further, the ministerial approval appeared to be at the minister's complete discretion and where approval was not given, there was no additional parliamentary accountability.[58]

The effect of the Harradine Amendments was to stifle any attempt to introduce RU486 to Australia under the therapeutic goods regulatory regime. At the very least, the circumstances were discouraging for any potential sponsor of RU486.[59] The Minister of Health at the time, Tony Abbott, was well known for his conservative position and pro-life values and was clearly unlikely to provide the exceptional approval needed.[60] The Harradine Amendments amounted to a prohibition on medical abortion for Australian

---

their importation and had notified the Chief Executive Officer of Customs: *Therapeutic Goods Amendment Act 1996* (Cth) s 5.

54 Baird, 'Medical Abortion in Australia' (n 3) 170; de Costa, *RU-486: The Abortion Pill* (n 16) 90.

55 de Costa, *RU-486: The Abortion Pill* (n 16) 91.

56 See, eg, Commonwealth, *Parliamentary Debates*, House of Representatives, 29 May 1996, 1806 (Michael Lee, Shadow Minister for Health); Commonwealth, *Parliamentary Debates*, Senate, 21 May 1996, 818 (Robert Woods, Parliamentary Secretary to the Minister for Health and Family Services).

57 *Therapeutic Goods Act 1989* (Cth), ss 25–27, as at 12 August 1996.

58 The Minister's decision may be subject to the normal constraints of administrative law: see, eg, *Therapeutic Goods Act 1989* (Cth) ss 60, 60A; Peter Cane, Leighton McDonald and Kristen Rundle, *Principles of Administrative Law* (Oxford University Press, 2nd ed, 2018) ch 4.

59 de Costa, *RU-486: The Abortion Pill* (n 16) 92 quoting Senator Meg Lees.

60 Marian Sawer, 'What Makes the Substantive Representation of Women Possible in a Westminster Parliament? The Story of RU486 in Australia' (2012) 33(3) *International Political Science Review* 320, 324; O'Rourke et al (n 21) 224. See also Bede Harris, *Constitutional Reform as a Remedy for Political Disenchantment in Australia: The Discussion We Need* (Springer, 2020) 23.

women. The reforms realised the anti-abortion, right-to-life values and objectives of their creator. It was not until over a decade that an attempt was made to introduce RU486 into Australia.[61]

The Repeal of the Harradine Amendments

A realistic opportunity to repeal the Harradine Amendments in the Commonwealth Parliament did not present itself until 2006.[62] It arose through the rare cooperation of four female senators from different political parties, ably supported by advocacy from parts of the medical community, activism by the Australian women's movement and the timing of the election cycle. These elements combined to produce the *Therapeutic Goods Amendment (Repeal of Ministerial responsibility for approval of RU486) Act 2006* (the 'Repeal Act').[63] The Repeal Act was clear in its intent: 'to remove the responsibility for approval of RU486 from the Minister and to provide responsibility for approval of RU486 to the Therapeutic Goods Administration'.[64]

The Repeal Act removed the Harradine Amendments from the statute book, including the provision for 'restricted goods' and the associated special treatment of abortifacients.[65] It was passed in February 2006 following a rare conscience vote in Parliament,[66] which was preceded by a broad-based

61 During the intervening period some clinicians were able to obtain access to abortifacients under the special access or authorised prescriber schemes. Further, there were two instances in which the drug had been imported for clinical trials in Western Australia for use with an approved contraceptive: de Costa, *RU-486: The Abortion Pill* (n 16) 95; 'Abbott Won't Approve Use of Abortion Pill', *PM* (ABC Radio, 15 November 2005) <https://www.abc.net.au/listen/programs/pm/abbott-wont-approve-use-of-abortion-pill/741434>; Caroline de Costa, 'RU486 a Safe Option for Abortion: Access Needs to Be Expanded', *Crikey* (online, 9 May 2011) <https://www.crikey.com.au/2011/05/09/ru486-a-safe-option-for-abortion-access-needs-to-be-expanded/>.

62 A failed attempt to repeal the Harradine Amendments was made in 2001 by the Australian Democrats: de Costa, *RU-486: The Abortion Pill* (n 16) 94-5.

63 Sawer (n 60) 326–7. The particular contribution of Professor Caroline de Costa, as a clinician, activist and commentator, is worth noting here: see especially de Costa, *RU-486: The Abortion Pill* (n 16) chs 15–17. The lobbying from right-to-life activists in the lead up to the Repeal Act's passage was equally intense and compounded by the defensive tactics of the Minister of Health at the time: Sawer (n 60) 331; de Costa, op cit 101–2.

64 *Therapeutic Goods Amendment (Repeal of Ministerial Responsibility for Approval of RU486) Act 2006* (Cth) s 3.

65 Ibid s 4, sch 1.

66 Members of Australian Parliaments typically vote as determined by the political party to which they belong. Conscience or 'free' votes occur when the political party leader determines that its parliamentary members can vote according to their 'individual conscience'. Similar observations can be made in relation to other Westminster parliamentary systems: John Warhurst, 'Conscience Voting in the Australian Federal Parliament' (2008) 54 *Australian Journal of Politics and History* 579, 582–3.

inquiry by the Senate's Community Affairs Legislation Committee.[67] Both of these elements arguably assisted in generating far more open debate than had occurred in relation to the Harradine Amendments ten years earlier.[68] While the Repeal Act was small in length – a total of four sections and one schedule – its potential impact for Australian women was significant.

The Approval of RU486 in Australia

It was not until 2012 that an application for the supply of RU486 in Australia was made and approved – six years after the removal of the exceptional treatment of abortifacients under the therapeutic goods regulatory regime.[69] Commentators have stated that one reason for the delay was that potential sponsors of the drug perceived the regulatory environment as controversial and risky in the aftermath of the Harradine Amendments.[70] Consistent with the remarkable path worn by the drug, the ultimate sponsor of the drug in Australia was itself unusual. Marie Stopes International Australia (now MSI Australia) – a not-for profit reproductive health organisation – established a new entity (MS Health) which obtained approval for RU486 and misoprostol in October 2012.[71] The approval was subject to comprehensive requirements in relation to informed consent, patient follow-up and after-care service,

67 de Costa, *RU-486: The Abortion Pill* (n 16) 107–10; Kerry Ross, Susan Dodds and Rachel A Ankeny, 'A Matter of Conscience? The Democratic Significance of "Conscience Votes" in Legislating Bioethics in Australia' (2009) 44(2) *Australian Journal of Social Issues* 121, 128–9; Helen Pringle, 'The Greatest Heights of Parliament? Conscience Votes and the Quality of Parliamentary Debate' (2008) 23(1) *Australasian Parliamentary Review* 195, 195. However, Morgan notes that parliamentary votes on abortion are typically conscience votes: Morgan (n 31) 143.

68 See, eg, Sawer (n 60) 330, quoting Senator Lyn Allison's statement about women's experiences, including her own, in terminating a pregnancy. However, Pringle (n 67) argues that while, for conscience votes, the length of speeches may be longer and the number of speakers greater, this did not necessarily equate to an enhanced quality of debate: at 200–1.

69 Baird (n 21) 153–4; TGA, *Australian Public Assessment Report for Mifepristone (RU486) (Abortifacient)* (n 17); TGA, *Australian Public Assessment Report for Misoprostol* (October 2012). This was followed by approval of a combined product – 'MS-2 Step' in October 2014: Baird (n 21) 156; TGA, *Australian Public Assessment Report for Mifepristone/Misoprostol* (October 2014).

70 See, eg, 'MJA Podcasts 2019 Episode 14: Lifting Restrictions on Medical Abortion, with Prof Caroline de Costa AM', *The Medical Journal of Australia* (Cate Swannell, 1 April 2019) <https://www.mja.com.au/podcast/210/6/mja-podcasts-2019-episode-14-lifting-restrictions-medical-abortion-prof-caroline-de>; Harris (n 60) 23; Buckmaster (n 43) 2.

71 Marie Stopes International Australia established MS Health Pty Ltd to market RU486 in Australia: 'About Us', *MS Health* (Web Page, 2019) <http://www.mshealth.com.au/about-us>; Caroline de Costa, Kirsten I Black and Darren B Russell, 'Medical Abortion: It Is Time to Lift Restrictions' (2019) 210(6) *Medical Journal of Australia* 248, 248.

prescriber and pharmacist registration and education.[72] In these respects, RU486 continued to be treated as 'special' in comparison with other drugs included on the ARTG.[73] In 2019 there were approximately 1500 clinicians registered to prescribe RU486 in Australia; despite the battle to enable access to the drug in Australia, this represented a low proportion of the approximately thirty-five thousand potential prescribers.[74]

The Social and Ethical Issues Surrounding RU486

The above discussion describes the journey of RU486 through the therapeutic goods regulatory regime over almost two decades. I now turn to the social and ethical elements in which surgical and medical abortion is embedded and how these elements shape distinct conceptualisations of abortion. Such social and ethical issues constitute key normative tension points in relation to women's access to abortion and were highly relevant to the regulation of RU486 from 1996 to 2012.[75] I begin by describing the close relationship between different conceptualisations of abortion and these social and ethical issues by using the science and technology studies' concept of 'co-production'.[76] I then describe two common social and political conceptualisations of abortion that are co-produced with such issues. The first is the 'traditional' conceptualisation of abortion, which is shaped by three social and ethical elements: a culture of silence and shame surrounding abortion; the significant role and control of medical professionals in relation to abortion; and arguments supporting the sanctity of the life of the foetus. The second conceptualisation of abortion is described as 'subversive'. It is overwhelmingly shaped by the link between women's autonomy and equality and access to abortion. In this discussion I analyse the conceptualisation of both surgical and medical abortion. This provides a basis for the subsequent discussion regarding what the case study of RU486 reveals about the political legitimacy of the regulation of therapeutic goods in Australia.

72 de Costa et al (n 71) 248; TGA, *Australian Public Assessment Report for Mifepristone (RU486) (Abortifacient)* (n 17). See also 'MS-2 Step: User Registration', *MS2Step: Mifepristone, Misoprostol* (Web Page, July 2018) <https://www.ms2step.com.au/register/>.

73 de Costa et al (n 71) 249; Baird (n 21) 154–55.

74 'MJA Podcasts 2019 Episode 14' (n 70).

75 The term 'normative' is used here in a broad sense to describe 'standards that can be adopted and … enacted, thereby articulating a way in which the world could be shaped or reshaped … so that it fits those norms': Onora O'Neill, *From Principles to Practice: Normativity and Judgement in Ethics and Politics* (Cambridge University Press, 2018) 41. Many more such issues exist beyond the four identified here, for example, the question of 'fathers' rights': see, eg, Morgan (n 31) 152.

76 Jasanoff, 'The Idiom of Co-Production' (n 8) 3–6.

The Social and Ethical Co-production of Abortion

Science and technology scholar Sheila Jasanoff describes co-production as a mechanism by which knowledge is 'made' in society, in particular in the scientific and technological realms, which, in turn, influences the ordering and understanding of society.[77] Jasanoff posits that scientific and technological knowledge 'embeds and is embedded in social practices, identities, norms, conventions, discourses, instruments and institutions – in short, in all the building blocks of what we term the *social*'.[78]

Jasanoff considers that the concept of co-production is best considered an 'idiom' and 'interpretive framework', rather than as a comprehensive theory.[79] Its usefulness lies in its attempt to explicate 'the intersections of science and technology with politics and culture'.[80] In instances of controversy, the concept of co-production can be applied to illuminate how 'one set of ideas gains supremacy over competing, possibly better established ones, or fails to do so'.[81] This is particularly relevant to conflicting social and ethical claims around abortion and its resulting and divergent conceptualisations. Abortion, including via RU486, is 'produced' by the social, ethical and political environment in which it is embedded and which, simultaneously, 'produces' that social, ethical and political context. Consequently, abortion is fundamentally a 'political technology' – one of biotechnology's 'sites of domination and contest in social and political life'.[82] The following discussion highlights this interrelationship between two conceptualisations of abortion and significant social and ethical issues.

The Traditional Conceptualisation of Abortion

The act of abortion is traditionally conceptualised in the social and political sphere as a shameful act of criminality against life itself, which should be silenced and suppressed.[83] Further, it has been constructed as an act dictated and monopolised by the expertise of the medical profession, rather than as

77 Ibid.

78 Ibid 3 (original emphasis).

79 Ibid 3–4.

80 Sheila Jasanoff, 'Ordering Knowledge, Ordering Society' in Sheila Jasanoff (ed), *States of Knowledge: The Co-production of Science and the Social Order* (Routledge, 2004) 13, 17.

81 Jasanoff, 'The Idiom of Co-production' (n 8) 5.

82 Rosalyn Diprose also describes RU486 as a 'site of *contestation* of government authority': Diprose (n 5) 213 (emphasis in the original).

83 In her article on the regulation of biotechnology, including abortion, in three countries, Jasanoff describes how, in the context of American conservative politics, 'it is important for those in power to sell the rhetoric of "life" directly to their consuming publics, as a transcendental *political* commodity': Sheila Jasanoff, 'In the Democracies of DNA' (n 1) 152 (emphasis in the original).

a choice determined by women themselves. This traditional construction of abortion has been significantly shaped by three social and ethical issues: the silencing of abortion, the medicalisation of abortion and the sanctity of life. Collectively these issues, discussed below, co-produce a conceptualisation of abortion that prioritises the voice of political and social conservatives, the medical profession and the imagined voice of the foetus over and above that of women. Abortion has consequently been traditionally constructed, and therefore regulated, as a means with which to control women's reproductive health and lives.[84] Further, it is a socially dominant construction of abortion that denies women full reproductive control and restricts their capacity to participate as equals in the social and political domains.

The Silencing of Abortion

Historically, abortion was commonly viewed as an 'unspeakable crime'. Haigh's account of the 'underground' and opaque provision of abortion services in early 20th-century Victoria is testament to the silencing of abortion as a means by which women sought control over their reproductive health.[85] He documents a 'twilight world' of abortionists, who were 'visible enough to be accessible, not so visible as to invite interference' from law enforcement.[86] De Costa observes that the attitude of the contemporary medical profession is one of silence ('we don't talk about abortion') and that relatively few doctors perform surgical abortion.[87] Another commentator similarly notes that abortion is 'marginalised and stigmatised as a health service' and that even following the approval of RU486, this 'stigma' discourages practitioners from offering the service.[88]

In broader Australian society, abortion is arguably still perceived as a shameful act surrounded by silence. De Costa observes that it is 'a topic little discussed socially' and that '[m]any women will conceal such information from their closest friends and family'.[89] This is despite polling since the 1980s indicating support for legal access to abortion.[90] The perceived shame is argu-

84 See, eg, Diprose (n 5) 218.
85 See, eg, Haigh (n 15) 10, 24, 58.
86 Ibid 22.
87 de Costa, *RU-486: The Abortion Pill* (n 16) 11–12.
88 Baird, 'Medical Abortion in Australia' (n 3) 170, 173. See also Danielle Newton et al, ''A One Stop Shop in Their Own Community': Medical Abortion and the Role of General Practice' (2016) *Australian and New Zealand Journal of Obstetrics and Gynaecology* 2.
89 de Costa, *RU-486: The Abortion Pill* (n 16) 11; Justine Landis-Hanley, 'Doctors Crippled by Religious Backlash', *The Saturday Paper* (online, 29 February–6 March 2020) <https://www.thesaturdaypaper.com.au/news/health/2020/02/29/doctors-crippled-religious-backlash/15828948009443>.
90 de Costa, *RU-486: The Abortion Pill* (n 16) 10; Graycar and Morgan (n 6) 217. Further, a Newspoll poll in the lead up to the repeal of the Harradine Amendments showed that only 21% of people opposed the supply of RU486: Sawer (n 60) 329.

ably reflected in the historical failure of Australian jurisdictions to clarify the criminal status of abortion, encouraging, through legal ambivalence, a view that abortion is 'something unsavoury, something disreputable'.[91] It is a view reflected in the popular political mantra that there are 'too many abortions' – a position adopted by both supporters and opponents of reforms to the criminal status of abortion in Australia and the United States. As commentators have observed, this position 'presupposes that abortion is wrong' and that those who undergo the procedure are acting wrongfully.[92] Absent from these debates, Morgan argues, are women who are pregnant, women who have experienced abortion and – it should be added – women who have had children and are consequently able to attest to their diverse experiences.[93]

The tradition of silence around abortion is reflected to some extent in the Commonwealth parliamentary debates on RU486. The speeches by members of parliament about the Harradine Amendments rarely articulated the act of surgical or medical abortion.[94] Parliamentarians instead focussed on the intention of the amendments to enhance 'public accountability'.[95] In repealing the amendments in 2006, members of parliament on both sides of the issue commented that the number of abortions performed in Australia was 'alarming and too high'.[96] However, despite these allusions to the shame of abortion, there were also parliamentarians who spoke about the reality of abortion and that the Harradine Amendments would require women 'to terminate a pregnancy only by surgical means'.[97] To similar effect were state-

91 de Costa, *RU-486: The Abortion Pill* (n 16) 81. See also Morgan, quoting John Pandazopoulos MP in the Victorian Parliament stating, in support of the Abortion Law Reform Bill 2008 (Vic) that 'we still have a sort of underground discussion because we have a Crimes Act that does not allow for a proper informed discussion to give members of the medical fraternity the confidence they need': Morgan (n 31) 148 fn 41, citing Victoria, *Parliamentary Debates*, Legislative Assembly, 9 September 2008, 3368 (John Pandazopoulos).

92 Morgan (n 31) 169–70.

93 Ibid 170–1.

94 The exception to this is a 'Background' paper incorporated into the parliamentary record (Hansard) by Senator Harradine which outlines what RU486 does and that it 'delivers death to the unborn': Commonwealth, *Parliamentary Debates*, Senate, 9 May 1996, 620–22 (Brian Harradine).

95 Ibid 625; Commonwealth, *Parliamentary Debates*, Senate, 21 May 1996, 818 (Robert Woods, Parliamentary Secretary to the Minister for Health and Family Services); Commonwealth, *Parliamentary Debates*, House of Representatives, 29 May 1996, 1806 (Michael Lee, Shadow Minister for Health); Commonwealth, *Parliamentary Debates*, House of Representatives, 16 February 2006, 22 (Margaret May), 25 (Harry Jenkins).

96 Commonwealth, *Parliamentary Debates*, House of Representatives, 16 February 2006, 14 (Ian Macfarlane, Minister for Industry, Tourism and Resources), 27 (Teresa Gambaro, Parliamentary Secretary (Foreign Affairs)), 33 (John Howard, Prime Minister).

97 Commonwealth, *Parliamentary Debates*, Senate, 8 May 1996, 577 (Meg Lees, Deputy Leader of the Australian Democrats); Commonwealth, Parliamentary Debates, Senate, 28 November 2005, 124 (Fiona Nash); Commonwealth, *Parliamentary Debates*, House

ments by academic and clinical health professionals appearing before the Senate Committee Inquiry on the Repeal Act attesting to the occurrence of abortion as part of women's everyday lives. These witnesses asserted that 'women will get an abortion if they need one, whatever it takes' and that '[t]here has always been an amount of abortions that women seek and need over time'.[98] Like its surgical predecessor, RU486 was perceived by some as reflecting a shameful act that should be muted. Also present, however, was an emerging openness to the 'reality' of the role of abortion in women's lives as a means of reproductive control.[99]

The Medicalisation of Reproduction and Abortion

The traditional conceptualisation of abortion is also influenced by the view that abortion is, and should be, controlled by medical professionals.[100] This so-called 'medicalisation' of female reproduction is illustrated by early attempts to liberalise the criminalisation of abortion in Australia. South Australian law, for example, provided that abortion was legal where two doctors formed an opinion about the risk to the physical or mental health of the pregnant woman or the physical health of the child.[101] Similarly, in Victoria and New South Wales, the judicial interpretations of the then applicable statutes meant that access to legal abortion was dependent on the 'honest belief' of a medical practitioner that a woman's health was at risk.[102] This reliance on medical professionals to provide women with a legal means of accessing abortion was also evident in Western Australia. There, legislative reform in 1998 required the involvement of two doctors to render the

---

of Representatives, 16 February 2006, 27–8 (Teresa Gambaro, Parliamentary Secretary (Foreign Affairs)).

98 Evidence to Senate Standing Committee on Community Affairs, Parliament of Australia, Melbourne, 3 February 2006, 2 (Jo Wainer, Director of the Centre for Gender and Medicine, Monash University), 6 (Lynne Jordan, Chief Executive Officer, Family Planning Authority).

99 This openness has arguably been cemented since the controversy around RU486: see, eg, Kylie Maslen, 'I Had One Too: An Online Storytelling Platform Taking the Stigma Out of Abortion', *The Adelaide Review* (8 May 2019).

100 See, eg, Baird, 'Abortion Politics during the Howard Years' (n 44) 246–7.

101 Or alternatively where the abortion was needed immediately to prevent 'grave injury to the physical or mental health' of the pregnant woman. Further, the abortion must have been performed in a hospital: *Criminal Law Consolidation Act 1935* (SA) s 82A; Graycar and Morgan (n 6) 204–5.

102 While in Victoria this defence was for practical purpose most likely to apply to a medical professional and his or her belief, in New South Wales the common law position was that the defence was available only to doctors: Graycar and Morgan (n 6) 201–2; Mark Rankin, 'The Disappearing Crime of Abortion and the Recognition of a Woman's Right to Abortion: Discerning a Trend in Australian Abortion Law?' (2011) 13(2) *Flinders Law Journal* 1, 13–14.

termination lawful – one to perform the abortion and a second to refer the patient to counselling.[103] Writing in 2011, Rankin concluded that a number of Australian jurisdictions failed to deliver a woman's 'right to abortion' partly because of their reliance on the medical profession to render the abortion lawful.[104]

This tendency to 'pathologise' abortion is also evident in the expression of concern, identified above, by parliamentarians about the number and impact of abortions on women.[105] In her analysis of the 2008 Victorian reforms to abortion law, Morgan identifies that some members of that parliament spoke of abortion 'as hurting women'.[106] Such arguments typically expressed a concern for the mental and physical health of women as a result of abortion. Morgan concludes that by adopting the language of 'women's rights' to champion the health of pregnant women, the anti-abortion movement cloaks itself as 'pro-woman'.[107] The same characterisation can be made about those parliamentarians who adopted the language of concern for women's health while advocating anti-abortion positions.

The debates surrounding RU486 also drew on aspects of the medicalisation of abortion. Senator Harradine expressed significant concern about the health impacts for women of RU486 – both in Australia and in developing countries.[108] In doing so he adopted a view articulated by a small group of pro-choice feminists based in the United States and Australia who were critical of the potential health impacts of RU486.[109] This group was concerned about the 'de-medicalisation' of abortion – that is, that abortion could become a 'do-it yourself' procedure.[110] Other parliamentarians followed the senator's lead. Their more extreme observations included that there was a risk of infection arising from the 'mummification' of the terminated foetus.

103 *Health (Miscellaneous Provisions) Act 1911* (WA) s 334; *Criminal Code Act Compilation Act* s 199 (WA); Graycar and Morgan (n 6) 205–6; Rankin, 'The Disappearing Crime of Abortion' (n 102) 31–5.

104 The exception, at the time of Rankin's article, was Victoria, because 'the medical profession must accede to [the] demand' of a woman for an abortion (where the woman is no more than 24 weeks pregnant): Rankin, 'The Disappearing Crime of Abortion' (n 102) 45–6.

105 Baird, 'Abortion Politics during the Howard Years' (n 44) 246, quoting Sally Sheldon that 'women were "decriminalised in order to be pathologised"': Sally Sheldon, *Beyond Control: Medical Power and Abortion Law* (Pluto Press, 1997) 31.

106 Morgan (n 31) 164.

107 Ibid 164, 166–8.

108 A document tabled by Senator Harradine refers to 'documented reports of death, heart attack ... post abortion bleeding ... lasting effect on tissue of the cervix and uterus': Commonwealth, *Parliamentary Debates*, Senate, 9 May 1996, 621 (Brian Harradine).

109 Commonwealth, *Parliamentary Debates*, Senate, 8 May 1996, 580–1 (Brian Harradine). This view was reflected in the position of anti-abortionists in Canada's subsequent approval of RU486: Patricia Campbell, 'Making Sense of the Abortion Pill: A Sociotechnical Analysis of RU486 in Canada' (2018) 27(2) *Health Sociology Review* 121, 126.

110 de Costa, *RU-486: The Abortion Pill* (n 16) 34–6.

A more moderate example was the concern about access to emergency medical services for women in remote areas who were prescribed RU486 and later experienced complications.[111] Similar views were presented by pro-life groups advocating for the retention of the Harradine Amendments before the Senate Committee Inquiry on the Repeal Bill in 2006.[112]

Arguably, the medicalisation of abortion also influenced the therapeutic goods regulatory regime to impose conditions on the approval of RU486 in 2012. As discussed above, these included prescriber training and registration, the availability of an information service, access to emergency medical treatment if needed and a 'follow up' clinician appointment.[113] There is some evidence that these requirements contributed to a lower uptake of RU486 in Australia than originally anticipated, and reinforced the stigmatisation of abortion.[114] While the World Health Organization specifies that some of the requirements were necessary for the provision of safe abortion services, others, such as provider registration and mandatory follow-up appointments, were not.[115] Further, numerous studies now attest to the safety and efficacy of the drug.[116] In contrast with other countries, Australia's 'highly regulated and medicalised system of provision' of RU486 underlines how the approach

111 Commonwealth, *Parliamentary Debates*, Senate, 6 December 2005, 177 (Barnaby Joyce).

112 Evidence to Senate Standing Committee on Community Affairs, Parliament of Australia, Melbourne, 3 February 2006, 21 (Kath Woolf, Spokesperson, Australian Federation of Right to Life Associations), 23 (Charles Francis), 26 (Margaret Tighe, President, Right to Life Australia), 31–2 (Mathew Piercy, Medical Adviser, Right to Life Australia).

113 de Costa et al (n 71) 248; Baird, 'Medical Abortion in Australia' (n 3) 171.

114 Baird, 'Medical Abortion in Australia' (n 3) 172–3. There is some, limited, evidence that the requirements of registration and training may discourage the provision of medical abortion by clinicians: Angela J Dawson et al, 'Medical Termination of Pregnancy in General Practice in Australia: A Descriptive-Interpretive Qualitative Study' (2017) 14 *Reproductive Health* 39, 46–7; de Costa et al (n 71) 249.

115 Since at least 2014 the WHO has advised that in in the case of medical abortion, '[w]omen must be able to access advice and emergency care in the event of complications, if necessary' and recommends that 'all women have access to information and services to support successful completion of the abortion procedure, address common side-effects and manage any complications that may arise'. However, in the case of the combined use of mifepristone and misoprostol for a pregnancy at less than 12 weeks, and in the absence of other symptoms, the WHO considers that '[t]here is no medical need for a mandatory routine follow-up. Women should be able to have a follow-up visit if they desire': World Health Organization, *Clinical Practice Handbook for Safe Abortion* (n 22) 28, 30, 33. The WHO supports the need for 'well-trained health care providers' to enable safe abortion. But in relation to the registration of clinicians who provide abortions the WHO states that 'where certification of abortion providers is required ... it should not create barriers to accessing legal services ... and should not be a barrier to the availability and provision of abortion care': World Health Organization, *Safe Abortion* (n 15) 67.

116 de Costa et al (n 71) 248–9.

of the therapeutic goods regulatory regime to the drug was influenced by the historical medicalisation of abortion.[117]

Sanctity of Life

A further issue of social and ethical significance for the traditional construction of abortion is the sanctity of foetal life. This was perhaps the most prominent, but least articulated, normative issue in which RU486 was enmeshed in Australia from 1996 to 2012. This issue has been extensively discussed elsewhere from a range of philosophical, ethical, legal and sociopolitical perspectives in relation to both surgical and medical abortion.[118] In summary, the questions raised by this concern include: when does human life 'begin'; do all 'human' organisms have a 'right to life'; and does termination of a pregnancy constitute an unethical destruction of human life that should be made unlawful?[119]

The perspective of 'pro-life' or 'right-to-life' advocates on this topic is broadly self-explanatory – that an embryo is human from the moment of conception, and that abortion is consequently murder and should be criminalised. This is the perspective that has largely influenced the traditional conceptualisation of abortion. It is a view which, in the West, is typically (although not exclusively) drawn from, and reflected in, Catholic Church doctrine.[120] In contrast, the traditional feminist or 'pro-choice' position is that it is up to a pregnant woman to decide whether to continue with a pregnancy or to seek a termination. Consequently, abortion should be available, to varying extents, 'on demand' (that is, on the request of the pregnant woman and not subject to any restrictions or pre-conditions).[121] This view may be based on a range of beliefs, including that an embryo is not human; that women's rights to autonomy and equality outweigh any foetal rights;

117 Baird, 'Medical Abortion in Australia' (n 3) 174.

118 Michael Tooley, 'Abortion' in *Oxford Bibliographies: Philosophy* (Oxford University Press, 2013); Graycar and Morgan (n 6) 212.

119 Tooley (n 119).

120 See, eg, Rosemary Radford Ruether, 'Women, Reproductive Rights and the Catholic Church' (2008) 16(2) *Feminist Theology* 184; Rishona Fleishman, 'The Battle against Reproductive Rights: The Impact of the Catholic Church on Abortion Law in Both International and Domestic Areas' (2000) 24 *Emory International Law Review* 277. Fundamentalist Protestants, Hindus and Buddhists may also adopt what can broadly be described as 'anti-abortion' perspectives: see, eg, Gloria H Albrecht, 'Contraception and Abortion within Protestant Christianity' in Daniel C Maguire (ed), *Sacred Rights: The Case for Contraception and Abortion in World Religions* (Oxford University Press, 2003) 79, 98; Sandhya Jain, 'The Right to Family Planning, Contraception, and Abortion: The Hindu View' in Maguire (n 120) 129, 136; Parichart Suwanbubbha, 'The Right to Family Planning, Contraception, and Abortion in Thai Buddhism' in Maguire (n 120) 145, 152–3.

121 See, eg, Rankin, 'The Disappearing Crime of Abortion' (n 102) 45–6.

that foetal rights are dependent on the mother; and that certain circumstances (for example, cases of foetal 'abnormality') morally justify abortion irrespective of the rights of the foetus.[122] It is important to acknowledge, however, that advocates for a pro-choice or anti-abortion approach can hold views along a continuum between the two extreme ends of these perspectives.[123] Similarly, contemporary criminal law in Australia has typically reflected a compromise between complete prohibition of abortion, on the one hand, and the availability of abortion 'on demand' on the other.[124]

The diverse range of opinions on these questions surrounded the political consideration of RU486 in Australia. Senator Harradine's long-held pro-life perspective was clearly the basis from which the Harradine Amendments sprang, despite his reticence to articulate such views.[125] Consequently, the Harradine Amendments clearly reflected and reinforced the traditional conceptualisation of abortion. During the 1996 parliamentary debate, senators who opposed or were concerned about the Harradine Amendments referred to Senator Harradine's established pro-life position on abortion and similar issues that raised 'sanctity of life' dilemmas.[126] Parliamentarians debating both the amendments and later the Repeal Act also described the possible status of an embryo following conception:

> The fundamental question that must be posed over the abortion pill RU486 is whether it deals with one person or two. If you believe that a human life which is killed by this medication is not a human life then what is it? ... Well, this is abhorrent state-sanctioned killing.[127]

The relevance of the question of the life of a foetus to the RU486 debate in Australia was perhaps most emphatically illustrated by the range of organisations represented at the Senate Committee's Inquiry into the repeal of the Harradine Amendments. These included Reproductive Choice Australia,

122 See, eg, Ian Kerridge, Michael Lowe and Cameron Stewart, *Ethics and Law for the Health Professions* (The Federation Press, 4th ed, 2013); Graycar and Morgan (n 6) 212–13; Kate Gleeson, 'Bracket Creep in Australian Abortion Indications: When Did Rubella Arrive?' (2007) 15 *Journal of Law and Medicine* 423.

123 Kerridge et al (n 122) 546–9.

124 See, eg, Kerry Petersen, 'Abortion Laws: Criminalisation and Decriminalisation' in Ian Freckleton and Kerry Petersen (eds), *Tensions & Traumas in Health Law* (The Federation Press, 2017) 657.

125 See, eg, Stephen Cordner and Kathy Ettershank, 'RU486 in Australia' (1996) 4(1) *Journal of Law and Medicine* 18; Marr (n 47).

126 Commonwealth, *Parliamentary Debates*, Senate, 9 May 1996, 624 (Belinda Neal, Shadow Minister for Consumer Affairs and Assistant to the Shadow Minister for Health).

127 Commonwealth, *Parliamentary Debates,* Senate, 6 December 2005, 176 (Barnaby Joyce). A different perspective is offered by Senator Margetts in 1996: Commonwealth, *Parliamentary Debates,* Senate, 9 May 1996, 623 (Diane Margetts).

Family Planning Victoria, the National Union of Students and the Women's Electoral Lobby. Amongst the 'pro-life' organisations represented were Catholic Health Australia, the Australian Catholic Bishops Conference, Right to Life Australia and Festival of Light.[128]

The Subversive Conceptualisation of Abortion

The traditional conceptualisation of abortion and its co-production with the social and ethical issues described above contrasts starkly with a second construction of abortion. The subversive conceptualisation of abortion is that abortion is a positive act of liberation to facilitate women's social, economic and political agency and equality. Accordingly, abortion is a means to emancipation. This conceptualisation of abortion not only conflicts with the traditional conceptualisation, it actively seeks to overthrow it. In its place it seeks to instil a construction of abortion that amplifies women's voices to freely choose and access abortion as a means of social and political empowerment. The above analysis of the traditional conceptualisation of abortion identified three influential social and ethical issues. The subversive conceptualisation of abortion is similarly co-produced by its social and ethical context. This includes reacting against the social and ethical positions surrounding the traditional conceptualisation and adopting more moderate alternatives, such as those described above in relation to the sanctity of life. Even more prominent in the co-production of the subversive conceptualisation of abortion is the issue of women's autonomy and equality.

Women's Autonomy and Equality

The close link between women's access to legal abortion, reproductive control and their autonomy and equality has been written about extensively.[129] The law regarding abortion, both in Australia and overseas, reflects this relationship. Morgan notes that where abortion continues to be unlawful it sends a message that women are 'incapable of making their own thoughtful decisions, as either unworthy to do so, and/or at the mercy of the all-powerful doctor'.[130] Similarly, Graycar and Morgan highlight the direct link made by the common law between restrictions imposed on the availability of abortion in the United States and Canada and a woman's constitutional right to liberty.[131] The authors argue that restrictions on access to abortion (at least in the

128 Evidence to Senate Standing Committee on Community Affairs, Parliament of Australia, Melbourne, 3 February 2006.

129 See, eg, Morgan (n 31) 164–6; Graycar and Morgan (n 6) 209–11.

130 Morgan (n 31) 149.

131 Graycar and Morgan (n 6) 202–4, 208.

United States) reflect social and political disquiet about gender equality.[132] In early post-federation Australia, parts of the medical establishment and government (including two Royal Commissions) similarly expressed concern that women were exercising control over their reproductive freedom, driving down the country's birth rate and consequently harming the 'young' nation.[133]

Rosalyn Diprose analyses this link between autonomy, equality and access to abortion in relation to Australia's RU486 controversy. She concludes that the Commonwealth Government's significant restrictions on RU486 were an exercise of 'biopower' to diminish women's agency to a 'biological life determined by natural [reproductive] forces'.[134] From this perspective, medical abortion in the form of RU486 is itself subversive.[135] Both symbolically and literally, RU486 offers the potential for women to control their reproductive status without medical intervention and to do so at a time and place of their own choosing. In one pill, RU486 offers reproductive, economic, social and political liberation. In this respect, analogies with the revolutionary nature of the contraceptive pill are appropriate.[136] Diprose consequently argues that the imposition of ministerial control over RU486, as introduced by the Harradine Amendments, constituted 'direct scrutiny' of women's ability to achieve the full potential of their future selves, particularly in a public context.[137] The 'battle over RU486', she states, 'is really about ... women's agency'.[138]

The RU486 debates in parliament similarly reflected this relationship between access to abortion, women's autonomy and, to some extent, equality. Those members of parliament who opposed the Harradine Amendments, and those subsequently in favour of the Repeal Act, articulated concerns about the impact on the 'freedom' and 'choice' of women regarding reproduction.[139] In contrast, those supporting the amendments emphasised that their purpose was to ensure 'public accountability' for any future approval

132 Ibid 209–11.

133 Haigh (n 15) 26–7; *Royal Commission on Secret Drugs, Cures and Foods* (Report, 1907) vol 1; *Royal Commission on the Decline of the Birth-Rate and on the Mortality of Infants in New South Wales* (Report, 1904).

134 Diprose (n 5) 217–18.

135 See, eg, Margaret Matthews, *Safe and Subversive: Medication Abortion's Potential to Reshape Patterns of Access and Power* (BA Thesis, Vassar College, 2020).

136 See, eg, Alam et al (n 27) 22.

137 Diprose (n 5) 222–8; 232–5.

138 Ibid 222.

139 Commonwealth, *Parliamentary Debates*, Senate, 9 May 1996, 623 (Diane Margetts), 624–5 (Meg Lees, Deputy Leader of the Australian Democrats); Commonwealth, *Parliamentary Debates*, Senate, 28 November 2005, 125 (Fiona Nash); Commonwealth, *Parliamentary Debates*, House of Representatives, 16 February 2006, 14 (Ian Macfarlane, Minister for Industry, Tourism and Resources).

of abortifacients. The aim was not, they contended, about 'denying people choice'.[140] This argument explicitly rejects a link between restrictions on abortion and women's autonomy. Implicitly however, as Diprose contends, it relegates women to a role that requires protecting by the Commonwealth executive government and parliament. Women are silent in this role, lacking autonomy and denied equality.[141]

RU486 and the Harradine Amendments: A Challenge to the Political Legitimacy of the Therapeutic Goods Regulatory Regime

The following discussion reengages with the concept of political legitimacy and asks what the case study of RU486 tells us about the legitimacy of the therapeutic goods regulatory regime. The 1996 Harradine Amendments were, at minimum, a stark challenge to the political legitimacy of the therapeutic goods regulatory regime. The amendments effectively transferred the power to make key regulatory decisions about abortifacients from decision-makers under the existing regulatory regime to the Minister for Health.[142] In doing so, the amendments embodied an absence of Beetham's third legitimacy element – the consent or acknowledgement of an existing power relationship. In this instance the Harradine Amendments demonstrated an absence of consent to the existing regulatory regime's approach to the regulation of RU486. Beetham's consent or acknowledgement element was explored in Chapter 3.[143] To recap, the presence of this element can be illustrated by subordinates' actions of support for, recognition of, or engagement with, a power relationship. Conversely, the absence of this element can be found in 'public acts of protest, disobedience and withdrawal of endorsement or recognition' of that relationship.[144] The Harradine Amendments constituted the latter. They were a deviation from the political legitimacy of the therapeutic goods regulatory regime. The amendments, the senator's accompanying speeches in Parliament and the passage of the legislative reforms with the support of both major

140 Commonwealth, *Parliamentary Debates*, Senate, 9 May 1996, 625 (Brian Harradine); Commonwealth, *Parliamentary Debates*, House of Representatives, 16 February 2006, 42 (Mark Baker).

141 In comparison, Morgan draws on the work of Rebecca Albury to argue that women were portrayed as 'active social agent[s]' and as 'independent decision maker[s]' in the debates about the 2008 reform of abortion in the Victorian Parliament: Morgan (n 31) 173, quoting Rebecca M Albury, *The Politics of Reproduction: Beyond the Slogans* (Allen and Unwin, 1999) 106–7.

142 Buckmaster (n 43) 3.

143 See Chapter 3.

144 David Beetham, 'Revisiting Legitimacy, Twenty Years On' in Justice Tankebe and Alison Liebling (eds), *Legitimacy and Criminal Justice: An International Exploration* (Oxford University Press, 2013) 19, 26.

political parties collectively constituted an absolute 'withdrawal of endorsement' for the existing regulatory regime.[145] The amendments undermined, or in Beetham's terms 'delegitimise[d]', the existing power relationship that the regime had established.[146]

In this section I examine the two primary reasons for this challenge to the political legitimacy of the therapeutic goods regulatory regime. Together, these reasons establish that the regulatory regime's failure to adopt a constant dialogic approach to legitimacy contributed significantly to the Harradine Amendments' challenge to the regime's legitimacy. The first reason is the failure by the regulatory regime to engage in the social and ethical issues surrounding RU486 and to instead focus on questions of a predominantly scientific and technical nature. The consequences of this blinkered approach were twofold: that the regime was unable to seek to establish a set of shared normative beliefs and values between the multiple interested parties in the regulatory relationship, as advocated by the constant dialogic approach; and a destabilising shift away from the 'scientific' source of legitimacy of the regulatory regime, as described by Beetham. The second reason contributing to the Harradine Amendments' challenge to the political legitimacy of the therapeutic goods regulatory regime was its failure to engage in a relationship-based dialogue with all relevant parties to the regulatory regime as required by the constant dialogic approach to political legitimacy.[147] These two reasons are discussed in turn.

A Failure to Engage with the Social and Ethical Issues Surrounding RU486

The preceding section discussed how surgical and medical abortion is co-produced with significant social and ethical issues – the silencing and subversion of abortion as an explicit form of fertility control; abortion's medicalisation; the sanctity of life; and the autonomy and equality of women. This results in distinct and often conflicting conceptualisations of the act of abortion. This

145 Ibid 26.

146 David Beetham, *The Legitimation of Power* (MacMillan Education, 2013) 19. Although Beetham refers in his framework to the consent of the 'subordinate' to the power relationship with the 'dominant', the constant dialogic approach to legitimacy emphasises the significance of multiple dominant and subordinate parties to a power relationship. Consequently, it is argued here that even if the Senator can be construed as one of the 'dominant' parties in the power relationship with the therapeutic goods regulatory regime, his role in providing or, in this case, withdrawing 'consent' as to the legitimacy of that relationship is significant: see Chapter 3; Anthony Bottoms and Justice Tankebe, 'Police Legitimacy and the Authority of the State' in Antje du Bois-Pedain, Magnus Ulvang and Petter Asp (eds), *Criminal Law and the Authority of the State* (Hart Publishing, 2017) 47, 73–4.

147 See Chapter 3.

social and ethical dynamic is therefore highly relevant to the regulatory treatment of RU486. Yet, as this section discusses, the therapeutic goods regulatory regime was impervious to the importance of these issues and their role in the conceptualisation of abortion.

The failure by the therapeutic goods regulatory regime to engage in the social and ethical issues in which RU486 was embedded arguably enabled the challenge by the Harradine Amendments to the legitimacy of the regulatory regime. The senator was explicitly motivated to move the Amendments because he did not support leaving these issues to the 'bureaucrats' administering the existing therapeutic goods regulatory regime. [148] The regulation of abortifacients was a decision, he considered, of such importance that it should be made by the Minister for Health, who was directly accountable to parliament.[149] This sentiment was reflected by the senator in parliament:

> The purpose of these amendments is perfectly clear: to ensure that these particular drugs, which are significantly different in nature to other drugs which are termed therapeutic goods, should not be left entirely in the hands of science technologists and the sponsors of the particular drugs.[150]

Similar statements were expressed by the Labor Party in supporting the amendments:

> [W]e acknowledge that this issue raises large concerns within the community. *It raises issues beyond purely health issues.* These issues need to be addressed by the executive of this government and addressed with absolute and direct accountability and absolute and complete transparency.[151]

Such concerns were echoed by members of parliament who objected to the repeal of the Harradine Amendments in 2006:

> [W]e, representing community values, principles and ethics, should be the ones who should make a decision about whether a drug that cause the level of unease and debate within the community should be released into that community ... [t]he members of *the TGA were not elected to*

148 Commonwealth, *Parliamentary Debates*, Senate, 9 May 1996, 622 (Brian Harradine).
149 Ibid.
150 Commonwealth, *Parliamentary Debates*, Senate, 8 May 1996, 580 (Brian Harradine).
151 Commonwealth, *Parliamentary Debates*, Senate, 9 May 1996, 624 (Belinda Neal, Shadow Minister for Consumer Affairs and Assistant to the Shadow Minister for Health) (emphasis added).

contemplate the moral, ethical and values based reasons as to why a good should not be released.[152]

The Harradine Amendments, and the statements made in support of them, reflect a dissatisfaction with the restriction of the TGA's regulatory responsibilities to the *quality*, *safety*, *efficacy* and *timely availability* of such goods. In contrast, the normative issues within which RU486 was embedded were of a broader social and ethical nature.[153] The inability of the regulatory regime to identify and engage with these issues appeared to play a significant role in the pursuit of the amendments through the parliament and the Minister for Health. For example, Senator Harradine expressed his concerns about the comparatively narrow focus of the TGA and its regulatory regime in relation to correspondence received from pharmaceutical industry groups:

> I have had correspondence ... strongly opposing the proposed amendments on the basis that the [TGA] processes require an independent scientific and clinical assessment as to the *safety, quality and efficacy of particular drugs sponsored. It was these processes which moved me to propose this amendment.*[154]

The TGA made clear its avoidance of these broader normative issues when appearing before a 2005 Senate Committee Inquiry on the repeal of the Harradine Amendments. Representatives of the TGA and Department of Health and Ageing (as it was then known) side-stepped questions relating to the potential impact of RU486 on the unborn. Their responses appear obtuse, even in light of the restriction on public servants offering opinions on policy issues to parliamentary committees:[155]

Senator Joyce: So if the question was 'Is this going to affect the life of this unborn child?' that would be a consideration that you would then have to take into account?

Ms Halton: It would depend on what the drug is and what the application is in respect of.

152 Commonwealth, *Parliamentary Debates*, House of Representatives, 16 February 2006, 17–18 (Anthony Byrne) (emphasis added).

153 See, eg, Karinne Ludlow, 'More Than Science: Ethical and Socio-legal Concerns in Nanotechnology Regulation in Australia' in Graeme Hodge, Diana Bowman and Karinne Ludlow (eds), *New Global Frontiers in Regulation: The Age of Nanotechnology* (Edward Elgar, 2007) 166, 176–7.

154 Commonwealth, *Parliamentary Debates*, Senate, 8 May 1996, 580 (Brian Harradine) (emphasis added).

155 See, eg, Lorraine Finlay, 'The McMullan Principle: Ministerial Advisors & Parliamentary Committees' (2016) 35(1) *The University of Tasmania Law Review* 69, 93–4.

Senator Joyce: RU486 – there is a drug.

Ms Halton: We do not have an application for RU486 and the TGA has not put in place any speculative arrangements in that regard.

Senator Joyce: I will change it around. Are there any other drugs that are currently under your auspices for which you have to consider the effects on the unborn child?

Prof. Horvath [Chief Medical Officer, TGA]: Every drug that is considered – and I will answer this clinically and my colleague from the TGA can give you a technical answer – looks at the effects on the unborn child potentially, because there are some drugs that affect different growth pathways in a teratogenic effect.[156]

The avoidance of ethical issues relating to RU486 is expressed even more explicitly in the following excerpt of the Senate Committee's proceedings:

Chair: I have a second question for the TGA. When a doctor administers a drug or a procedure to a patient there are, of course, ethical considerations which are part of that doctor's training. In your opinion, are there any ethical dimensions of the process that the TGA employs in assessing the effectiveness or suitability of a drug?

Dr Graham: What we try to do is evaluate the evidence that is given to us. In that sense, we are very objective about that evidence and make a judgment, as I said earlier, on the basis of the three principles: quality, safety and efficacy.

Ms Halton: I think it is important to understand that the TGA operates within the legislative framework that it is given. There are a number of places, for example, under the special access arrangements where a medical practitioner is required to have ethical clearance before they can actually use a product. But we require the TGA to make a technical assessment in respect of the criteria in the legislation.

Chair: And ethical considerations are not one of the criteria.

Prof. Horvath: No.[157]

The TGA's responses in this instance are firmly situated in the existing legislative requirements of the regulatory regime and by the demands of 'evidence'

156 Evidence to Senate Standing Committee on Community Affairs, Parliament of Australia, Canberra, 15 December 2005, 24–5 (Barnaby Joyce; Jane Halton, Secretary, Department of Health and Ageing; John Horvath, Chief Medical Officer, Therapeutic Goods Administration, Department of Health and Ageing).

157 Ibid 30–1 (Gary Humphries, Chair; David Graham, National Manager, Therapeutic Goods Administration, Department of Health and Ageing; Jane Halton, Secretary, Department of Health and Ageing; John Horvath, Chief Medical Officer, Therapeutic Goods Administration, Department of Health and Ageing).

and its 'technical assessment'.[158] There is no room given for an alternative dialogue on normative issues.

In many respects the concerns expressed by Senator Harradine and his supporters mirror the extensive literature critiquing governance dominated by a scientific and technological ethos and by experts or 'technocrats'.[159] This criticism is aimed at the ideologies of scientism and technocracy which, as discussed in Chapter 2, significantly shaped the establishment and ongoing operation of the therapeutic goods regulatory regime. Broader conclusions about these ideologies and the regulatory regime will be discussed in Chapter 7. However, it is useful at this point to articulate how this critique is relevant to the case study of RU486.

First, the literature observes an aversion to non-scientific, normative issues by governments and regulators broadly, and in particular, in relation to technology itself.[160] Similarly, in the case of RU486 the broader ethical and social issues in which the drug was embedded were not addressed by the therapeutic goods regulatory regime. The elements of the co-production of different conceptualisations of medical abortion, discussed earlier, were ignored. Yet, judicial and academic commentators have historically urged that abortion be considered as 'not just a medical decision' but a 'profound social and ethical one as well'.[161]

Second, critics of a 'technocratic' approach to regulation refer to the overwhelming tendency to treat technological developments as 'politically neutral' and as objectively assessable.[162] But science, technology and their regulation are rarely, if ever, 'objective' and are produced by epistemologies, decisions and implications with their own social, moral and political meaning.[163] However, the above comments by the TGA clearly highlight its view

158 This recalls the significance of jargon and epistemics in the making of claims to legitimacy by powerholders, as identified in the analysis of the Sarah Bland 'traffic-stop' incident outlined in Chapter 3: Belén V Lowrey-Kinberg and Grace Sullivan Buker, '"I'm Giving You a Lawful Order": Dialogic Legitimacy in Sandra Bland's Traffic Stop' (2017) 51(2) *Law & Society Review* 379, 398–403.

159 See, eg, Frank Fischer, *Technocracy and the Politics of Expertise* (SAGE Publications, 1990) 14–17; Sheila Jasanoff, *The Ethics of Invention: Technology and the Human Future* (WW Norton & Company, 2016) 19–21.

160 See, eg, Fischer (n 159) *Technocracy and the Politics of Expertise* (SAGE Publications, 1990) 40–9.

161 Graycar and Morgan (n 6) 204, quoting *Morgentaler v The Queen* [1988] 1 SCR 30, 171–2 (Wilson J).

162 See, eg, Massimiano Bucchi, *Beyond Technocracy: Science, Politics and Citizens* (Springer, 2009) 78. See, also Keith Syrett's analysis of allocation of funding for the drug Herceptin in the United Kingdom: Keith Syrett, *Law, Legitimacy and the Rationing of Health Care* (Cambridge University Press, 2007) 7–8.

163 Julia Black, 'Regulation as Facilitation: Negotiating the Genetic Revolution' in Roger Brownsword, WR Cornish and Margaret Llewelyn (eds), *Law and Human Genetics: Regulating a Revolution* (Hart Publishing, 1998) 29, 63; Bucchi (n 162) 83.

that the regulatory regime enabled an objective assessment of therapeutic goods such as RU486 and that engagement with social and ethical issues was unnecessary and undesirable. Further, certain parliamentarians considered that the Harradine Amendments undermined the TGA's perceived objectivity – 'its scientific arm's length approach to assessment'.[164] Similar to the regulatory regime, these members explicitly and repeatedly sought to distance themselves from 'the philosophical or moral debate' regarding the use of RU486.[165] They advocated instead to 'allow the TGA to evaluate RU486 in the same impartial manner that it has done with almost 50,000 therapeutic goods' and to 'take the politics out of the issue and put the science back'.[166] They arguably considered that the therapeutic goods regulatory regime prior to the Harradine Amendments supported the apparent 'neutrality' of science itself.

Further, one of the most telling observations regarding the TGA's apparent neutrality is reflected in its eventual 2012 assessment and approval of RU486. While the assessment is predominantly discussed in clinical terms consistent with the scientific tradition, there is one notable exception: '[f]or a woman who has come to the difficult decision to have an abortion, when choice of method is available this is a separate and subsequent decision'.[167] This sentence attempts to separate the social and ethical issues surrounding RU486 from assessment by the therapeutic goods regulatory regime, and from the role of the TGA itself. However, the statement also highlights the criticism about the purported neutrality of the regulation of science and technology. It assumes that all women consider the decision to terminate a pregnancy as 'difficult' and that their choice of method is always separate from that decision. The regulator has clearly made a judgment about women, their views and values regarding abortion and their approach to decision-making. While the TGA's attempt at objectivity and neutrality here is clear, its effectiveness is not.

This section has described the aversion of the therapeutic goods regulatory regime to the normative issues surrounding RU486 and aspects of the broader critique of such an approach. As stated, these broader criticisms will be revisited in Chapter 7. The avoidance of the social and ethical issues regarding RU486 had two key consequences for the political legitimacy of the regime. These effects, and their influence after the repeal of the Harradine Amendments, are now discussed.

164 Commonwealth, *Parliamentary Debates*, Senate, 8 May 1996, 575 (Rosemary Crowley).
165 Ibid.
166 Commonwealth, *Parliamentary Debates*, Senate, 28 November 2005, 125 (Fiona Nash).
167 TGA, *Australian Public Assessment Report for Mifepristone (RU486) (Abortifacient)* (n 17) 26.

The Absence of a 'Shared Moral Order' about RU486

The first consequence of the therapeutic goods regulatory regime's resistance to the social and ethical issues surrounding RU486 was that the regulatory regime was not able to support any congruence in the beliefs and values about the regulation of the drug between all parties to the regulatory relationship.[168] This congruence or 'shared moral order' is an essential aspect of political legitimacy according to the constant dialogic approach and it is the second, or 'normative', element of Beetham's framework.[169] It is acknowledged that, given the contentious nature of abortion, such a congruence may not have been possible. However, there was no opportunity for the therapeutic goods regulatory regime to even seek normative congruence about the regulation of RU486. This was because the regulatory regime was unable to explicitly engage with these normative issues; and because it inadvertently suppressed any alternative to the traditional conceptualisation of abortion. This meant that there was no opportunity for the TGA to facilitate dialogue and decision-making about the control of RU486 that was informed by different views on highly relevant social and ethical issues.[170]

In the previous chapter I observed that normative congruence was absent in relation to medicinal cannabis. In that instance, arrival at a set of shared normative beliefs and values was inhibited by the regulatory regime's inability to engage with the alternative voices of medicinal cannabis regulation. In the case of RU486, a set of shared normative beliefs and values was not possible because the explicit foci of the therapeutic goods regulatory regime were the issues of quality, safety and efficacy, not the fundamental normative issues surrounding the drug. These scientific issues, and the expertise and traditions applied to answer them, were an insufficient normative justification of the power asserted by the regulatory regime in relation to RU486.[171] As Beetham states, '[s]cientific theories are logically incapable of generating normative principles on their own'.[172] In 1996, therefore, it was not possible for the TGA and its supporters to develop a 'narrative of legitimation' around the approach to RU486 that engaged with relevant social and ethical issues, such as women's autonomy and equality, or the proper protection to be given to the life of a foetus. The Harradine Amendments flowed from this failure, as did regulatory instability.[173]

168 Beetham, *The Legitimation of Power* (n 146) 11.

169 Ibid 82.

170 An alternative and preferable course of events to this approach is briefly discussed in Chapter 7.

171 Bottoms and Tankebe (n 146) 57.

172 Beetham, *The Legitimation of Power* (n 146) 73.

173 Bottoms and Tankebe (n 146) 48–50. Parallels can be drawn here with the work of Keith Syrett on the legitimacy of the allocation or 'rationing' of healthcare resources in the UK and the instability that may result from such decisions. Syrett observes that the allocation

Further, the focus of the therapeutic goods regulatory regime on the scientific characteristics of medical abortion reinforced, albeit inadvertently, the traditional conceptualisation of abortion described above. By avoiding the broader social and ethical issues surrounding RU486, the regulatory regime effectively suppressed their articulation. This regulatory environment reflected and reinforced the traditional conceptualisation of abortion as a shameful act that should be silenced. Similarly, by exercising regulatory power through a singular focus on scientific-based criteria and methodology, the regulatory regime emulated the historical medicalisation of abortion. The voices and values that were effectively articulated were those of the medical profession, political conservatives and, through them, the imagined voice of the unborn. There was no space for the many women whose voices and values were reflected in the subversive conceptualisation of abortion. The regulatory regime's blinkered perspective on the broader social and ethical issues surrounding abortion meant that it had failed to recognise when it was itself blindly following, and therefore reinforcing, the traditional conceptualisation of abortion. This further inhibited any chance of seeking and achieving a shared normative congruence in relation to the regulation of RU486. Such a regulatory environment arguably emboldened the Harradine Amendments.

From Science to Society: A Change in the Authoritative Source of Normative Legitimacy

The second consequence of the regulatory regime's inability to engage with the social and ethical issues around RU486 was a change in the authoritative 'source' of the regime's normative legitimacy. This transition was the crux of the Harradine Amendments: they enabled a transfer of power over abortifacients from the regulatory regime and its traditional decision-making criteria to the Minister for Health and his or her discretion.[174] The Harradine Amendments made it possible for the minister to consider the normative issues which the therapeutic goods regulatory regime could and would not. Indeed, it was likely that this would occur given Senator Harradine's political power and his narrow social and ethical views around abortion.

of finite healthcare resources can never be value neutral where human health is significantly compromised. This is despite attempts to present outcomes as the objective result of 'technocratic modes of decision making', analogous to those made in relation to therapeutic goods. He explains that fault lines about what constitutes the 'right' decision in these circumstances, once revealed, reflect competing ethical perspectives, and result in 'profound moral outrage' that 'jeopardises the cohesiveness of society': Syrett (n 162) 7, 78–9, 95.

174 Abortifacients could not be 'evaluated' under the criteria of the therapeutic goods regulatory regime unless first approved by the Minister: *Therapeutic Goods Amendment Act 1996* (Cth) s 25(1).

According to Beetham's approach to political legitimacy, the change in the authoritative source of normative legitimacy (which the Harradine Amendments reflected) represented much more than a transfer of responsibilities from one entity or individual to another. In outlining the second 'normative' element of his legitimacy framework, Beetham describes societal beliefs as constituting the authoritative source of legitimate power.[175] As described in Chapter 3, sources of normative legitimacy may be 'external' to a particular society (e.g., religion; secular natural law; scientific theories) and 'internal' to that society (e.g., societal traditions such as heredity power or present-day decisions by a society's governing representatives).[176] The Harradine Amendments represented a transition from the external source of science (reflected in the pre-Amendments regime) to the external sources of religion (reflected in the 'sanctity of life' doctrine of the Catholic Church) or natural law doctrines (reflected in the social and ethical issues discussed above).[177]

It is also arguable that the reforms reflected a change in the internal source of normative legitimacy for the regulatory regime. That is, the internal source of normative legitimacy shifted from decision-makers pursuant to the therapeutic goods regulatory regime, to 'the people' as represented by parliament and to which the Minister for Health was accountable.[178] Beetham considers that transitions such as this constitute 'profound social changes': '[s]uch shifts in belief, as gradual as they are also fundamental, will leave a society's established power rules intellectually unsupported, like a bridge whose foundations have been weakened by the slow processes of erosion'.[179]

In the absence of an ability to address the social and ethical issues around RU486, the therapeutic goods regulatory regime was vulnerable to such a shift. In the face of the broader normative issues the regulatory regime was unable to justify power as emanating purely from the scientific tradition and its associated beliefs. The reforms introduced by Senator Harradine were an attempt to address this resulting 'legitimacy gap or deficit' and to do so in a

175 Beetham, *The Legitimation of Power* (n 146) 70.

176 See ibid 71–5. See also Chapter 3.

177 RU486 is a noteworthy case study in the context of Beetham's work on external 'authoritative sources' for legitimacy. Beetham describes the typical, historical transition between external sources as progressing from religion, to natural law doctrines to the disciplines of science. This trend is reversed in the case of RU486: Beetham, *The Legitimation of Power* (n 146) 74.

178 The Minister was required to report to Parliament if he approved RU486. There was extensive criticism, however that the Harradine Amendments did not require a similar parliamentary reporting mechanism if the Minister rejected an application for the approval of RU486. This omission served as a basis to undermine the Harradine Amendments during the debate on their ultimate repeal in 2006: see, eg, Buckmaster (n 43) 3.

179 Beetham, *The Legitimation of Power* (n 146) 75.

way that facilitated his particular social and ethical values and conceptualisation of abortion.[180]

A Reestablishment of Normative Legitimacy Following the Repeal of the Harradine Amendments?

As a counterargument, it may be suggested that the eventual repeal of the Harradine Amendments and the approval of RU486 marked, at least, the reestablishment of the normative aspect of the regulatory regime's political legitimacy. This argument assumes, however, that these later events were evidence of a congruence of values regarding the regulation of RU486 and the reemergence of 'science' as the authoritative source of the regulatory regime's normative legitimacy.

But there are indications that these assumptions are incorrect. The TGA's assessment of RU486 in 2012 shows that social and ethical issues continued to be influential and contentious at that time. For example, the TGA requested that Marie Stopes establish a patient registry and expressed strong concern that it may not be possible to prevent prescribers who had not undergone Marie Stopes education program from prescribing the drug.[181] When viewed through the so-called objective veneer of 'science', these matters appear to relate to the legislative objective of 'safety'. But the TGA's concerns are also imbued with implicit decisions about women's autonomy and assumptions regarding the medicalisation of abortion discussed earlier.[182] Arguably, they therefore amounted to a regulatory affirmation of the traditional conceptualisation of abortion.

Marie Stopes, as sponsor of the drug, argued that the TGA's expectation that certain clinicians would be prevented from prescribing the drug went beyond that normally required of other drugs approved by the regulator.[183] Further, Marie Stopes objected to the suggested patient registry, in part because of concerns about the privacy of women to whom the drug was prescribed.[184] While the TGA's assessment of RU486 was largely formal in tone, the exchanges on these issues with Marie Stopes suggests the ongoing significance of, and divergence in, normative values. The approval of RU486 by the regulatory regime was certainly a pragmatic victory for Australian women's

180 Ibid 75–6.

181 Patient registries are typically implemented as a basis on which to continue to assess the efficacy and safety of a drug or device following its approval: TGA, *Australian Public Assessment Report for Misoprostol* (n 69) 74, 85–7.

182 This is indicated by the 'special' requirements and restrictions placed on the supply of RU486 including the registration and education of clinicians and pharmacists: de Costa et al (n 71) 248.

183 TGA, *Australian Public Assessment Report for Misoprostol* (n 69) 85–6.

184 Ibid 87.

reproductive freedom. But in light of the above analysis, the approval of RU486 did not represent a definitive normative congruence around 'pro-choice' values consistent with the subversive construction of abortion, nor the reestablishment of 'science' as the authoritative source of such norms.

A Failure to Engage in a Constant Dialogue with All Relevant Parties

The second reason for the challenge posed by the Harradine Amendments to the political legitimacy of the therapeutic goods regulatory regime was the absence of a constant dialogue with all relevant parties to the regulatory power relationship. The constant dialogic approach proposes that the 'relational' dimension of political legitimacy is fundamental to its establishment and endurance.[185] An ongoing dialogue between all parties is necessary to support the formulation of a shared set of normative beliefs and values. For example, the previous chapter outlined how, in relation to medicinal cannabis, the TGA and its supporters limited dialogue to governments and producers of medicinal cannabis and communicated its own views in a formal, non-discursive manner.

In the case of RU486, statements made before the Senate Committee Inquiry regarding the repeal of the Harradine Amendments indicate that the TGA was not prepared to enter into any discourse about RU486 until an application for the drug's approval was made. For example, when asked about what guidelines the TGA may require to be provided to women if an application for the approval of RU486 was received, the then Secretary of the Department of Health and Ageing replied:

> The Therapeutic Goods Administration has no role in speculative consideration in relation to drugs that are not listed and for which there have been no applications received ... In the event that there is an application from a sponsor in respect of this drug ... [a]ll of the circumstances and all of the evidence would be considered by the evaluators ... But at this moment *the TGA has no role in doing any work of a speculative nature. That is not the role of the regulator.*[186]

A subsequent statement indicates that the TGA viewed itself strictly as a creature and administrator of its legislative scheme. When asked if the TGA approval processes were appropriate for RU486, the Secretary replied: '[y]ou

185 See Chapter 3.

186 Evidence to Senate Standing Committee on Community Affairs, Parliament of Australia, Canberra, 15 December 2005, 21 (Jane Halton, Secretary, Department of Health and Ageing).

are asking for an opinion … we cannot provide you with an opinion. We can say that we administer the legislation as it is provided to us, and I believe that we administer it with due diligence'.[187] It is consistent with the role of public servants appearing before Commonwealth parliamentary committees to not provide opinions about public policy.[188] Even given this, it appears that the TGA was at the very least unable, and perhaps also unwilling, to engage with a dialogue about RU486 outside strict legislative parameters. This observation is also reflected in the answers to questions about the impact of RU486 on the unborn, discussed earlier.

The above questions asked by the Senate Committee are equivalent to a 'basic legitimation demand'. As outlined in Chapter 3, the basic legitimation demand commonly constitutes a request by a subordinate party to the powerholder to provide a normative reason or justification for exercising that power.[189] The responses given here by the representatives of the TGA to the basic legitimation demand are formal and legalistic. As in the case of medicinal cannabis, this recalls the observation of Beetham that the status quo will often refer to the 'legal' element of political legitimacy even though it is insufficient. The TGA's statements do not form a narrative that attempts to normatively justify the power exercised by it in relation to RU486. Further, the responses given do not provide the basis for an ongoing dialogue between all parties to the regulatory relationship about that power.

Finally, it is not clear that the regulatory regime engaged effectively with all relevant parties in relation to RU486. Despite opinion polls indicating acceptance of abortion in the Australian community, there was an absence of strong opposition in parliament to the Harradine Amendments. This perhaps indicates a failure by the regulatory regime to engage, and engage early, with supporters of medical abortion, including MPs, non-government groups, clinicians and women themselves.[190] This failure – at least as far as the public record reveals – to engage in a dialogue with pro-choice groups and individuals occurred despite Australia's long history of women's rights

187 Ibid 24.

188 Finlay (n 155) 93–4.

189 See Chapter 3; Lowrey-Kinberg and Sullivan Buker (n 158) 391; Bottoms and Tankebe (n 146) 57, 60, 73 citing Bernard Williams (selected and edited by Geoffrey Hawthorn), *In the Beginning Was the Deed: Realism and Moralism in Political Argument* (Princeton University Press, 2005).

190 This is despite the indication that a strong opposition to the Harradine Amendments existed at the time that they were proposed, including, for example, by Senator Crowley, the Labor Senator for South Australia, Senator Lees, the Australian Democrats Senator for South Australia, the National Council of Women, the AMA Women's Committee, Family Planning Australia, the Doctors Reform Society, Australian Women's Health Network and the National Association of Leading Women's Hospitals: Commonwealth, *Parliamentary Debates*, Senate, 21 May 1996, 818, 824–5 (Rosemary Crowley), 827–8 (Meg Lees, Deputy Leader of the Australian Democrats).

activism in relation to fertility control.[191] Further, in the decade between the Harradine Amendments and their repeal there appears to have been little, if any, engagement or dialogue by the TGA with relevant parties in relation to RU486.[192] This was despite the extensive approval of the drug overseas,[193] the call for a 'watching brief' following the Harradine Amendments on any adverse effects they may have on the community,[194] and the cross-party campaign to repeal the Harradine Amendments.[195] Despite the early indications of controversy surrounding RU486,[196] the therapeutic goods regulatory regime did not appear to establish a dialogue with all parties to the regulatory relationship, nor to do so with a narrative that justified its approach to the drug in normative terms.

Recent Developments

In mid-2023 the TGA approved an application by MS Health to relax the conditions that had been imposed on the approval of RU486 in 2012. The changes included allowing any health practitioner (including certain nurses) to prescribe the drug and any pharmacist to dispense it – not just one registered

191 See, eg, Barbara Baird, 'Abortion and the Limits of the Personal Becoming Political' (2018) 33(95) *Australian Feminist Studies* 129, 131–5; Women's Liberation Centre, 'Abortion' (1974) 7 *Vashti's Voice: A Women's Liberation Newspaper* 5; Zelda D'Aprano, *Zelda* (Spinifex, 1995) 229, 401–2.

192 See, eg, Evidence to Senate Standing Committee on Community Affairs, Parliament of Australia, Canberra, 2 November 2005, 175–6 (Kerry Nettle and Jane Halton, Secretary, Department of Health and Ageing). It is unclear on the face of publicly available material whether the TGA engaged with relevant stakeholders, other than the sponsor which applied for the eventual approval of RU486, following the repeal of the Harradine Amendments.

193 TGA, *Australian Public Assessment Report for Mifepristone (RU486) (Abortifacient)* (n 17) 5.

194 Commonwealth, *Parliamentary Debates*, Senate, 21 May 1996, 824 (Christabel Chamarette).

195 See, eg, Adele Lausberg, 'Women and Representation: Cross-Party Collaboration in the Australian Federal Parliament' (2016) 69(2) *Parliamentary Affairs* 249, 258–60.

196 For example, Senator Harradine's questioning of TGA representatives appearing before a Senate Committee in 1995 was arguably indicative of his values regarding RU486 and the need for the regulatory regime to engage with them: Evidence to Senate Standing Committee on Community Affairs Legislation, Parliament of Australia, Canberra, 23 November 1995 (Brian Harradine). Further, two years prior to the Harradine Amendments, the Right to Life Association of NSW brought proceedings in the Federal Court of Australia against the Secretary of the Commonwealth Department of Human Services and Health. The proceedings challenged, unsuccessfully, the conduct of clinical trials of RU486 under the *Therapeutic Goods Act 1989* (Cth) and subordinate regulations: *Right to Life Association (NSW) Inc v Secretary, Department of Human Services and Health and Family Planning Inc (Vic)* (1995) 128 ALR 238; Natasha Cica, 'Abortion Law in Australia' (Research Paper, Parliamentary Library, Parliament of Australia, 31 August 1998) 9–12.

to do so after receiving specified training.[197] The restrictions originally placed on the drug were, in the view of MSI Australia, unwarranted and 'created unnecessary obstacles for people seeking to access vital healthcare'.[198] The Commonwealth Labor government and medical professionals hoped that access to medical abortion would improve as a result of the changes.[199]

From the perspective of political legitimacy, the reforms were welcome considering the high rates of public approval for access to abortion across the country. Nevertheless there were aspects of the TGA's decision that were concerning in light of the complex social and moral history of abortion. The TGA issued a media release about the changes but provided no additional information about the changes or the reasons behind them. This relative lack of information risks feeding the view of abortion as shameful and as something that should therefore be hidden, and it represents a missed opportunity for the TGA to engage in broader public discourse about aspects of medical abortion.

Conclusion

The examination of the regulation of RU486 between 1996 and 2012 reveals that the Harradine Amendments challenged the political legitimacy of the therapeutic goods regulatory regime. The failure by the regulatory regime to embrace aspects of the constant dialogic approach to political legitimacy created an environment which was vulnerable to this challenge. This is evident in the regulatory regime's lack of engagement with the social and ethical issues in which medical abortion is embedded and constructed; an almost purist reliance on its legislative objectives and their purported objectivity; and the inadvertent reinforcement of the traditional conceptualisation of abortion. Consequently, a congruence between the normative beliefs and values held by parties to the regulatory relationship about RU486 was unobtainable. Further, the Harradine Amendments constituted a destabilising shift in the authoritative source of the regulatory regime's normative legitimacy – from the scientific tradition represented by the regulatory regime prior to the Harradine Amendments to the natural law or religious principles which motivated those reforms. Finally, the regulatory regime failed to engage in the

197 'Amendments to Restrictions for Prescribing of MS-2 Step (Mifepristone and Misoprostol)' (Media Release, Therapeutic Good Administration, Department of Health and Aged Care (Cth), 11 July 2023).

198 'TGA Decision Improving Access to Abortion Care for All Australians Welcomed' (Media Release, MSI Australia, 11 July 2023).

199 Claudia Long, 'Changes to Abortion Regulation Will Come Into Effect Next Month In a Bid to Increase Access' *ABC News* (Online, 11 July 2023) <https://www.abc.net.au/news/2023-07-11/changes-to-abortion-regulation-in-a-bid-to-increase-access/102584108>.

ongoing, relational dialogue that is central to the constant dialogic approach to political legitimacy.

I do not suggest that an attempt to construct an ongoing dialogue between all parties affected by the regulation of medical abortion will inevitably result in a single set of shared normative values or a common conceptualisation of abortion. This is particularly given the protracted and virulent debate between the pro-choice and right-to-life positions. However, the analysis of this case study indicates that the regulatory regime attempted to control these diverse and impassioned views on contested normative issues by funnelling them into containable scientific methods and traditions. This camouflaged significant social and ethical issues and prevented any possibility of the therapeutic goods regulatory regime substantively engaging with these issues as part of its regulatory mandate and in the pursuit of normative congruence. Inevitably, however, these fundamental normative questions could not be contained. As I will argue in Chapter 7, the therapeutic goods regulatory regime should instead support the instigation and facilitation of a dialogue between all parties to the regulatory relationship. This dialogue should enable the identification of relevant and diverse normative issues and their integration in regulatory decision-making with the traditional objectives of the quality, safety and efficacy of therapeutic goods.

Chapter 6

Shouting to Be Heard

The Regulation of Urogynaecological Mesh Devices in Australia

Introduction

The preceding case studies considered the therapeutic goods regulatory regime's treatment of pharmaceuticals in the form of medicinal cannabis and abortifacients. In this chapter I turn to an area of increasing focus for regulatory regimes of medical products – that of medical devices and, in particular, the control of urogynaecological mesh devices (UMDs). UMDs have been the subject of public complaint and controversy in a number of countries since at least the mid-2000s. Along with breast implants, hip and knee prostheses, artificial cardiac stents and others, the regulatory experience of mesh devices has led to calls in Australia and internationally for reform to device regulation more broadly.[1]

In this chapter I describe the urogynaecological mesh device and its regulation as a medical device in Australia. The regulatory regime for medical devices is polycentric in nature, characterised 'by fragmentation, complexity and interdependence between actors'.[2] The roles of the key actors in the regulation of UMDs are outlined, along with how each actor collectively contributes to the polycentric nature of the regulatory regime. Despite the multiple regulatory actors, many rely on the central role played by the TGA. The first part of this chapter further describes a 'loop' of information generation and exchange between the regulatory actors, which is essential to the polycentric regulatory arrangements for medical devices. The effective operation of this

1 See, eg, Wendy Bonython and Bruce Baer Arnold, Submission No 12 to Senate Community Affairs References Committee, Parliament of Australia, *Number of Women in Australia Who Have Had Transvaginal Mesh Implants and Related Matters* (2017) 1–2; 'Medical Devices Harm Patients Worldwide as Governments Fail on Safety', *International Consortium of Investigative Journalists* (online, 25 November 2018) <https://www.icij.org/investigations/implant-files/medical-devices-harm-patients-worldwide-as-governments-fail-on-safety/>.

2 Julia Black, 'Constructing and Contesting Legitimacy and Accountability in Polycentric Regulatory Regimes' (2008) 2 *Regulation & Governance* 137, 137.

DOI: 10.4324/9781003293811-6

loop supports a constant dialogue between the regulatory actors, consistent with the constant dialogic approach to political legitimacy.

Following an outline of the history of the regulation of UMDs and how events regarding failures in the safety and efficacy of the device unfolded from 2006 to 2021, I identify and explain the key factors that contributed to these failures. These are the training and conduct of clinicians; the risk profile of UMDs; the inadequacy of informed consent for device implantation; and the under-reporting of adverse events related to the devices, which, in turn, contributed to their delayed withdrawal from the market.

In the final part of the chapter I explore what can be learnt about the political legitimacy of the therapeutic goods regulatory regime from the controversy surrounding UMDs. This question is addressed by demonstrating how criticism from individuals, civil society, parliamentary representatives and the judiciary constituted a challenge to the regulatory regime's political legitimacy. A key reason for this challenge was the collective absence of a constant dialogic approach to political legitimacy in relation to the regulation of UMDs. This is illustrated in two key respects: first, a limited dialogue between polycentric regulatory parties about the potential for harm – that is, risks – of the devices; and, second, a similarly inadequate dialogue regarding the actual harm caused by the devices. Consequently, there were clear incongruencies between the values and beliefs held by the regulatory parties about what constituted an acceptable risk of harm, and what harm amounted to an adverse event under the therapeutic goods regulatory regime. It is argued that failings in the information loop contributed significantly to these constrained dialogues and the resulting absence of a constant dialogic approach to political legitimacy by the regulatory regime. Steps taken by the TGA in the wake of the urogynaecological mesh device controversy have the potential to address these failings, and to enable the avoidance of future challenges to the regulatory regime's political legitimacy.

Urogynaecological Mesh and its Regulation

What Is Urogynaecological Mesh?

Urogynaecological mesh devices have been described as 'net-like substance[s] that [provide] extra support to repair weakened or damaged internal tissue'.[3] The devices were introduced to the medical device market to treat pelvic

3 'Transvaginal Mesh', *Better Health Channel* (Web Page, March 2018) <https://www.betterhealth.vic.gov.au/health/conditionsandtreatments/Transvaginal-mesh>.

organ prolapse (POP)[4] and stress urinary incontinence (SUI).[5] POP and SUI are urogynaecological conditions experienced by women, either as separate conditions or simultaneously.[6] Symptoms of POP vary between patients but may include 'back and pelvic pain, vaginal pressure, vaginal discomfort, urinary incontinence or urinary obstruction, bowel incontinence or other bowel dysfunction, bleeding or unusual vaginal discharge and pain during exercise and/or sex'.[7] Some estimates place the extent of incidence of the condition at half of all women. Despite this, and the potential significant impact of POP on a women's quality of life, the condition is often undiagnosed.[8] Depending on severity, both POP and SUI can be treated conservatively via non-surgical measures, including pelvic floor exercises, bladder strengthening and pessaries.[9] More severe or chronic cases frequently require surgery. For POP, surgical treatment involved repairing weakened tissue using the patient's own tissue.[10] However, this approach was considered relatively unsuccessful for POP, often requiring follow-up surgery.[11] For POP in particular, therefore, the introduction of UMDs was welcomed by clinicians.

Surgical mesh was initially introduced for the successful repair of hernias. The product was subsequently developed using synthetic material and adapted for urogynaecological purposes in the mid- to late 1990s.[12] Urogynaecological mesh was initially used for SUI in the form of the mid-

4 'Pelvic Organ Prolapse is where the lower pelvic organs – bladder, uterus or bowel – have prolapsed, or moved down, into the vagina or anus. The most common cause is pregnancy, labour and childbirth. POP is a common condition, and up to 50 per cent of women who have been through childbirth will have some prolapse present': Department of Health (Cth), Submission No 19 to Senate Community Affairs References Committee, Parliament of Australia, *Number of Women in Australia Who Have Had Transvaginal Mesh Implants and Related Matters* (31 May 2017) 9 ('Department of Health (Cth) Submission 2017').

5 'Stress Urinary Incontinence (SUI) is the leaking of urine during activities such as coughing, lifting and playing sport. The causes of SUI are similar to POP. SUI affects about one-third of women of childbearing age': ibid 9.

6 Senate Community Affairs References Committee, Parliament of Australia, *Number of Women in Australia Who Have Had Transvaginal Mesh Implants and Related Matters* (Report, March 2018) 6 ('Senate Community Affairs References Committee Report 2018').

7 Department of Health (Cth) Submission 2017 (n 4) 11.

8 See, eg, Sherrie J Palm, 'Medical Device Innovation and Errors: The Patient Perspective' in S Abbas Shobeiri (ed), *The Innovation and Evolution of Medical Devices: Vaginal Mesh Kits* (Springer, 2019) 125, 125–6.

9 *Department of Health (Cth) Submission 2017* (n 4) 11.

10 Ibid 12.

11 Christopher Maher and Nir Haya, 'The Transvaginal Mesh Decade' (2013) 8(5) *Expert Review of Obstetrics & Gynecology* 485, 485–6.

12 See, eg, Bruce Patsner, 'Medical-Legal Aspects of Transvaginal Mesh Kit Complications: A Historical Perspective and the US Food and Drug Administration Review Process' in S Abbas Shobeiri (ed), *The Innovation and Evolution of Medical Devices: Vaginal Mesh Kits* (Springer, 2019) 71; Valerie Leiter and Shelley K White, 'Enmeshed in Controversy: Claims About the Risks of Vaginal Mesh Devices' (2015) 17 *Health, Risk & Society* 64, 66.

urethral sling or vaginal tape inserted transvaginally (via an incision in the vagina). This procedure was considered as good as, or better than, traditional surgical approaches and resulted in a reduction in procedure and recovery time. The device was subsequently adopted for surgical treatment of POP in the hope of achieving similar results, particularly given the sub-optimal outcomes of existing surgical approaches.[13] While different forms of mesh devices and surgical techniques are used to treat SUI and POP, the mesh device is typically inserted to support the vaginal walls, bladder or urethra and with the intention that the mesh is held in place by scar tissue.[14]

The uptake of UMDs by specialists in the United States and Europe was swift.[15] Mesh was similarly embraced in Australia when it was introduced in the early 2000s. Clinicians were encouraged by the perception of positive results and by strong marketing and education campaigns by the medical device industry.[16] Hospitals and health systems were similarly motivated by the apparent reduction in surgery and recuperation time compared with traditional surgical methods.[17] The existence of data, however, to support the rush of health professionals to the use of urogynaecological mesh was more equivocal. The use of mesh for SUI surgery was established as the 'gold standard'.[18] Initial data for the use of mesh to treat POP was positive; however, subsequent randomised controlled trials were not published until some years following its introduction for the treatment of that disorder.[19] The subsequent data were less positive about effectiveness and indicated a larger number of complications in relation to its use.[20]

The Polycentric Regulation of Urogynaecological Mesh Devices in Australia

This section outlines the polycentric regulation of UMDs in Australia, and their regulatory status prior to the initial receipt and investigation of adverse

13 Senate Community Affairs References Committee Report 2018 (n 6) 1; Maher and Haya (n 11) 485–6.
14 Senate Community Affairs References Committee Report 2018 (n 6) 7–8.
15 See, eg, Patsner (n 12) 71, 84; Independent Medicines and Medical Devices Safety Review (UK), *First Do No Harm: The Report of the Independent Medicines and Medical Devices Safety Review* (Report, 8 July 2020) 145–8.
16 Chloe Thompson and Thomas Faunce, 'Australian Senate Committee Report on Transvaginal Mesh Devices' (2018) 25 *Journal of Law and Medicine* 934, 934–5.
17 See, eg, Christopher Maher, Urogynaecologist, Submission No 154 to Senate Community Affairs References Committee, Parliament of Australia, *Number of Women in Australia Who Have Had Transvaginal Mesh Implants and Related Matters* (25 May 2017) 2 ('Maher Submission 2017').
18 Senate Community Affairs References Committee Report 2018 (n 6) 7–8.
19 Ibid 1.
20 Ibid 1, citing Maher Submission 2017 (n 17), 5.

events between 2006 and 2008. Black describes polycentric regulatory regimes as

> marked by fragmentation, complexity and interdependence between actors, in which state and non-state actors are both regulators and regulated. … The greater the dispersal and fragmentation of actors in the performance of regulation … the greater the polycentricity of the regime.[21]

In polycentric regimes, regulation occurs at 'multiple sites', typically including the 'sub-national, national and transnational'.[22] Commentators have, for example, invoked the concept of polycentric regulation to describe environmental governance arrangements.[23] For instance, the regulation of Australia's Great Barrier Reef has historically included actors from government (the state of Queensland, the Commonwealth and UNESCO) and non-government sectors ('Indigenous Peoples groups, local marine advisory committees, scientists, natural resources management groups, E[nvironmental]NGOs, the media and industry associations').[24] Polycentric regulatory regimes contrast with monocentric regulatory arrangements in which, for example, a single source of public power exercises regulatory control.[25] An illustration of monocentric regulatory regimes includes the direction and control over monetary policy by many central banks.[26]

The polycentric nature of the regulation of UMDs was recognised by the Australian Senate Community Affairs References Committee in its 2018 Inquiry into transvaginal mesh implants ('Senate Committee Inquiry'). The Senate Committee Inquiry was established following extensive lobbying by mesh-injured women to investigate the circumstances surrounding the use of UMDs in Australia.[27] The Senate Committee Inquiry identified that the regulatory bodies responsible for 'the introduction and use of transvaginal mesh devices in Australia sit across a number of entities, principally: the TGA, the

21 Black, 'Constructing and Contesting Legitimacy' (n 2) 137, 139.

22 Ibid 140.

23 Tiffany H Morrison, 'Evolving Polycentric Governance of the Great Barrier Reef' (2017) 114(15) *Proceedings of the National Academy of Sciences of the United States of America* E3013, E3013.

24 Ibid E3015.

25 Tiffany Morrison et al, 'Mitigation and Adaptation in Polycentric Systems: Sources of Power in the Pursuit of Collective Goals' (2017) 8(5) *WIREs Climate Change* 3.

26 See, eg, Alexander William Salter and Vlad Tarko, 'Governing the Banking System: An Assessment of Resilience Based on Elinor Ostrom's Design Principles' (2019) 15 *Journal of Institutional Economics* 505.

27 Senate Community Affairs References Committee Report 2018 (n 6) 117 (Appendix 1). Regarding the context for the establishment of the Senate Committee Inquiry, see, eg, Commonwealth, *Parliamentary Debates*, Senate, 22 November 2016, 2958 (Derryn Hinch).

medical colleges, and the ACSQHC'[28] (the Australian Commission on Safety and Quality in Health Care). However, there are other 'actors' that, consistent with Black's definition above, also contribute to the composition of an intricate and interdependent regulatory web for urogynaecological mesh. These actors include overseas medical device regulators, the medical device industry (including the sponsors and manufacturers of the product) and its representative industry bodies, clinicians (specialists and general practitioners) and their regulators, hospitals and the patients themselves. The roles of the key actors in the polycentric regulation of urogynaecological mesh will now be briefly examined.

The TGA

Urogynaecological mesh was first included on the ARTG in 1998.[29] In approving these devices for inclusion on the ARTG the TGA and its regulatory regime were purporting to ensure 'the safety and satisfactory performance'[30] of urogynaecological mesh.[31] The regulatory regime generally achieves this through a three stage process – first, a pre-market assessment of the device; second, authorisation to include the device on the ARTG; and, finally, post-market monitoring.[32]

Pre-market Assessment

The pre-market aspect of the regulatory regime specifies that certain requirements – the 'essential principles' and the 'conformity assessment procedures' – are met.[33] As described in Chapter 2, it is the sponsor of the device who provides information to the TGA to substantiate that the device meets these requirements as part of the application for the inclusion of the device on the ARTG.[34]

The essential principles are requirements about the safety and performance of the device, including health and safety; risk identification and management; suitability for intended purpose; and that the benefits of the medical

28 Senate Community Affairs References Committee Report 2018 (n 6) 8.

29 Department of Health (Cth) Submission 2017 (n 4) 26.

30 *Therapeutic Goods Act 1989* (Cth) s 41B.

31 Broadly speaking, urogynaecological mesh falls within the definition of a 'medical device' under the Act: ibid s 41BD(1).

32 While the inclusion of the first nine urogynaecological mesh products on the ARTG predated the current legislative framework for medical devices, the vast majority of devices on the ARTG were included after its introduction in 2002: Department of Health (Cth) Submission 2017 (n 4) 26.

33 *Therapeutic Goods Act 1989* (Cth) s 41BA.

34 See Chapter 2; *Therapeutic Goods Act 1989* (Cth) pt 4-5.

device outweigh 'any undesirable effects'.[35] Most relevantly for UMDs, the essential principles include, for example, a requirement that 'the device will not compromise the clinical condition or safety of a patient'[36] and that 'any risks associated with the use of the device are (i) acceptable risks when weighed against the intended benefit to the patient; and (ii) compatible with a high level of protection of health and safety'.[37] The essential principles also require that certain information be provided with medical devices.[38] This information includes the 'intended purpose ... the kind of patient on whom the device is intended to be used (if this information is not obvious)' and 'any warnings, restrictions, or precautions that should be taken, in relation to use of the device'.[39] Further, 'Instructions for the use' of UMDs are required to be provided including 'any undesirable side effects caused by use of the device'.[40] Conformity assessment procedures are 'about the application of quality management systems' for medical devices to ensure compliance with the Essential Principles.[41]

Medical devices are classified according to a 'risk-based classification system' which, in turn, determines the degree of regulatory scrutiny applied to the device.[42] Until 2018, the majority of UMDs registered on the ARTG were classified as Class IIb – that is, as 'moderate risk' devices.[43] Class IIb devices must receive a conformity assessment certificate from the TGA or the equivalent from 'a designated EU Notified Body' in order to be included on the ARTG. The majority of UMDs were imported and therefore possessed a certificate of European conformity recognised by the Australian therapeutic

35 *Therapeutic Goods Act* 1989 (Cth) s 41BA(a), pt 4-2; *Therapeutic Goods (Medical Devices) Regulations 2002* (Cth) reg 2.1, sch 1.

36 *Therapeutic Goods (Medical Devices) Regulations 2002* (Cth) reg 2.1, sch 1, cl 1(a).

37 Ibid reg 2.1, sch 1, cl 1(b). These requirements have existed since the commencement of the *Therapeutic Goods (Medical Devices) Regulations 2002* (Cth) in 2003.

38 Ibid reg 2.1, sch 1, cl 13.

39 Ibid reg 2.1, sch 1, cl 13.3.

40 Ibid reg 2.1, sch 1, cl 13.4.

41 *Therapeutic Goods Act 1989* (Cth) s 41BA(b), pt 4-3; 'Conformity Assessment Overview' *Therapeutic Goods Administration* (Web Page, 19 June 2024) <https://www.tga.gov.au/how-we-regulate/manufacturing/medical-devices/conformity-assessment/conformity-assessment-bodies/tga-conformity-assessment-certification/conformity-assessment-overview>.

42 Department of Health (Cth) Submission 2017 (n 4) 22. See also Petahn McKenna, 'Australian Medical Device Regulations: An Overview' in Jack Wong and Raymond Tong (eds), *Medical Regulatory Affairs: An International Handbook for Medical Devices and Healthcare Products* (3rd ed, Jenny Stanford Publishing, 2) 387, 390–1.

43 Ibid 25–6. In December 2018 certain urogynaecological mesh devices were reclassified as Class III (high risk) devices: Therapeutic Goods Administration, Department of Health (Cth), *Reclassification of Surgical Mesh Devices* (November 2018).

goods regulatory regime.[44] The role of overseas regulatory regimes in relation to Australia's regulation of UMDs will be discussed shortly.

Inclusion on the ARTG

The Secretary of the Department of Health determines whether to accept an application for the inclusion of an urogynaecological mesh device on the ARTG.[45] In doing so, the Secretary may request advice from the Advisory Committee on Medical Devices ('ACMD').[46] The highest number of UMDs on the ARTG, approximately 100 UMDs or 42 entries, was reached in 2013.[47] Australian Public Assessment Reports ('AusPARs') are publicly searchable documents that set out 'information about the evaluation' of certain therapeutic goods and the 'considerations' that result in their inclusion or otherwise on the ARTG.[48] However AusPARs are not provided for medical devices.[49] It has been suggested that the unavailability of AusPARs for devices is due to industry concerns about commercially sensitive information.[50] In contrast, AusPARs are provided for many prescription medicines. The typical length of an AusPAR for a prescription medicine is 40 pages and includes information such as a 'Risk Management Plan'[51]; by way of comparison, a decision to approve a medical device such as urogynaecological mesh on the ARTG is accompanied by a two-page 'Public Summary'. This document sets

44 Department of Health (Cth) Submission 2017 (n 4). The conformity assessment procedure for high risk (Class III) and specific moderate (Class IIa or IIb) devices requires an additional 'design examination' at the pre-market assessment phase and a TGA audit in the case of devices accompanied by an EU notified body certificate : at 21–6.

45 *Therapeutic Goods Act 1989* (Cth) ss 41FC(1), 41FDB, 41FF–41FI.

46 *Therapeutic Goods Regulations 1990* (Cth) reg 38A.

47 Senate Community Affairs References Committee Report 2018 (n 6) 32–3, Appendix 4.

48 'Australian Public Assessment Reports for Prescription Medicines (AusPARs)' *Therapeutic Goods Administration* (Web Page, 11 October 2021) <https://www.tga.gov.au/australian-public-assessment-reports-prescription-medicines-auspars>.

49 Australian Government, *An Action Plan for Medical Devices* (April 2019) 9.

50 Lloyd Sansom, Will Delaat and John Horvath, *Review of Medicines and Medical Devices Regulation: Discussion Paper* (November, 2014) 84. In contrast, an 'approval summary' is provided by the United States' FDA in relation to medical devices which obtain pre-market approval: Lloyd Sansom, Will Delaat and John Horvath, *Review of Medicines and Medical Device Regulation: Report on the Regulatory Framework for Medicines and Medical Devices* (March 2015) 153 ('*Report*').

51 See, eg, the AusPAR for an application to extend the age range for which a particular influenza vaccine can be prescribed: Therapeutic Goods Administration, Department of Health and Ageing (Cth), *Australian Public Assessment Report for Influenza Virus Haemagglutinin* (November 2018). See also Therapeutic Goods Administration, Department of Health and Ageing (Cth), *Australian Public Assessment Report (AusPAR) Guidance: For Prescription Medicines* (version 3.0, October 2023).

out a brief description of the ARTG entry, the product, its intended purpose and any conditions attached to the ARTG inclusion.[52]

Post-market Monitoring

After UMDs were included on the ARTG they were, like all approved medical devices, subject to post-market monitoring.[53] The broad aim of post-market monitoring is to ensure that devices continue to meet the essential principles. In evidence given to the Senate Committee Inquiry, the head of the TGA explained that pre- and post-market monitoring effectively combine to provide a feedback loop to regulators about whether or not the device should continue to remain on the ARTG:

> [T]he evidence that you use to look at whether it is appropriate for a product to be on the [ARTG] is a combination of the evidence that was provided and reviewed at the time of the application to be put on the market as well as the continuously evolving nature of evidence from clinical studies and day-to-day experience with these products worldwide.[54]

One of the most relevant aspects of the post-market monitoring regime for UMDs is the reporting of adverse events.[55] Once included on the ARTG, sponsors of UMDs are required to notify the Secretary of the Department of Health of adverse events relating to the device.[56] Adverse events are defined

52 See, eg, the 'Public Summary' for five devices, sponsored by Johnson & Johnson and intended for use as slings for the treatment of SUI: Therapeutic Goods Administration, Department of Health, *Public Summary for ARTG Entry 99193* (2018).

53 Department of Health (Cth) Submission 2017 (n 4) 25.

54 Senate Community Affairs References Committee Report 2018 (n 6) 88.

55 It should be noted, however, that post-market monitoring also may include the exchange of information regarding medical device incidents with international regulatory agencies; inspections of manufacturers and/or sponsors' records and post-market reviews of medical device consistency with regulatory compliance: Therapeutic Goods Administration, Department of Health and Ageing (Cth), *Australian Regulatory Guidelines for Medical Devices*. These Guidelines are under review: 'Australian Regulatory Guidelines for Medical Devices (ARGMD), *Therapeutic Goods Administration, Department of Health (Cth)* (Web Page, 2 November 2023) <https://www.tga.gov.au/publication/australian-regulatory-guidelines-medical-devices-argmd>.

56 This requirement is a condition of inclusion on the ARTG and failure to do so within the prescribed period of time may constitute a criminal offence and incur a civil penalty unless there is a 'reasonable excuse' for failing to do so, or if the contravening person 'ought fairly to be excused for the contravention'. The Secretary of the Department of Health may also require information regarding adverse events to be provided: *Therapeutic Goods Act 1989* (Cth) ss 41FN(3)(d), 41MP-41MR, 41JA(1)(j); *Therapeutic Goods (Medical Devices) Regulations 2002* (Cth) regs 5.7, 10.4, 10.4AA, 8.1A (k). Amendments to the *Therapeutic Goods*

broadly by the *Therapeutic Goods Act 1989* (Cth) ('the Act') in relation to a range of information about a medical device.[57] Adverse events include, for example, 'information relating to ... any malfunction or deterioration in the characteristics or performance of the kind of device ... that might lead, or might of led to the death of a patient ... or to a serious deterioration in his or her state of health'.[58]

While device sponsors must report adverse events, in the view of the TGA (at the time of the controversy surrounding UMDs) it was at the discretion of any other person – including patients, doctors, hospitals and other parts of the health system – to also do so.[59] As will be elaborated below, this indicates a high degree of interdependence between a range of actors in the regulation of UMDs.

The TGA 'manages' reports of adverse events for medical devices via the Incident Reporting and Investigation Scheme ('IRIS').[60] Adverse events are subject to a risk assessment conducted by 'a panel of scientific, engineering and clinical experts'.[61] The events may also be the subject of 'a detailed evaluation to establish the possible role of the therapeutic good in causing the adverse event'.[62] The TGA website states that 'incidents that led to injury or may lead to injury or with unusually high levels of occurrence are routinely investigated'.[63] In evidence given before the Senate Committee Inquiry, the head of the TGA described this evaluation as follows:

Act 1989 (Cth), which, at the time of writing were still to commence, will also introduce mandatory reporting of certain adverse events by healthcare facilities: *Therapeutic Goods Amendment (2022 Measures No. 1) Act 2023* (Cth).

57 *Therapeutic Goods Act 1989* (Cth) ss 41MP(2), 41 MPA(2); 'Reporting Adverse Events', *Therapeutic Goods Administration* (Web Page, 19 August 2021) <http://www.tga.gov.au/reporting-adverse-events> ('*Reporting Adverse Events*').

58 *Therapeutic Goods Act 1989* (Cth) ss 41MP (2)(a)(i), 41MPA(2)(a)(i).

59 'Reporting Adverse Events' (n 57). There is, however, an alternative view that doctors are required to report such events as part of a fiduciary duty to their patient: Thompson and Faunce (n 16) 935–6. The TGA's website specifies that the Quality or Risk Manager of a health facility should be notified of any medical device adverse event of harm (or one that could have caused harm) to a patient or caregiver: 'Medical Device Incident Reporting & Investigation Scheme (IRIS)', *Therapeutic Goods Administration* (Web Page, 30 October 2019) <https://www.tga.gov.au/medical-device-incident-reporting-investigation-scheme-iris>.

60 'Reporting Adverse Events' (n 57). See also 'Medical Device Incident Reporting & Investigation Scheme (IRIS)' (n 59).

61 Therapeutic Goods Administration, Department of Health and Ageing (Cth), *Australian Regulatory Guidelines for Medical Devices* (Version 1.1, May 2011) 310.

62 'Reporting Adverse Events' (n 57).

63 'Overview of How TGA Manages Medical Device Adverse Event Reports', *Therapeutic Goods Administration* (Web Page, 3 November 2023) <https://www.tga.gov.au/overview-how-tga-manages-medical-device-adverse-event-reports>.

> [W]hat we do in looking for problems with any medical product is what is known as signal detection. You are looking at an aggregate of signals to see if there is a pattern saying, 'We're seeing a problem with that product because it is causing X'.[64]

Ultimately information about adverse events is made publicly available on a searchable database.[65] Similar databases are available internationally.[66] Investigations into adverse events by the TGA can lead to the recall of devices, safety alerts, further inspections and suspensions or cancellations of the devices from the ARTG.[67]

Overseas Regulatory Regimes for Medical Devices

As observed above, many of the UMDs imported into Australia possessed a certificate of European conformity.[68] In broad terms, such certificates constitute evidence of compliance by those devices with conformity assessment procedures under the Australian regulatory regime. This facilitates pre-market approval under the Australian regime.[69] These arrangements reflect the close alignment between aspects of the Australian and European regulatory frameworks for medical devices. They also reflect the considerable role that the European regulatory regime plays in relation to the Australian therapeutic goods regulatory regime. The TGA has stated, for example, that '[i]n practice ... EC certificates support more than 90% of existing ARTG entries'.[70] This trend towards regulatory harmonisation, discussed in Chapter 1, reflects one of the recommendations of the 2015 Government-appointed Review of Medicines and Medical Device Regulation. Since 2018 the therapeutic goods regulatory regime has recognised regulatory assessments under

64 Evidence to Senate Community Affairs References Committee, Parliament of Australia, Melbourne, 3 August 2017, 48 (John Skerritt, Deputy Secretary, Therapeutic Goods Administration).

65 'Database of Adverse Event Notifications (DAEN)', *Therapeutic Goods Administration* (Web Page, 16 February 2023) < https://www.tga.gov.au/database-adverse-event-notifications-daen>.

66 'Adverse Event Monitoring Internationally', *Therapeutic Goods Administration* (Web Page, 30 October 2018) <https://www.tga.gov.au/safety/safety/safety-monitoring-medicines/adverse-event-monitoring-internationally>.

67 Department of Health (Cth) Submission 2017 (n 4) 25. See also 'Reporting Adverse Events' (n 57).

68 Senate Community Affairs References Committee Report 2018 (n 6) 9.

69 'Using Assessments from Comparable Overseas Regulators for Medical Devices, *Therapeutic Goods Administration* (Web Page, 7 October 2022) <https://www.tga.gov.au/resources/guidance/using-assessments-comparable-overseas-regulators-medical-devices>..

70 Therapeutic Goods Administration, Department of Health (Cth) *Comparable Overseas Regulators – Medical Devices: Criteria and Implementation* (May 2017).

additional overseas regulatory schemes, including the United States, Canada and Japan.[71]

The Medical Device Industry

To achieve its regulatory objects, the therapeutic goods regime imposes obligations on the sponsors and manufacturers of medical devices, including urogynaecological mesh, via the Act and associated legislative instruments.[72] The sponsors and manufacturers of UMDs include large pharmaceutical and medical device companies such as Boston Scientific and Johnson & Johnson.[73] Obligations to meet the pre- and post-market regulatory requirements fall on such entities, including the provision of mandated information and the reporting of adverse events.[74] The Medical Technology Association of Australia ('MTAA') describes itself as 'the national association representing companies in the medical technology industry', including over 70 'manufacturers and suppliers' of medical devices.[75] Its role includes supporting its members and advocating on their behalf. Entities who are members of the MTAA agree to comply with the Medical Technology Industry Code of Practice, which outlines an 'ethical framework' of conduct.[76]

Health Practitioners

In contrast to its role regulating sponsors and manufacturers of medical devices, the TGA emphasised throughout the urogynaecological mesh controversy that it 'does not regulate clinical practice' and has no powers to do so.[77] The TGA did, however, recognise the role of clinicians in relation to advising, treating and responding to women who had had UMDs implanted.[78] Indeed, health practitioners form a key part of the polycentric regulatory arrangements around UMDs. Most obviously, specialist clinicians play a key role in consulting with, diagnosing and treating the urogynaecological

71 Ibid 7.
72 See, eg, *Therapeutic Goods (Medical Devices) Regulations 2002* (Cth).
73 Department of Health (Cth) Submission 2017 (n 4) 26.
74 The Act provides that it is a criminal and civil offence for a sponsor of a medical device to fail to report an adverse event: *Therapeutic Goods Act 1989* (Cth) ss 41MP, 41MPA, 41MPB.
75 'About Us', *Medical Technology Association of Australia* (Web Page, 2020) <https://www.mtaa.org.au/about-us>; Medical Technology Society of Australia, Submission No 40 to Senate Community Affairs References Committee, Parliament of Australia, *Number of Women in Australia Who Have Had Transvaginal Mesh Implants and Related Matters* (20 July 2017) 1.
76 'About the Code', *Medical Technology Association of Australia* (Web Page, 2020) <https://www.mtaa.org.au/about-the-code>.
77 Department of Health (Cth) Submission 2017 (n 4) 16.
78 Ibid 16–17.

complaints that resulted in the use of mesh device implants. Further, specialists, GPs and other health professionals were a source of information about adverse events associated with the devices. By the beginning of the Senate Committee Inquiry in early 2017, 11% of adverse event reports regarding UMDs came from health professionals.[79] In evidence given to the Senate Committee Inquiry by the Royal Australian College of General Practitioners, it was recognised that GPs 'are the key providers of care to women ... to listen to patients ... to make ourselves available for patients who present with problems and to actually think about what they're actually experiencing and to take that seriously'.[80]

The role of health practitioners as actors in the polycentric regulatory arrangements for urogynaecological mesh is also arguably evident in the pre-market stage of device development – that is, prior to the regulatory approval of the device and its clinical use. Clinicians have historically been involved in the invention of medical devices.[81] While the development of modern medical devices is undoubtedly now dominated by private commercial industry,[82] the clinician's role as 'physician-inventor' continues.[83] In the case of UMDs, for example, an Australian gynaecologist had designed a mesh device which he subsequently implanted in patients during surgery. He was later found guilty of professional misconduct for failing to disclose a financial interest in relation to the device to his patients and to the hospitals in which he worked.[84]

79 Evidence to Senate Community Affairs References Committee, Parliament of Australia, Canberra, 6 February 2018, 6 (Adriana Platona, First Assistant Secretary, Medical Devices and Product Quality, Department of Health).

80 Evidence to Senate Community Affairs References Committee, Parliament of Australia, Canberra, 19 September 2017, 13 (Magdalena Simonis, Member, Expert Committee, Quality Care, Royal Australian College of General Practitioners). Further, the National Association of Specialist Obstetricians and Gynaecologists recognised that specialist clinicians 'should' be reporting adverse events to the TGA, even though it considered that this was not required by law: at 26 (Gary Swift, President, National Association of Specialist Obstetricians and Gynaecologists).

81 Including now familiar items such as the stethoscope and for measuring blood pressure: see, eg, Jacalyn Duffin, *To See with a Better Eye: A Life of RTH Laennec* (Princeton University Press, 1998); Andras Gedeon, *Science and Technology in Medicine: An Illustrated Account Based on Ninety-Nine Landmark Publications from Five Centuries* (Springer, 2006) 351–6.

82 See, eg, Alex Faulkner, *Medical Technology into Healthcare and Society: A Sociology of Devices, Innovation and Governance* (Palgrave Macmillan, 2009) 31.

83 See, eg, Aaron K Chatterji et al, 'Physician-Industry Cooperation in the Medical Device Industry' (2008) 27(6) *Health Affairs* 1532;Faulkner (n 82) 51.

84 *Health Care Complaints Commission v Petros* [2019] NSWCATOD 83. See, also, Joanne McCarthy, 'Dr Peter Petros Assured a Colleague He Could "Mollify" Investigators Looking for Answers', *The Newcastle Herald* (online, 2 April 2019) <https://www.newcastleherald.com.au/story/5986291/mesh-doctors-drip-feed-of-misinformation/>; Joanne McCarthy, 'Pelvic Mesh a Global Medical Scandal with Origins Close to Home', *The Newcastle Herald* (online, 3 August 2017).

Regulators of Health Practitioners

The regulatory arrangements for health practitioners are broad and diverse.[85] Most relevant for this case study are the roles of medical colleges and the Australian Health Practitioners Regulatory Agency ('Ahpra'). Medical colleges are professional organisations which broadly provide 'education and training ... guidance for the management of clinical conditions ... and standards for professional behaviour and research'.[86] These include the Royal Australian and New Zealand College of Obstetricians and Gynaecologists ('RANZCOG'), the Urogynaecological Society of Australasia, the Royal Australasian College of Surgeons and the Royal Australian College of General Practitioners. The Colleges do not, however, oversee the clinical practice of their members.[87] In this respect, their role in relation to the regulatory arrangements for UMDs was to 'influence the standard of care delivered by practitioners' rather than to oversee or dictate it.[88] Overseeing the accreditation and registration of a range of health practitioners, including by the Medical Board of Australia, is the Ahpra. Broadly, the Ahpra also sets out certain professional requirements and handles complaints and disciplinary matters.[89]

Hospitals and the ASQHC

It is the hospitals themselves that determine, through a credentialling process, which doctors can perform which services, including procedures involving UMDs. Ideally, this ensures 'that only suitably experienced, trained and qualified medical practitioners provide particular types of services'.[90] Prior to the controversy involving UMDs, however, no such credentialling requirements existed in relation to those devices. A decision as to whether to implant the device was therefore a matter for each clinician.[91] There were indications

---

<https://www.newcastleherald.com.au/story/4493496/scandals-australian-backstory/>. See also Miriam Wiersma, Ian Kerridge and Wendy Lipworth, 'Transvaginal Mesh, Gender and the Ethics of Clinical Innovation (2020) 40 *Internal Medicine Journal* 523, 524.

85 They include regulatory schemes across the Commonwealth, states and territories and obligations under private law, including tort law: see, eg, Senate Community Affairs References Committee Report 2018 (n 6) 10.

86 Ibid.

87 Ibid.

88 Ibid.

89 See, eg, Ian Kerridge, Michael Lowe and Cameron Stewart, *Ethics and Law for the Health Professions* (The Federation Press, 4th ed, 2013) 166–80.

90 Australian Commission on Safety and Quality in Health Care, Submission No 46 to Senate Community Affairs References Committee, Parliament of Australia, *Number of Women in Australia Who Have Had Transvaginal Mesh Implants and Related Matters* 2 ('Australian Commission on Safety and Quality in Health Care Submission').

91 Thompson and Faunce (n 16) 940.

that the well-established supervisory and training arrangements of the larger teaching hospitals in Australia meant that the performance of surgery in which such devices were used was typically limited to appropriately trained practitioners.[92] In smaller hospitals, however, these arrangements were not as well established or supported.[93] The ASQHC plays a role in the regulation of health services, including hospitals. Specifically, its role relates to the safety and quality of healthcare such as the formulation and implementation of safety and quality standards and the accreditation of healthcare service organisations.[94]

Patients

Finally, it is critical to highlight the role that patients played as additional regulatory actors in relation to UMDs. Patients have not only been the recipients of regulatory outcomes. As will be examined shortly, they have also played a pivotal role in the regulation of these devices: as receivers of information regarding mesh devices, as communicators of adverse events (typically to health practitioners) and as, effectively, the subjects on which the risk of UMDs has been assessed and determined in the post-market environment. Ultimately, the experiences of patients formed a key part of subsequent risk analysis by the TGA and its international counterparts. In this way, patients were not just the recipients of the regulatory decisions relating to UMDs but were also key actors in the regulatory regime itself.

Polycentric Regulation of Urogynaecological Mesh Devices and the Regulatory Information Loop

The above summary of the regulation of UMDs in Australia highlights its polycentric nature. This is not unusual for contemporary regulatory regimes, including in relation to technology and contemporary healthcare.[95] Like other polycentric regulatory arrangements, the regime for UMDs is arguably characterised by 'complexity, fragmentation, interdependencies, ungovernability, and the rejection of a clear distinction between public and private'.[96]

92 See, eg, Evidence to Senate Community Affairs References Committee, Parliament of Australia, Melbourne, 3 August 2017, 41 (Debora Picone, Chief Executive Officer, Australian Commission on Safety and Quality in Health Care).

93 See, eg, ibid.

94 *National Health Reform Act 2011* (Cth) ch 2.

95 See, eg,Faulkner(n 82) 201; Karen Lee, *The Legitimacy and Responsiveness of Industry Rule-Making* (Hart, 2018).

96 Julia Black, 'Legitimacy and the Competition for Regulatory Share' (LSE Law, Society and Economy Working Papers No 14/2009, London School of Economics and Political Science, Law Department, 2009) 3. See also Robert Baldwin, Martin Cave and Martin Lodge, *Understanding Regulation: Theory, Strategy, and Practice* (Oxford University Press, 2011);

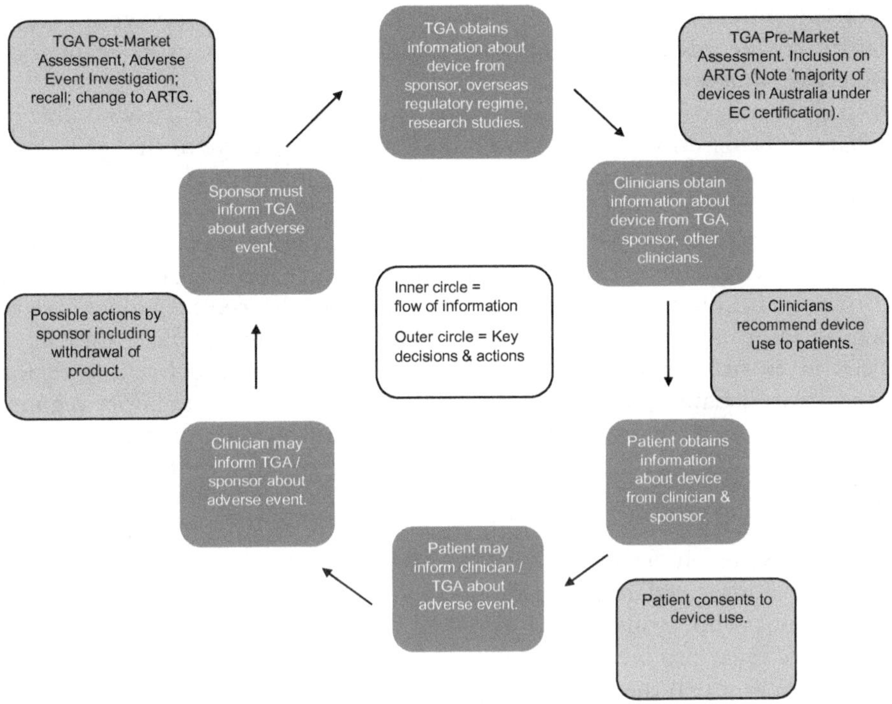

Figure 6.1 Medical Devices Regulatory Information Loop.

Source: Certain information drawn from Kiki He, Medical Devices and Product Quality, Therapeutic Goods Administration 'Process of Conformity Assessments for Higher Risk Devices: Conformity Assessment Overview' (Conference Paper, Symposium on Regulatory Fundamentals in Medical Devices) 28 August 2018.

Such arrangements can be described as occurring within a 'regulatory space' in which relationships between numerous actors are 'complex, dynamic and horizontal, involving negotiated interdependence'.[97] The TGA and its regulatory regime is one regulator and regulatory scheme operating interdependently with many others and their respective actors – the medical device industry, health practitioners, hospitals and patients themselves.[98]

Elinor Ostrom, 'Beyond Markets and States: Polycentric Governance of Complex Economic Systems' (2010) 100 *American Economic Review* 641.

97 Colin Scott, 'Analysing Regulatory Space: Fragmented Resources and Institutional Design' (2001) *Public Law* 283, 330.

98 Evidence given to the Senate Committee Inquiry provided a range of examples of the polycentric, interdependent operation of the regulation of urogynaecological mesh devices: see, eg, Evidence to Senate Community Affairs References Committee, Parliament of Australia, Canberra, 19 September 2017, 24, 30 (Stephen Robson, President, Royal Australian and

Consequently, in the context of medical devices, the therapeutic goods regulatory regime effectively co-opts or 'enrols' other parties in its regulatory objectives and arrangements.[99]

This characteristic of regulatory interdependence is particularly notable in what can be described as an information loop at the centre of the regulatory arrangements for medical devices. The following diagram sets out the essential aspects of this loop (

From the patient's perspective, for example, the loop begins when their clinician recommends the implantation of an urogynaecological mesh device. Typically, in consenting to the implantation of the device, the patient is relying on information provided by their clinician; any information they have been given or themselves obtained about the device; and the knowledge that the device must conform with the therapeutic goods regulatory regime. Consequently, patients adversely affected by UMDs described their initial reliance on, and later disappointment with, this regulatory information loop and the TGA's role in it:

> I feel extremely let down by the TGA, who we rely on to make good, safe and informed decisions about products they approve for use. ..... The surgeons who promote and use these meshes may honestly believe that they're great products based on what the manufacturers are telling them and the fact that the TGA had approved them for use ... perhaps it is time for the surgeons to take more responsibility and independently research the products ... before just assuming that they are safe.[100]

From the clinician's perspective, the operation of the information loop and the reliance on the TGA's role in it is highlighted in the following terms: '[i] nitially, there was certainly a sense of: "Mesh had been around for a long time. The general surgeons have been using it. It has TGA approval, presumably." That's it'.[101]

The information loop continues after the device has been implanted in the patient. As described earlier, the therapeutic goods regulatory regime relies (during the post-market stage) on the reporting of adverse events about medical devices to inform its ongoing risk assessment. That is, in order to do its job, the TGA is dependent on information from other regulatory actors to tell it about harmful, or potentially harmful, events associated with the device.

New Zealand College of Obstetricians and Gynaecologists), 31, 32 (Christopher Maher) 45 (Tim Greenaway, Acting Deputy Secretary, Health Products Regulation Group).

99 Black, 'Constructing and Contesting Legitimacy' (n 2) 148.

100 Evidence to Senate Community Affairs References Committee, Parliament of Australia, Perth, 25 August 2017, 20 (Katrina).

101 Ibid.

While, at the time of writing, the Act obliges sponsors of medical devices to report adverse events, it is also apparent that significant information can be received from health practitioners, hospitals and patients themselves. In this respect, these regulatory actors potentially take on the role of 'intermediaries' or 'gatekeepers' in the regulation of medical devices by facilitating the post-market assessment of those devices by the therapeutic goods regulatory regime.[102] This again reflects the enrolment of other parties in the regulatory regime.

Completing the loop is the subsequent reliance by those same actors – health practitioners, hospitals and patients – on the analysis by the TGA of the information they provide and on the TGA's regulatory decisions. Collectively patients, their clinicians and the hospitals are all regulatory actors that ultimately rely on the TGA and the regulatory regime to determine whether a particular medical device is safe to purchase, to recommend to patients, to use and, in the case of patients, to consent to.

This loop of information generation, provision and regulatory decision-making is a defining feature of the polycentric regulation of medical devices.[103] When working effectively, it can support the exchange of information for the consideration of, and decision-making and action by, regulatory actors. In this respect, the loop may be described as a form of 'regulatory dialogue'.[104] In terms consistent with the constant dialogic approach to political legitimacy, the loop can potentially support a constant dialogue between all regulatory parties through which a shared set of normative beliefs and values is formulated in relation to medical devices. The information loop therefore constitutes an important mechanism to support the political legitimacy of the therapeutic goods regulatory regime according to the constant dialogic approach. Similarly, failings in the information loop may contribute to deficiencies in, or the absence of, political legitimacy according to the

102 See, eg, Kenneth W Abbott, David Levi-Faur and Duncan Snidal, 'Introducing Regulatory Intermediaries' (2017) 670 *The Annals of the American Academy of Political and Social Science* 6, 7–8; Kenneth W Abbott, David Levi-Faur and Duncan Snidal, 'Theorizing Regulatory Intermediaries: The RIT Model' (2017) 670 *Annals of the American Academy of Political and Social Science* 14, 14–21. In relation to regulatory intermediaries for therapeutic goods, see Martino Maggetti, Christian Ewert and Philipp Trein, 'Not Quite the Same: Regulatory Intermediaries in the Governance of Pharmaceuticals and Medical Devices' (2017) 670 *The Annals of the American Academy of Political and Social Science* 152. In relation to the role of 'gatekeepers', see Julia Black, 'Paradoxes and Failures: "New Governance" Techniques and the Financial Crisis' (2012) 75(6) *The Modern Law Review* 1037, 1048-52.

103 See a similar description of feedback involving regulatory intermediaries in Abbott et al, 'Theorizing Regulatory Intermediaries: The RIT Model' (n 102) 26–8.

104 Abbott, Levi-Faur and Snidal describe the ideal role of regulatory intermediaries as 'facilitators and mediators, enhancing trust and strengthening "regulatory dialogues" between regulators and targets' of a regulatory regime: ibid 23–4.

constant dialogic approach. The operation of the information loop with respect to UMDs and its relationship with political legitimacy is further discussed below.

Having described the key regulatory actors in the polycentric regulation of urogynaecological mesh in Australia, and the loop of information generated, provided and relied on by these regulatory actors under the therapeutic goods regulatory regime, I now turn to the question of whether and how this loop operated in the case of UMDs in Australia from 2006 to 2021.

The Events of 2006 to 2021

From the mid-2000s, UMDs were characterised by legal, media and clinical controversy. In this section I outline this controversy and how it was triggered by an increased incidence, and visibility, of reports of adverse events involving UMDs. I summarise the responses to these reports by patient groups, the media, the TGA, those in the political arena and finally the courts. A chronology of the key events is included at Appendix 1.

The first adverse event in relation to an urogynaecological mesh device was reported to the TGA in 2006.[105] For most patients, the implantation of an urogynaecological mesh device was a successful procedure, alleviating the otherwise challenging symptoms of SUI or POP.[106] But for a minority of women, the implantation of the device was followed by extensive and chronic side effects. The TGA received 63 reports of adverse events between 2006 and 2012,[107] and a further 32 between 2012 and 2014.[108] By May 2017, the total number of adverse reports was 226.[109] As will be discussed shortly, the Senate Committee Inquiry concluded that data limitations meant that it was impossible to accurately determine the number of UMDs that had been implanted in Australian women. Accordingly, it was also impossible to determine the number of women adversely affected by the devices.[110] The Health Issues Centre, a non-government health organisation, told the Senate Committee Inquiry that it had received accounts of adverse events

105 'About Transvaginal Surgical Mesh Devices' *Therapeutic Goods Administration* (Web Page,19 December 2023) <https://www.tga.gov.au/products/urogynaecological-transvaginal-surgical-mesh-hub/about-transvaginal-surgical-mesh-devices>.

106 Senate Community Affairs References Committee Report 2018 (n 6) 13, 31–6.

107 Department of Health (Cth) Submission 2017 (n 4) 15.

108 J Oliver Daly et al, 'The Australasian Pelvic Floor Procedure Registry: Not before Time' (2019) 59 *Australian and New Zealand Journal of Obstetrics and Gynaecology* 473.

109 Department of Health (Cth) Submission 2017 (n 4) 15.

110 Senate Community Affairs References Committee Report 2018 (n 6) 41–58. The Committee concluded that it was 'likely' that the number of women who had 'undergone transvaginal mesh procedures in Australia' was 150,000: at 56.

from 2,400 women by August 2017.[111] In New Zealand, four per cent of POP and SUI patients made subsequent claims for government compensation as a result of their procedures. RANZCOG submitted that the proportion of adverse events may be similar in Australia.[112]

For women who had been negatively affected, symptoms varied depending on the nature of the procedure and type of device use.[113] These symptoms included:

- 'punctures or lacerations of vessels, nerves, structures or organs
- mesh extrusion, exposure or erosion into the vagina or other structures or organs
- lower urinary tract obstructions
- acute and/or chronic pain
- voiding dysfunction
- pain during intercourse
- neuromuscular problems including acute and/or chronic pain in the groin, thigh, leg, pelvic and/or abdominal area
- recurrence of incontinence
- bleeding including haemorrhage
- urinary frequency
- atypical vaginal discharge
- exposed mesh may cause pain or discomfort to the patient's partner during intercourse
- mesh migration
- recurrent prolapse'[114]

The frequency and severity of the side effects were much more pronounced in women treated for POP than for women with SUI.[115] Women reported that the non-physical implications of side effects included under- or unemployment; financial pressure; a reduced capacity to participate in everyday activities; sexual inactivity; negative family and social impacts, including marital breakdown and the inability to care for their children or grandchildren; stress, anxiety and suicidal thoughts. [116]

111 Ibid 42.
112 Ibid 52.
113 Ibid 14, 16.
114 'Urogynaecological Surgical Mesh Complications' *Therapeutic Goods Administration* (Web Page, 1 August 2024).
115 Senate Community Affairs References Committee Report 2018 (n 6) 13.
116 Ibid 22–30.

Patient and Media Response

Many mesh-injured women reported experiencing significant feelings of 'physical, emotional and social isolation' as a result of symptoms which left them unable to fully participate in everyday activities.[117] Despite this, or perhaps because of it, women soon connected with each other about their experiences, including through social media.[118] In Australia and internationally, affected patients formed support groups. Some groups adopted agendas calling for regulatory reform for UMDs and enhanced treatment options and support for those adversely affected.[119] Consumer health advocacy groups in Australia rallied around the issue, convening forums with affected patients, carers, clinicians and regulatory parties and conducting research to better understand the harm experienced by women.[120] The Victoria-based Health Issues Centre stated that its research, conducted over a six-week period in 2017, identified that over 1200 respondents experienced 'severe...debilitating...or unendurable' ongoing pain since implant mesh surgery. This was certainly more than the number of adverse outcomes reported to the TGA in the preceding years. [121]

Patients initiated class actions in Australia against the sponsors and manufacturers of the devices, mirroring similar proceedings in the United States, the United Kingdom and Canada.[122] One class action was filed in the Federal Court of Australia in 2012. These applicants, and the over 700 members of the class they represented, were all women who claimed to have suffered

117 Teresa O'Connor, 'Surgical Mesh Complications: A Study in Pain, Loss and Isolation' (2019) 25(7) *Kai Tiaki: Nursing New Zealand* 14. See also Amanda Hooton and Joanne McCarthy, 'The Nightmare Within', *The Age: Good Weekend Magazine* (Melbourne, 16 June 2019) 19.

118 See, eg, @MeshAwareness (Mesh Awareness); @WAPMSG (WA Pelvic Mesh Support Group); @nswpmsg (NSW Pelvic Mesh Support Group); @AngelaSpaniak (Gold Coast Pelvic Mesh Support) (Twitter/X).

119 See, eg, Senate Community Affairs References Committee Report 2018 (n 6); Thompson and Faunce (n 16) 936; *Australian Pelvic Mesh Support Group* (Web Page) <https://www.facebook.com/groups/AustralianPelvicMeshSupportGroup/>; *Sling the Mesh: Raising Awareness of the Life Changing Risks of a 'Simple' Day Case Operation* (Web Page) <https://slingthemesh.co.uk/>; *Scottish Mesh Survivors: Hear Our Voice* (Web Page) <http://www.scottishmeshsurvivors.com/news-media.html>.

120 For example, a forum on mesh implants in April 2019 was co-convened by the Health Issues Centre (based in Victoria), Health Consumers NSW, Health Consumers Queensland, Health Consumers' Council (WA), Health Consumers Alliance of South Australia, Health Care Consumers (ACT) and Health Consumers Tasmania: 'Unfinished Business: A National Forum on the Impact of Mesh Implants', *Health Consumers Queensland* (Web Page, 2019) <https://www.hcq.org.au/unfinished-business-a-national-forum-on-the-impact-of-mesh-implants/>.

121 Health Issues Centre, Submission No 115 to Senate Community Affairs References Committee, Parliament of Australia, *Number of Women in Australia Who Have Had Transvaginal Mesh Implants and Related Matters* ('Health Issues Centre Submission').

122 *Jodie Philipsen v American Medical Systems LLC*, NSD 35/2018; *Kathryn Gill v Ethican Sàrl*, NSD 1590/2012; *Senate Community Affairs References Committee Report 2018* (n 6) 2, 5.

mesh-related injuries.[123] The class action focussed on nine UMDs used to treat SUI and POP. The respondents were Johnson & Johnson Medical Pty Ltd (the sponsor of the devices) and Ethicon Sàrl and Ethicon Inc (the manufacturers), both of whom were members of the Johnson & Johnson group of companies.[124] The applicants alleged that the respondents had breached Commonwealth law intended to protect consumers (the *Competition and Consumer Act 2010* (Cth) and its predecessor the *Trade Practices Act 1974* (Cth)) and negligently manufactured and supplied the relevant mesh devices. The respondents denied liability.[125] The resulting trial lasted seven months, from July 2017 to February 2018.[126] The outcome of the case represented the first significant response by an Australian court to the urogynaecological mesh controversy. It will be discussed shortly.

The safety and effectiveness of the surgical use of UMDs ultimately became a focus not only of the academic medical literature but also of the popular press.[127] In 2019, the International Consortium of Investigative Journalists[128] identified UMDs as one of a number of medical devices characterised by poor outcomes and unjustified side effects, and which therefore warranted the reform of device regulation.[129] An analysis of the Australian media reporting of urogynaecological mesh to the end of 2021 concludes that it presented injured women as facing up to the device manufacturers, clinicians

123 *Gill v Ethicon Sàrl (No 5)* [2019] FCA 1905, 21 [13].
124 Ibid 19 [7]–[9].
125 Ibid 21 [13]–[17].
126 Ibid 22 [19].
127 See, eg, Maher and Haya (n 11); Alexandra E Mowat and Christopher Maher, 'Transvaginal Mesh: Let's Not Repeat the Mistakes of the Past' (2017) 57 *Australian and New Zealand Journal of Obstetrics and Gynaecology* 108; Joanne McCarthy, 'Australian Medical Association President Confirms AMA Role in Pelvic Mesh Scandal', *WA Today* (online, 22 August 2017) <https://www.watoday.com.au/national/western-australia/australian-medical-association-president-confirms-ama-was-role-in-pelvic-mesh-scandal-20170822-gy1hzj.html>; Editorial, '80,000 Deaths. 2 Million Injuries. It's Time for a Reckoning on Medical Devices', *The New York Times* (online, 4 May 2019) <https://www.nytimes.com/2019/05/04/opinion/sunday/medical-devices.html>.
128 The International Consortium of Investigative Journalists is a US-based non-governmental organisation. It operates its own newsroom and collaborates with a wide network of members who are news reporters. It describes itself as using 'the expertise and reach of our network' to 'collaborate on groundbreaking investigations that expose the truth and hold the powerful accountable, while also adhering to the highest standards of fairness and accuracy': 'About', *International Consortium of Investigative Journalists* (Web Page, 2020) <https://www.icij.org/about/>.
129 'Implant Files', *International Consortium of Investigative Journalists* (Web Page, 2019) <https://www.icij.org/investigations/implant-files/>.

and regulatory regime.[130] The media were crucial in 'engaging with women's accounts of experienced epistemic injustice'.[131]

Regulatory Response

In Australia, the TGA's first significant response to the concerns of patients harmed by urogynaecological mesh was an investigation into adverse event reports in 2008. At this time, the TGA obtained advice from the predecessor of the ACMD under the Act. On its advice, the TGA decided to 'continue to monitor mesh reports and emerging clinical evidence'.[132] Between 2009 and 2010, international regulatory bodies issued public statements communicating their concerns about potential side effects and the efficacy of certain UMDs.[133] The TGA responded by conducting an initial review of a report that certain mesh devices were hard for surgeons to see after they were implanted, therefore making them difficult to remove. No regulatory action was taken.[134] In 2012 the TGA communicated 'concerns' about UMDs on its website and initiated a fuller post-market literature review. In 2013, the TGA established a review of all mesh devices available in Australia.[135] The review resulted in the TGA cancelling nine entries for mesh devices from the ARTG, the vast number for failure to comply with the essential principles.[136] Device sponsors withdrew a further fourteen devices. The TGA imposed additional conditions on UMDs remaining on the ARTG.[137] Also in 2013, the ACSQHC formed an expert reference group consisting of health consumers and their advocacy groups, clinical experts, state and territory health representatives and the TGA.[138] Its primary purpose was to develop material for patients, clinicians and health providers about the 'use, complications and removal of transvaginal mesh products'.[139]

By mid-2017, the TGA had reached the view that there was 'uncontroverted evidence about the unfavourable benefit and risk profile for this product for pelvic organ prolapse [POP] when used transvaginally'.[140] It subsequently

130 Mina Motamedi, Stacy M Carter and Chris Degeling, 'Transvaginal Mesh in Australia: An Analysis of News Media Reporting from 1996 to 2021' (2023) 26 *Health Expectations* 1189, 1196.

131 Ibid 1190, where epistemic injustice is defined by the authors as where 'a person's contribution to the production of knowledge is unjustly excluded or dismissed'.

132 Department of Health (Cth) Submission 2017 (n 4) 27, 32.

133 Ibid 5, 32.

134 Ibid.

135 Senate Community Affairs References Committee Report 2018 (n 6) 32–3, Appendix 4.

136 See this Chapter regarding the 'essential principles'.

137 Department of Health (Cth) Submission 2017 (n 4) 5–6.

138 Australian Commission on Safety and Quality in Health Care Submission (n 90) 2, 8–9.

139 Ibid.

140 Senate Community Affairs References Committee Report 2018 (n 6) 74–5.

removed all mesh devices intended for that purpose from the ARTG along with certain devices used in the treatment of SUI.[141] In November 2018 the TGA announced that all surgical mesh devices, including urogynaecological mesh, would be reclassified from a medium-risk, Class IIb device, to a high-risk, Class III device 'due to serious concerns about risks associated with the use of these devices'.[142] Manufacturers of UMDs that had been approved for inclusion on the ARTG were required to apply for registration again or face having the device removed from the ARTG.[143]

Other actors in the regulatory system also responded to the emerging controversy. RANZCOG, for example, cautioned its members in relation to the use of UMDs and recommended that they not be used 'as the first line of treatment for any vaginal prolapse'.[144]

Political Response

The controversy associated with the adverse events around UMDs also involved Australia's politicians. The Australian Senate voted in early 2017 to establish the Senate Committee Inquiry into a range of matters concerning transvaginal mesh devices and their regulation in Australia. These matters included 'the role of the TGA in approving and monitoring UMDs for use in Australia'.[145] The Inquiry was conducted by the Senate Standing Community Affairs References Committee.[146] It should be noted that while the Senate Committee Inquiry appears to have covered the *regulation* of *urogynaecological* mesh devices broadly, in relation to the *experiences* of patients and clinicians it limited itself to considering mesh devices inserted *transvaginally* (through incisions in the vagina, as opposed to through incisions in the pelvic area).[147]

141 'TGA Actions after Review into Urogynaecological Surgical Mesh Implants' *Therapeutic Goods Administration* (Web Page, 17 May 2019) <https://www.tga.gov.au/alert/tga-actions-after-review-urogynaecological-surgical-mesh-implants>.

142 This was broadly consistent with action taken in the USA and Europe: Therapeutic Goods Administration, Department of Health (Cth), *Reclassification of Surgical Mesh Devices* (November 2018) 4.

143 'Australian Regulatory Actions – About Transvaginal Surgical Mesh' *Therapeutic Goods Administration, Department of Health and Aged Care (Cth)* (Web Page, 20 December 2023) <https://www.tga.gov.au/products/urogynaecological-transvaginal-surgical-mesh-hub/australian-regulatory-actions-about-transvaginal-surgical-mesh>.

144 Thompson and Faunce (n 16) 936; see also Senate Community Affairs References Committee Report 2018 (n 6) 105, Appendix 4 at 34.

145 Senate Community Affairs References Committee Report 2018 (n 6) 3.

146 Ibid 3, 4 n 16.

147 While this distinction is not explicitly stated in the report of the Senate Committee Inquiry, it can be ascertained from its stated purpose and the summary of its Report structure: ibid 3, 5 (emphasis added).

Following the conduct of extensive hearings and the receipt of a significant number of submissions the Committee tabled its thirteen recommendations in March 2018.[148] Broadly the recommendations focussed on the need for regulatory improvements in relation to the reporting of adverse events, patient consent and support, post-market monitoring, clinician training and the recording of procedures involving UMDs. The government responded by broadly supporting the recommendations with a number of qualifications.[149] In providing the government's response, the Minister for Health issued an apology, on behalf of the Australian government, for the harm suffered by women that was caused by UMDs.[150]

Judicial Response

In November 2019, the Federal Court of Australia handed down its decision in relation to the class action, described earlier, brought against three Johnson & Johnson companies.[151] The judgment, running to almost 1,500 pages, was the first significant response by an Australian court to the urogynaecological mesh controversy. The decision was subsequently affirmed by the Full Court of the Federal Court.[152] In summary, Katzmann J found that the UMDs in question, and the methods used to implant them, 'exposed patients to risks of significant and serious injury'.[153] She concluded that the respondents had breached the *Competition and Consumer Act 2010* (Cth) and the *Trade Practices Act 1974* (Cth). In particular, she found that the devices were unsafe and therefore defective, unfit for the purpose for which they were purchased and of insufficient ('unmerchantable') quality.[154] Further, the

148 Ibid ix–xii, 15.

149 Australian Government, *Australian Government Response to the Senate Community Affairs References Committee Report: The Number of Women in Australia Who Have Had Transvaginal Mesh Implants and Related Matters* (October 2018) ('Australian Government Response').

150 Sophie Scott and Alison Branley, 'Mesh Implants: Government Issues National Apology Over "Agony and Pain" Caused by Device', *ABC News* (online, 10 October 2018) <https://www.abc.net.au/news/2018-10-10/mesh-implants-government-issues-apology-to-women/10355546>.

151 *Gill v Ethicon Sàrl (No 5)* [2019] FCA 1905.

152 *Ethicon Sàrl v Gill* (2021) 288 FCR 338. The High Court subsequently denied special leave to appeal: Transcript of Proceedings, Ethicon Sàrl v Gill [2021] HCATrans 187, 630 (Keane J). See also Julia Symons and Marco Rizzi, 'Consumers or Patients? Medical Device Recipients Under Australian Law Straddle Two Worlds (2023) 30 *Journal of Law and Medicine* 572, 573; Marco Rizzi, Penny Gleeson and Jeannie Marie Paterson, 'Floors and Ceilings: Coordination, Coherence and Consistency in the Relationship between Therapeutic Goods Regulation and Consumer Protection (2023) 47(2) *Melbourne University Law Review* (forthcoming) 33.

153 *Gill v Ethicon Sàrl (No 5)* [2019] FCA 1905..

154 Ibid 905 [3458], 914–15 [3496]–[3500], 918 [3515]–[3517], 924–5 [3542]–[3544].

information provided by the respondents in relation to the devices failed to warn about risks of harm associated with the devices which the respondents knew, or should have known. That information was therefore misleading.[155] Katzmann J also found that the respondents were negligent because they had not taken reasonable care to assess the safety of the devices during their pre-market and post-market assessment phases.[156] The Court concluded that the injuries suffered by the women who had brought the case were the result of the respondents' breaches in law.[157] Katzmann J ordered that the respondents pay approximately A$2.3 million in damages.[158]

In assessing the conduct of the respondents, the Federal Court made certain observations about the therapeutic goods regulatory regime.[159] Katzmann J described the regime in relation to medical devices as 'largely self-regulating'.[160] In reaching this conclusion she noted that the Class IIb classification of the devices meant that certificates of European conformity enabled the relevant mesh devices to be included on the ARTG. This was permissible under the regulatory regime 'without the TGA conducting any independent assessment of [the devices'] safety or efficacy and without the need for the manufacturer to demonstrate that independent pre-market testing of their safety and efficacy had been carried out'.[161] Consequently, '[a]ll the sponsor needed to do in order to have the devices listed on the ARTG was to produce the [European] certificates'.[162] Further, the European certificate could effectively be obtained via an audit of the manufacturer's procedures, rather than any substantive examination of the devices.[163] In assessing the claims against the respondents, the Court found that none of the devices in question 'met the essential requirements of the applicable' European regulatory obligations.[164]

While the focus of the media reports about the Federal Court's decision was the respondent's breaches of the law, attention was also drawn to Katzmann J's observations in relation to the therapeutic goods regulatory regime. In that context, the reports noted the Court's findings of substantive

155 Ibid 933–9 [3581]–[3607].
156 Ibid 958–9 [3672]–[3680], 981–5 [3762]–[3778], 987 [3784], 996 [3826]–[3827], 1007–8 [3878]–[3884].
157 Ibid 1147 [4428]–[4430], 1151 [4445]–[4447], 1163 [4496]–[4497], 1163–4 [4498]–[4499], [4502], 1168 [4514]–[4517], 1170 [4521], 1177–8 [4556]–[4560].
158 *Gill v Ethicon Sàrl (No 6)* [2020] FCA 279.
159 See, eg, *Gill v Ethicon Sàrl (No 5)* [2019] FCA 1905, 362–4 [1364]–[1374].
160 Ibid 961 [3687]. See also at 374 [1408].
161 Additional regulatory requirements are imposed on Class III devices: *Gill v Ethicon Sàrl (No 5)* [2019] FCA 1905, 369–370 [1391].
162 Ibid.
163 Ibid 390 [1455].
164 Ibid 981 [3762]. See also Rizzi et al (n 152) 31–37.

noncompliance with the European regulatory requirements, and the absence of separate assessments by the TGA.[165]

Factors Contributing to the Urogynaecological Mesh Device Controversy

In this section I identify four of the key reasons for the complications associated with UMDs and, ultimately, the controversy surrounding them. I draw on certain findings of the Senate Committee Inquiry and others to outline what the ACSQHC described as the 'multifactorial' basis for the complications arising from UMDs.[166] This description highlights again the diverse number of actors involved in the regulation of UMDs and, consequently, its inherently polycentric nature.

The Conduct and Training of Clinicians

The Senate Committee Inquiry found that there were a range of concerns experienced and expressed by patients about their treatment by their health professionals in relation to the implantation of UMDs. These included the inappropriate selection of patients for implantation of UMDs and inadequate training for clinicians performing the implantation procedures.[167] Incomplete diagnosis of some patients and an unjustified enthusiasm for UMDs resulted in the implantation of devices in women for whom they were inappropriate and/or for whom more conservative treatment options should have been considered in the first instance. In the more extreme cases, young women had been implanted with UMDs as a 'first line treatment' and one had received the implant 'just in case she later developed SUI'.[168] The Senate Committee Inquiry stated that these factors were compounded by heavy marketing of devices, and associated training and education provided by device sponsors to clinicians, which encouraged the use of UMDs.[169]

165 See, eg, Christopher Knaus, 'Australian Women Win Landmark Vaginal Mesh Class Action against Johnson & Johnson', *The Guardian* (online, 21 November 2019) <https://www.theguardian.com/australia-news/2019/nov/21/australian-women-win-landmark-vaginal-mesh-class-action-against-johnson-johnson>; Rachel Clun, 'Johnson & Johnson Lose Pelvic Mesh Case to Women in Landmark Judgment', *Sydney Morning Herald* (online, 21 November 2019) <https://www.smh.com.au/national/johnson-and-johnson-lose-pelvic-mesh-case-to-women-in-landmark-judgment-20191121-p53coe.html>.

166 Evidence to Senate Community Affairs References Committee, Parliament of Australia, Melbourne, 3 August 2017, 42 (Dr Robert Herkes, Clinical Director, Australian Commission on Safety and Quality in Health Care).

167 Senate Community Affairs References Committee Report 2018 (n 6) 59–60, 71.

168 Ibid 75–6.

169 Ibid 71–2, 75. There were also suggestions of conflicts of interest in relation to instances of the medical profession's involvement in the development of urogynaecological mesh

In relation to the education and training of clinicians, the Senate Committee Inquiry concluded that there was 'a need to review the current training models' set and overseen by the specialist medical colleges 'to ensure that the skill levels of medical practitioners to diagnose and treat POP and SUI meet minimum quality standards'.[170] This, it was hoped, would help address a lack of oversight of the use of newly developed devices by clinicians without adequate training.[171] Further, the Committee supported the development by the ACSQHC of guidance for hospital credentialing of clinicians to undertake transvaginal mesh procedures. The Committee recommended that medical colleges improve governance arrangements in relation to clinician training for UMDs. The Committee's hope was that this would 'go some way to restoring faith in medical professionals' for women adversely affected.[172]

The Risk and Efficacy Profile of Urogynaecological Mesh Devices

The Senate Committee Inquiry identified concerns about the TGA's premarket and post-market assessment of the risk, and effectiveness, of UMDs. Certain submissions to the Senate Committee Inquiry alleged that the evidence of efficacy and safety on which the TGA approved UMDs at the premarket stage was 'paper-thin'.[173] This was emphasised in the case of devices approved for the treatment of particular types of POP.[174] The implications of

devices: see, eg, McCarthy, 'Australian Medical Association President Confirms AMA Role in Pelvic Mesh Scandal' (n 127).

170 Senate Community Affairs References Committee Report 2018 (n 6) 106; Joanne McCarthy, 'America Has Banned a Group of Problem Pelvic Mesh Devices with Origins in Australia in the 1980s', *The Newcastle Herald* (online, 26 April 2019) <https://www.newcastleherald.com.au/story/6086959/pelvic-mesh-era-ends-as-the-us-bans-devices-18-years-after-fda-approved-them/>.

171 See, eg, Evidence to Senate Community Affairs References Committee, Parliament of Australia, Canberra, 19 September 2017, 23–4 (Skye Kakoschke-Moore and Stephen Robson, President, Royal Australian and New Zealand College of Obstetricians and Gynaecologists).

172 Senate Community Affairs References Committee Report 2018 (n 6) 108.

173 Evidence to Senate Community Affairs References Committee, Parliament of Australia, Canberra, 19 September 2017, 31 (Peter Maher). See also Maurice Blackburn Lawyers, Submission No 45 to Senate Community Affairs References Committee, Parliament of Australia, *Number of Women in Australia Who Have Had Transvaginal Mesh Implants and Related Matters* (29 May 2017); Health Consumers Councils across Australia (Health Issues Centre (Vic), Health Consumers Queensland, Health Consumers' Council (WA), Health Consumers Alliance of SA, Health Care Consumers Assocation (ACT) and Health Consumers New South Wales), Submission No 21 to Senate Community Affairs References Committee, Parliament of Australia, *Number of Women in Australia Who Have Had Transvaginal Mesh Implants and Related Matters* (31 May 2017) ('Health Consumers Councils Submission').

174 Maher Submission 2017 (n 17) 6–7, 10; Maher and Haya (n 11).

these allegations were that the devices did not satisfy the essential principles, including that the benefits of their use did not 'outweigh any undesirable effects'.[175]

The TGA informed the Committee that its pre-market assessment of medical devices, including urogynaecological mesh, was limited by two factors that were inherent in the nature of medical devices generally. The first was the 'tension for regulators between acceding to the desire to gain timely access to new treatments and the need to assess the evidence regarding the efficacy and safety of each device'.[176] The second was the inability 'to conduct "double blind, randomised clinical controlled trails [sic] on a device, especially an implanted device" in the same way as can be done with medicines', and for the same length of time.[177] This second factor in particular was presented by the TGA in response to the criticism that it had failed to adequately assess the risk and efficacy of UMDs before their approval.[178] In summary, the TGA's view was that the 'regulation of devices poses greater challenges than that of prescription medicines'.[179]

Some clinicians submitted to the Senate Committee Inquiry that, given such limitations, 'new' devices should be introduced for medical use only after approval by an established ethics committee and application of that committee's consent and governance procedures.[180] However, the Senate Committee Inquiry acknowledged, and appeared to accept, the inherent nature of the two limitations presented by the TGA and the TGA's approach to its 'pre-market' assessment of urogynaecological mesh.[181] The Committee further agreed that 'the assessment and approval of medical devices is a *continuous* process of review and that regulatory responses to emerging issues need to be carefully considered and evidence based'.[182] The role of 'post-market' assessment as part of this 'continuous' process was therefore pivotal.

In relation to the TGA's post-market analysis of the risk and efficacy of UMDs, the Senate Committee Inquiry was critical 'of the lag in regulatory

175 *Therapeutic Goods Act 1989* (Cth) s 41BA(a), pt 4-2; *Therapeutic Goods (Medical Devices) Regulations 2002* (Cth) reg 2.1, Sch 1.

176 Senate Community Affairs References Committee Report 2018 (n 6) 89.

177 Ibid 89 quoting Evidence to Senate Community Affairs References Committee, Parliament of Australia, Melbourne, 3 August 2017, 46 (John Skerritt, Deputy Secretary, Therapeutic Goods Administration). See also Evidence to Senate Community Affairs References Committee, Parliament of Australia, Canberra, 6 February 2018, 9–10.

178 Senate Community Affairs References Committee Report 2018 (n 6) 89.

179 John Skerritt, 'Medical Device Regulation – a Challenging and Changing Area' (2017) 21 *Health Voices: Journal of the Consumers Health Forum of Australia*.

180 Senate Community Affairs References Committee Report 2018 (n 6) 89–90, 105.

181 Ibid 95. The Government subsequently reiterated these limitations as a necessary part of the TGA's role 'in the constantly evolving and increasingly complex medical technology sector': Australian Government Response (n 149) 2.

182 Senate Community Affairs References Committee Report 2018 (n 6) 95 (emphasis added).

response to emerging evidence of complications in relation to transvaginal mesh products'.[183] The absence of robust data regarding the use of, and complications arising from, transvaginal mesh devices was a key contributing factor in the Committee reaching this conclusion.[184] It formed the basis for the Committee's recommendation that the Government establish 'a more comprehensive post-market monitoring scheme'. The Committee further recommended that all state, territory and Commonwealth governments request the ACSQHC to conduct an audit of transvaginal mesh procedures in order to establish the extent and impact of the devices and their use.[185] In addition, it recommended the development of a national register of all 'implantable' medical devices to gain 'an understanding of the true scale of the risk' and to 'tailoring an effective regulatory response'.[186] Also significant to the Senate Committee Inquiry's conclusion in relation to 'post-market' assessment of risk and efficacy by the TGA were the problems identified with the reporting of adverse events.[187] This will be discussed in more detail shortly.

The Inadequacy of 'Informed Consent' for Use of Urogynaecological Mesh Devices

The terms of reference for the Senate Committee Inquiry specified that it investigate the information provided to women prior to surgery, and to doctors, about transvaginal mesh implants and 'possible complications and side effects'.[188] In doing so, the Committee expressed that it was

> deeply concerned by the evidence received regarding the information provided to women to enable them to provide their informed consent to a transvaginal mesh procedure. The committee is particularly concerned that, despite the availability of detailed guidance and patient information leaflets produced by specialist colleges and societies, many women appear

183 Ibid.
184 Ibid.
185 Ibid 100–1, 108–9. The government supported the establishment of an enhanced post-market monitoring scheme. It noted, but did not explicitly support the recommendation to conduct an audit of transvaginal mesh procedures: Australian Government Response (n 149) 8, 12.
186 Senate Community Affairs References Committee Report 2018 (n 6) 97. Notably, many of the Senate Committee Inquiry's recommendations in relation to the post-market monitoring of urogynaecological mesh devices specifically, and medical devices generally, reflected the recommendations of the 2015 Sansom Review of Medicines and Medical Devices: Sansom et al, *Report* (n 50); Bonython and Arnold (n 1) 3–4.
187 Senate Community Affairs References Committee Report 2018 (n 6) 95–6.
188 Ibid 117.

> to have received little or no information to assist them to make a decision or provide their informed consent.[189]

This, the Committee believed, reflected poorly on the medical profession.[190] It observed that consent for transvaginal mesh surgery was often obtained in a manner that was 'inconsistent' and 'cursory' despite clear legal obligations for clinicians to ensure adequate consent is provided.[191] Further the Committee found that women had limited access to information about the risks and the likely success of the procedure, including in relation to their individual circumstances.[192] In certain cases women were not told that urogynaecological mesh was going to be implanted prior to the procedure, and only discovered this had occurred following the onset of complications.[193] The Committee concluded that, despite the trust many women had placed in the judgment of their clinician, their experiences cast 'the medical profession in a very poor light'.[194] What was therefore required was 'clear and accessible information ... for both patients and medical practitioners'.[195] The Committee supported the preparation by the ACSQHC of material to inform women about transvaginal mesh procedures. In addition, the Committee requested that the ACSQHC prepare 'guidance material on effective informed consent processes' to facilitate an appropriate 'dialogue' between a patient and their clinician. The Committee considered that this dialogue should include the reasons for the treatment; treatment options and 'the likely success and potential complications ... as they relate to the individual patient'.[196]

189 Ibid 101.
190 Ibid 59.
191 Ibid 47, 60. See also Thompson and Faunce (n 16) 938.
192 Senate Community Affairs References Committee Report 2018 (n 6) 59–69.
193 Ibid 66–7. The Senate Committee Inquiry's conclusions were reflected in findings of the ACSQHC and the Health Consumers Councils, drawing on forums and surveys that had been conducted with patients across Australia: *Australian Commission on Safety and Quality in Health Care Submission* (n 90) 10; Health Issues Centre Submission (n 121). In particular, the Senate Committee Inquiry noted the Health Consumers Councils' concerns that these circumstances had been allowed to eventuate despite a previous Inquiry into medical devices recommending improvements to ensure that clinicians provided patients with 'all the information needed to allow them to give fully informed consent': Senate Community Affairs References Committee Report 2018 (n 6) 63–4, citing the Senate Community Affairs References Committee, Parliament of Australia, *The Role of the Government and the Therapeutic Goods Administration (TGA) regarding Medical Devices, particularly Poly Implant Protheses (PIP) Breast Implants* (Report, 31 May 2012).
194 Senate Community Affairs References Committee Report 2018 (n 6) 69, 84.
195 Ibid 85.
196 Ibid 102–3. The Senate Committee Inquiry further recommended that treatment guidelines, to be written by the ACSQHC, 'should clearly indicate that transvaginal mesh implantation should only be undertaken with fully informed consent': at 104. The Government

The Underreporting of Adverse Events

A significant additional factor found to have contributed to the urogynaecological mesh device controversy in Australia was the underreporting of adverse events associated with the devices.[197] Notably, underreporting of adverse events, particularly by patients, has been suggested as occurring in relation to medical devices more broadly.[198] As stated earlier, the therapeutic goods regulatory regime requires that sponsors of medical devices notify the Secretary of the Department of Health about any adverse event relating to the device. At the time of the controversy surrounding UMDs, other actors in the regulatory regime including clinicians and patients could report such events voluntarily.[199]

The Senate Committee Inquiry concluded that in relation to transvaginal mesh procedures 'the number of women who have experienced adverse events is unknown'.[200] Importantly, the Committee was 'particularly concerned by the level of underreporting of adverse events to the TGA', especially in light of the 'significance of adverse event reports to post-market monitoring by the TGA'. The extent of the underreporting of adverse events to the TGA was illustrated by the divergence in the number of accounts of adverse events associated with UMDs presented to the Senate Committee Inquiry. While the TGA had received 'formal' adverse event reports from 349 patients by early 2018, the non-government Health Issues Centre had received stories of adverse events from 2,400 women by August 2017.[201]

The Implications of Adverse Event Underreporting

The therapeutic goods regulatory regime relies on the post-market reporting of adverse events to assist the regime to ensure that devices continue to comply with the essential principles. This is particularly important in light of the TGA's view (accepted by the Senate Committee Inquiry) that the regulatory assessment of medical devices at the pre-market stage is inherently

---

subsequently supported these two recommendations: Australian Government Response (n 149) 9–10.

197 Senate Community Affairs References Committee Report 2018 (n 6) 41.

198 See, eg, Parisa Aslani et al, 'Consumer Opinions on Adverse Events Associated with Medical Devices' (2019) 15 *Research in Social and Administrative Pharmacy* 568, 569. Note that this study was funded, and one author employed, by the TGA: at 573.

199 Department of Health (Cth) Submission 2017 (n 4) 30.

200 This finding was closely related to the paucity of information regarding the number of transvaginal mesh implant procedures that had been performed in Australia: Senate Community Affairs References Committee Report 2018 (n 6) 56–7.

201 The TGA acknowledged the underreporting 'challenge' in evidence given to the Committee: ibid 42.

limited.[202] The Senate Committee Inquiry consequently concluded that the underreporting of adverse events associated with mesh devices was 'likely to have resulted in delays in identifying the problems with transvaginal mesh and resulted in more women suffering adverse impacts of these products'.[203] In other words, the underreporting 'provided a false indication of the safety of such devices'.[204] It can be concluded from this that the underreporting of adverse events in this instance constituted a breakdown in the 'loop' of information generation, provision and decision-making for the polycentric regulation of medical devices.[205]

The Reasons for the Underreporting of Adverse Events

There were multiple reasons for the underreporting of adverse events associated with UMDs. These reasons emanated from different actors in the polycentric regulatory arrangements for the devices – patients, clinicians and medical device sponsors.[206]

Sponsors of UMDs rely partly on information provided by clinicians and their patients in order to meet their regulatory obligations to report adverse events.[207] However, it was submitted by the MTAA, representing medical device sponsors, that the provision of this information by clinicians to sponsors may have been restricted because of the obligation of patient confidentiality owed by clinicians.[208] Further, the Senate Committee Inquiry was concerned about the 'significant scope' available for sponsors 'to determine whether an event should be reported'. It is possible, for example, that sponsors may receive information from clinicians regarding the performance of urogynaecological devices but fail to assess that information as constituting

202 See, eg, ibid 41.
203 Ibid 57–8.
204 Ibid 95.
205 See, eg, ibid 41.
206 In evidence given to the Senate Committee, the TGA submitted that 50% of adverse event reports regarding urogynaecological mesh devices were from patients; 37.6% were from sponsors and 11% from 'doctors and other health professionals'. The TGA stated, however, that in the months leading up to its testimony, 'the source of the information has now changed from industry to individual patients and consumers'. The head of the TGA stated that the Senate Committee Inquiry had raised 'awareness' about the ability for individuals to report adverse events (and presumably had influenced this change in reporting numbers): Evidence to Senate Community Affairs References Committee, Parliament of Australia, Canberra, 6 February 2018, 4 (John Skerritt, Deputy Secretary, Health Products Regulation Group, Department of Health), 6 (Adriana Platona, First Assistant Secretary, Medical Devices and Product Quality, Department of Health).
207 Senate Community Affairs References Committee Report 2018 (n 6) 48.
208 Ibid 49. Other commentators have argued, however, that doctors are obliged to report adverse events in order to fulfil a fiduciary duty to patients: Thompson and Faunce (n 16) 935–6, 940.

an adverse event under the regulatory regime. This, the Senate Committee Inquiry stated, 'led to inconsistency in the reporting of events' and warranted 'that clear criteria should be available to guide the reporting of adverse events' in relation to all medical devices.[209]

The Senate Committee Inquiry extended its concerns regarding the inappropriate use of discretion in the reporting of adverse events, and their consequential underreporting, to medical professionals.[210] Evidence given before the Committee indicated that both specialists and GPs were often unclear about what constituted an adverse event and what did not; whether symptoms experienced by a patient were associated with an urogynaecological mesh device; or even if such a device had been implanted.[211] The Committee acknowledged that the TGA had attempted to improve awareness and understanding of the adverse event reporting process in the medical and general community. However, the Committee concluded that the regulator 'is not funded to undertake large-scale consumer/community information programs'. It therefore relies on 'partnerships' with other actors in the regulatory regime, such as 'clinical and consumer groups'.[212]

Further, women adversely affected by UMDs considered 'that the medical professionals they approached simply did not have sufficient awareness of knowledge of symptoms of adverse events after a surgical mesh implant'.[213] Alarmingly, the Committee concluded that in many instances women who reported symptoms to clinicians about UMDs were ignored, dismissed, treated with disrespect or anger, and/or told that they were imagining their symptoms.[214] The consequence for many of these women was to feel 'humiliated, embarrassed and upset' and, ultimately, that their voices had been 'invalidated'.[215] This combination of ignorance, arrogance and disrespect on the part of Australian clinicians contributed to a deficit in the reporting of the adverse events experienced by women with urogynaecological mesh implants.

209 Senate Community Affairs References Committee Report 2018 (n 6) 57.
210 Ibid.
211 Ibid 46–7.
212 Ibid 96–7.
213 Ibid 4.
214 Ibid 77–8, 103. The Government response to the Senate Committee Inquiry's Report acknowledged the 'lack of support from some in the medical profession' for women experiencing adverse events: Australian Government Response (n 149) 12.
215 Senate Community Affairs References Committee Report 2018 (n 6) 77–9. In some instances, women reported being asked by their clinicians about their sexual activity in response to expressing concerns about their symptoms: see, eg, at 77–8. See also Mina Motamedi, Chris Degeling and Stacy M Carter, 'Patients' Perspectives on Quality and Patient Safety Failures: Lessons Learned from an Inquiry Into Transvaginal Mesh in Australia' (2024) 24 *BMC Health Services Research* 436.

The view presented to, and accepted by, the Senate Committee Inquiry was that many women experiencing adverse events reported their symptoms to their clinicians and that the clinicians failed to report these events to the TGA or to sponsors of medical devices.[216] The Senate Committee Inquiry also noted, however, that many women were not aware that they could directly report their experiences to the TGA or to sponsors.[217] This observation is supported by a separate study regarding the reporting of adverse events by patients in relation to medical devices. It found that only two of a total of 29 study participants knew about the TGA, and only one of those was aware that adverse events could be reported to the regulator.[218]

The Senate Committee Inquiry further observed that women who did try to report adverse events directly to the TGA found that the process was 'daunting' and complex and that they could not access the information they needed to do so (e.g., their medical records).[219] Women may also have relied on their clinicians to report their experience of adverse events to the TGA, rather than do so directly, because they felt 'alone' in their experience, that their symptoms were 'deeply private and personal' and that they were 'embarrassed'.[220] In this respect, and as indicated above, consumer health advocates played a significant role in encouraging women to eventually communicate their experiences.[221]

Reforms and Recommendations to Address Underreporting of Adverse Events

The underreporting of adverse events associated with UMDs by a range of regulatory actors contributed significantly to the harm and controversy that ultimately arose regarding these devices. Consequently, the Senate Committee Inquiry welcomed previous actions taken by the TGA in an

216 For example, in evidence given to the Senate Committee Inquiry, the head of the ACSQHC stated that 'women have reported these problems. For anyone to suggest that they have not reported them is nothing short of nonsense. It is what people have done or have not done with those reports; that is the issue': Evidence to Senate Community Affairs References Committee, Parliament of Australia, Melbourne, 3 August 2017, 40 (Debora Picone, Chief Executive Officer, Australian Commission on Safety and Quality in Health Care).

217 Senate Community Affairs References Committee Report 2018 (n 6) 96.

218 Aslani at al (n 198) 572.

219 Senate Community Affairs References Committee Report 2018 (n 6) 43–5, 96. The TGA acknowledged these challenges and the need to encourage patient reporting: at 45. In some instances, women were not aware that they had been implanted with an urogynaecological mesh device and therefore did not initially associate their symptoms with the implant: at 66–8.

220 Ibid 29, 43.

221 See, eg, Danny Vadasz, 'Trans Vaginal Mesh Injuries – Is Anyone Accountable?' (2017) (21) *Health Voices: Journal of the Consumers Health Forum of Australia*.

attempt to address underreporting, including targeted awareness-raising campaigns.[222] Nevertheless, the Committee recommended that, in light of 'the vital role of adverse reporting in post-market surveillance', the regulatory regime should be reformed to make it mandatory for medical practitioners to report adverse events.[223] This, it was hoped, would significantly reduce the discretion available to clinicians in determining whether to report an adverse event.[224] Further, the Committee recommended that improvements be made to the guidance for, and awareness and simplification of, the adverse event reporting system.[225] The need to amplify the voices of patients who had undergone urogynaecological mesh procedures was a prominent theme of the Senate Committee Inquiry's Report, in particular in relation to adverse event reporting.[226]

What Does This Case Study Indicate about the Political Legitimacy of the Regulation of Therapeutic Goods?

The above discussion provides a comprehensive overview of the polycentric regulation of UMDs in Australia and the range of factors that contributed to the controversy associated with these devices. As in the preceding chapters, I next explore what can be learned from this case study about the political legitimacy of the therapeutic goods regulatory regime. I contend that the political legitimacy of the regulatory regime was, at the very least, challenged in relation to UMDs, and arguably in relation to medical devices more broadly. The fundamental reason for this challenge is the collective absence of all aspects of the constant dialogic approach to political legitimacy: a constant dialogue; through which a set of shared normative beliefs and values are formulated; between all parties to a power relationship.

The absence of a constant dialogic approach is evident from the regulatory regime's apparent reluctance to adopt a relational approach to the polycentric regulation of medical devices. It is further illustrated by two key examples of the regulation of UMDs. First, there was a limited dialogue between regulatory parties about the potential for harm – that is risks, relating to the devices. Consequently, there was a clear incongruence between the values and beliefs held by these parties about what constituted an acceptable risk of harm. Second, there was a similarly limited dialogue between parties about

222 Senate Community Affairs References Committee Report 2018 (n 6) 96–7.

223 Ibid 97. This recommendation reflected a previous recommendation made following a 2011 Inquiry about the regulation of medical devices: at 47, citing Senate Community Affairs References Committee, Parliament of Australia, *Inquiry into the Regulatory Standards for the Approval of Medical Devices in Australia* (Report, 22 November 2011).

224 See, eg, ibid 47.

225 Ibid 97, 115.

226 See, eg, ibid 4, 13, 115.

the actual harm caused by UMDs. As a result, there was a divergence between parties about what they believed constituted an adverse event. The discussion about these two reasons for the challenge to the regulatory regime's political legitimacy will emphasise a significant contributing factor: the breakdown in the regulatory information loop that is at the centre of the regulation of medical devices. This supports the view, expressed earlier, that the effective operation of this information loop is crucial to the political legitimacy of the regulatory regime according to the constant dialogic approach.

The Challenge to Political Legitimacy

The preceding discussion highlighted instances in which regulatory actors expressed negative views about the therapeutic goods regulatory regime and the TGA in relation to UMDs. These views were expressed strongly by affected patients, patient advocacy and consumer health groups and parts of the media. Representatives of the Australian Pelvic Mesh Support Group,[227] for example, stated in evidence to the Senate Committee Inquiry that '[w]omen have been let down by their doctors, by RANZCOG and by the TGA as the regulator'.[228] They were further critical of the TGA's assessment that UMDs complied with the essential principles and of the effectiveness of the adverse event database.[229] Over 500 women made submissions to the Senate Committee Inquiry, many of whom had suffered adverse events.[230] In doing so, individual patients expressed their dissatisfaction with the regulatory arrangements and called for the Senate Committee Inquiry to 'investigate the TGA's current approval policies and procedures for approving implantable medical devices'.[231] Health Consumer Councils across Australia explicitly supported the submission of the Australian Pelvic Mesh Support Group.

227 The Australian Pelvic Mesh Support Group was initiated on Facebook in November 2014 to support mesh injured women.: *Australian Pelvic Mesh Support Group* (Web Page) <https://www.facebook.com/groups/AustralianPelvicMeshSupportGroup/>. In many respects the Group illustrates what Grabosky describes as the 'enormous potential for digital technology to enhance the regulatory capacity of ordinary citizens': Peter Grabosky, 'Beyond Responsive Regulation: The Expanding Role of Non-State Actors in the Regulatory Process' (2013) 7 *Regulation & Governance* 114, 118.

228 Evidence to Senate Community Affairs References Committee, Parliament of Australia, Perth, 25 August 2017, 3 (Stella Channing, Director and Administrator, Australian Pelvic Mesh Support Group).

229 Carolyn Chisolm and the Committee on Behalf of the Australian Pelvic Mesh Support Group, Submission No 130 to Senate Community Affairs References Committee, Parliament of Australia, *Number of Women in Australia Who Have Had Transvaginal Mesh Implants and Related Matters* (17 May 2017) 24–117.

230 Senate Community Affairs References Committee Report 2018 (n 6) 4.

231 Evidence to Senate Community Affairs References Committee, Parliament of Australia, Perth, 25 August 2017, 19 (Katrina).

They described the impetus behind the Senate Committee Inquiry as the 'catastrophic failure by Australian clinicians and our medical device regulator (the TGA) to provide evidence-based care and protect women from harm'.[232] Both the domestic and the international media published in-depth and critical reports of the regulation and use of UMDs.[233]

The lobbying of these individuals and groups led to the establishment of the Senate Committee Inquiry and guided the manner in which the Inquiry was conducted. The Senate Committee Inquiry was 'struck by the extent to which women who have had adverse experiences following transvaginal mesh surgery have struggled to be heard' and therefore 'sought to place these women at the forefront' of the Inquiry.[234] The dissent expressed by these individuals and their representative groups was therefore amplified following a period of relative obscurity. The first recommendation of the Senate Committee Inquiry at its conclusion was directed at the therapeutic goods regulatory regime (including the TGA). It recommended that the Government 'review the current system of reporting adverse events to the Therapeutic Goods Administration'.[235] Subsequently, the Minister for Health made a wide-ranging apology in which he appeared to accept that the regulatory system had failed patients:

> On behalf of the Australian Government, I say sorry to all of those women with the historic agony and pain that has come from mesh implantations, which have led to horrific outcomes … [t]his has been an issue over some decades in many cases and *on our time and on our watch we both recognise the problem and we're moving to take sweeping action to repair it.*[236]

Adding to this strong tone of dissent were the comments made by the Federal Court of Australia in its judgment in favour of women injured by UMDs. As noted earlier, the Court described the regime in relation to medical devices as 'largely self-regulating'. This was arguably a significant criticism of the regulatory regime in light of the extensive and ostensibly independent regulatory framework through which medical devices are regulated in Australia and the 'excellent reputation' of the TGA.

Collectively the views of patients, civil society, the courts and the government constituted a wide-ranging dilution of consent to, or acknowledgement

232 Health Consumers Councils Submission (n 173) 3.

233 See, eg, McCarthy, 'America Has Banned a Group of Problem Pelvic Mesh Devices' (n 170); Hooton and McCarthy (n 117); 'Medical Devices Harm Patients Worldwide as Governments Fail on Safety' (n 1).

234 Senate Community Affairs References Committee Report 2018 (n 6) 4. See also at 13.

235 Ibid ix. See also at 95–6.

236 'Greg Hunt Says Sorry for Vaginal Mesh Damage', *ABC News* (10 October 2018) (emphasis added).

of, the power exercised by the therapeutic goods regulatory regime in relation to UMDs. In some instances, these views extended beyond those devices to implantable devices more broadly.[237] Many of the views noted above were expressed to the Senate Committee Inquiry or in the media. According to Beetham, such views constituted 'public acts of protest'.[238] In addition, the apology issued by the Minister for Health, responsible to Parliament for the therapeutic goods regulatory regime, may be considered a 'withdrawal of endorsement or recognition' for the regulatory regime in relation to UMDs.[239] These actions and beliefs consequently constitute, at the very least, a challenge to, if not a deviation from, the political legitimacy of the therapeutic goods regulatory regime.[240]

It may be argued that some of the delegitimating views expressed during the UMDs controversy more broadly do not relate to the therapeutic goods regulatory regime or to the TGA alone. Such views have also been articulated in relation to the power exercised by other regulatory actors as part of that, and other, regulatory regimes. This is particularly the case in relation to clinicians and their particular regulators, and the sponsors and manufacturers of certain devices.[241] Indeed, the multiple factors that led to the harm caused by UMDs have been described as 'Swiss cheese systematic failure' in which 'failure occurred at multiple levels concurrently' and which involved a range of other regulatory actors.[242] However, this does not mean that the TGA was untouched by delegitimating beliefs and actions directed at other regulatory actors. As highlighted earlier, the regulation of UMDs was polycentric and interdependent. This means that the legitimacy of each regulatory actor was enmeshed with others. As Black states:

> [I]n polycentric regimes, regulators enrol others in the performance regulation ... [e]nrollment can enhance legitimacy within some legitimacy communities, as where the regulator aligns itself with another regulator who is considered legitimate ... but if the actor enrolled is not considered legitimate, it may well erode it.[243]

237 See, eg, 'Medical Devices Harm Patients Worldwide as Governments Fail on Safety' (n 1).

238 David Beetham, 'Revisiting Legitimacy, Twenty Years On' in Justice Tankebe and Alison Liebling (eds), *Legitimacy and Criminal Justice: An International Exploration* (Oxford University Press, 2013) 19, 26.

239 Ibid.

240 David Beetham, *The Legitimation of Power* (MacMillan Education, 2nd ed, 2013) 14, 18, 91, 267.

241 See, eg, *Gill v Ethicon Sàrl (No 5)* [2019] FCA 1905.

242 S Abbas Shobeiri, 'Introduction: Why a Case Study of Vaginal Mesh Kits?' in S Abbas Shobeiri (ed), *The Innovation and Evolution of Medical Devices: Vaginal Mesh Kits* (Springer, 2019) 1, 4–5. See also Evidence to Senate Community Affairs References Committee, Parliament of Australia, Perth, 25 August 2017, 41 (Hans Peter Dietz).

243 Black, 'Constructing and Contesting Legitimacy' (n 2) 148.

As discussed earlier, the therapeutic goods regulatory regime effectively co-opts or enrols other regulatory actors, such as device sponsors and clinicians, in the regulation of medical devices. Consequently, not only did interdependent regulatory actors 'share' the regulation of UMDs, they also shared in the initial benefit of each other's political legitimacy – and the subsequent loss of that legitimacy. Therefore, public statements and actions of criticism and protest about the medical profession and its regulators, hospitals and sponsors of medical devices also constitute acts of delegitimation against the TGA and its regulatory regime. This was particularly evident in the November 2019 decision of the Federal Court against the Johnson & Johnson companies. While the Court focussed on the failings of the respondents, the therapeutic goods regulatory regime was arguably portrayed by the Court and reporting media as complicit in the harm endured by mesh-injured women.

The Absence of the Constant Dialogic Approach to Political Legitimacy

Underpinning the challenge to the political legitimacy of the therapeutic goods regulatory regime was its failure to adopt and enable a constant dialogic approach in relation to the regulation of UMDs: that is, a constant dialogue, between all regulatory parties, through which a set of shared normative beliefs and values can be formulated. While the constant dialogic approach is fundamentally relational, the polycentric nature of the regulation of implantable medical devices requires a particular focus on dialogue with a large number of regulatory actors.[244] The absence of the constant dialogic approach can be broadly observed from the apparent reluctance of the TGA to accept the interconnected nature of the regulatory regime. In the midst of the UMD controversy, the TGA expressed the view that it was starkly distinct and distant from other regulatory actors:[245]

> The TGA has no regulatory powers with respect to the clinical practice of medical practitioners. The Australian framework for regulation of medical practitioners and the services they provide is complex, with different responsibilities for each of the Commonwealth, state and territory governments, professional organisations, independent statutory bodies and public and private hospitals.[246]

244 See, eg, Anthony Bottoms and Justice Tankebe, 'Beyond Procedural Justice: A Dialogic Approach to Legitimacy in Criminal Justice' (2012) 102(1) *Journal of Criminal Law and Criminology* 119, 128–9; Anthony Bottoms and Justice Tankebe, 'Police Legitimacy and the Authority of the State' in Antje du Bois-Pedain, Magnus Ulvang and Petter Asp (eds), *Criminal Law and the Authority of the State* (Hart Publishing, 2017) 47, 73–4.

245 See, eg, Skerritt (n 179).

246 Department of Health (Cth) Submission 2017 (n 4) 16.

As was evident in the case of medicinal cannabis and RU486, the TGA here emphasised its legal powers and, in particular, the limits of those legal powers.[247] However, as the earlier discussion in this chapter highlighted, the multiple actors involved in the regulation of UMDs (and implantable medical devices generally) are closely connected. For example, the practice of medicine by a clinician is inseparable from the device that she or he recommends to a patient and later implants.[248] The above assertion by the TGA arguably represented an attempt by the regulator to exclude itself from responsibility for the harm associated with UMDs. It also reflected an attempt by the TGA to excuse itself from dialogue with other regulatory actors in relation to such devices. The TGA's tendency to distance itself from other regulatory actors, instead of facilitating a dialogue with them, undermined its ability to justify its role and power in this polycentric regulatory arrangement.

Two specific examples further illustrate the absence of the constant dialogic approach which resulted in the challenge to the political legitimacy of the regulatory regime in relation to UMDs. The first example relates to the potential for harm, or risks, associated with these devices; the second concerns the actual harm, or adverse events, resulting from their use. Both examples highlight the breakdown in the regulatory information loop that is pivotal to the polycentric regulation of medical devices, including urogynaecological mesh.[249] This loop of information generation, provision and regulatory decision-making also supports the constant dialogic approach to political legitimacy. In both examples, failures in the information loop contributed significantly to the absence of a constant dialogue between all regulatory parties and a divergence in their respective beliefs and values regarding UMDs.

The Potential for Harm: A Failure in the Dialogue about Risk

From a patient's perspective, a constant dialogue with other regulatory actors, in particular clinicians, is crucial to achieving a mutual understanding about the risks of harm associated with medical devices, including UMDs. Such a dialogue is also fundamental to a patient's ability to provide informed consent to the implantation of a device. Broadly speaking, during such a dialogue a clinician shares information about the risks of the device with the patient, the patient asks questions and highlights issues important to him or her and the clinician listens and responds with additional information and advice. This

247 As expressed by Beetham, legality is an insufficient basis on which to establish political legitimacy: Beetham (n 240) 68.

248 See, eg, S Abbas Shobeiri, 'The Innovation of Medical Devices' in S Abbas Shobeiri (ed), *The Innovation and Evolution of Medical Devices: Vaginal Mesh Kits* (Springer, 2019) 13, 18, 37–41; Chatterji et al (n 83); Faulkner (n 82) 51.

249 See a similar description of feedback involving regulatory intermediaries in Abbott et al, 'Theorizing Regulatory Intermediaries' (n 102) 26–8.

represents a constant dialogue – the first aspect of the constant dialogical approach. It is akin to 'an ongoing process of claim and response' between the patient and their clinician about the safety of the device.[250] As stated, the aim of the dialogue is for the patient and clinician to reach a shared belief or understanding about the risks of the medical device and their acceptability. This constitutes the second element of the constant dialogic approach. An analogous dialogue may also occur between the patient and the TGA in relation to the information the regulator provides, or makes available, to the patient about the medical device. This additional interaction is an example of the third aspect of the constant dialogic approach – the engagement of all regulatory parties in dialogue. The regulatory information loop can therefore support the constant dialogic approach through the exchange of information between regulatory parties about the risks of medical devices. However, in the case of UMDs, the operation of the information loop was inadequate and the constant dialogic approach was absent. This is illustrated in two respects.

First, as described earlier, there were significant deficiencies in the information women received from their clinicians about UMDs.[251] Consequently, patients did not understand the risks posed by the device and were unable to provide consent that was adequately informed.[252] It was also contended that informed consent could not have been given by patients because there was inadequate data on which clinicians could provide an accurate, statistically based risk profile about the device to patients.[253] Further, some women described limited opportunities and little encouragement to raise and discuss questions and concerns about the devices with their clinicians.[254] These failures in the exchange of information between clinicians and patients meant that a constant dialogue to reach a shared understanding of the risks posed by UMDs was, in many instances, impossible.

Second, information was not available to women from the TGA about the basis on which UMDs were included on the ARTG. While patients could search the TGA's public database to confirm that a device was on the ARTG, AusPARs are not available for medical devices. Therefore, no information

250 See Belén V Lowrey-Kinberg and Grace Sullivan Buker, '"I'm Giving You a Lawful Order": Dialogic Legitimacy in Sandra Bland's Traffic Stop' (2017) 51(2) *Law & Society Review* 379, 384. The consent process between patient and clinician has itself been described as a 'dialogue': see, eg, Senate Community Affairs References Committee Report 2018 (n 6) x (Recommendation 6), 102.

251 See Melissa Oxlad, Georgina Edwards and Kate A McKinlay, 'Patients' Perspectives about Doctor–Patient Communication Regarding Transvaginal Mesh Implant Surgery' (2022) 105 *Patient Education and Counseling* 3534.

252 See, eg, Senate Community Affairs References Committee Report 2018 (n 6) 101.

253 Health Issues Centre Submission (n 121) 26. See also Shelley K White and Abigail N Walters, 'Assessing Risk by Analogy: A Case Study of US Medical Device Risk Management Policy' (2018) 20 *Health, Risk & Society* 358, 363–4.

254 Senate Community Affairs References Committee Report 2018 (n 6) 68–9.

about the risks of medical devices, or their TGA approved risk management plan, was available to patients.[255] In the absence of information about UMDs from the regulator it was not possible for patients to engage in a dialogue with other regulatory actors, such as clinicians, and, vice versa, about the risks associated with the devices.

During the term of the Senate Committee's Inquiry, three significant reforms were made to the therapeutic goods regulatory regime with the potential to enhance dialogue between future patients and regulatory actors about the risks associated with UMDs. The first reform was to require sponsors of UMDs to include additional information, including 'certain adverse events' on the '[i]nstructions for use' of the device.[256] However, as this information was intended for clinicians, it would not necessarily be communicated to the patients themselves.[257] Additional reforms required that device manufacturers make 'available' a 'patient implant' card and a 'patient information leaflet' with a range of 'implantable medical devices', including UMDs.[258] Any 'undesirable side effects that could be caused by use of the device' are required to be included on the leaflet.[259] However, neither the information leaflet nor the card is required to be provided to the patient *prior* to the implantation of the device. The reforms only require that the card and leaflet be 'made available' for the patient. This strongly suggests that this additional patient information, partly intended to facilitate informed consent,[260] may be provided *after* the device has been implanted.[261] The reforms will not, therefore, assist to encourage a constant dialogue with patients about the risks associated with UMDs.

255 Australian Government, *An Action Plan for Medical Devices* (n 49) 9.

256 'TGA Actions after Review into Urogynaecological Surgical Mesh Implants' (n 141); Senate Community Affairs References Committee Report 2018 (n 6) 94–5.

257 Senate Community Affairs References Committee Report 2018 (n 6) 95.

258 *Therapeutic Goods (Medical Devices) Regulations 2002* (Cth) regs 1.3, 13A, Dictionary (definition of 'implantable medical device').

259 Ibid reg 13A.3.

260 Explanatory Statement, Therapeutic Goods (Medical Devices) Amendment (Implantable Medical Devices) Regulations 2017 (Cth) 1; Therapeutic Goods Administration, Department of Health (Cth), *Medical Device Patient Cards and Leaflets: Requirements for New and On-Market Implantable Medical Devices* (October 2018).

261 A publicly available educational resource produced by the TGA indicates that, consistent with the EU model, the cards should be provided at the time that the patient is discharged: Elizabeth McGrath, A/g Assistant Secretary, Medical Devices Branch, Therapeutic Goods Administration, 'MMDR Reform – Patient Implant Cards and Information Leaflets' (Conference Presentation, Association of Regulatory and Clinical Scientists (Australia) Annual Conference, 22 August 2018) 19. In contrast, a document produced by the Consumers Health Forum of Australia states that the leaflets will be given to consumers 'prior to providing consent': Consumers Health Forum of Australia, *Consumer Guide to Reforms* (12 June 2018).

This discussion highlights the breakdown in the regulatory information loop in relation to UMDs, and the related absence of a constant dialogue between patients, clinicians and the TGA, about their associated risks. In the absence of a constant dialogue it is not surprising to find that regulatory actors held incongruent beliefs about what constituted an acceptable risk of harm.[262] Broadly, commentary on different conceptions of 'risk', what is an appropriate level of risk and how risk should be addressed is diverse and comprehensive.[263] Such an extensive debate cannot be covered within the limits of this chapter. However, it is illuminating to briefly point to one of the key differences in the views about risk held by regulatory actors in relation to UMDs in Australia. The TGA, for example, appeared to hold the view that greater risks of harm should be tolerated in relation to implantable medical devices than for pharmaceuticals because those devices cannot be tested to the same standards or degree.[264] The TGA instead emphasised that evidence of the risk of devices is 'evolving' and is gained from the 'day-to-day experience' of patients.[265] In contrast, the patients harmed by UMDs and their advocates protested that the TGA's perspective on risk accepts that some patients will inevitably be harmed as 'collateral damage' in the evolution of medical devices.[266] They consider that the regulator's approach reflects an unreasonably utilitarian perspective on the regulation of implantable medical devices.[267] This incongruency in normative beliefs between regulatory actors

262 See, eg, Mina Motamedi, Stacy M Carter and Chris Degeling, 'Women's Experiences of and Perspectives on Transvaginal Mesh Surgery for Stress Urine Incontinency and Pelvic Organ Prolapse: A Qualitative Systematic Review' (2022) 15 *The Patient* 157.

263 See, eg, David Demortain, *Scientists and the Regulation of Risk: Standardising Control* (Edward Elgar Publishing, 2011); Sheila Jasanoff, 'The Songlines of Risk' in Sheila Jasanoff (ed), *Science and Public Reason* (Routledge, 2012) 133; Sheila Jasanoff, 'Technologies of Humility: Citizen Participation in Governing Science' in Sheila Jasanoff (ed), *Science and Public Reason* (Routledge, 2012) 167; Laurence Boisson de Chazournes, 'New Technologies, the Precautionary Principle, and Public Participation' in Therese Murphy (ed), *New Technologies and Human Rights* (Oxford University Press, 2009) 161.

264 Senate Community Affairs References Committee Report 2018 (n 6) 89, quoting Evidence to Senate Community Affairs References Committee, Parliament of Australia, Melbourne, 3 August 2017, 46 (John Skerritt, Deputy Secretary, Therapeutic Goods Administration). See also Evidence to Senate Community Affairs References Committee, Parliament of Australia, Canberra, 6 February 2018, 9–10.

265 Senate Community Affairs References Committee Report 2018 (n 6) 88. See also commentary confirming that '[t]he typical innovation pathway of medical devices ... involves "postmarketing" usership feedback in building incremental developments of a device': Faulkner (n 82) 34.

266 Vadasz (n 221).

267 Similarly, in the United States commentators observed that regulatory actors made different 'claims' about the risk associated with vaginal mesh and sought to 'assert control over the definition of risk attached to vaginal mesh' during FDA hearings into mesh devices: Leiter and White (n 12) 67–8. Further, one American commentator considers that the adoption of an approach to risk such as that advanced by the TGA has meant that medical devices

about what constitutes acceptable risks of harm to patients is reflected in the following statement from the Health Issues Centre:

> Much of the debate about the severity of this problem has been framed in terms of the good outcomes for the many outweighing the unfortunate experiences of a few. Health spokespeople continue to refer to [transvaginal mesh] as the 'gold standard' in dealing with prolapse. Our health system is built on social equity values such as universal duty of care, not on a cost/benefit analysis that accepts the unavoidability of collateral damage.[268]

This divergence in beliefs and values associated with the risk of UMDs illustrates the absence of a constant dialogic approach to political legitimacy by the therapeutic goods regulatory regime. It also illuminates the dominance of the regulator's own perspective and ideology on risk, a contention I will return to in Chapter 7.

Actual Harm: A Failure in the Dialogue about Adverse Events

The limited dialogue between regulatory parties about the harm caused by UMDs also illustrates the absence of the constant dialogic approach to political legitimacy and failings in the regulatory information loop. The concerns expressed by patients to the TGA, clinicians and other regulatory actors that they had been harmed by UMDs arguably constituted 'basic legitimation demands'.[269] As described in Chapter 3, a basic legitimation demand can form part of the constant dialogue between regulatory parties. It is a request by a subordinate party (here the patient) of a dominant party (the TGA or clinician) to justify the power they exercise and to do so in 'normative' terms.[270]

A patient's suggestion that she has experienced harm from a mesh device raises the possibility that such harm may constitutes an adverse event and that the device should no longer remain on the ARTG. A patient's basic legitimation demand in this context therefore challenges the justification of the power of regulatory actors to develop, approve, sell, recommend and use UMDs. As discussed earlier, clinicians, sponsors and the TGA failed to

are 'introduced, trialed [sic] on patients, litigated, and then withdrawn from the market: Shobeiri (n 248) 42. See also Julie Kent, 'Lay Experts and the Politics of Breast Implants' (2003) 12 *Public Understanding of Science* 403, 413–14.

268 Health Issues Centre Submission (n 121) 3.

269 Senate Community Affairs References Committee Report 2018 (n 6) 48–9.

270 Bottoms and Tankebe, 'Police Legitimacy and the Authority of the State' (n 244) 57, 60 quoting Bernard Williams (selected and edited by Geoffrey Hawthorn), *In the Beginning Was the Deed: Realism and Moralism in Political Argument* (Princeton University Press, 2005). See also Lowrey-Kinberg and Sullivan Buker (n 250).

facilitate, support and adequately respond to claims of adverse events by patients. Such inaction arguably amounted to a failure to justify the exercise of power by these regulatory actors. In these circumstances a constant dialogue between all regulatory actors about the harm caused by UMDs was not possible. This was illustrated by the following exchange between the Senate Committee Inquiry and the head of the ACSQHC:

Prof Picone: So as we made our preliminary inquiries ..... we were told that the complication rates were very low, that there were really no big issues. Of course, as time has gone by, that has not been the case at all

Senator Kakoschke-Moore: What does that mean for patients?

Prof Picone: It confirms what the women are telling us – that these complications they are experiencing are quite real.[271]

The regulatory information loop failed to support the exchange of information about harm and adverse events experienced by patients in relation to UMDs. Consequently, it also failed to support the constant dialogue necessary to achieve political legitimacy around their regulation. The TGA relied on the information loop to receive reports of adverse events from sponsors, clinicians and patients as intermediaries to enable the post-market regulation of medical devices.[272] However, as discussed earlier, this feedback was curtailed.[273] Instead, a significant underreporting of adverse events to the TGA reflected a collective regulatory deafness to women's voices and experiences.[274]

In the absence of a constant dialogue it was impossible for regulatory actors to arrive at a set of shared beliefs and values about whether and what harm associated with UMDs was an adverse event under the regulatory regime. For example, as described above, the Senate Committee Inquiry

271 Evidence to Senate Community Affairs References Committee, Parliament of Australia, Melbourne, 3 August 2017, 11 (Debora Picone, Chief Executive Officer, Australian Commission on Safety and Quality in Health Care).

272 See, eg, Abbott et al, 'Introducing Regulatory Intermediaries' (n 103) 7–8; Abbott et al, 'Theorizing Regulatory Intermediaries: The RIT Model' (n 103) 14–21. In relation to regulatory intermediaries and therapeutic goods, see Maggetti et al (n 102).

273 In relation to the role of feedback from regulatory intermediaries, see Maggetti et al (n 102) 23–4.

274 In relation to the 'marginalised' patient voice, see Leiter and White (n 12) 78; Miles Sibley, 'Evidence-Based Practice – A Double Standard?', *The BMJ Opinion* (Blog Post, 24 April 2019) <https://blogs.bmj.com/bmj/2019/04/24/miles-sibley-evidence-based-practice-a-double-standard/>. In relation to women's voices in particular, see, eg, Katrina Hutchison, 'Gender Bias in Medical Implant Design and Use: A Type of Moral Aggregation Problem?' (2019) 34(3) *Hypatia: A Journal of Feminist Philosophy* 570; Arianne Shahvisi, 'Medicine Is Patriarchal, but Alternative Medicine Is Not the Answer' (2019) 16 *Journal of Bioethical Inquiry* 113.

concluded that clinicians were often unclear about what harm constituted an adverse event, and it was concerned about the discretion exercised by clinicians and sponsors in reaching conclusions about adverse events.[275] For many clinicians and sponsors an adverse event is objectively and empirically measurable, and clearly caused by the device rather than the procedure to implant the device or the clinical care provided.[276] The view of patients and carers about what constituted an adverse event was quite different. From a patient's perspective, the adverse event they endure is highly subjective in nature, reflected in their 'lived experience' of a range of symptoms (e.g., pain) and resulting from a procedure in which the clinical care they receive, and the device that is implanted, are inseparable.[277]

The therapeutic goods regulatory regime appears to support and enable the perspective of clinicians and sponsors about what harm constitutes an adverse event. For example, at the time of writing, the regulatory regime relies on the mandatory reporting of adverse events from sponsors alone. That is, from regulatory actors associated solely with the *product* and its measurable characteristics. This arguably reflects the dominant influence of scientism on the regulatory regime, discussed in Chapter 2. However, this perspective is inconsistent with the polycentric nature of the regulatory arrangements for medical devices. The experiences, values and beliefs of all regulatory actors, in particular the historically silenced voice of patients, should have been part of a constant dialogue to reach a shared set of beliefs about what constitutes an adverse event in relation to UMDs.[278] In the next chapter I will return to the comparative absence of the views of patients and carers in relation to the control of therapeutic goods.

Conclusion

The head of the TGA, in giving evidence before the Senate Committee Inquiry in 2017, described the urogynaecological mesh controversy as 'a

275 Senate Community Affairs References Committee Report 2018 (n 6) 4–7, 57, 79–82.

276 See, eg, in the American context, Leiter and White (n 12) 71–2; 76–7. However, it was notable that the RANZCOG submitted to the Senate Committee that a register of implantable medical implants should include subjective measures of 'patient satisfaction': Senate Community Affairs References Committee Report 2018 (n 6) 54.

277 See, eg, Senate Community Affairs References Committee Report 2018 (n 6) 77–9. See also, in the American context, Leiter and White (n 12) 76–7. In relation to the importance of a patient's subjective experience in the evaluation of transvaginal mesh, see Maher and Haya (n 11) 486; Christine Kilgore, 'FDA Panel Tackles Mesh for Anterior Repair of POP' (2019) 54(3) *Obstetrics & Gynaecology News* 6.

278 See also proposals for patients collaborating with the medical profession and the medical device industry: Palm (n 8) 134, 140.

learning journey'.[279] In the period leading up to and following the Inquiry, the TGA took certain steps to address aspects of the controversy that led to the challenge to the political legitimacy of the therapeutic goods regulatory regime. Most significantly this appeared to include an acknowledgement that the regulation of UMDs was polycentric in nature. For example, the TGA announced that it was working with other regulatory actors in relation to the credentialing of clinicians for the implantation and removal of mesh devices and to support the reporting of adverse events.[280] Other steps taken by the TGA included attempts to increase awareness amongst regulatory actors, including patients, about adverse event reporting[281] and the establishment of a 'unique device identification database for medical devices' to further facilitate adverse event reporting.[282] The TGA also participated in a Reference Group convened by the ACSQHC to develop resources on the use of transvaginal mesh[283] and worked with consumer health groups on resources to assist patients in their dialogue with clinicians about implantable medical devices.[284]

These steps may represent an acknowledgement by the TGA of past failings and a recognition of the benefits of applying a constant dialogic approach to the polycentric regulatory arrangements for medical devices. This was arguably further reflected in the reforms announced by the Commonwealth Government in the lead up to the 2019 Australian election. The Minister for Health announced funding for a register, which was subsequently established, to collate information on transvaginal mesh surgery with the aim

279 Evidence to Senate Community Affairs References Committee, Parliament of Australia, Melbourne, 3 August 2017, 45 (John Skerritt, Deputy Secretary, Therapeutic Goods Administration).

280 Evidence to Senate Community Affairs References Committee, Parliament of Australia, Canberra, 6 February 2018, 3, 5–6 (John Skerritt, Deputy Secretary, Health Products Regulation Group, Department of Health and Tim Greenaway, Chief Medical Adviser, Health Products Regulation Group, Department of Health); Department of Health (Cth) Submission 2017 (n 4) 16, 30.

281 Department of Health (Cth) Submission 2017 (n 4) 16.

282 Australian Government, *Final Report on the Australian Government Response to the Recommendations of the Senate Community Affairs References Committee Report: The Number of Women in Australia Who Have Had Transvaginal Mesh Implants and Related Matters* (July 2021) 4 ('*Final Report*').

283 'Transvaginal Mesh', *Australian Commission on Safety and Quality in Healthcare* (Web Page, 2019) <https://www.safetyandquality.gov.au/our-work/health-conditions-and-treatments/transvaginal-mesh>.

284 Australian Government Response (n 149) 6. See, eg, 'Urogynaecological (Transvaginal) Surgical Mesh Hub' *Therapeutic Goods Administration, Department of Health and Aged Care (Cth)* (Web Page) https://www.tga.gov.au/products/medical-devices/urogynaecological-transvaginal-surgical-mesh-hub. See also Australian Government, *Final Report* (n 282).

of improving post-market monitoring of mesh devices.[285] In addition, he announced 'An Action Plan for Medical Devices' to enhance 'Australia's medical device regulatory framework'. The Plan includes three 'strategies' to enhance pre- and post-market device assessment and to 'provide more information to patients' about medical devices. Notably, this included a proposal to 'co-design a strategy to raise awareness ... about how regulatory decisions were reached about individual products' and the 'publication of consumer friendly information on each new higher risk device'.[286] Further, the Plan stated that 'all perspectives', and 'particularly those of consumers who use medical devices', will be considered in the development and implementation of the Plan.[287] The proposal therefore represented a significant step towards a constant dialogue with all regulatory actors in relation to medical device regulation under the therapeutic goods regime. At the time of writing, the TGA had released a 'Progress Report Card' against the 'Action Plan' for December 2023 indicating that a number of actions had been completed or were underway.[288] Significantly this included, in early 2023, legislative amendments to require the CEO of a healthcare facility to report any adverse event involving prescribed medical devices where the device 'has resulted in the death, or a serious deterioration in the health' of a patient. While these reforms were, at the time of writing, yet to commence, it is hoped that they will partly rectify a significant regulatory deficiency identified earlier in relation to the reporting of adverse events. The December 2023 'Progress Report Card' also detailed the establishment of a number of Working Groups which appear to have a strong patient focus.[289]

This chapter has considered the controversy surrounding UMDs in Australia from the perspective of a constant dialogic approach to political legitimacy. It outlines the polycentric and interdependent nature of the regulation of UMDs and identifies the factors that contributed to the controversy. In particular, I have highlighted the failures in the regulatory information

285 Daly et al (n 108) 473; Jenny King, 'Transvaginal Mesh for Incontinence and Pelvic Organ Prolapse: Where Are We Now and How Did We Get Here?' (2024) 53 *Australian Journal of General Practice* 23, 23; 'Australian Regulatory Actions – About Transvaginal Surgical Mesh' *Therapeutic Goods Administration, Department of Health and Aged Care (Cth)* (Web Page, 20 December 2023) <https://www.tga.gov.au/products/urogynaecological-transvaginal-surgical-mesh-hub/australian-regulatory-actions-about-transvaginal-surgical-mesh>.

286 Australian Government, *An Action Plan for Medical Devices* (n 49) 9.

287 Ibid 4.

288 'Action Plan for Medical Devices – Progress Report Card: December 2023', *Therapeutic Goods Administration, Department of Health and Aged Care (Cth)* (Web Page, 23 May 2024) <https://www.tga.gov.au/resources/publication/publications/action-plan-medical-devices-progress-report-card-december-2023>. See also Australian Government, *Final Report* (n 282).

289 'Action Plan for Medical Devices – Progress Report Card: December 2023' (n 289).

loop at the centre of this polycentric regulatory arrangement. In light of these failings, the therapeutic goods regulatory regime was unable to support a constant dialogue between all regulatory actors. This was evident in incongruent beliefs between regulatory actors about the risk of harm posed by UMDs and what harm constituted associated adverse events. It is arguable that it was the resulting challenge to the political legitimacy of the therapeutic goods regulatory regime in the wake of this controversy that motivated the reforms announced by the TGA and the Commonwealth Government. While too late for those harmed by UMDs,[290] these reforms perhaps indicate an acknowledgement of the benefits of a constant dialogic approach to the polycentric regulation of medical devices.

290 See, eg, Kate Gorman, 'Report on National Forum on Mesh Implants' *Health Care Consumers* (Web Page, 9 September 2019) <https://www.hcca.org.au/2019/04/30/report-on-national-forum-on-mesh-implants-by-kate-gorman/>.

Chapter 7

Regulatory Challenges, Courage and Evolution

Introduction

This book set out to explore the question: what does political legitimacy tell us about the regulation of medical products? In the preceding chapters I examined controversial case studies involving the regulatory regime. Each case study was analysed using the constant dialogic approach to provide insights about the political legitimacy of the Australian regulatory regime. The case studies involved different types of therapeutic goods, regulated at different points in time and involving various means by which political legitimacy was undermined in each case. Despite these differences there are commonalities which emerge from this analysis. In this chapter I argue that two key challenges relating to the nature of the Australian therapeutic goods regulatory regime explain its deficiencies in political legitimacy. In doing so, I present a broad or 'meta' perspective about the regulatory regime's failings in political legitimacy.

The first broad challenge is its technocratic-based *approach* to expertise. This challenge is demonstrated in the regulatory regime's directive and unilateral approach to expertise. The directive and unilateral expressions of the regulatory regime's technocratic character and their contribution to undermining political legitimacy are discussed in turn.

The second challenge that further explains the regulatory regime's failings in political legitimacy is the dominance of scientism in relation to the *content* of the expertise relied on by the regulatory regime. This challenge is evident in the regulatory regime's near singular reliance on scientific expertise. This feature of the therapeutic goods regulatory regime results in two epistemic obstacles to political legitimacy – an over-confidence or 'arrogance' in the solutions offered by scientific knowledge, and a 'scarcity' of other types and sources of knowledge with which to adequately address regulatory questions.

I argue that these two meta challenges – the directive and unilateral approach to expertise, and a singular reliance on scientific knowledge – are fundamentally at odds with the constant dialogic approach to political legitimacy. The therapeutic goods regulatory regime must address these

DOI: 10.4324/9781003293811-7

challenges, and their foundations in scientism and technocracy, in order to regulate future difficult cases with enhanced legitimacy.

My argument responds to the two challenges facing the therapeutic goods regulatory regime by making a case for the evolution of its ideological foundations. Drawing on the notion of regulatory 'courage', it argues for a consistent and incremental change in the nature of the regulatory regime.[1] I propose two fundamental goals for change to the therapeutic goods regulatory regime: first, to embrace normative pluralism, and, second, to adopt an approach to expertise that is facilitative in nature. Regulatory courage is advocated to enable the regulatory regime to achieve such change, including the contemplation and adoption of new values and norms in a sometimes controversial and unstable regulatory environment.

It is not my intention in this book to lay out a comprehensive plan for reform for the therapeutic goods regulatory regime. The changes proposed in this chapter, and the challenges they address, primarily focus on the 'norms and ideas' underpinning the regulatory regime.[2] A plan for reform is, however, a necessary next step in the development of scholarship related to the therapeutic goods regulatory regime and in the evolution of the regime itself.

Regulatory Challenge 1: The Regulatory Regime as Expert

A fundamental characteristic of the therapeutic goods regulatory regime is the notion of expertise. However, this characteristic is also one of its significant challenges. In the following discussion I highlight the origins of the regime's approach to expertise in its technocratic foundations – a thread begun in Chapter 2. I discuss the regulatory regime's directive and unilateral approach to expertise as illustrated by the case studies examined earlier and contend that this approach to, and exercise of, expertise, contributes to the deficiencies in the regime's political legitimacy.

A Directive and Unilateral Approach to Expertise

Chapter 2 introduced the concept of technocracy as power held and used by those with technical expertise or knowledge.[3] Further, it discussed how

1 Oren Perez, 'Courage, Regulatory Responsibility, and the Challenge of Higher-Order Reflexivity' (2014) 8 *Regulation & Governance* 203.

2 In Fuchs's terms, the 'discursive' dimension of the regulatory regime's power: see Chapter 3; Jennifer Clapp and Doris Fuchs, 'Agrifood Corporations, Global Governance, and Sustainability' in Jennifer Clapp and Doris Fuchs (eds), *Corporate Power in Global Agrifood Governance* (MIT Press, 2009) 1, 9–10.

3 Richard Olson, *Scientism and Technocracy in the Twentieth Century: The Legacy of Scientific Management* (Lexington Publications, 2016) ix, citing Robert Putnam 'Elite Transformation in Advanced Industrial Societies' (1977) 10 *Comparative Political Studies* 383.

expertise is a dominant element of the therapeutic goods regulatory regime and the primary conduit of its regulatory power. Yet, while expertise establishes and maintains the regulatory regime's power, it is also a source of its failings in relation to political legitimacy. There are two fundamental and related expressions of the regulatory regime's approach to expertise that have contributed significantly to these deficiencies. The first is the regulatory regime's *directive* approach to expertise, and the second its *unilateral* approach to expertise.

The Directive Approach to Expertise

The directive approach to expertise professes to offer an authoritative position on an issue. In relation to the therapeutic goods regulatory regime it is exhibited by the purported provision of 'the' answer to questions regarding the control of such goods. That is, directive expertise is knowledge given with a high degree of certainty as to its ability to comprehensively and objectively solve any societal, policy or regulatory challenges such as those facing the regulatory regime.[4] The directive characteristic is inherent in the technocratic-based and scientism-based foundations of the regulatory regime. It pervades the notion of technocratic advice as 'all-knowing' and as advice to be unquestioningly accepted and followed.[5]

CERTAINTY

The directive approach reflects a traditional perception of a link between the acquisition of knowledge and that of certainty: '[o]nly knowledge that has shed the attribute of "uncertain" could pass as stringent knowledge'.[6] In particular, scientific knowledge is commonly regarded as inherently certain and its use discourages dissent. It therefore often represents the 'end' of dialogue regarding an unresolved question or issue.[7] But this perspective has been challenged by contemporary commentators.[8] Adolf and Stehr regard scientific knowledge as, at best, able to 'offer more or less plausible assumptions, scenarios or probability statements'.[9] Scientific knowledge, they contend, is not able to provide constant certainty, particularly in the face of 'historically

4 See, eg, Nico Stehr and Reiner Grundmann, *Experts: The Knowledge and Power of Expertise* (Routledge, 2011) 105.
5 See, eg, Olson (n 3) 40.
6 Marian Adolf and Nico Stehr, *Knowledge: Is Knowledge Power?* (Routledge, 2017) 74.
7 Ibid 100, 165.
8 See, eg, Sheila Jasanoff, *The Fifth Branch: Science Advisers as Policymakers* (Harvard University Press, 1998) 7–8, 42.
9 Adolf and Stehr (n 6) 165.

novel problems'.[10] This can be seen most recently in relation to regulatory responses to the COVID-19 pandemic. More specifically, and relevantly to the therapeutic goods regulatory regime, are the promises and techniques of risk assessment, which have similarly been accused of generating a fallacy of certainty.[11] That is not to say, however, that scientific knowledge is unable to provide clear, stable and certain answers in many instances. But its fallibility means that scientific knowledge should be regarded as 'both a provider of reliable knowledge *and* a source of uncertainty'.[12]

The case study of medicinal cannabis illustrates the notion that certainty is assumed in the directive approach to expertise adopted by the regulatory regime, and that this approach discouraged dialogue in relation to regulation of the drug. In that case, the regulatory regime embraced and echoed the 'dominant' voice, which conceived of medicinal cannabis as an appropriately 'prohibited substance'. In the TGA's view there was insufficient certainty attached to the 'moderate' or 'radical' voices to support an alternative view to that of the 'dominant' status quo.[13] From the regulator's perspective, only its knowledge and expertise was sufficiently certain and, therefore, compelling. This view appeared to influence the extent to which the regulator was prepared to engage in a 'constant dialogue' with other parties to the regulatory relationship. In contrast, the Victorian Labor government and the Victorian Law Reform Commission invoked the 'moderate' voice and embraced the uncertainty associated with knowledge about the drug. According to this perspective, uncertainty was interpreted as 'potential' in relation to the drug's unknown medicinal qualities. The knowledge and expertise that was valued was less certain but was nonetheless regarded as highly pertinent. The Victorian government and the Victorian Law Reform Commission were consequently more receptive to dialogue with alternative voices than were those supporting the regulatory status quo.

NEUTRALITY

Also inherent in the directive approach to expertise is that the knowledge it imparts is 'value neutral' or objective. This is a core feature of the technocratic foundations of the regulatory regime.[14] Technocratic expertise posits

10 Ibid.

11 Fiona Haines, *The Paradox of Regulation: What Regulation Can Achieve and What It Cannot* (Edward Elgar, 2011) 40–3.

12 Adolf and Stehr (n 6) (emphasis in the original). Indeed, as Jasanoff points out, greater scientific knowledge does not relate to greater or lesser policy agreement: Jasanoff (n 8) 8.

13 See, eg, John Skerritt, 'Medicinal Cannabis – What's Happening?' (Conference Presentation, Association of Regulatory and Clinical Scientists, August 2016).

14 See, eg, Boris Hauray, 'From Regulatory Knowledge to Regulatory Decisions: The European Evaluation of Medicines' (2017) 55 *Minerva: A Review of Science, Learning & Policy* 187; Olson (n 3) xi, 55.

that 'non-technical', and in particular 'non-scientific', expertise is biased and irrational, and is consequently inappropriate to solve problems such as the control of therapeutic goods.[15] This assertion of a rational, unbiased source of expertise nurtured by the technocratic tradition has, however, been comprehensively criticised.[16] In her seminal work on the role of scientific expertise in policy formulation, Jasanoff surmises that so-called 'scientific "facts" are, for the most part, socially constructed'[17] and that subjective judgment is frequently and necessarily employed by scientific advisers acting in a regulatory capacity in order to appropriately respond to an uncertain evidence base.[18] Concepts such as 'safety', a central objective of the therapeutic goods regulatory regime, 'are not governed by mechanical procedures' but 'involve interpretive decisions'.[19] Consequently, '[t]he "neutral" expert is at best a convenient fiction'.[20]

Jasanoff criticises the 'artificiality' of technocratic attempts to keep politics at arms-length from science in the regulatory context.[21] Eriksen, in examining the role of normative values in public agencies, labels such attempts as the 'avoidance model'.[22] While this approach 'sounds a warning against expert agencies taking a politically activist or partisan stance', he argues that it 'does not secure neutrality' but, instead, results in 'decisions that are political yet not acknowledged as such'.[23] Similarly, Wood argues in an analysis of the intersection between expertise, politics and policymaking that '*all* forms

15 See, eg, Stehr and Grundmann (n 4) 105.

16 See, eg, Jasanoff (n 8) 6–7. Esmark, summarising such a critique by Habermas, asks whether the exclusion of moral and social norms and experiences renders, 'the technocratic "fetish of science", functionally equivalent to an ideology insofar as it even more efficiently impedes broad political thought, reflection, and debate about the foundations of society': Anders Esmark, 'Maybe It Is Time to Rediscover Technocracy? An Old Framework for a New Analysis of Administrative Reforms in the Governance Era' (2017) 27(3) *Journal of Public Administration Research and Theory* 501, 503–4. See also Jürgen Habermas, *Toward a Rational Society: Student Protest, Science and Politics*, tr Jeremy J Shapiro (Beacon Press, 1971) 67.

17 Jasanoff (n 8) 12. See also at 16–7.

18 Ibid 94.

19 Andreas Eriksen, 'Political Values in Independent Agencies' (2021) 15 *Regulation & Governance* 785. See also, in relation to risk assessment, Jasanoff (n 8) 232–4; Julie Kent, 'Lay Experts and the Politics of Breast Implants' (2003) 12 *Public Understanding of Science* 403, 411, 416.

20 Jasanoff (n 8) 93.

21 Ibid 230.

22 Eriksen (n 19) 2–4.

23 Ibid.

of allegedly expert policymaking are embedded within political networks. Politics may be suppressed in this process, but ... it is bound to rise up'.[24]

The misguided attempts at neutrality inherent in the directive approach to expertise are well illustrated by the analysis in Chapter 4 concerning the abortifacient RU486. In that instance, assertions about the neutrality of the therapeutic goods regulatory regime did not prevent controversy about the social and ethical issues surrounding the drug. The regulatory regime was not, however, equipped with the ideological foundations or mechanisms to identify and address these normative issues. The regime's sole focus in fulfilling its regulatory mandate was to assess therapeutic goods according to the purportedly objective criteria of quality, safety and efficacy through the application of science-based methodology. The regulatory regime was not tasked with the objective of addressing broader normative issues, nor was it empowered with the legislative means to do so. It was therefore fundamentally outside the mandate of the regulatory regime to identify and consider broader normative concerns. What remained was a regulatory vacuum for values-based issues, created and sustained by a fundamental assumption of regulatory neutrality.

In this context, Senator Harradine and his supporters arguably had little choice but to prosecute their claims about RU486 through the parliament and the Minister for Health.[25] This approach was supported and vindicated by the major political parties, which identified the need for broader ethical and social concerns to be addressed and the absence of an appropriate regulatory arrangement to do so.[26] Consequently, the normative questions surrounding RU486, such as the sanctity of human life, became subject to the vagaries of much broader political forces. This included the fact that Senator Harradine partly held the balance of power in the senate and that the government of the day needed his support for the privatisation of the nation's telecommunication's carrier.[27] Senator Harradine was therefore politically empowered to enable his narrow ethical and social opinions to shape the parliamentary debate around the amendments to control RU486. In such circumstances, the

24 Matthew Wood, *Hyper-Active Governance: How Governments Manage the Politics of Expertise* (Cambridge University Press, 2019) 17 (emphasis in original).

25 Similar observations are made in Syrett's analysis of the United Kingdom's National Institute for Clinical Excellence ('NICE'). He observes that 'debate and discussion between different interests and the articulation of conflicting social, ethical and political values are ... inevitable' despite the dominant and broad technocratic approach of NICE: Keith Syrett, 'Legitimating "Fourth Hurdle" Pharmaceutical Regulation in Europe: Learning the NICE Way?' (2003) 9(4) *European Public Law* 509, 522. See also Keith Syrett, *Law, Legitimacy and the Rationing of Health Care* (Cambridge University Press, 2007) 7.

26 See, eg, Commonwealth, *Parliamentary Debates*, Senate, 9 May 1996, 624 (Belinda Neal, Shadow Minister for Consumer Affairs and Assistant to the Shadow Minister for Health) (emphasis added).

27 See, eg, Caroline de Costa, *RU-486: The Abortion Pill* (Boolarong Press, 2007) 89–90.

debate around the Harradine Amendments was unable to reflect a breadth of diverse and well-reasoned views about the normative issues at stake and the resulting different conceptualisations of abortion. Instead, the normative vacuum of the 'neutral' therapeutic goods regulatory regime was filled by the particular values of a politically influential Senator and his supporters.

An alternate and preferable course of events would have seen the broader normative issues surrounding RU486 explicitly identified, deliberated and decided on as part of the therapeutic goods regulatory regime. This would have required the regulatory regime to be equipped with sufficient powers, capabilities and, as will be discussed, the underpinning ethos to do so. Consistent with the constant dialogic approach to political legitimacy, such an alternative approach would have included a comprehensive and soundly reasoned dialogue between all parties about their respective social and moral views. In contrast to the narrow views that framed the parliamentary debates, this approach would have reflected the more diverse and liberal voices of health practitioners, activists and the broader public about reproductive freedom and its social implications.[28] The consideration of normative issues by the regulatory regime would have been inevitably contentious and have required difficult regulatory decisions. It would, however, have been highly preferable to the (so-called) neutral normative vacuum that ultimately undermined the political legitimacy of the regulatory regime.

It may be argued that the eventual repeal of the Harradine Amendments means that such a regulatory change is unnecessary. Yet, while the repeal was a pragmatic political victory for the pro-choice movement, it too was arguably won on the back of the misguided promotion of the neutrality of the regulatory regime. It was not achieved through well-reasoned, well-articulated deliberation of the applicable social and ethical issues. During the repeal debates the normative issues were arguably downplayed in favour of an emphasis on the superiority of 'science' to support regulatory decision-making. Yet despite their opacity, these issues continued to be relevant to the regulatory regime. This is evident, for example, in the requirements that the regulatory regime attempted, and in some cases did, impose on the eventual supply of RU486, including the training of clinicians and pharmacists.[29] I

28 This approach has been further developed by Parker, Haines and Boehm in advocating for 'ecological'-based regulation to frame 'the enormity of intersecting ecological, social and political challenges' in order to better protect the environment: Christine Parker, Fiona Haines and Laura Boehm, 'The Promise of Ecological Regulation: The Case of Intensive Meat' (2018) 59 *Jurimetrics* 15, 27. See also Christine Parker and Fiona Haines, 'An Ecological Approach to Regulatory Studies?' 45(1) *Journal of Law and Society* 136.

29 See, eg, Caroline de Costa, Kirsten I Black and Darren B Russell, 'Medical Abortion: It Is Time to Lift Restrictions' (2019) 210(6) *Medical Journal of Australia* 248; 'MJA Podcasts 2019 Episode 14: Lifting Restrictions on Medical Abortion, with Prof Caroline de Costa AM', *The Medical Journal of Australia* (Cate Swannell, 1 April 2019).

discuss the ideological shifts required to achieve an alternative, normative-rich approach in the final part of this chapter.

The Unilateral Approach to Expertise

The unilateral character of the regulatory regime's approach to expertise also constitutes a challenge for the regime and contributes to its legitimacy failings. The one-sided approach of the regulatory regime is highlighted in two key respects. The first is the regime's apparent failure to adequately receive and consider the knowledge and experiences of 'laypeople' in relation to the control of therapeutic goods. The scientific pedigree of the regulatory regime is perceived as granting it a higher status than that of members of the public:

> [T]he scientific voice is that which is granted the status of objectivity, and thus, in the current rules of debate, authority and legitimacy. Lay views are often seen as irrational, based in ignorance, as mere emotions or prejudices. ... For 'lay' views to be accepted ... they have to re-translate themselves into the language of science.[30]

The relative neglect of lay expertise is illustrated by the case study of medicinal cannabis. In that instance, the 'traditional' science-based expertise, qualifications and focus of the members of the regulatory regime's Advisory Committee on Medicines Scheduling ('ACMS') operated to the exclusion of the experience and knowledge of patients, carers and cannabis societies.[31] In contrast, the Victorian Law Reform Committee embraced 'lay' expertise as an additional source of knowledge that was highly relevant to its Inquiry.[32] Similarly, in the case of UMDs, the experiences of patients and their carers were effectively silenced by the regulatory regime, contributing to a breakdown in the information loop at the centre of medical device regulation and an underreporting of adverse events. It also appears that the regulatory regime failed to engage effectively with women and pro-choice advocates in relation to RU486. I will elaborate on the epistemic obstacles and limitations

30 Julia Black, 'Regulation as Facilitation: Negotiating the Genetic Revolution' in Roger Brownsword, WR Cornish and Margaret Llewelyn (eds), *Law and Human Genetics: Regulating a Revolution* (Hart Publishing, 1998) 29, 30. See also Kent (n 19).

31 *Therapeutic Goods Regulations 1990* (Cth) regs 35B; Therapeutic Goods Administration, Department of Health (Cth), *Final Decisions and Reasons for Decisions by a Delegate of the Secretary to the Department of Health* (31 August 2016).

32 Victorian Law Reform Commission, *Medicinal Cannabis,* (Report, August 2015) 214–7; Kari Lancaster, Kate Seear and Alison Ritter, 'Making Medicine; Producing Pleasure: A Critical Examination of Medicinal Cannabis Policy and Law in Victoria, Australia' (2017) 49 *International Journal of Drug Policy* 117, 123.

created by this dominance of scientific sources of knowledge on the regulatory regime later in this chapter.

There are also significant indications that, beyond these case studies, the regulatory regime may not regard the opinions of the broader public as highly as those of industry, health professionals, academia and government. In 2015 the Commonwealth Government-appointed Review of Medicines and Medical Device Regulation observed that public health and consumer organisations 'were frustrated by the TGA's failure to engage with them on their issues'.[33] There is some evidential support for this claim in the consultative practices and outcomes of the TGA itself. Since 2016 the TGA has conducted an annual 'stakeholder survey'.[34] In 2016 only 2.3% of those answering the survey identified as a 'community member, consumer or community representative'.[35] In 2017 this figure was 0.6%.[36] This contrasts with responses from the 'medical products industry', which made up 69% and 63% of the sample, respectively.[37] In 2018 the response rate from the community cohort was 1%.[38] In that year the TGA conducted its first 'Consumer Survey' 'to ensure a range of community views were captured' and, in a positive sign, such surveys have continued.[39] Nevertheless, this consultative history is arguably indicative of a traditionally weak relationship between the regulatory regime and regulator, on the one hand, and the broader community and its advocates, on the other.[40] Further, it arguably reflects the observation by Olson in his examination of scientism that 'it has rarely been the case that technocrats have felt the need to consult or consider public sentiment because they feel more competent to understand the general good than members of the general public'.[41] The unilateral tendencies of the regulatory

33 'Public health' organisations appeared to include non-government health advocacy groups such as the Consumers Health Forum of Australia: Lloyd Sansom, Will Delaat and John Horvath, *Review of Medicines and Medical Device Regulation: Report on the Regulatory Framework for Medicines and Medical Devices* (March, 2015) 8, 164–5.

34 Therapeutic Goods Administration (TGA), 'TGA Stakeholder Surveys', *Resources* (Web Page, 1 December 2023) <https://www.tga.gov.au/resources/publication/publications/tga-stakeholder-surveys>.

35 TGA, *TGA Stakeholder Survey 2016* (2016) 11.

36 TGA, *TGA Stakeholder Survey 2017* (2017) 15. The participants in this category identified themselves as either a 'consumer', 'consumer health representative or advocate', 'patient', 'carer' or 'other': at 14–5.

37 TGA, *TGA Stakeholder Survey 2016* (n 35) 11; *TGA Stakeholder Survey 2017* (n 36) 15.

38 TGA, *TGA Stakeholder Survey 2018* (2018) 17–8.

39 Ibid 10; TGA, 'TGA Stakeholder Surveys' (n 34).

40 More positive conclusions may be drawn from the subsequent surveys: see 'TGA Stakeholder Surveys' (n 34).

41 Olson (n 3) 181.

regime have consequently established a rigid 'boundary' between the expertise of the regulator and that of the lay public.[42]

The unilateral approach to expertise by the regulatory regime is also evident in a second key aspect. This is its insufficient dialogue with other regulatory actors, including other regulators, clinicians, hospitals and their representative bodies. This was most prominently illustrated in the case of UMDs and the breakdown in the information loop at the centre of their regulation. In that instance, the TGA arguably held information tightly and appeared to begin to share it with other regulatory actors such as patients and clinicians only as problems with UMDs began to emerge. This was apparent in the unavailability of Australian Public Assessment Reports ('AusPARs') for medical devices including urogynaecological mesh.[43] As discussed in Chapter 6, AusPARs are publicly searchable documents that set out information regarding the evaluation of certain therapeutic goods for inclusion on the ARTG.[44] Pertinent information (such as that contained in AusPARs) relating to urogynaecological mesh and other medical devices continues to be unavailable to the public.[45] This is arguably underpinned by a view that only the therapeutic goods regulatory regime is able to provide answers in relation to the control of such goods and that there is therefore no need to provide such information for the consideration of others. This perspective fails to recognise that the political legitimacy of each regulatory actor is closely connected with all other actors. It also fails to recognise that legitimacy can be built only through dialogue about the construction and interpretation of key values at the heart of the regulation of medical devices. This dialogue is essential to facilitate a shared understanding, and congruence, about value-laden regulatory concepts such as 'risk' and 'harm'.

42 Harry Collins and Robert Evans, *Rethinking Expertise* (University of Chicago Press, 2007) 10.

43 While AusPARs are available for pharmaceuticals they are not for medical devices: see Chapter 6.

44 See Chapter 6. See also TGA, *Australian Public Assessment Reports for Prescription Medicines* (Web Page, 11 October 2021) <https://www.tga.gov.au/australian-public-assessment-reports-prescription-medicines-auspars>.

45 The government-appointed Review of Medicines and Medical Devices Regulation noted the anomaly and broadly recommended greater transparency of the regulatory regime's 'policies and processes': Sansom et al. (n 33) 153, 163. More recently, the third part of the TGA's 'strategy to strengthen Australia's regulatory system' around medical devices specified a need to '[p]rovide more information to patients about the devices they use', with a particular focus on the absence of AusPARs for medical devices: Australian Government, *An Action Plan for Medical Devices* (April 2019) 4, 9.

Regulatory Challenge 2: The Regulatory Regime as Scientist

The second broad challenge facing the therapeutic goods regulatory regime focuses less on its approach to expertise per se, and more on the content of that expertise. Science is the source of knowledge, and consequently of regulatory power, exercised by the regulatory regime. As discussed in Chapter 2, science-based expertise is the fulcrum of the regulatory regime's establishment and objectives. It is central to the regulatory regime's identity. Underpinning this pivotal characteristic is the ideology of scientism. This part will return to this principle and explain how it operates to undermine the political legitimacy of the regulatory regime in two respects. First, the ideology of scientism encourages an over-confidence or 'arrogance' in scientific knowledge to provide complete and almost infallible solutions to the questions posed by the regulation of therapeutic goods, including those questions raised by difficult cases. A second and related way in which scientism operates to undermine political legitimacy is by significantly limiting the types of knowledge relied on by the regulatory regime in answering such questions.

Epistemic Arrogance

Inherent in the therapeutic goods regulatory regime is the perspective that scientific disciplines and sources of knowledge alone are capable of supporting the control of therapeutic goods.[46] As discussed in Chapter 2, this reflects the dominant influence of scientism and its position that science is the superior source of knowledge with which to approach and solve a range of societal challenges. Scientism arguably, therefore, establishes and perpetuates 'epistemic arrogance' on the part of the therapeutic goods regulatory regime.[47]

Epistemic arrogance has been expressed as 'an unwillingness to learn from others ... a kind of bad faith'.[48] Those who possess it project a 'conviction that they have it all figured out; that they know it all, that the light of truth shines within them'.[49] While this description is typically one that conjures images of individuals who hold and exercise power, it is also one that can be attributable to institutions and to regulatory arrangements. Like the constant dialogic approach to political legitimacy, epistemic arrogance 'is relational' and is

46 This has been described by some commentators as a form of scientism equivalent to '[s]cientific fundamentalism': Collins and Evans (n 42) 10.

47 See, eg, Ian James Kidd, 'Is Scientism Epistemically Vicious?' in Jeroen de Ridder, Rik Peels and Rene van Woudenberg (eds), *Scientism: Prospects and Problems* (Oxford University Press, 2019) 149, 149–50.

48 Michael Patrick Lynch, 'Arrogrance, Truth and Public Discourse' (2018) 15(3) *Episteme* 283, 284.

49 Ibid.

> both ... self-regarding by being an orientation towards one's own worldview, the sense of knowing it all ... [and] other-regarding in that it is an attitude that, by definition, concerns your worldview's possible relation to other people or sources of information.[50]

The attribute of epistemic arrogance is consequently deeply problematic for 'real dialogue and deliberation' and accordingly for the political legitimacy of the therapeutic goods regulatory regime.[51] Epistemic arrogance need not be widespread or affect every aspect of the regulatory regime for it to pose a fundamental threat to the political legitimacy of the regime.[52] It is therefore sufficient to provide an illustrative sketch of the existence of epistemic arrogance in relation to the therapeutic goods regulatory regime.

At a general level, and as was highlighted in Chapter 2, the regulatory concepts of quality, efficacy and safety and the techniques of standardisation and risk assessment are fundamentally determined by scientific knowledge and method. They are formed to the exclusion of other perspectives and sources of knowledge. For example, in relation to the FDA, Carpenter observes that

> the definition of pharmaceutical politics in terms of 'safety' and 'efficacy' excludes other important questions from discussion ... [such as] the continued operation of placebo effects in markets for prescription pharmaceuticals, and the therapeutic implications of drug advertising and labeling.[53]

More particularly, the case study of medicinal cannabis highlights how epistemic arrogance is conveyed by the Australian therapeutic goods regulatory regime. As discussed in Chapter 4, the regulatory regime engaged almost entirely with established scientific and medical sources of knowledge in relation to the drug. Other sources of knowledge – or 'voices' – in the form of patients, carers, cannabis societies and non-'dominant' sources of medical knowledge were perceived as insignificant or irrelevant. Scientific expertise 'trumped' any dialogue with these non-traditional sources of knowledge. A very similar pattern can be observed in relation to UMDs. That case study highlights the initial failure by the regulatory regime to take adequate account of the range of experiences and knowledge of patients, carers and their advocates in relation to fundamental concepts such as risk and harm (and, consequently, what constitutes an adverse event). The regime exhibited an inherent assumption that the substantive meaning of these terms can be determined

50 Ibid 286 (emphasis omitted).

51 Ibid 284.

52 Epistemic arrogance 'can vary in degree' and 'in scope': ibid 287.

53 Daniel P Carpenter, *Reputation and Power: Organizational Image and Pharmaceutical Regulation at the FDA* (Princeton University Press, 2010) 16–7.

only by scientific methodology and knowledge. This constituted epistemic arrogance. It failed to recognise patients, carers, and others outside the traditional scientific domain as being 'a possible source of reasons and knowledge' that are essential to the dialogue at the heart of political legitimacy.[54]

Epistemic Scarcity

Epistemic arrogance is closely linked to a second fundamental challenge for the regulatory regime – that of epistemic scarcity. In a wide-ranging article on the challenges faced by modern regulators, Perez describes epistemic scarcity as 'the gap between the questions regulators ask regarding various risks and the epistemologically warranted answers provided by science'.[55] An answer that is premised on 'good reasons' is one that is epistemologically warranted.[56] Accordingly, a response by the regulatory regime which is not founded on good reasons highlights a 'gap' between the regulatory response and the question it sought to answer.

Arguably, this gap and the corresponding indication of epistemic scarcity arises because the regulatory regime relies almost solely on scientific principles and methodology to meet the challenges confronting it. However, as indicated by the difficult cases explored in this book, the scientific ethos of the regulatory regime is inadequate to answer many of the questions such cases raise. These questions are fundamentally normative. They raise issues of a social and ethical nature which cannot be adequately responded to by a regulatory regime dominated by the ideology of scientism.[57] The regulatory regime is unable to identify, access and apply the normative breadth of knowledge and expertise – such as sociology, ethics or psychology – that such cases demand of it.[58] The result is a significant gap, to use Perez's term, between the answers provided by the regulatory regime and the questions that are asked of it. Epistemic scarcity is therefore a consistent and pervasive

54 In his analysis of epistemic arrogance, Lynch describes such recognition as 'basic epistemic recognition respect'. He distinguishes it from acknowledging someone as an 'expert', which he describes as 'appraisal respect', that is assessing someone 'as having the skills and knowledge base to warrant that respect': Lynch (n 48) 292.

55 Perez (n 1) 204, n 4.

56 This is a basic summary of the description of 'epistemic warrant' adopted by Perez, referring to Siegel and Biro: ibid 204, n 4, citing Harvey Siegel and John Biro, 'Epistemic Normativity, Argumentation, and Fallacies' (1997) 11 *Argumentation* 277, 278.

57 Similarly, Perez observes that one of the common approaches of regulatory regimes to the challenges of decision-making is to rely on 'regulatory techniques' such as 'cost-benefit analysis' and 'risk assessment': ibid 204.

58 See, eg, Olson's discussion of Robert Putnam's 'defining attitudes' of technocrats includes that 'practical considerations were paramount and always trumped ideology or any non-consequentialist moral claims': Olson (n 3) 41.

meta-challenge to the political legitimacy of the therapeutic goods regulatory regime.

This challenge is illustrated most clearly in the RU486 case study. There, the regulatory regime was unable to address the broader normative issues so obviously relevant to the regulation of abortifacients. A purely scientific basis for regulation was inadequate to address the complexities surrounding this therapeutic good and the multifaceted issues that it raised. The response to the epistemic scarcity provided by the regulatory regime was support for, and enactment of, the Harradine Amendments, and the regulatory regime's loss of political legitimacy. Similarly, the case study of UMDs highlighted how the dominance of scientific knowledge in the construction of notions of risk and harm excluded alternative 'world views' about such concepts.[59] In that case, the regulatory regime's interpretation of what constituted risk and harm was inadequate to capture other sources of knowledge that could usefully contribute to relevant and comprehensive understandings of such concepts. Such sources of knowledge could include insights from the disciplines of psychology or sociology, particularly where they provide an enhanced perspective about the experiences of patients and their carers.

These case studies highlight the inadequacy of the scientific epistemic tradition to address complex and controversial normative issues. To bridge this gap, the regulatory regime must be prepared to build its expertise and power on a broader epistemological base. Currently, however, the building blocks of the regulatory regime provide it with limited epistemological tools. This is illustrated by the predominantly narrow scientific and medical backgrounds of members of its advisory bodies such as the ACMS and the Advisory Committee on Medical Devices, as outlined in Chapter 2.[60] As discussed earlier, it is further highlighted in the historical dominance of stakeholders from the medical products industry, and its associated epistemological base, as compared with patients and the broader public.

59 Perez argues that 'regulatory reliance on techniques ... may lock regulators into a particular world view, causing them to lose sight of opposing world views': Perez (n 1) 206.

60 See *Therapeutic Goods Regulations 1990* (Cth) regs 35B (Advisory Committee on Medicines), 38B (Advisory Committee on Medical Devices). Jasanoff similarly advocates a need for 'disciplinary breadth' on the part of regulatory advisory committees in the United States: Jasanoff (n 8) 244. See also Karinne Ludlow, 'More Than Science: Ethical and Socio-legal Concerns in Nanotechnology Regulation in Australia' in Graeme Hodge et al. (eds), *New Global Frontiers in Regulation: The Age of Nanotechnology* (Edward Elgar, 2007) 166, 175. For a perspective on this issue from the United Kingdom, see John Abraham and Julie Sheppard, 'Democracy, Technocracy, and the Secret State of Medicines Control: Expert and Nonexpert Perspectives' (1997) 22(2) *Science, Technology and Human Values* 139.

The Regulatory Challenges and Political Legitimacy in Conflict

I have argued above that the therapeutic goods regulatory regime's directive and unilateral approach to expertise and the significant epistemic limitations of the content of that expertise constitute significant challenges for the achievement of political legitimacy by the regulatory regime. These two broad challenges stem from the dominant influence of scientism and technocracy on the regulatory regime. They are also fundamentally at odds with the constant dialogic approach to political legitimacy.

The constant dialogic approach to political legitimacy argues that legitimacy is established through a constant dialogue between all parties to a power relationship through which a set of shared normative beliefs and values are formulated. As discussed in Chapter 3, at the core of this approach to political legitimacy is its relational nature – that is, legitimacy is developed over the course of a dialogue between those exercising power – in this case the regulatory regime, largely through the TGA – and those that are subject to such regulation. The establishment of the regulatory regime's political legitimacy is therefore dependent on the cultivation of an ongoing relationship with all parties that are subject to its power. Legitimacy relies on the development of a narrative by the regulatory regime about why it deserves to hold and exercise power and a willingness to alter that narrative in response to perpetual discussion with all parties that are subject to that power.

There is, however, a fundamental dissonance between the regulatory regime's directive and unilateral approach to expertise and the constant dialogic approach to political legitimacy. The regulatory regime's all-knowing approach, and its exclusive focus on apparently 'neutral' subject matter, impedes the exchange that is necessary to formulate congruent normative beliefs and values. Compounding this is the regulatory regime's historical propensity to exclude the lay public and other regulatory actors from the ongoing discussion necessary to achieve political legitimacy. Similar conclusions can be reached in relation to the regulatory characteristics of epistemic arrogance and scarcity, which inhibit a genuine exchange of a range of perspectives and diverse disciplinary knowledge. They prohibit 'attitudes conducive of inquiry – those that encourage' both the regulatory regime, and those subject to its power, 'to participate in the give and take of reasons in a landscape of plural and conflicting opinions'.[61]

In some respects, the above conclusions are unsurprising given that they spring from the fundamental influence of scientism and its technocratic

61 Lynch (n 48) 284. Lynch expands on how epistemic arrogance limits the 'ability to engage in reasonable public discourse' by discouraging participation in such discourse; undermining accountability between discourse participants; undermining epistemic trust and the concern for 'objective truth': at 290–5.

manifestations in the therapeutic goods regulatory regime. As has been observed by a number of commentators, the ideologies of scientism and technocracy are antithetical to key liberal democratic principles on which the constant dialogic approach to political legitimacy is based.[62] What is surprising, however, is that despite these broader observations, the regulatory regime has historically failed to adequately identify and address these conflicts and the resulting deficiencies in the regime. The reasons for this are unclear. A pessimistic perspective would suggest that because the regulatory regime has been shaped by scientism and technocracy, it is in the regulatory regime's self-interest to preserve the dominant influence of those ideologies in an attempt to preserve power.[63] However, as the preceding chapters have shown, difficult cases fundamentally challenge the political legitimacy of the therapeutic goods regulatory regime. The regulatory regime will continue to face such cases. It is therefore in the interests of those exercising regulatory power, and those subject to it, to contemplate what changes are necessary to achieve enhanced legitimacy. The next section addresses this concern.

Confronting the Regulatory Paradox: Regulatory Courage and Evolution

In the final part of this chapter I argue for an evolution in the ethos of the therapeutic goods regulatory regime, underpinned by the notion of regulatory 'courage'.[64] I argue that the evolution of the regulatory regime should comprise two broad ideological changes. First, the regulatory regime should embrace a perspective on regulatory knowledge and expertise which elevates normative pluralism. Second, the regulatory regime should adopt the concept of facilitative expertise as an inherent part of its *raison d'être*. These two changes both contribute to the evolution of the approach to, and content of, expertise by the therapeutic goods regulatory regime. They are, therefore, changes directed at the regulatory regime's ideological foundations of scientism and technocracy.

The two recommendations for regulatory change made here can be contrasted with the arguably more pragmatic responses of many commentators to deficits in political legitimacy. For example, Bottoms and Tankebe advocate certain 'mechanisms' to support political legitimacy such as 'lawfulness;

62 See, eg, '[t]he commitment to scientific management makes the technocratic project, sometimes aggressively, anti-political, anti-ideological, and in no small measure also anti-democratic': Esmark (n 16) 503; Olson (n 3) 138, 153–60; Colin Scott, 'Governing Without Law or Governing Without Government? New-Ish Governance and the Legitimacy of the EU' (2009) 15(2) *European Law Journal* 160, 170–1; David Beetham and Christopher Lord, *Legitimacy and the European Union* (Longman, 1998) 3, 16–22.

63 See, eg, David Beetham, *Bureaucracy* (Open University Press, 1996) 99.

64 Perez (n 1).

procedural justice; distributive justice; and effectiveness'.[65] However, this book has consistently advocated that the challenges facing the therapeutic goods regulatory regime are located in its ideological foundations and that such challenges should be, in the first instance, addressed accordingly. This approach reflects arguments of Julia Black on regulatory reform, to which I will return throughout this part.[66] Black advocates that before functional and 'structural solutions' for regulatory regimes can be identified, there is a need to address their 'cognitive' and 'communicative' dimensions. That is, rather than primarily considering 'the institutional context in which regulation occurs', attention should first focus on 'the perceptions of participants ... their rationalities' and 'the communicative interaction between participants' to a regulatory regime.[67] Elsewhere, Black describes the 'problem solving' focus of regulation as 'contingent on what we value' and consequently 'on our knowledge and understanding of the world, and our ideas of how it operates'.[68] The changes advocated in this chapter are accordingly aimed at what Fuchs would describe as the 'discursive' dimension of the therapeutic goods regulatory regime's power, rather than its structural or instrumental dimensions of power.[69] It is, however, acknowledged that such changes will have inevitable implications for these other dimensions of the regulatory regime.

The suggested changes also reflect an aspect of Bottoms's and Tankebe's perspective on dialogic legitimacy. They emphasise the importance of 'power-holders' perspectives' about the legitimacy of their own authority and the relationship between such perspectives and 'a person's identity

65 Justice Tankebe, 'Legitimacy and Regulatory Compliance' in Maria Krambia-Kapardis (ed), *Financial Compliance: Issues, Concerns and Future Directions* (Palgrave Macmillan, 2019) 47, 52. See also, for a discussion of 'procedural', 'structural' and 'consequential' legitimacy, Camilla Pondel, 'Legitimacy in Australia's Financial System External Dispute Resolution Framework: New and Improved or Simply New?' (2019) 42(1) *University of New South Wales Law Journal* 335, 353–72; Donal Casey and Colin Scott, 'The Crystallization of Regulatory Norms' (2011) 38(1) *Journal of Law and Society* 76, 87.

66 Black, 'Regulation as Facilitation' (n 30).

67 Ibid 31. See also at 32, 58–68. See also Julia Black, 'Regulatory Conversations' (2002) 29(1) *Journal of Law and Society* 163, 165. Further, there are similarities here with the notion of 'cultural capture, in which regulators are limited not by a covert bargain, but their own ideas'. Cultural capture is 'especially insidious ... because it hides in plain sight in the assumptions shared more or less unthinkingly by the actors' and 'is the product of the [regulatory] actors themselves': Charles Sabel, Gary Herrigel and Peer Hull Kristensen, 'Regulation under Uncertainty: The Coevolution of Industry and Regulation' (2018) 12 *Regulation & Governance* 371, 388.

68 Julia Black, 'Learning from Regulatory Disasters' (LSE Law, Society and Economy Working Papers 24/2014, London School of Economics and Political Science, Law Department, 2014) 13–4.

69 See Clapp and Fuchs (n 2) 8–10.

as a power-holder'.[70] Black similarly highlights the role of communication between regulatory parties to 'constitute their identities'.[71] Consequently the evolution that is argued for focuses on the ideological identity of the regulatory regime.

Although I will not attempt to set out a comprehensive roadmap for regulatory reform, examples of possible reform will be provided for illustrative purposes. While it is not the focus of this book, such a plan is a logical extension of its conclusions.

Regulatory Courage

It is a significant undertaking to transform the ideological foundations and ethos of the therapeutic goods regulatory regime beyond scientism and technocracy. A starting point from which to do so may be taken from Perez's notion of 'regulatory courage'.[72] As referred to earlier, Perez describes contemporary regulators as 'perplexed' in the face of 'ever-increasing societal demands ... under conditions of extreme epistemic scarcity and deep ideological divide'.[73] Notably, this aptly describes key aspects of the difficult case studies explored here. In contrast, regulatory courage should embolden a regulatory regime to adopt a perseverant and open-minded stance in the face of such 'moral-epistemic challenge[s]',[74] and to do so in the midst of the public controversy, contention and uncertainty associated with difficult cases. Perez argues that regulatory courage enables

> [t]he [regulatory] decisionmaker to cut short the regress associated with deeply introspective reasoning by providing him [sic] with the emotive force and moral resolve needed to make difficult choices in the face of epistemic scarcity and value pluralism; courage thus, reflects the capacity to 'take a stand'. But the idea of courage also requires agents to be able to provide an articulated moral justification for their choices and to take responsibility for their choices.[75]

70 Anthony Bottoms and Justice Tankebe, '"A Voice Within": Power-Holders' Perspectives on Authority and Legitimacy' in Justice Tankebe and Alison Liebling (eds), *Legitimacy and Criminal Justice: An International Exploration* (Oxford University Press, 2013) 60, 61, 68 (emphasis omitted), discussing R Rodney Barker *Legitimating Identities: The Self-Presentation of Rulers and Subjects* (Cambridge University Press, 2001).

71 Black, 'Regulatory Conversations' (n 67) 182. See also at 183–6.

72 Perez (n 1).

73 Ibid 203.

74 Ibid 205.

75 Ibid 212.

Regulatory courage should embolden a regulator – and the regulatory regime as a whole – to 'take action' in controversial circumstances; to draw on 'moral and epistemic convictions', including an 'openness' to those 'of the community'; and to do so unbounded by existing and 'entrenched' regulatory approaches and ideologies.[76] It advocates a 'willingness ... to engage in a collaborative, open-minded discussion, which could advance the understanding of the correct epistemic and moral response to a particular regulatory dilemma'.[77] Regulatory courage therefore addresses and supports the two key recommended changes to be discussed below – that of normative pluralism and facilitative expertise. As will be seen, these two changes draw on the work of Black, Jasanoff and others. For current purposes regulatory courage should be thought of as an ideal ideological basis from which to address the regulatory regime's challenges and on which a new ethos for the regime can be built.

Regulatory Evolution 1 – Normative Pluralism

The first element in the evolution of the ethos of the therapeutic goods regulatory regime should be to embrace normative pluralism – that is, to embrace a diversity of sources, types and traditions of knowledge, values and propositions. One promise of normative pluralism is to counter epistemic arrogance and scarcity. Normative pluralism offers to dispel the inherent assumption that scientific knowledge and expertise is solely capable of supporting the control of therapeutic goods. Further, it offers to narrow the 'gap' between the regulatory regime's task and the inadequate features of the response offered by scientific knowledge alone. As will be evident, a pluralistic approach to the normative sources of expertise endorsed by the regulatory regime is fundamentally consistent with the constant dialogic approach to political legitimacy.

Normative pluralism requires that the regulatory regime recognise when dominant scientific-based norms are operating to the exclusion of other, relevant norms that should be contemplated in order to address the questions it faces. It obliges the regulatory regime to be willing to adopt a greater range of sources of knowledge beyond that of the sciences in seeking to control therapeutic goods. This includes humanities-based disciplines and knowledge offered from the perspectives of the lay public.[78] The regulatory regime will consequently need to embrace the substantive and methodological approaches found in the social sciences, including sociology and ethics.

76 Ibid 213–4.

77 Ibid 214.

78 See, eg, Morag McDermont et al. (eds), *Imagining Regulation Differently: Co-creating for Engagement* (Bristol University Press, 2021).

In this sense, normative pluralism reflects the observations of Jasanoff in relation to scientific advisers: '[t]he most valued expert is one who not only transcends disciplinary boundaries and synthesizes knowledge from several fields but also understands the limits of regulatory science and the policy issues confronting the [regulatory] agency'.[79]

What normative pluralism advocates is, in Black's terms, 'the integration of scientific and non-scientific views' and therefore a replacement of 'the idea of scientific objectivity *versus* lay irrationality' with 'one which recognises different rationalities'.[80] Such an approach ensures that science 'adopt ... this questioning of itself' through the incorporation of a diversity of views in the regulatory space.[81]

In practical terms, normative pluralism may be applied to explicitly expand the legislative basis on which some or all therapeutic goods are considered for supply, such as their social and ethical implications. Normative pluralism may also support a greater diversity of sources of information used in the assessment of the quality, safety and efficacy of therapeutic goods. Further, it could be reflected in a broader scope of disciplines and backgrounds from which the regulatory regime's advisory committees draw their members.[82] The TGA has shown more recently its capacity to do this through the formation and work of apparently patient-focussed working groups in relation to medical devices.[83]

Normative pluralism will require the therapeutic goods regulatory regime to not only embrace a broader range of perspectives beyond that of the sciences, but also to engage in 'courageous' discourse with such perspectives. Perez has suggested that a regulatory regime must approach the 'range of moral, epistemic and policy choices' available to it in a way that is 'elenctically justifiable' – that is, as 'a "search for moral truth "through two-part question-and-answer adversative argument", which is used to expose inconsistencies and points of agreement in the participants' beliefs'.[84] As will be

79 Jasanoff (n 8) 243. In relation to the need for disciplinary depth in expertise, see also Olson (n 3) xvii, 135.

80 Black, 'Regulation as Facilitation' (n 30) 60. See also at 66.

81 Ibid 66–7.

82 See, eg, Jasanoff (n 8) 243–5. These suggestions are consistent with commentary advocating for policy and regulatory schemes to draw on diverse sources of knowledge and to implement supportive procedural and institutional mechanisms: see, eg, Sujatha Raman, 'Science, Uncertainty and the Normative Question of Epistemic Governance in Policymaking' in Emilie Cloatre and Martin Pickersgill (eds), *Knowledge, Technology and Law* (Routledge, 2015) 17.

83 TGA, 'Action Plan for Medical Devices – Progress Report Card: December 2023', *Resources* (Web Page, 23 May 2024) <https://www.tga.gov.au/resources/publication/publications/action-plan-medical-devices-progress-report-card-december-2023>.

84 Perez (n 1) 214, quoting Gregory Vlastos, 'The Socratic Elenchus' (1982) 79 *The Journal of Philosophy* 711, 711–2. See also Joe Mintoff, 'Teaching to the Elenchus' (2015) 15(1) *Teaching Ethics* 97, 99–101.

discussed in the next section, the regulatory regime may play a particular, 'facilitative', role in such an exchange.

It is hoped that through a 'courageous' discourse the regulatory regime can, and can be seen to, endorse an ethos that accepts and articulates that knowledge, and in particular scientific knowledge, is fallible. Such an approach enhances 'the power of sincere and open-minded deliberation to improve ... understanding'.[85] This contrasts with the regulatory regime's current directive approach to expertise, which asserts certainty and therefore discourages dialogue. In contrast, what is sought to be achieved through normative pluralism is an 'epistemic humility' that encompasses the acceptance of the limitations of knowledge and the recognition of mistakes in reasoning and in decision-making.[86] Through the adoption of a regulatory practice that is open to the knowledge, perspectives and experiences of others, epistemic humility may also embrace the notion of empathy.[87] This is particularly relevant in enhancing the future response of the regulatory regime to cases such as UMDs and the experiences of patients in relation to the 'safety' of therapeutic goods.

Further, inherent to the adoption of normative pluralism is the consideration and deliberation of perspectives outside the supposedly neutral or objective technocratic sphere. Eriksen, for example, advocates that regulatory entities should engage with the 'interpretation of political values'.[88] He argues that in order for such normatively informed decisions to be made 'in a responsible way', regulatory experts must embrace value judgments as 'a field of disciplined reasoning'.[89] This requires that, in a case such as RU486, the regulatory regime should explicitly identify and deliberate the relevant social and ethical issues and consider a plurality of normative perspectives.[90] Clough addresses the concern that the resulting introduction of political norms to answer traditionally 'science'- based questions will result in relativism-based regulatory outcomes. She argues instead that

85 Perez (n 1) 214.

86 Sharon Clough, 'Charity, Peace, and the Social Epistemology of Science Controversies' in Natalie Ashton et al. (eds), *Social Epistemology and Relativism* (Oxford University Press, 2020) 122.

87 Ibid 15–9. See also Lynch (n 48) 289; Sheila Jasanoff, 'Technologies of Humility: Citizen Participation in Governing Science' in Sheila Jasanoff (ed), *Science and Public Reason* (Routledge, 2012) 167.

88 Eriksen (n 19) 1, 10.

89 Ibid 3.

90 Ibid 10–2. Eriksen advocates more specifically for the adoption of 'the public reason model' by regulatory entities in engaging with political values, based on the work of John Rawls. While the elements of this model that align with the conclusions advocated here are appealing, it is not necessary for this book to engage in detail with Eriksen's chosen model: at 6–13.

> where relevant and well-supported by evidence, political values ... can increase objectivity, by increasing the empirical adequacy of scientific hypothesis, opening up new avenues for empirical investigation that were previously ignored, and explaining more variation in the data than rival hypotheses.[91]

For example, the initially low number of adverse events in relation to UMDs did not indicate an absence of harm in relation to the devices. A broader perspective on the deeply subjective question of the relationship and dialogue between clinicians and their (female) patients would have instead indicated to the regulatory regime that there was an alternative explanation for the lack of adverse events reported.

It may be argued that by embracing normative pluralism, the therapeutic goods regulatory regime will be at risk of displacing the guidance of scientific knowledge and become subject to the self-interested whims of political actors. That is not what is advocated here. What is instead proposed is a reimagining of the regulatory power of the regime to encompass scientific knowledge *in addition to* a range of other normative perspectives and sources of knowledge. Expertise should be broadened, not devalued. As the discussion in this book has illustrated, this is particularly pertinent to the maintenance of the regulatory regime's political legitimacy when faced with controversial and contested cases.

Regulatory Evolution 2 – Facilitative Expertise

The second shift in the ideological precept of the therapeutic goods regulatory regime is to adopt the notion of facilitative expertise. The fundamental aim of this change is to reconfigure regulatory power obtained through the use of expertise to speak 'to' the public, into power earned through the use of expertise to speak 'with' the public. Consequently, the purpose of the regulatory regime should be a transformative one that *facilitates* identifying, deliberating, interpreting and decision-making about a breadth of normative issues and knowledge relevant to the control of therapeutic goods. This perspective is grounded in the work of Black, who argues for 'regulators to adopt a different role: that of facilitators, of negotiators'.[92]

Black's thesis aligns with the preceding proposal in favour of normative pluralism. Collectively, these arguments for regulatory evolution envisage

91 She illustrates her assertion by explaining the reasons underlying the reluctance of some parents to vaccinate their children in terms of 'political and moral issues of trust', rather than a lack of understanding of scientific evidence: Clough (n 86) 2, 21. Also relevant here is Jasanoff's concept of 'civic epistemologies': Sheila Jasanoff, *Designs on Nature: Science and Democracy in Europe and the United States* (2005) 247–70.

92 Black, 'Regulation as Facilitation' (n 30) 60.

that the regulatory regime for therapeutic goods should bring together experts with backgrounds in the science and humanities, any relevant regulators, members of the lay public and those with other pertinent knowledge. Inherent in the notion of facilitative expertise, therefore, is the rejection of the unilateral approach to expertise criticised in the preceding section. The adoption of facilitative expertise will require the regulatory regime to become adept at determining which knowledge is needed, from which sources and at what point in time. It will also require the regulatory regime to be open to other perspectives about the answers to those questions. For example, commentators have adopted different views as to the appropriate 'balance' between technocratic expertise and more democratic approaches to regulation and, in particular, when and how the views of the lay public should be considered.[93] It is likely that there is no one conclusive answer to such questions. The exercise of facilitative expertise by the regulatory regime will require it to navigate such issues of participation and deliberation on a case-by-case basis and with humility. What is suggested here is, at the very least, a broader and more nuanced approach to where and from whom relevant expertise and experience is sought and how it may be used in relation to the mandate of the regulatory regime.

To enable diverse types and sources of knowledge to engage and deliberate, the therapeutic goods regulatory regime will also, as Black describes more broadly, 'need to take on the role of interpreters: of re-translating the views of different groups and putting them into a language that the others can understand … to facilitate the integration of contending views'.[94] To achieve this, the regulatory regime will need to draw on the vast literature on democratic deliberation and the co-production of public policy and services, a topic that greatly exceeds the constraints of this book.[95] Specific instances in which comparable regulatory regimes have adopted deliberative practices – and their related critiques – may be particularly instructive.[96] Interpreting

93 See, eg, ibid 63, 65; Olson (n 3) 155; Jasanoff (n 8) 234–6; Stehr and Grundmann (n 4) 66–8; Collins and Evans (n 42) 7–8.

94 Black, 'Regulation as Facilitation' (n 30) 60.

95 See, eg, Amy Gutmann and Dennis Thompson, *Why Deliberative Democracy?* (Princeton University Press, 2004); John S Dryzek, *Foundations and Frontiers of Deliberative Governance* (Oxford University Press, 2010); Anna Durnova, Frank Fischer and Philippe Zittoun, 'Discursive Approaches to Public Policy: Politics, Argumentation, and Deliberation' in Guy B Peters and Philippe Zittoun (eds), *Contemporary Approaches to Public Policy: Theories, Controversies and Perspectives* (Palgrave Macmillan, 2016) 35; Taco Brandsen, Bram Verschere and Trui Steen (eds), *Co-Production and Co-Creation: Engaging Citizens in Public Services* (Routledge, 2018). See also Alex Faulkner and Poort Lonneke, 'Stretching and Challenging the Boundaries of Law: Varieties of Knowledge in Biotechnologies Regulation' (2017) 55 *Minerva: A Review of Science, Learning & Policy* 209.

96 See, eg, Michael Gusmano, 'FDA Decisions and Public Deliberation: Challenges and Opportunities' (2013) 73 *Public Administration Review* 115; Syrett (n 25) 527–30; Alex

and integrating diverse perspectives aligns with Jasanoff's 'negotiated model of regulatory science' in which 'negotiation commits scientists, no less than other actors, to moderating their views toward a societal mean'.[97] In doing so, she advocates that the ultimate regulatory focus should be on 'how to harness the collective expertise of the scientific community so as to advance the public interest'. This requires, she argues, the pursuit not of one singular directive 'answer' or 'truth' but instead

> a serviceable truth: a state of knowledge that satisfies tests of scientific acceptability and supports reasoned decisionmaking, but also assures those exposed to risk that their interests have not been sacrificed on the altar of an impossible scientific certainty.[98]

An acknowledgement that there are multiple 'truths' arrived at through facilitation, translation, integration and negotiation will also recognise that such a process may never be ultimately 'finished'. Consistent with the constant dialogic approach to political legitimacy, the regulatory regime will need to maintain ongoing relationships with those contributing to the regulatory mandate in order to revisit and potentially revise positions as new information and new perspectives are illuminated.[99]

There have been some positive indications that the regulatory regime has taken steps to adopt aspects of the facilitative expertise ethos. For example, the TGA has hosted public forums in response to concerns about proposed changes to the regulation of alkyl nitrites.[100] These meetings were held in partnership with non-government organisations and academic institutions.[101] As discussed above, the TGA also conducted a 'Consumer Survey' in 2018 in

---

Faulkner, *Medical Technology into Healthcare and Society: A Sociology of Devices, Innovation and Governance* (Palgrave Macmillan, 2009) 10–12; Barbel Dorbeck-Jung, 'Challenges to the Legitimacy of International Regulation: The Case of Pharmaceuticals Standardisation' in Andreas Follesdal, Ramses Wessel and Jan Wouters (eds), *Multilevel Regulation and the EU: The Interplay between Global, European and National Normative Processes* (Martinus Nijhoff Publishers, 2008) 51, 56–7, 64–6.

97 Jasanoff (n 8) 250.

98 Ibid.

99 See, eg, ibid.

100 Alkyl nitrites are a group of drugs, commonly known as 'poppers', used as a muscle relaxant and to heighten sexual experience. See, eg, TGA, *Testing of Alkyl Nitrite 'Poppers': TGA Laboratory Testing* (Web Page, 6 June 2019) <https://www.tga.gov.au/testing-alkyl-nitrite-poppers>; Staff Writers, 'The TGA Has Decided Not to Ban Poppers', *Star Observer* (online, 7 June 2019) <https://www.starobserver.com.au/news/national-news/the-tga-has-decided-not-to-ban-poppers/183671>; Ange McCormack, 'Should Amyl Be Banned? The TGA Wants You to Have Your Say', *Triple J Hack* (Web Page, 17 September 2018) <https://www.abc.net.au/triplej/programs/hack/should-amyl-be-banned/10256338>.

101 TGA, *Public Meeting Communique: Regulatory Options for Appropriate Access and Safety Controls for Alkyl Nitrites* (Web Page, 7 March 2019) <https://www.tga.gov.au

order to increase the survey participation of community members and consumers.[102] Since 2019 the TGA has included consumers in a broader survey of all stakeholders but has focussed on the recruitment of 'consumers' and 'consumer representatives'.[103] In 2023 these groups constituted around 35% of survey participants,[104] a significant increase on previous surveys. Further, following the controversy associated with UMDs, the TGA implemented 'An Action Plan for Medical Devices'; significantly, this Action Plan states that '[t]he TGA will work closely with consumer groups to develop a range of consumer focussed documents that explain the options' for reform and that the regulator 'will ensure that all perspectives, but particularly of those consumers who use medical devices, are taken into account'.[105]

Conclusion

In this chapter I have set out the two key challenges that explain why the political legitimacy of the therapeutic goods regulatory regime has been undermined in relation to the difficult case studies examined in this book. The first 'meta' challenge for the regulatory regime is its directive and unilateral approach to expertise, driven by the inherently technocratic characteristics of the regime. The second challenge is the fundamental reliance on scientific-based expertise and the epistemological constraints this imposes on the regulatory regime. I propose that these challenges can be met by harnessing the concept of regulatory courage and embracing a new ideological ethos. This regulatory evolution requires the regime to adopt an approach to expertise which is both normatively pluralistic and facilitative in nature. In doing so, it is to be hoped that the regulatory regime will be better able to face difficult and contentious cases in the future.

/public-meeting-communique-regulatory-options-appropriate-access-and-safety-controls-alkyl-nitrites>.

102 See TGA, *TGA Consumer Survey 2018* (2018).

103 'TGA Stakeholder Surveys' (n 34); TGA, *TGA Consumer Survey 2019* (2020).

104 TGA, *TGA Stakeholder Survey Report 2023* (September 2023).

105 Australian Government, *An Action Plan for Medical Devices* (n 45).

Chapter 8

Conclusion

Introduction

This book began with a description of a press conference at the height of the COVID-19 pandemic led by the Prime Minister and Health Minister of Australia along with the then head of the TGA. The COVID-19 pandemic, like the case studies in this book, was a crucial test for the therapeutic goods regulatory regime in Australia and for the regulation of medical products worldwide. Regulators grappled with heightened uncertainty in the face of a new virus and the challenge of meeting an urgent need for safe and effective vaccines and anti-virals. They were frequently pulled into the limelight by political leaders, in a way that had never occurred with such frequency and under such levels of public attention. Press conferences such as the one described arguably enhanced the political legitimacy of regulators like the TGA because they constituted an 'endorsement' of the regulator by other powerholders.[1] This book does not analyse the performance of these regulators during the pandemic, a task addressed elsewhere.[2] It is hoped, however, that the analysis presented here will encourage a perspective on all work of the regulators of medical products, including during a health crisis, to be viewed through the lens of political legitimacy and, in particular, the constant dialogic approach.

This final chapter begins by summarising the findings of this book. I then describe the anticipated expectations, challenges and opportunities for these regulatory regimes in a 'post-pandemic' world with a keen eye to the

1 Richard Martin and Ben Bradford, 'The Anatomy of Police Legitimacy: Dialogue, Power and Procedural Justice' (2021) 25 *Theoretical Criminology* 559.

2 See, eg, Marco Rizzi, Penny Gleeson and Jeannie Marie Paterson, 'Floors and Ceilings: Coordination, Coherence and Consistency in the Relationship between Therapeutic Goods Regulation and Consumer Protection' (2023) 47(2) *Melbourne University Law Review* (forthcoming); Raymond J March, 'The FDA and the COVID-19: A Political Economy Perspective' (2021) 87 *Southern Economic Journal* 1210; Rafael Dal-Re and Odile Launay, 'Public Trust on Regulatory Decisions: The European Medicines Agency and the AstraZeneca COVID-19 Vaccine Label' (2021) 39 *Vaccine* 4029

DOI: 10.4324/9781003293811-8

requirements of political legitimacy. Importantly, in doing so, I set out the lessons[3] from controversial case studies in relation to the Australian therapeutic goods regulatory regime, which are broadly applicable to similar regimes worldwide.

Findings

This book sought to understand what can be learned about the regulation of medical products from the theoretical perspective of political legitimacy. This was achieved through an analysis of the political legitimacy of three case studies involving the Australian therapeutic goods regulatory regime: medicinal cannabis, RU486 and UMDs. In each instance the political legitimacy of the regulatory regime was found to have been challenged because it failed to adopt and act consistently with the constant dialogic approach to legitimacy.

In the case of the regulation of medicinal cannabis, this was highlighted by the therapeutic goods regulatory regime's failure to engage in a constant dialogue with all regulatory parties, in particular those that voiced a perspective contrary to the regulatory status quo. In relation to the abortion drug RU486, deficiencies in political legitimacy were evident in the regulatory regime's failure to engage in a dialogue about the significant social and ethical issues surrounding the drug and different conceptualisations of abortion. This inhibited any potential congruence in relation to the divergent values and beliefs held by the regulatory parties. Finally, failings in political legitimacy regarding the regulation of UMDs were evident in the divergence of values and beliefs held by the regulatory parties about what constituted an acceptable risk of harm associated with the devices, and what should be considered an adverse event arising from their use. Significant failings in the information loop at the centre of the polycentric regulatory arrangements for these devices contributed to the absence of a constant dialogic approach to political legitimacy. Collectively, these shortcomings in the political legitimacy of the regulatory regime pointed to two broad shortcomings facing the regime.

The first is the technocratic-based characteristics of the therapeutic goods regulatory regime manifest in its directive or authoritative approach to expertise. The purported certainty and neutrality of this approach inhibits the regime's recognition that knowledge is fallible and inherently imbued with meaning. This is evident in the case studies regarding medicinal cannabis and RU486 and, in particular, the regulatory regime's failure to engage with alternative and additional issues, values and beliefs. Further, the regulatory

3 See, eg, Julia Black, 'Learning from Regulatory Disasters' (LSE Law, Society and Economy Working Papers 24/2014, London School of Economics and Political Science, Law Department, 2014).

regime's technocratic nature is reflected in its unilateral approach to expertise. This approach fails to consider the knowledge of laypeople and inhibits an effective dialogue with other regulatory actors, as illustrated by the case study of UMDs.

The second shortcoming, the dominant influence of scientism on the therapeutic goods regulatory regime, is demonstrated by its reliance on science as the only source and content of relevant knowledge and expertise. Science-based knowledge is central to the regulatory regime's exercise of power. This creates two epistemic obstacles for the regulatory regime. Epistemic arrogance – the assumption that scientific knowledge is a superior source of knowledge – precludes an engagement with other sources of expertise. This was illustrated in the regulatory regime's failure to adequately consider the experiences and knowledge of patients in relation to the regulation of medicinal cannabis and UMDs. These alternative sources of knowledge, and their respective values and beliefs, formed the basis of a challenge to the political legitimacy of the regulatory regime in each of those cases. A second consequence of the dominance of scientism on the regulatory regime is epistemic scarcity, which is the gap between the broad, normative issues that the regulatory regime should consider relevant, and the comparatively narrow sources of knowledge on which it is required to rely. This was highlighted in the inability of the regulatory regime to engage in dialogue about the social and ethical issues surrounding RU486.

This book constitutes the first significant critical contribution to the literature on the Australian therapeutic goods regulatory regime and the first analysis of the influence of the concepts of scientism and technocracy on the history and operation of the therapeutic goods regulatory regime. Further, it adds to the currently limited literature applying Bottoms's and Tankebe's dialogic approach to political legitimacy beyond the field of criminal justice. I next consider how these contributions might assist regulatory regimes for medical products as they face a 'post-pandemic' environment.

The 'Post-Pandemic' Regulation of Medical Products

Expectations

The COVID-19 pandemic arguably forced the general public to engage with public health to an extent and degree that had not been seen for a significant period. Governments, workplaces, families, individuals and the media were required to grapple with how such a virus could be prevented, controlled and treated. All of this required an engagement with medical products (masks, vaccines, hand sanitisers) and consequently with the regulation of such products. Arguably in a 'post-pandemic' environment, the general public and media will be more aware, informed and vocal about issues affecting individual and public health. Regulatory decisions and actions in relation to medical products will therefore be subject to higher levels of scrutiny than prior to the start of the pandemic. Regulators of medical products will be expected to meet these expectations and to do so in a way that is politically legitimate: that embraces a constant dialogue between all parties and through which a set of shared normative beliefs and values can be formulated.

Further public calls for regulatory change in relation to the selected case studies have continued throughout the writing of this book,[4] and these case studies are not the only examples of difficult issues facing the regulatory regimes for medical products. Disagreement with regulatory approaches adopted by the therapeutic goods regulatory regime have also occurred in relation to stem cell therapies and complementary and alternative medicines.[5] Finally the range of normative issues raised by advanced and anticipated technologies (such as nanotechnology, medical devices employing artificial intelligence, gene therapy, other precision medicines and technological responses to viruses such as COVID-19) suggests that their control will also pose future challenges for this and other regulatory regimes of medical products.[6] Such instances should be interpreted as new opportunities for regulatory regimes to embrace regulatory courage and ideological evolution. They are examples

4 See, eg, Senate Community Affairs References Committee, Parliament of Australia, *Current Barriers to Patient Access to Medicinal Cannabis in Australia* (Report, March 2020); Caroline de Costa, Kirsten I Black and Darren B Russell, 'Medical Abortion: It Is Time to Lift Restrictions' (2019) 210(6) *Medical Journal of Australia* 248.

5 See, eg, Chris Rudge and Megan Munsie, 'The Promise of Stem Cell Treatments: What Are They and How Are They Regulated Down Under?' (2020) 156 *Precedent* 25; Ken Harvey, 'Editorial: Regulation of Complementary Medicines' (2017) 47 *Internal Medicine Journal* 983; Catherine Elizabeth Brophy, 'The Integration of Complementary and Alternative Medicine into Health Care: Regulating for Consumer Choice, Autonomy and Responsibility' (PhD Thesis, The University of Melbourne, 2007) chs 3, 4; Jonathan Breach et al, 'Regulation of Complementary Medicines' (2003) 2(4) *Journal of Complementary Medicine* 44; Karinne Ludlow, 'More Than Science: Ethical and Socio-Legal Concerns in Nanotechnology Regulation in Australia' in Graeme Hodge et al (eds), *New Global Frontiers in Regulation: The Age of Nanotechnology* (Edward Elgar, 2007) 166, 175–6.

6 See, eg, Ludlow (n 5) 175–6; Therapeutic Goods Administration, *Consultation: Regulation of Software, Including Software as a Medical Device (SaMD)* (February 2019) 5–7; Dianne Nicol et al, 'Precision Medicine: Drowning in a Regulatory Soup?' (2016) 3(2) *Journal of Law and the Biosciences* 281, 288–9, 292–3; Glenn Smith, Director, Scientific Evaluation Branch, Therapeutic Goods Administration, 'Regulation, Ethics and Reimbursement of Novel Biological Therapies in Australia – An Update' (Conference Presentation, Association of Regulatory and Clinical Scientists (Australia) Annual Conference, 6 August 2019) (note that despite the acknowledgement of a role for ethics in the title of this presentation, these issues do not appear to have been addressed); Rhema Vaithianathan et al, 'Digital Contact Tracing for COVID-19: A Primer for Policymakers' (Working Paper, Centre for Social Data Analytics, Auckland University of Technology, Institute for Social Science Research, The University of Queensland, 2 June 2020).

of where past 'teachable moments' can be applied by regulatory regimes 'to build more legitimate relationships'.[7]

Challenges and Opportunities

To meet these expectations the Australian therapeutic goods regulatory regime, and arguably regulatory regimes for medical products worldwide, must address the two challenges of technocracy and scientism. What is advocated in response is not, however, an immediate program of legislative or other regulatory reform. While such a program is an inevitable consequence of the changes proposed, it should be preceded by an evolution in the ideological foundations of the regulatory regime.

For example, the changes to the underlying ideology of the therapeutic goods regulatory regime are proposed to together address the two challenges facing the regulatory regime. Normative pluralism should be embraced as a means of expanding the diversity of sources, types and traditions of knowledge and values considered by the regulatory regime. These new forms of expertise should not replace those of science, but rather be integrated with them as a new basis for dialogue. In doing so, the epistemic obstacles facing the regulatory regime will diminish. Further, the regulatory regime should adopt the concept of facilitative expertise, that is, using expertise to speak 'with' the public rather than 'to' it. This will require the regime to become adept at a nuanced and ongoing dialogue with those who possess a range of relevant expertise and experience. These two evolutionary goals – normative pluralism and facilitative expertise – will require significant courage on the part of the Australian regulatory regime, given the substantial foundations and continued influence of scientism and technocracy.[8] They are, however, crucial if Australia's regulatory regime, and those of other countries, is to face future challenges.

There are four main areas of future research which should be pursued to support these ideological changes and ultimate reform. As briefly discussed in Chapter 7, this may include research on the application of principles and practices associated with deliberative democracy and co-production to the objectives and work of the regulatory regime. Second, research on other difficult cases involving the regulatory regime from the perspective of the constant dialogic approach to political legitimacy will test and build on the

7 Anthony Bottoms and Justice Tankebe, '"A Voice Within": Power-Holders' Perspectives on Authority and Legitimacy' in Justice Tankebe and Alison Liebling (eds), *Legitimacy and Criminal Justice: An International Exploration* (Oxford University Press, 2013) 60, 62, 75, quoting Tom Tyler, 'Trust and Legitimacy: Policing in the USA and Europe' (2011) 8 *European Journal of Criminology* 254, 257.

8 Oren Perez, 'Courage, Regulatory Responsibility, and the Challenge of Higher-Order Reflexivity' (2014) 8 *Regulation & Governance* 203.

generalisability of the conclusions reached here. Further insights about the therapeutic goods regulatory regime could also be gained from the application of public health perspectives, which were outside the scope of this book.[9] Finally, the interactions and relationships between regulatory arrangements for medical products in other jurisdictions should continue to be a subject for examination. For example, the influence of the regulatory decisions of other countries on the operation of the therapeutic goods regulatory regime, in particular in relation to medical devices, and the broader impact of regulatory harmonisation should be the subject of further enquiry. This is particularly the case in light of the Federal Court's observations regarding the effect of such arrangements on the regulation of UMDs in Australia.[10]

As stated, the proposed evolution in the ideological basis of the regulatory regimes for medical products should be followed by an agenda for reform. The detail of such a reform program will obviously be different for different jurisdictions. In Australia, for example, such a reform program should begin with work started, but left unfinished, in relation to the regulatory regime. This includes a reconsideration of the recommendations made by the expert panel in 2015 to review the Act and, in particular, its objectives.[11] In addition, the Commonwealth government's 2019 commitment to 'strengthen and improve' the regulation of medical devices should continue to be prioritised.[12] A range of countries should be surveyed to determine if and where more effective mechanisms for the engagement of a broader diversity of perspectives have been successfully adopted.[13]

The regulatory regimes for medical products worldwide play a significant role in providing the public with safe and effective medical products. Despite this ostensibly uncontroversial role, these regulatory regimes continue to be challenged by instances of public contest. It is only by addressing the fundamental ideological basis of these regulatory regimes that failings in their political legitimacy can be addressed, and the resulting opportunities for evolution and change successfully achieved.

9 See, eg, John Coggon, *What Makes Health Public? A Critical Evaluation of Moral, Legal and Political Claims in Public Health* (Cambridge University Press, 2012).

10 See, eg, *Gill v Ethicon Sàrl (No 5)* [2019] FCA 1905, 369–70, 390, 981.

11 Lloyd Sansom, Will Delaat and John Horvath, *Review of Medicines and Medical Device Regulation: Report on the Regulatory Framework for Medicines and Medical Devices* (March 2015) 161–3.

12 Australian Government, *An Action Plan for Medical Devices* (April 2019) 3.

13 See, eg, Theresa Mullin, Pujita Vaidya and Meghan Chalasani, 'Recent US Food and Drug Administration Efforts to Integrate the Patient's Perspective in Drug Development and Decision Making (2019) 105 *Clinical Pharmacology and Therapeutics* 789.

Appendix 1

Chronology of Key Events Relating to Urogynaecological Mesh Devices ('UMDs')[1]

Year	*Event*	*Country*
1996	UMDs approved in USA.	USA
1998	UMDs approved in Australia.	Australia
2006	First UMD adverse event reported to the TGA.	Australia
2006–2012	TGA receives 63 reports of adverse events.[2]	Australia
2008	TGA investigates Australian adverse events with experts. TGA decides to continue to oversee adverse events and new clinical evidence.	Australia
2009	FDA: a literature review shows conflicting reports of success for transvaginal mesh. Additional investigation needed.	USA
2010	TGA conducts post-market review of certain UMDs following report that implanted UMDs difficult to see. Larger review and consultation indicates most mesh marked with colour or other markers.	Australia
2011	FDA advises that adverse events no longer regarded as rare and that patients should be told of limited long-term safety data. Alternatives should be considered.	USA
2012	TGA posts 'Concerns with urogynaecological surgical mesh implants' on Internet. TGA conducts post-market review of UMD research.	Australia
2012	Legal proceedings against Johnson & Johnson and Ethicon filed in Federal Court of Australia.[3]	Australia

1 Unless indicated otherwise, the entries in this table have been summarised from the chronology supplied by the Therapeutic Goods Administration ('TGA') to the Senate Committee Inquiry: Senate Community Affairs References Committee, Parliament of Australia, *Number of Women in Australia Who Have Had Transvaginal Mesh Implants and Related Matters* (Report, March 2018) 153 ('Senate Community Affairs References Committee Report 2018').

2 Department of Health (Cth), Submission No 19 to Senate Community Affairs References Committee, Parliament of Australia, *Number of Women in Australia Who Have Had Transvaginal Mesh Implants and Related Matters* (31 May 2017) 15.

3 *Kathryn Gill v Ethican Sàrl*, NSD 1590/2012; *Gill v Ethicon Sàrl (No 5)* [2019] FCA 1905, 22.

Year	*Event*	*Country*
2012–2014	TGA receives further 32 reports of adverse events.[4]	Australia
2013	The ACSQHC and Department of Health (Cth) establish Urogynaecological Devices Working Group.	Australia
2013	TGA starts larger review of all UMDs.	Australia
2014	Health Canada continues to receive adverse event reports.	Canada
2014	According to UK's Medicines and Healthcare products Regulatory Agency there is no regulatory need to remove UMDs from hospitals.	UK
2014	TGA concludes post-market UMD review and limits UMDs available in Australia.	Australia
2014	Australian Pelvic Mesh Support Group formed.[5]	
2015	European Commission recommends restricting mesh surgery, surgeon certification, and changes to which patients undergo the surgery and their counselling.	EC
2016	FDA changes classification of UMD POP mesh to (higher risk) Class III. Gives manufacturers time to update evidence with FDA.	USA
2016	Meeting between Australian Pelvic Mesh Support Group, Ministerial Advisors and Department of Health (Cth) covers improving adverse event reporting.	Australia
2016	TGA publicly encourages UMD adverse event reporting.	Australia
2016	RANZCOG advises that transvaginal mesh should not be initial treatment for vaginal prolapse.	Australia and NZ
2016	Cochrane Review contrasts mesh with human tissue repair for POP.	International
2016	*The Lancet* publishes Scottish UMD PROSPECT trial. Concludes there is no advantage of mesh over traditional surgery for POP. TGA states it is considering response.	Scotland
2017	The ACSQHC patient / consumer consultations.[6]	Australia
2017	EC changes classification of all mesh to Class III. Australia proposes reclassification to Class III.	Australia and EC
2017	Australian Senate establishes Committee Inquiry into transvaginal mesh devices and their regulation.	Australia
July 2017	Federal Court proceedings for class action against Johnson & Johnson and Ethicon starts.[7]	Australia

4 J Oliver Daly et al, 'The Australasian Pelvic Floor Procedure Registry: Not before Time' (2019) 59 *Australian and New Zealand Journal of Obstetrics and Gynaecology* 473, 474.

5 *Australian Pelvic Mesh Support Group* (Web Page) <https://www.facebook.com/groups/AustralianPelvicMeshSupportGroup/>.

6 Daly (n 4) 474.

7 Melissa Sweet, 'New Report: A Damning Indictment of Health System's Failure to Care for Women' *Croakey* (online, 5 April 2018) <https://croakey.org/new-report-a-damning-indictment-of-health-systems-failure-to-care-for-women/>.

Year	Event	Country
November 2017	TGA announces removal of UMDs for treatment of POP from ARTG (benefits of using UMD did not outweigh the risks).[8]	Australia
January 2018	TGA requires amended information to be provided with UMDs to patients about potential adverse events. Johnson & Johnson withdraws UMDs from market. Seven entries (14 devices) remain on ARTG from other sponsors / manufacturers.[9]	Australia
March 2018	Senate Committee Inquiry tables Report in Parliament.[10]	Australia
October 2018	Australian government responds to Senate Committee Inquiry Report by broadly supporting recommendations, with qualifications.[11] Minister for Health issues apology.	Australia
November 2018	TGA announces that all UMDs to be reclassified from medium-risk, Class IIb device to a high-risk, Class III devices 'due to serious concerns about risks'.[12]	Australia
2019	International Consortium of Investigative Journalists identifies UMDs as one of the medical devices characterised by poor outcomes and unjustified side effects.[13]	International
2019	Australian government releases 'An Action Plan for Medical Devices'.[14]	Australia
2019	Australian government announces funding for establishment of a Pelvic Floor Surgery Clinical Quality Registry.[15]	Australia
November 2019	Single Judge of the Federal Court of Australia decides in favour of litigants in class action against Johnson & Johnson companies.[16]	Australia
April 2020	Ethicon and Johnson & Johnson file appeal of Federal Court judgment.[17]	Australia

8 Ibid.
9 Ibid.
10 Senate Community Affairs References Committee Report 2018 (n 1).
11 Australian Government, *Australian Government Response to the Senate Community Affairs References Committee Report: The Number of Women in Australia Who Have Had Transvaginal Mesh Implants and Related Matters* (October 2018).
12 Therapeutic Goods Administration, *Reclassification of Surgical Mesh Devices* (November 2018).
13 'Implant Files', *International Consortium of Investigative Journalists* (Web Page, 2019) <https://www.icij.org/investigations/implant-files/>.
14 Australian Government, *An Action Plan for Medical Devices* (April 2019).
15 Greg Hunt, '$2.3 Million to Improve Safety of Pelvic Floor Surgery' (Media Release, 5 April 2019) <https://www.health.gov.au/ministers/the-hon-greg-hunt-mp/media/23-million-to-improve-safety-of-pelvic-floor-surgery>.
16 *Gill v Ethicon Sàrl (No 5)* [2019] FCA 1905.
17 Jerome Doraisamy, 'Appeal Lodged in Mesh Class Action Judgment', *Lawyers Weekly* (online, 7 April 2020) <https://www.lawyersweekly.com.au/biglaw/27935-appeal-lodged-in-mesh-class-action-judgment >.

Year	*Event*	*Country*
March 2021	Full Federal Court dismisses Johnson & Johnson appeal and affirms Single Judge's decision.[18] High Court subsequently denies special leave to appeal.[19]	Australia
July 2021	Commonwealth government releases 'Final Report on the Australian Government Response to the Recommendations of the Senate Community Affairs References Committee Report'.[20]	Australia
2024	TGA releases latest 'Progress Report Card' against the *Action Plan for Medical Devices*.[21]	Australia

18 *Ethicon Sàrl v Gill* (2021) 288 FCR 338.

19 Transcript of Proceedings, *Ethicon Sarl v Gill* [2021] HCATrans 187, 630 (Keane J).

20 Australian Government, *Australian Government Response to the Senate Community Affairs References Committee Report: The Number of Women in Australia Who Have Had Transvaginal Mesh Implants and Related Matters* (October 2018).

21 'Action Plan for Medical Devices – Progress Report Card: December 2023', *Therapeutic Goods Administration, Department of Health and Aged Care (Cth)* (Web Page, 23 May 2024) <https://www.tga.gov.au/resources/publication/publications/action-plan-medical-devices-progress-report-card-december-2023>.

Bibliography

A Articles

Abbott, Kenneth W, David Levi-Faur and Duncan Snidal, 'Introducing Regulatory Intermediaries' (2017) 670 *The Annals of the American Academy of Political and Social Science* 6

Abbott, Kenneth W, David Levi-Faur and Duncan Snidal, 'Theorizing Regulatory Intermediaries: The RIT Model' (2017) 670 *Annals of the American Academy of Political and Social Science* 14

Abraham, John and Julie Sheppard, 'Democracy, Technocracy, and the Secret State of Medicines Control: Expert and Nonexpert Perspectives' (1997) 22(2) *Science, Technology and Human Values* 139

Albrecht, Gloria H, 'Contraception and Abortion within Protestant Christianity' in Daniel C Maguire (ed), *Sacred Rights: The Case for Contraception and Abortion in World Religions* (Oxford University Press, 2003) 79

Aslani, Parisa et al, 'Consumer Opinions on Adverse Events Associated with Medical Devices' (2019) 15 *Research in Social and Administrative Pharmacy* 568

Baird, Barbara, 'Abortion and the Limits of the Personal Becoming Political' (2018) 33(95) *Australian Feminist Studies* 129

Baird, Barbara *Abortion Care is Health Care* (Melbourne University Press, 2023)

Baird, Barbara, 'Abortion Politics During the Howard Years: Beyond Liberalisation' (2013) 44(2) *Australian Historical Studies* 245

Baird, Barbara, 'Medical Abortion in Australia: A Short History' (2015) 23(46) *Reproductive Health Matters* 169

Berridge, Virginia, 'Drugs and Social Policy: The Establishment of Drug Control in Britain 1900–30' (1984) 79(4) *Addiction* 17

Black, Julia, 'Constructing and Contesting Legitimacy and Accountability in Polycentric Regulatory Regimes' (2008) 2 *Regulation & Governance* 137

Black, Julia, 'Learning from Regulatory Disasters' (LSE Law, Society and Economy Working Papers 24/2014, London School of Economics and Political Science, Law Department, 2014)

Black, Julia, 'Legitimacy and the Competition for Regulatory Share' (LSE Law, Society and Economy Working Papers 14/2009, London School of Economics and Political Science, Law Department, 2009)

Black, Julia, 'Paradoxes and Failures: "New Governance" Techniques and the Financial Crisis' (2012) 75(6) *The Modern Law Review* 1037

Black, Julia, 'Regulation as Facilitation: Negotiating the Genetic Revolution' in Roger Brownsword, WR Cornish and Margaret Llewelyn (eds), *Law and Human Genetics: Regulating a Revolution* (Hart Publishing, 1998) 29

Black, Julia, 'Regulatory Conversations' (2002) 29(1) *Journal of Law and Society* 163

Blasche, Rowena EC, Anthoney Worsley and Mark Lawrence, 'The Effects of an Apparent Breach of Therapeutic Regulations on Consumers: The Pan Pharmaceuticals Recall' (2008) 18(3) *Critical Public Health* 367

Boam, Ashley and Theresa Mullin, 'FDA Voices: Harmonization – Convergence in the Global Regulatory Village' (2023) *Pharmaceutical Technology* 30

Bodor, Nicola, 'Regulation of the Abortion Drug RU 486: The Collission of Politics, Ethics and Morals in Australia' (2020) 27 *Journal of Law and Medicine* 928

Bottoms, Anthony and Justice Tankebe, 'Beyond Procedural Justice: A Dialogic Approach to Legitimacy in Criminal Justice' (2012) 102(1) *Journal of Criminal Law and Criminology* 119

Breach, Jonathan et al, 'Regulation of Complementary Medicines' (2003) 2(4) *Journal of Complementary Medicine* 44

Broadhead, Lee-Anne and Sean Howard, 'Nanotechnology and the Developing Critique of Scientism' (2010) 74(4) *Science & Society* 553

Buckley, Nick A and Thomas A Faunce, 'Trials and Tribulations in the Removal of Dextropropoxyphene from the Australian Register of Therapeutic Goods' (2013) 199(4) *Medical Journal of Australia* 257

Buckmaster, Luke, 'RU486 for Australia?' (Research Note, Parliamentary Library, Parliament of Australia, 28 November 2005)

Bushra, Alam, Amy Kaler and Zubia Mumtaz, 'Women's Voices and Medical Abortions: A Review of the Literature' (2020) 249 *European Journal of Obstetrics & Gynecology and Reproductive Biology* 21

Campbell, Patricia, 'Making Sense of the Abortion Pill: A Sociotechnical Analysis of RU486 in Canada' (2018) 27(2) *Health Sociology Review* 121

Carney, Terry, 'The History of Australian Drug Laws' (1981) 7 *Monash University Law Review* 165

Carpenter, DP, 'Protection without Capture: Product Approval by a Politically Responsive, Learning Regulator' (2004) 98 *American Political Science Review* 613

Casey, Donal and Colin Scott, 'The Crystallization of Regulatory Norms' (2011) 38(1) *Journal of Law and Society* 76

Chatterji, Aaron K, et al, 'Physician-Industry Cooperation in the Medical Device Industry' (2008) 27(6) *Health Affairs* 1532

Cheng, Katherine, Joanna Harnett and Sharon Davis, 'Conversations About Cannabis: The Supply Process in Australia' (2023) 10 *Advances in Integrative Medicine* 190

Chisolm, Orin and Helen Critchley, 'Future Directions in Regulatory Affairs' (2023) 9 *Frontiers in Medicine* 1

Cica, Natasha, 'Abortion Law in Australia' (Research Paper, Parliamentary Library, Parliament of Australia, 31 August 1998)

Cockburn, W Chas, 'The International Contribution to the Standardization of Biological Substances I. Biological Standards and the League of Nations 1921–1946' (1991) 19(1) *Biologicals* 161

Cordner, Stephen and Kathy Ettershank, 'RU486 in Australia' (1996) 4(1) *Journal of Law and Medicine* 18

Dal-Re, Rafael, and Odile Launay, 'Public Trust on Regulatory Decisions: The European Medicines Agency and the AstraZeneca COVID-19 Vaccine Label' (2021) 39 *Vaccine* 4029

Daly, J Oliver, Susannah Ahern, Robert Herkes and Helen E. O'Connell, 'The Australasian Pelvic Floor Procedure Registry: Not before Time' (2019) 59 *Australian and New Zealand Journal of Obstetrics and Gynaecology* 473

Dawson, Angela J, Rachel Nicolls, Deborah Bateson, Anna Doab, Jane Estoesta, Ann Brassil and Elizabeth A. Sullivan, 'Medical Termination of Pregnancy in General Practice in Australia: A Descriptive-Interpretive Qualitative Study' (2017) 14 *Reproductive Health* 39

de Costa, Caroline, Kirsten I Black and Darren B Russell, 'Medical Abortion: It Is Time to Lift Restrictions' (2019) 210(6) *Medical Journal of Australia* 248

de Costa, Caroline, Heather Douglas, Julie Hamblin, Philippa Ramsay and Mandy Shircore, 'Abortion Law across Australia – A Review of Nine Jurisdictions' (2015) 55 *Australian and New Zealand Journal of Obstetrics and Gynaecology* 105

Dellmuth, Lisa Maria, Jan Aart Scholte and Jonas Tallberg, 'Institutional Sources of Legitimacy for International Organisations: Beyond Procedure Versus Performance' (2019) 45(4) *Review of International Studies* 627

Demortain, David, 'Expertise, Regulatory Science and the Evaluation of Technology and Risk: Introduction to the Special Issue' (2017) 55 *Minerva: A Review of Science, Learning & Policy* 139

Dobson, Olivia, Michaela Barber, Myfanwy Graham, Adrian Carter and Michael Savic, '"The Wild West of Medicine": A Qualitative Investigation of the Factors Influencing Australian Health-Care Practitioners' Delivery of Medicinal Cannabis' (2024) 43 *Drug and Alcohol Review* 1280

Eckstein, Lisa and Dianne Nicol, 'Gene Editing Clinical Trials Could Slip through Australian Regulatory Cracks' (2019) 27 *Journal of Law and Medicine* 274

Eriksen, Andreas, 'Political Values in Independent Agencies' (2021) 15 *Regulation & Governance* 785

Esmark, Anders, 'Maybe It Is Time to Rediscover Technocracy? An Old Framework for a New Analysis of Administrative Reforms in the Governance Era' (2017) 27(3) *Journal of Public Administration Research and Theory* 501

Faulkner, Alex and Poort Lonneke, 'Stretching and Challenging the Boundaries of Law: Varieties of Knowledge in Biotechnologies Regulation' (2017) 55 *Minerva: A Review of Science, Learning & Policy* 209

Ferriera de Oliveira e Silva, Ricardo and Emilio Nabas Figueiredo, 'Current Legislation on Medical Cannabis in the European Union: Historical Background, Movements, Trends, and Counter-Trends Lessons for Brazil' (2023) 6(2) *Brazilian Journal of Pain* 90

Finch, Lynette, 'Soothing Syrups and Teething Powders: Regulating Proprietary Drugs in Australia, 1860–1910' (1999) 43 *Medical History* 74

Finlay, Lorraine, 'The McMullan Principle: Ministerial Advisors & Parliamentary Committees' (2016) 35(1) *The University of Tasmania Law Review* 69

Fleishman, Rishona, 'The Battle against Reproductive Rights: The Impact of the Catholic Church on Abortion Law in Both International and Domestic Areas' (2000) 24 *Emory International Law Review* 277

Flyvbjerg, Bent, 'Five Misunderstandings About Case-Study Research' (2006) 12(2) *Qualitative Inquiry* 219

Freckelton, Ian, 'Children as Voices and Images for Medicinal Cannabis Law Reform' (2021) 39 *Monash Bioethics Review* S4

Freckleton, Ian, 'Medicinal Cannabis Law Reform in Australia' (2016) 23 *Journal of Law and Medicine* 497

Gates, Peter, Stephanie Todd and Jan Copeland, 'Survey of Australian's Knowledge, Perception and Use of Cannabis for Medicinal Purposes' (2017) 5(1) *Journal of Addiction and Prevention* 10

Gibson, Liza, 'WHO Puts Abortifacients on Essential Drug List' (9 July 2005) 331(7508) *British Medical Journal* 68

Gleeson, Kate, 'Bracket Creep in Australian Abortion Indications: When Did Rubella Arrive?' (2007) 15 *Journal of Law and Medicine* 423

Gleeson, Penny, 'The Challenge of Medicinal Cannabis to the Political Legitimacy of Therapeutic Goods Regulation in Australia' (2019) 43(2) *Melbourne University Law Review* 558

Green, Judith, Edward F Fischer and Des Fitzgerald et al, 'The Publics of Public Health: Learning from COVID-19' (2022) 32 *Critical Public Health* 592

Goot, Murray, 'Public Opinion, Privatisation and the Electoral Politics of Telstra' (1999) 45(2) *Australian Journal of Politics and History* 214

Gostin, Lawrence O, Eric A Friedman and Sarah A Wetter, 'Responding to Covid-19: How to Navigate a Public Health Emergency Legally and Ethically' (2020) 50(2) *Hastings Center Report* 8

Grabosky, Peter, 'Beyond Responsive Regulation: The Expanding Role of Non-State Actors in the Regulatory Process' (2013) 7 *Regulation & Governance* 114

Graham, Myfanwy, Vivian Chiu, Daniel Stjepanovic and Wayne Hall, 'A Provisional Evaluation of Australia's Medical Cannabis Program' (2023) 122 *International Journal of Drug Policy* 1

Graves, Stephen E and Guy J Maddern, 'Device Regulation: What Next? Time to Improve Transparency and Communication to the Public' (2012) 196(4) *Medical Journal of Australia* 222

Greenwood, Stephen, 'Faulty Generics: A Ministerial Ticking Time Bomb' (2014) 95 (1127) *Australian Journal of Pharmacy* 40

Grunwald, Fabian and Tom Stargardt, 'Harmonizing Regulatory Market Approval of Products with High Safety Requirements: Evidence from the European Pharmaceutical Market' (2024) *Health Economics* 1

Gusmano, Michael, 'FDA Decisions and Public Deliberation: Challenges and Opportunities' (2013) 73 *Public Administration Review* 115

Hallinan, Christine Mary, and Yvonne Ann Bonomo, 'The Rise and Rise of Medicinal Cannabis, What Now? Medicinal Cannabis Prescribing in Australia 2017–2022' (2022) 19 *International Journal of Environmental Research and Public Health* 1

Hamm, Joseph A, Scott E Wolfe, Caitlin Cavanah and Sung Lee, '(Re)Organizing Legitimacy Theory' (2022) 27 *Legal and Criminological Psychology* 129

Haridy, Rich, 'Australia to Prescribe MDMA and Psyilocybin for PTSD and Depression in World First' (2023) 619 *Nature* 227

Harvey, Ken, 'Editorial: Regulation of Complementary Medicines' (2017) 47 *Internal Medicine Journal* 983

Harvey, Ken, 'Transparency and the Therapeutic Goods Administration' (2013) 36(4) *Australian Prescriber* 110

Hathaway, Andrew D and Kate Rossiter, 'Medical Marijuana, Community Building, and Canada's Compassionate Societies' (2007) 10(3) *Contemporary Justice Review* 283

Hauray, Boris, 'From Regulatory Knowledge to Regulatory Decisions: The European Evaluation of Medicines' (2017) 55 *Minerva: A Review of Science, Learning & Policy* 187

Herring, E Pendleton, 'The Balance of Social Forces in the Administration of the Pure Food and Drug Act' (1935) 13 *Social Forces* 358

Hinsch, Wilfried, 'Justice, Legitimacy, and Constitutional Rights' (2010) 13(1) *Critical Review of International Social and Political Philosophy* 39

Homel, Peter and Rick Brown, 'Marijuana Legalisation in the United States: An Australian Perspective' (2017) (535) *Trends & Issues in Crime & Criminal Justice* 1

Howe, Joanne and Suzanne Le Mire, 'Medical Referral for Abortion and Freedom of Conscience in Australian Law' (2019) 34(1) *Journal of Law and Religion* 85

Hutchison, Katrina, 'Gender Bias in Medical Implant Design and Use: A Type of Moral Aggregation Problem?' (2019) 34(3) *Hypatia: A Journal of Feminist Philosophy* 570

Jacobs, Sharon B, 'Crises, Congress, and Cognitive Biases: A Critical Examination of Food and Drug Legislation in the United States' (2009) 64 *Food and Drug Law Journal* 599

Jasanoff, Sheila, 'In the Democracies of DNA: Ontological Uncertainty and Political Order in Three States' (2005) 24(2) *New Genetics and Society* 139

Jonathan-Zamir, Tal and Amikam Harpaz, 'Police Understanding of the Foundations of Their Legitimacy in the Eyes of the Public: The Case of Commanding Officers in the Israel National Police' (2014) 54(3) *British Journal of Criminology* 469

Kent, Julie, 'Lay Experts and the Politics of Breast Implants' (2003) 12 *Public Understanding of Science* 403

Keogh, Louise A, Lyle C Gurrin and Patricia Moore, 'Estimating the Abortion Rate in Australia from National Hospital Morbidity and Pharmaceutical Benefits Scheme Data' (2021) 215 *Medical Journal of Australia* 375

Keogh, Louise A, D Newton, C Bayly, K McNamee, A Hardiman, A Webster and M Bismark, 'Intended and Unintended Consequences of Abortion Law Reform: Perspectives of Abortion Experts in Victoria, Australia' (2016) 43 *Journal of Family Planning and Reproductive Health Care* 18

Kilgore, Christine, 'FDA Panel Tackles Mesh for Anterior Repair of POP' (2019) 54(3) *Obstetrics & Gynaecology News* 6

Kim, James H and Anthony R. Scialli, 'Thalidomide: The Tragedy of Birth Defects and the Effective Treatment of Disease' (2011) 122(1) *Toxicological Sciences* 1

Kim, Sooyoung, Ariadna Capasso and Shahmir H Ali et al, 'What Predicts People's Belief in COVID-19 Misinformation? A Retrospective Study Using a Nationwide Online Survey Among Adults Residing in the United States' (2022) 22 *BMC Public Health* 2114

King, Jenny, 'Transvaginal Mesh for Incontinence and Pelvic Organ Prolapse: Where Are We Now and How Did We Get Here?' (2024) 53 *Australian Journal of General Practice* 23, 23

Lamkin, Matt, 'Prescription Psychedelics: The Road from FDA Approval to Clinical Practice' (2022) 135 *The American Journal of Medicine* 15

Lancaster, Kari, Kate Seear and Alison Ritter, 'Making Medicine; Producing Pleasure: A Critical Examination of Medicinal Cannabis Policy and Law in Victoria, Australia' (2017) 49 *International Journal of Drug Policy* 117

Lausberg, Adele, 'Women and Representation: Cross-Party Collaboration in the Australian Federal Parliament' (2016) 69(2) *Parliamentary Affairs* 249

Leiter, Valerie and Shelley K White, 'Enmeshed in Controversy: Claims About the Risks of Vaginal Mesh Devices' (2015) 17 *Health, Risk & Society* 64

Linn, Alanna, 'Raw Milk Is Always Risky: Stabilising the Danger of Raw Milk in Australia Food Safety Regulation' (2019) 21 *Journal of Health, Risk & Society* 304

Lintzeris, Nicholas, et al, 'Medicinal Cannabis in Australia, 2016: The Cannabis as Medicine Survey (Cams-16)' (2018) 209(5) *The Medical Journal of Australia* 211

London, Jillian, 'Tragedy, Transformation, and Triumph: Comparing the Factors and Forces That Led to the Adoption of the 1860 Adulteration Act in England and the 1906 Pure Food and Drug Act in the United States' (2014) 69 *Food and Drug Law Journal* 315

Lowrey-Kinberg, Belén V and Grace Sullivan Buker, '"I'm Giving You a Lawful Order": Dialogic Legitimacy in Sandra Bland's Traffic Stop' (2017) 51(2) *Law & Society Review* 379

Lynch, Michael Patrick, 'Arrogrance, Truth and Public Discourse' (2018) 15(3) *Episteme* 283

MacDonald, Margaret E, 'Misoprostol: The Social Life of a Life-Saving Drug in Global Maternal Health' (2021) 46 *Science, Technology and Human Values* 376

Maggetti, Martino, 'Legitimacy and Accountability of Independent Regulatory Agencies: A Critical Review' (2010) 2 *Living Reviews in Democracy* 1

Maggetti, Martino, Christian Ewert and Philipp Trein, 'Not Quite the Same: Regulatory Intermediaries in the Governance of Pharmaceuticals and Medical Devices' (2017) 670 *The Annals of the American Academy of Political and Social Science* 152

Maher, Christopher, 'The Way Forward after the Transvaginal Mesh Decade' (2018) 20 *The Obstetrician & Gynaecologist* 7

Maher, Christopher and Nir Haya, 'The Transvaginal Mesh Decade' (2013) 8(5) *Expert Review of Obstetrics & Gynecology* 485

March, Raymond J, 'The FDA and the COVID-19: A Political Economy Perspective' (2021) 87 *Southern Economic Journal* 1210

Martin, Jennifer H, Wayne Hall and Mary-Ann Fitzcharles et al, 'Ensuring Access to Safe, Effective, and Affordable Cannabis Based Medicines' (2020) 86 *British Journal of Clinical Pharmacology* 630

Martin, Richard and Ben Bradford, 'The Anatomy of Police Legitimacy: Dialogue, Power and Procedural Justice' (2021) 25 *Theoretical Criminology* 559

McEwen, John, 'Australian Drug Evaluation Committee (ADEC) 40th Anniversary' (2004) 18(4) *International Journal of Pharmaceutical Medicine* 225

McGee, Richard, Angela C Webster, Thomas E Rogerson and Jonathan C Craig, 'Medical Device Regulation in Australia: Safe and Effective?' (2012) 196(4) *Medical Journal of Australia* 256

McGuire, Amy L, Holly Fernandez Lynch and Lewis A Grossman et al, 'Pressing Regulatory Challenges for Psychedelic Medicine' (2023) 380 *Science* 347

Mintoff, Joe, 'Teaching to the Elenchus' (2015) 15(1) *Teaching Ethics* 97

Morgan, Jenny, 'Abortion Law Reform: The Importance of Democratic Change' (2012) 35(1) *UNSW Law Journal* 142

Morrison, Tiffany H, 'Evolving Polycentric Governance of the Great Barrier Reef' (2017) 114(15) *Proceedings of the National Academy of Sciences of the United States of America* E3013

Morrison, Tiffany H, et al, 'Mitigation and Adaptation in Polycentric Systems: Sources of Power in the Pursuit of Collective Goals' (2017) 8(5) *WIREs Climate Change* 3

Motamedi, Mina, Chris Degeling and Stacy M Carter, 'Patients' Perspectives on Quality and Patient Safety Failures: Lessons Learned from an Inquiry Into Transvaginal Mesh in Australia' (2024) 24 *BMC Health Services Research* 436

Motamedi, Mina, Stacy M Carter and Chris Degeling, 'Transvaginal Mesh in Australia: An Analysis of News Media Reporting from 1996 to 2021' (2023) 26 *Health Expectations* 1189

Motamedi, Mina, Stacy M Carter and Chris Degeling, 'Women's Experiences of and Perspectives on Transvaginal Mesh Surgery for Stress Urine Incontinency and Pelvic Organ Prolapse: A Qualitative Systematic Review' (2022) 15 *The Patient* 157

Mowat, Alexandra E and Christopher Maher, 'Transvaginal Mesh: Let's Not Repeat the Mistakes of the Past' (2017) 57 *Australian and New Zealand Journal of Obstetrics and Gynaecology* 108

Mullin, Theresa, Pujita Vaidya and Meghan Chalasani, 'Recent US Food and Drug Administration Efforts to Integrate the Patient's Perspective in Drug Development and Decision Making' (2019) 105 *Clinical Pharmacology and Therapeutics* 789

Newton, Danielle, et al, '"...A One Stop Shop in Their Own Community": Medical Abortion and the Role of General Practice' (2016) 56 *Australian and New Zealand Journal of Obstetrics and Gynaecology* 648

Newton, Danielle, Chris Bayly, Kathleen McNamee, Marie Bismark, Annarella Hardiman, Amy Webster and Louise Keogh, 'How Do Women Seeking Abortion Choose between Surgical and Medical Abortion? Perspectives from Abortion Service Providers' (2016) 56 *Australian and New Zealand Journal of Obstetrics and Gynaecology* 523

Ngum, Nancy, Margareth Ndomondo-Sigonda and Stuart Walker et al 'Regional Regulatory Harmonisation Initiatives: Their Potential Contribution to the Newly Established African Medicines Agency' (2023) 145 *Regulatory Toxicology and Pharmacology* 1

Nicol, Dianne, et al, 'Precision Medicine: Drowning in a Regulatory Soup?' (2016) 3(2) *Journal of Law and the Biosciences* 281

O'Connor, Teresa, 'Surgical Mesh Complications: A Study in Pain, Loss and Isolation' (2019) 25(7) *Kai Tiaki: Nursing New Zealand* 14

O'Kane, Rosemary, 'Against Legitimacy' (1993) XLI *Political Studies* 471

O'Rourke, Anne, Suzanne Belton and Ea Mulligan, 'Medical Abortion in Australia: What Are the Clinical and Legal Risks? Is Medical Abortion Over-Regulated?' (2016) 24 *Journal of Law and Medicine* 221

Ostrom, Elinor, 'Beyond Markets and States: Polycentric Governance of Complex Economic Systems' (2010) 100 *American Economic Review* 641

Oxlad, Melissa, Georgina Edwards and Kate A McKinlay, 'Patients' Perspectives about Doctor-Patient Communication Regarding Transvaginal Mesh Implant Surgery' (2022) 105 *Patient Education and Counseling* 3534

Parker, Christine, Rachel Carey, Josephine De Costa and Gyorgy Scrinis, 'Can the Hidden Hand of the Market Be an Effective and Legitimate Regulator? The Case of Animal Welfare under a Labeling for Consumer Choice Policy Approach' (2017) 11 *Regulation & Governance* 368

Parker, Christine and Fiona Haines, 'An Ecological Approach to Regulatory Studies?' 45(1) *Journal of Law and Society* 136

Parker, Christine, Fiona Haines and Laura Boehm, 'The Promise of Ecological Regulation: The Case of Intensive Meat' (2018) 59 *Jurimetrics* 15

Paterson, John, 'Trans-Science, Trans-Law and Proceduralization' (2003) 12(4) *Social & Legal Studies* 525

Perez, Oren, 'Courage, Regulatory Responsibility, and the Challenge of Higher-Order Reflexivity' (2014) 2014(8) *Regulation & Governance* 203

Pondel, Camilla, 'Legitimacy in Australia's Financial System External Dispute Resolution Framework: New and Improved or Simply New?' (2019) 42(1) *University of New South Wales Law Journal* 335

Pringle, Helen, 'The Greatest Heights of Parliament? Conscience Votes and the Quality of Parliamentary Debate' (2008) 23(1) *Australasian Parliamentary Review* 195

Rankin, Mark J, 'Contemporary Australian Abortion Law: The Description of a Crime and the Negation of a Woman's Right to Abortion' (2001) 27 *Monash University Law Review* 229

Rankin, Mark J, 'The Disappearing Crime of Abortion and the Recognition of a Woman's Right to Abortion: Discerning a Trend in Australian Abortion Law?' (2011) 13(2) *Flinders Law Journal* 1

Rizzi, Marco, Penny Gleeson and Jeannie Marie Paterson, 'Floors and Ceilings: Coordination, Coherence and Consistency in the Relationship Between Therapeutic Goods Regulation and Consumer Protection' (2023) 47(2) *Melbourne University Law Review* (forthcoming)

Rodrígez García, José María, 'Scientia Potestas Est – Knowledge Is Power: Francis Bacon to Michel Foucault' (2001) 28(1) *Neohelicon* 109

Roberts, Darren M and Alexandra Bennett, 'COVID-19 and the Quality Use of Medicines: Evidence, Risks and Fads' (2020) 43 *Australian Prescriber* 78

Roe, Michael, 'The Establishment of the Australian Department of Health: Its Background and Significance' (1976) 17(67) *Australian Historical Studies* 176

Ross, Kerry, Susan Dodds and Rachel A Ankeny, 'A Matter of Conscience? The Democratic Significance of "Conscience Votes" in Legislating Bioethics in Australia' (2009) 44(2) *Australian Journal of Social Issues* 121

Rudge, Christoper, Sara Attinger and Ian Kerridge et al, 'A New Priority Pathway for Biologicals in Australia: Contextualising and Evaluating the Proposed Reforms' (2022) 29 *Journal of Law and Medicine* 67

Rudge, Chris and Megan Munsie, 'The Promise of Stem Cell Treatments: What Are They and How Are They Regulated Down Under?' (2020) 156 *Precedent* 25

Ruether, Rosemary Radford, 'Women, Reproductive Rights and the Catholic Church' (2008) 16(2) *Feminist Theology* 184

Sabel, Charles, Gary Herrigel and Peer Hull Kristensen, 'Regulation under Uncertainty: The Coevolution of Industry and Regulation' (2018) 12 *Regulation & Governance* 371

Salter, Alexander William and Vlad Tarko, 'Governing the Banking System: An Assessment of Resilience Based on Elinor Ostrom's Design Principles' (2019) 15 *Journal of Institutional Economics* 505

Savell, Kristin, 'Life and Death Before Birth: 4D Ultrasound and the Shifting Frontiers of the Abortion Debate' (2007) 15 *Journal of Law and Medicine* 103

Sawer, Marian, 'What Makes the Substantive Representation of Women Possible in a Wesminster Parliament? The Story of RU486 in Australia' (2012) 33(3) *International Political Science Review* 320

Scott, Colin, 'Analysing Regulatory Space: Fragmented Resources and Institutional Design' (2001) (Summer) *Public Law* 283

Scott, Colin, 'Governing Without Law or Governing Without Government? New-Ish Governance and the Legitimacy of the EU' (2009) 15(2) *European Law Journal* 160

Shahvisi, Arianne, 'Medicine Is Patriarchal, but Alternative Medicine Is Not the Answer' (2019) 16 *Journal of Bioethical Inquiry* 113

Sharkey, Catherine M, 'The Opiod Litigation: The FDA is MIA' (2020) 124 *Dickinson Law Review* 669

Shirlow, Esme and Thomas Faunce, 'Recent Legal Developments and the Authority of the Australian Therapeutic Goods Administration' (2009) 16 *Journal of Law and Medicine* 764

Siegel, Harvey and John Biro, 'Epistemic Normativity, Argumentation, and Fallacies' (1997) 11 *Argumentation* 277

Skerritt, John, 'Medical Device Regulation – A Challenging and Changing Area' (2017) 21 *Health Voices: Journal of the Consumers Health Forum of Australia* <https://healthvoices.org.au/issues/november-2017/medical-device-regulation-challenging-changing-area/>

Stokes, Melvyn, 'American Progressives and the European Left' (1983) 17(1) *Journal of American Studies* 5

Suchman, Mark C, 'Managing Legitimacy: Strategic and Institutional Approaches' (1995) 30(3) *The Academy of Management Review* 571

Symons, Julia and Marco Rizzi, 'Consumers or Patients? Medical Device Recipients Under Australian Law Straddle Two Worlds (2023) 30 *Journal of Law and Medicine* 572

Syrett, Keith, 'Courts, Expertise and Resource Allocation: Is There a Judicial "Legitimacy Problem"' (2014) 7(2) *Public Health Ethics* 112

Syrett, Keith, 'Legitimating "Fourth Hurdle" Pharmaceutical Regulation in Europe: Learning the NICE Way?' (2003) 9(4) *European Public Law* 509

Terakawa, N, I Shimizu, O Tanizawa and K Matsumoto, 'RU486, a Progestin Antagonist, Binds to Progesterone Receptors in a Human Endometrial Cancer Cell Line and Reverses the Growth Inhibition by Progestins' (1988) 31(2) *Journal of Steroid Biochemistry* 161

Teixeira, Tania, Sandra L Kweder and Agnes Saint-Raymond 'Are the European Medicines Agency, US Food and Drug Administration, and Other International Regulators Talking to Each Other? (2020) 107 *Clinical Pharmacology & Therapeutics* 507

Thatcher, Mark and Alec Stone Sweet, 'Theory and Practice of Delegation to Non-Majoritarian Institutions' (2002) 25(1) *West European Politics* 1

Thompson, Chloe and Thomas Faunce, 'Australian Senate Committee Report on Transvaginal Mesh Devices' (2018) 25 *Journal of Law and Medicine* 934

Thornhill, Chris, 'Political Legitimacy: A Theoretical Approach between Facts and Norms' (2011) 18(2) *Constellations: An International Journal of Critical and Democratic Theory* 135

Tyler, Tom, 'Trust and Legitimacy: Policing in the USA and Europe' (2011) 8 *European Journal of Criminology* 254

Vadasz, Danny, 'Trans Vaginal Mesh Injuries – Is Anyone Accountable?' (2017) (21) *Health Voices: Journal of the Consumers Health Forum of Australia* <https://healthvoices.org.au/issues/november-2017/trans-vaginal-mesh-injuries-anyone-accountable/>

Vaithianathan, Rhema, M Ryan, N Anchugina, L Selvey, T Dare and A Brown, 'Digital Contact Tracing for COVID-19: A Primer for Policymakers' (Working Paper, Centre for Social Data Analytics, Auckland University of Technology, Institute for Social Science Research, The University of Queensland, 2 June 2020)

Veit, Markus, 'Quality Requirements for Medicinal Cannabis and Respective Products in the European Union – Status Quo' (2023) 89 *Planta Medica* 808

Villarreal, Pedro A, 'Pandemic Declarations of the World Health Organization as an Exercise of International Public Authority: The Possible Legal Answers to Frictions between Legitimacies' (2016) 7(1) *Goettingen Journal of International Law* 95

Waldby, Catherine, 'Autologous Stem Cell-Based Interventions in Australia: Exploring Patient Experience in Light of Regulatory Exceptionalism' (2019) 21(5) *Cytotherapy* S22

Warhurst, John, 'Conscience Voting in the Australian Federal Parliament' (2008) 54 *Australian Journal of Politics and History* 579

Weir, Michael, Brenda Marshall and John Wardle, 'Regulation of Complementary and Alternative Medicine: Interplay of Therapeutic Goods Legislation and Consumer Law' (2013) 25(1) *Bond Law Review* 13

Wheelwright, Karen, 'Commonwealth and State Powers in Health a Constitutional Diagnosis' (1995) 21(1) *Monash University Law Review* 53

White, Shelley K and Abigail N Walters, 'Assessing Risk by Analogy: A Case Study of US Medical Device Risk Management Policy' (2018) 20 *Health, Risk & Society* 358

Wiersma, Miriam, Ian Kerridge and Wendy Lipworth, 'Transvaginal Mesh, Gender and the Ethics of Clinical Innovation' (2020) 40 *Internal Medicine Journal* 523

Wright, Anthony, 'A Century of Fabianism 1884–1984' (1984) 34(5) *History Today* 50

Zarhin, Darna, et al, '"Medical Cannabis" as a Contested Medicine: Fighting over Epistemology and Morality' (2019) 45(3) *Science, Technology & Human Values* 488

Zettler, Patricia J, Margaret Foster Riley and Aaron S Kesselheim, 'Implementing a Public Health Perspective in FDA Drug Regulation' (2018) 73 *Food and Drug Law Journal* 221

B Books and Book Chapters

Abbott, Frederick M. and Graham Dukes, *Global Pharmaceutical Policy: Ensuring Medicines for Tomorrow's World* (Edward Elgar, 2009)

Abraham, John and Graham Lewis, *Regulating Medicines in Europe* (2000, Routledge)

Adolf, Marian and Nico Stehr, *Knowledge: Is Knowledge Power?* (Routledge, 2017)

Baldwin, Robert, Martin Cave and Martin Lodge, *Understanding Regulation: Theory, Strategy, and Practice* (Oxford University Press, 2011)

Barker, Rodney, *Political Legitimacy and the State* (Clarendon Press, 1990)

Barnard, Frederick, *Democratic Legitimacy: Plural Values and Political Power* (McGill-Queens University Press, 2001)

Beck, Ulrich, *Risk Society: Towards a New Modernity* (Sage, 1992)

Beetham, David, *Bureaucracy* (Open University Press, 1996)

Beetham, David, 'Revisiting Legitimacy, Twenty Years On' in Justice Tankebe and Alison Liebling (eds), *Legitimacy and Criminal Justice: An International Exploration* (Oxford University Press, 2013) 19

Beetham, David, *The Legitimation of Power* (Palgrave Macmillan, 1991)

Beetham, David, *The Legitimation of Power* (MacMillan Education, 2nd ed, 2013)

Beetham, David and Christopher Lord, *Legitimacy and the European Union* (Longman, 1998)

Boisson de Chazournes, Laurence, 'New Technologies, the Precautionary Principle, and Public Participation' in Therese Murphy (ed), *New Technologies and Human Rights* (Oxford University Press, 2009) 161

Bonython, Wendy Elizabeth and Bruce Baer Arnold, 'Transitioning Up to Best Practice, or Down to the Bare Minimum? Global Harmonisation of Regulation of Therapeutic Goods' in Umair Ghori, Mary Hiscock, Louise Parsons et al (eds) *Globalisation in Transition: Human and Economic Perspectives* (2023, Springer) 45

Booth, Martin, *Cannabis: A History* (Doubleday, 2003)

Bottoms, Anthony and Justice Tankebe, '"A Voice Within": Power-Holders' Perspectives on Authority and Legitimacy' in Justice Tankebe and Alison Liebling (eds), *Legitimacy and Criminal Justice: An International Exploration* (Oxford University Press, 2013) 60

Bottoms, Anthony and Justice Tankebe, 'Police Legitimacy and the Authority of the State' in Antje du Bois-Pedain, Magnus Ulvang and Petter Asp (eds), *Criminal Law and the Authority of the State* (Hart Publishing, 2017) 47

Bottoms, Anthony and Justice Tankebe, 'Procedural Justice, Legitimacy and Social Contexts' in Denise Meyerson, Catriona Mackenzie and Therese MacDermott (eds) *Procedural Justice and Relational Theory: Empirical, Philosophical, and Legal Perspectives* (Routledge, 2020) 85

Brand, Arie, *The Force of Reason: An Introduction to Habermas' Theory of Communicative Action* (Allen & Unwin, 1990)

Brandsen, Taco, Bram Verschere and Trui Steen (eds), *Co-Production and Co-Creation: Engaging Citizens in Public Services* (Routledge, 2018)
Brownlee, Kimberley, 'The Offender's Part in the Dialogue' in Rowan Cruft, Matthew H Kramer and Mark R. Reiff (eds), *Crime, Punishment, & Responsibility: The Jurisprudence of Antony Duff* (Oxford University Press, 2011) 54
Brunsson, Nils and Bengt Jacobsson, *A World of Standards* (Oxford University Press, 2002)
Bucchi, Massimiano, *Beyond Technocracy: Science, Politics and Citizens* (Springer, 2009)
Busch, Lawrence, *Standards: Recipes for Reality* (MIT Press, 2011)
Cane, Peter, Leighton McDonald and Kristen Rundle, *Principles of Administrative Law* (Oxford University Press, 2nd ed, 2018)
Carpenter, Daniel P, *Reputation and Power: Organizational Image and Pharmaceutical Regulation at the FDA* (Princeton University Press, 2010)
Caulkins, Jonathan P, Beau Kilmer and Mark AR Kleiman, *Marijuana Legalization: What Everyone Needs to Know* (Oxford University Press, 2016)
Charo, R Alta, 'A Political History of RU-486' in Kathi E Hanna (ed), *Biomedical Politics: Institute of Medicine (US) Committee to Study Decision Making* (National Academies Press, 1991) 43
Clapp, Jennifer and Doris Fuchs, 'Agrifood Corporations, Global Governance, and Sustainability' in Jennifer Clapp and Doris Fuchs (eds), *Corporate Power in Global Agrifood Governance* (MIT Press, 2009) 1
Clough, Sharon, 'Charity, Peace, and the Social Epistemology of Science Controversies' in Natalie Ashton et al (eds), *Social Epistemology and Relativism* (Oxford University Press, 2020) 122
Coggon, John, *What Makes Health Public? A Critical Evaluation of Moral, Legal and Political Claims in Public Health* (Cambridge University Press, 2012)
Coicaud, Jean-Marc, *Legitimacy and Politics: A Contribution to the Study of Political Right and Political Responsibility*, tr David Ames (Cambridge University Press, 2002)
Collins, Harry and Robert Evans, *Rethinking Expertise* (The University of Chicago Press, 2007)
D'Aprano, Zelda, *Zelda* (Spinifex, 1995)
Davis, Courtney and John Abraham, *Unhealthy Pharmaceutical Regulation: Innovation, Politics and Promissory Science* (Palgrave Macmillan, 2013)
de Costa, Caroline, *RU-486: The Abortion Pill* (Boolarong Press, 2007)
de Ridder, Jeroen, *Rik Peels and Rene van Woudenberg, Scientism: Prospects and Problems* (Oxford University Press, 2018)
Demortain, David, *Scientists and the Regulation of Risk: Standardising Control* (Edward Elgar Publishing, 2011)
Diprose, Rosalyn, 'The Political Technology of RU486: Time for the Body and Democracy' in Bruce Braun and Sarah J Whatmore (eds), *Political Matter: Technoscience, Democracy, and Public Life* (University of Minnesota Press, 2010) 211
Dorbeck-Jung, Barbel, 'Challenges to the Legitimacy of International Regulation: The Case of Pharmaceuticals Standardisation' in Andreas Follesdal, Ramses Wessel and Jan Wouters (eds), *Multilevel Regulation and the EU: The Interplay*

between Global, European and National Normative Processes (Martinus Nijhoff Publishers, 2008) 51
Dryzek, John S, *Foundations and Frontiers of Deliberative Governance* (Oxford University Press, 2010)
Duffin, Jacalyn, *To See with a Better Eye: A Life of RTH Laennec* (Princeton University Press, 1998)
Dukes, Graham, *The Law and Ethics of the Pharmaceutical Industry* (Elsevier BV, 2006)
Durnova, Anna, Frank Fischer and Philippe Zittoun, 'Discursive Approaches to Public Policy: Politics, Argumentation, and Deliberation' in Guy B Peters and Philippe Zittoun (eds), *Contemporary Approaches to Public Policy: Theories, Controversies and Perspectives* (Palgrave Macmillan, 2016) 35
Duster, Troy, *The Legislation of Morality: Law, Drugs and Moral Judgment* (The Free Press, 1970)
ElSohly, Mahmoud A and Waseem Gul, 'Constituents of Cannabis Sativa' in Roger G Pertwee (ed), *Handbook of Cannabis* (Oxford University Press, 2014)
Faulkner, Alex, *Medical Technology into Healthcare and Society: A Sociology of Devices, Innovation and Governance* (Palgrave Macmillan, 2009)
Feldschreiber, Peter, *The Law and Regulation of Medicines and Medical Devices* (2nd ed, 2021)
Fernandez Lynch, Holly and I Glenn Cohen, 'Introduction' in Holly Fernandez Lynch and I Glenn Cohen (eds) *FDA in the Twenty-First Century: The Challenges of Regulating Drugs and New Technologies* (Columbia University Press, 2015) 1
Fischer, Frank, *Technocracy and the Politics of Expertise* (SAGE Publications, 1990)
Fitzgerald, John L, *Framing Drug Use: Bodies, Space, Economy and Crime* (Palgrave Macmillan, 2015)
Flear, Mark L, Tamara Hervey, Anne-Maree Farrell and Thérèse Murphy (eds), *European Law and New Health Technologies* (Oxford University Press, 2013)
Fuchs, Doris, *Business Power in Global Governance* (Lynne Rienner, 2007)
Garton, Stephen, 'Eugenics in Australia and New Zealand: Laboratories of Racial Science' in Alison Bashford and Philippa Levine (eds), *The Oxford Handbook of the History of Eugenics* (Oxford University Press, 2010) 243
Gedeon, Andras, *Science and Technology in Medicine: An Illustrated Account Based on Ninety-Nine Landmark Publications from Five Centuries* (Springer, 2006)
Gerring, John, *Case Study Research: Principles and Practices* (Cambridge University Press, 2nd ed, 2016)
Gordon, Sanford C and Gregory A Huber, 'The Empirical Study of Legitimate Authority: Normative Guidance for Positive Analysis' in Jack Knight and Melissa Schwartzberg (eds), *Political Legitimacy* (New York University Press, 2019) 328
Graycar, Regina and Jenny Morgan, *The Hidden Gender of Law* (Federation Press, 2002)
Gutmann, Amy and Dennis Thompson, *Why Deliberative Democracy?* (Princeton University Press, 2004)
Habermas, Jurgen, *Toward a Rational Society: Student Protest, Science and Politics*, tr Jeremy J Shapiro (Beacon Press, 1971)
Haigh, Gideon, *The Racket: How Abortion Became Legal in Australia* (Melbourne University Press, 2008)

Haines, Fiona, *The Paradox of Regulation: What Regulation Can Achieve and What It Cannot* (Edward Elgar, 2011)

Hanus, Lumír O and Raphael Mechoulam, 'Cannabinoid Chemistry: An Overview' in Raphael Mechoulam (ed), *Cannabinoids as Therapeutics* (Birkhauser Verlag, 2005) 23

Harris, Bede, *Constitutional Reform as a Remedy for Political Disenchantment in Australia: The Discussion We Need* (Springer, 2020)

Haubenreisser, Sabine and Martin Harvey-Allchurch, 'The European Medicines Agency and the Regulation of Medicines in the European Union' in SF Halabi (ed) *Food and Drug Regulation in an Era of Globalized Markets* (Elsevier, 2015)

Hutter, Bridget M and Sally Lloyd-Bostock, *Regulatory Crisis: Negotiating the Consequences of Risk, Disasters and Crises* (Cambridge University Press, 2017)

Jackson, Jonathan et al, 'Empirical Legitimacy as Two Connected Psychological States' in Gorazd Mesko and Justice Tankebe (eds), *Trust and Legitimacy in Criminal Justice: European Perspectives* (Springer, 2015) 137

Jain, Sandhya, 'The Right to Family Planning, Contraception, and Abortion: The Hindu View' in Daniel C Maguire (ed), *Sacred Rights: The Case for Contraception and Abortion in World Religions* (Oxford University Press, 2003) 129

Jasanoff, Sheila, *Designs on Nature: Science and Democracy in Europe and the United States* (Princeton University Press, 2005)

Jasanoff, Sheila, 'Ordering Knowledge, Ordering Society' in Sheila Jasanoff (ed), *States of Knowledge: The Co-Production of Science and the Social Order* (Routledge, 2004) 13

Jasanoff, Sheila, *Science and Public Reason* (Routledge, 2011)

Jasanoff, Sheila, *States of Knowledge: The Co-Production of Science and the Social Order* (Routledge, 2004)

Jasanoff, Sheila, 'Technologies of Humility: Citizen Participation in Governing Science' in Sheila Jasanoff (ed), *Science and Public Reason* (Routledge, 2012) 167

Jasanoff, Sheila, *The Ethics of Invention: Technology and the Human Future* (WW Norton and Company, 2016)

Jasanoff, Sheila, *The Fifth Branch: Science Advisers as Policymakers* (Harvard University Press, 1998)

Jasanoff, Sheila, 'The Idiom of Co-Production' in Sheila Jasanoff (ed), *States of Knowledge: The Co-Production of Science and Social Order* (Routledge, 2004) 1

Jasanoff, Sheila, 'The Songlines of Risk' in Sheila Jasanoff (ed), *Science and Public Reason* (Routledge, 2012) 133

Kennedy, David, *A World of Struggle: How Power, Law and Expertise Shape Global Political Economy* (Princeton University Press, 2016)

Kennedy, Peter, 'Habermas and the Self-Regulation of Complementary and Alternative Medicine (CAM)' in Mark Murphy (ed), *Habermas and Social Research: Between Theory and Method* (Routledge, 2017) 56

Kerridge, Ian, Michael Lowe and Cameron Stewart, *Ethics and Law for the Health Professions* (The Federation Press, 4th ed, 2013)

Kidd, Ian James, 'Is Scientism Epistemically Vicious?' in Jeroen de Ridder, Rik Peels and Rene van Woudenberg (eds), *Scientism: Prospects and Problems* (Oxford University Press, 2019) 149

Marc T Law, 'History of Food and Drug Regulation in the United States' in Robert Whaples (ed) (2004) *Economic History Association: Encyclopedia* <https://eh.net/encyclopedia/history-of-food-and-drug-regulation-in-the-united-states/>

Lee, Karen, *The Legitimacy and Responsiveness of Industry Rule-Making* (Hart, 2018)

Levi, Margaret, 'Trustworthy Government and Legitimating Beliefs' in Jack Knight and Melissa Schwartzberg (eds), *Political Legitimacy* (New York University Press, 2019) 361

Levitov, Alex, 'Normative Legitimacy and the State' in *Oxford Handbooks OnLine* (Oxford University Press, 2016)

Ludlow, Karinne, 'More Than Science: Ethical and Socio-Legal Concerns in Nanotechnology Regulation in Australia' in Graeme Hodge et al (eds), *New Global Frontiers in Regulation: The Age of Nanotechnology* (Edward Elgar, 2007) 166

Manderson, Desmond, *From Mr Sin to Mr Big: A History of Australian Drug Laws* (Oxford University Press, 1993)

Mann, RD, 'The Historical Developments of Medicines Regulations' in Stuart R Walker and John P Griffin (eds), *International Medicines Regulations: A Forward Look to 1992* (Kluwer Academic Publishers, 1989) 3

Marion, Nancy E, *The Medical Marijuana Maze: Policy and Politics* (Carolina Academic Press, 2014)

Martin, Elizabeth, *Concise Medical Dictionary* (Oxford University Press, 9th ed, 2015)

McDermont, Morag, Tim Cole, Janet Newman and Angela Piccini (eds), *Imagining Regulation Differently: Co-Creating for Engagement* (Bristol University Press, 2021)

McEwen, John, *A History of Therapeutic Goods Regulation in Australia* (Commonwealth of Australia, 2007)

McEwen, John, 'Measuring Performance: The View of the TGA' in Neil McAuslane and Stuart Walker (eds), *Improving the Regulatory Review Process: Assessing Performance and Setting Targets* (Springer, 1997)

McKenna, Petahn, 'Australian Medical Device Regulations: An Overview' in Jack Wong and Raymond Tong (eds), *Medical Regulatory Affairs: An International Handbook for Medical Devices and Healthcare Products* (3rd ed, Jenny Stanford Publishing, 2022) 387

Mead, Alice, 'International Control of Cannabis' in Roger Pertwee (ed), *Handbook of Cannabis* (Oxford University Press, 2014) 44

Michael, Mike, 'Sticking Plasters and the Standardizations of Everyday Life' in Vaughan Higgins and Wendy Larner (eds), *Calculating the Social: Standards and the Reconfiguring of Governing* (Palgrave Macmillan, 2010) 131

Mills, James H, *Cannabis Britannica: Empire, Trade, and Prohibition* 1800–1928 (Oxford University Press, 2003)

Mills, James H, *Cannabis Nation: Control and Consumption in Britain, 1928–2008* (Oxford University Press, 2012)

Morgan, Brownwen and Karen Yeung, *An Introduction to Law and Regulation: Text and Materials* (Cambridge University Press, 2007)

National Academies, *Regulating Medicines in a Globalized World: The Need for Increased Reliance Among Regulators (2020)* (National Academies Press, 2020)

National Academies of Science, *Stronger Food and Drug Regulatory Systems Abroad* (The National Academies Press, 2020)

Novas, Carlos, 'Standards, Orphan Drugs, and Pharmaceutical Markets' in Vaughan Higgins and Wendy Larner (eds), *Calculating the Social: Standards and the Re-Configuration of Governing* (Palgrave Macmillan, 2010) 185

Nugent, Walter, *Progressivism: A Very Short Introduction* (Oxford University Press, 2010)

Olson, Richard, *Scientism and Technocracy in the Twentieth Century: The Legacy of Scientific Management* (Lexington Publications, 2016)

O'Neill, Onora, *From Principles to Practice: Normativity and Judgement in Ethics and Politics* (Cambridge University Press, 2018)

Palm, Sherrie J, 'Medical Device Innovation and Errors: The Patient Perspective' in S Abbas Shobeiri (ed), *The Innovation and Evolution of Medical Devices: Vaginal Mesh Kits* (Springer, 2019) 125

Parker, Christine and John Braithwaite, 'Regulation' in Mark Tushnet and Peter Cane (eds) *The Oxford Handbook of Legal Studies* (Oxford University Press, 2005) 119

Patsner, Bruce, 'Medical-Legal Aspects of Transvaginal Mesh Kit Complications: A Historical Perspective and the US Food and Drug Administration Review Process' in S Abbas Shobeiri (ed), *The Innovation and Evolution of Medical Devices: Vaginal Mesh Kits* (Springer, 2019) 71

Peter, Fabienne, *The Grounds of Political Legitimacy* (Oxford University Press, 2023)

Peter, Fabienne, 'Political Legitimacy', The Stanford Encyclopedia of Philosophy (*Web Page*, 24 April 2017) <https://plato.stanford.edu/archives/sum2017/entries/legitimacy/>

Peters, B Guy, 'Institutionalism and Public Policy' in B Guy Peters and Philippe Zittoun (eds), *Contemporary Approaches to Public Policy: Theories, Controversies and Perspectives* (Palgrave Macmillan, 2016)

Petersen, Alan, *Hope in Health: The Socio-Politics of Optimism* (Palgrave MacMillan, 2015)

Petersen, Kerry, 'Abortion Laws: Criminalisation and Decriminalisation' in Ian Freckleton and Kerry Petersen (eds), *Tensions & Trauams in Health Law* (The Federation Press, 2017) 657

Plato, Republic, *tr Robin Waterfield* (Oxford University Press, 1993)

Porter, Dorothy, *Health, Civilization and the State: A History of Public Health from Ancient to Modern Times* (Routledge, 1999)

Porter, Dorothy, 'Introduction' in *The History of Public Health and the Modern State* (Editions Rodopi BV, 1994)

Principe, Lawrence M, 'Scientism and the Religion of Science' in Richard N Williams and Daniel N Robinson (eds), *Scientism: The New Orthodoxy* (Bloomsbury, 2015) 41

Rago, Lembit and Budiono Santoso, 'Drug Regulation: History, Present and Future' in Chris J van Boxtel, Budiono Santoso and I Ralph Edwards (eds), *Drug Benefits and Risks: International Textbook of Clinical Pharmacology* (IOS Press, 2nd ed, 2008)

Raman, Sujatha, 'Science, Uncertainty and the Normative Question of Epistemic Governance in Policymaking' in Emilie Cloatre and Martin Pickersgill (eds), *Knowledge, Technology and Law* (Routledge, 2015) 17

Robbins, Brent Dean, *The Medicalized Body and Anesthetic Culture: The Cadaver, the Memorial Body, and the Recovery of Lived Experience* (Palgrave Macmillan, 2018)

Robinson, Daniel N, 'Science, Scientism and Explanation' in Richard N Williams and Daniel N Robinson (eds), *Scientism: The New Orthodoxy* (Bloomsbury, 2015) 23

Rottger-Wirtz, Sabrina, *The Interplay of Global Standards and EU Pharmaceutical Regulation: The International Council for Harmonisation*' (Hart Publishing, 2021)

Russo, Ethan, 'Cannabis in India: Ancient Lore and Modern Medicine' in Raphael Mechoulam (ed), *Cannabinoids as Therapeutics* (Birkhauser Verlag, 2005) 1

Schneider, Steffen, A. Hurrelmann, Zuzana Krell-Laluhová, F. Meier, Achim Wiesner and Kenneth A. Loparo , *Democracy's Deep Roots: Why the Nation State Remains Legitimate* (Palgrave Macmillan, 2010)

Schwartzberg, Melissa, 'Introduction' in Jack Knight and Melissa Schwartzberg (eds), *Political Legitimacy* (New York University Press, 2019)

Scruton, Roger, 'Scientism and the Humanities' in Richard N Williams and Daniel N Robinson (eds), *Scientism: The New Orthodoxy* (Bloomsbury, 2015) 131

Seddon, Toby and William Floodgate, *Regulating Cannabis: A Global Review and Future Directions* (Palgrave MacMillan, 2020)

Sekeres, Mikkael A, *Drugs and the FDA: Safety, Efficacy, and the Public's Trust* (MIT Press, 2022)

Shapiro, Stuart, *Analysis and Public Policy: Successes, Failures and Directions for Reform* (Edward Elgar, 2016)

Sheridan, Alan, *Michael Foucault: The Will to Truth* (Tavistock Publications, 1980)

Shobeiri, S Abbas, 'The Innovation of Medical Devices' in S Abbas Shobeiri (ed), *The Innovation and Evolution of Medical Devices: Vaginal Mesh Kits* (Springer, 2019) 13

Shobeiri, S Abbas, 'Introduction: Why a Case Study of Vaginal Mesh Kits?' in S Abbas Shobeiri (ed), *The Innovation and Evolution of Medical Devices: Vaginal Mesh Kits* (Springer, 2019) 1

Sorell, Tom, *Scientism: Philosophy and the Infatuation with Science* (Routledge, 1991)

Stehr, Nico and Reiner Grundmann, *Experts: The Knowledge and Power of Expertise* (Routledge, 2011)

Stenmark, Mikael, *Scientism: Science, Ethics and Religion* (Routledge, 2016)

Steup, Mattias, 'Epistemology', The Stanford Encyclopedia of Philosophy (*Web Page*, 14 December 2005) <https://plato.stanford.edu/archives/win2018/entries/epistemology/>

Suwanbubbha, Parichart, 'The Right to Family Planning, Contraception, and Abortion in Thai Buddhism' in Daniel C Maguire (ed), *Sacred Rights: The Case for Contraception and Abortion in World Religions* (Oxford University Press, 2003) 145

Syrett, Keith, *Law, Legitimacy and the Rationing of Health Care* (Cambridge University Press, 2007)

Tankebe, Justice, 'Legitimacy and Regulatory Compliance' in Maria Krambia-Kapardis (ed), *Financial Compliance: Issues, Concerns and Future Directions* (Palgrave Macmillan, 2019) 47

Tannenberg, Marcus, 'Legitimacy as Congruence: Matching Expert-Coded and Public Opinion Data' (Working Paper No 2023:124, The Varieties of Democracy Institute, 2023).

Taylor, Frederick Winslow, *The Principles of Scientific Management* (The Floating Press, 2012)

Thakur, Dinesh S and Prashant T Reddy, *The Truth Pill: The Myth of Drug Regulation in India* (Simon & Schuster, 2022)

Tooley, Michael, 'Abortion' in Duncan Pritchard (ed), *Oxford Bibliographies: Philosophy* (Oxford University Press, 2013)

Tyler, Tom R and Yuen J Huo, *Trust in the Law: Encouraging Public Cooperation with the Police and Courts* (Russell Sage Foundation, 2002)

Vesa Rope Kojonen, Erikki, *The Intelligent Design Debate and the Temptation of Scientism* (Routledge, 2016)

Weber, Max, 'Bureaucracy' in Hans Heinrich Gerth and Charles Wright Mills (eds), *Max Weber: Essays in Sociology* (Routledge, 1948) 196

Westlaw AU, *The Laws of Australia* (online at 1 September 2019)

Williams, Richard N, 'Introduction' in Richard N Williams and Daniel N Robinson (eds), *Scientism: The New Orthodoxy* (Bloomsbury, 2015) 1

Wood, Matthew, *Hyper-Active Governance: How Governments Manage the Politics of Expertise* (Cambridge University Press, 2019)

Woolner, David B and John M Thompson (eds), *Progressivism in America: Past, Present and Future* (Oxford University Press, 2016)

Yin, Robert K, *Case Study Research: Design and Methods* (SAGE Publications, 5th ed, 2014)

C Reports

Australian Government, *Final Report on the Australian Government Response to the Recommendations of the Senate Community Affairs References Committee Report: The Number of Women in Australia Who Have Had Transvaginal Mesh Implants and Related Matters* (July 2021).

Australian Institute of Health and Welfare, *National Drug Strategy Household Survey 2019* (Survey, 2020)

Gorman, Kate, 'Report on National Forum on Mesh Implants', *Health Care Consumers* (Web Page, 9 September 2019) <https://www.hcca.org.au/2019/04/30/report-on-national-forum-on-mesh-implants-by-kate-gorman/>

House of Representatives Standing Committee on Health, Aged Care and Sport, Parliament of Australia, *The New Frontier – Delivering Better Health for All Australians: Inquiry into Approval Processes for New Drugs and Novel Medical Technologies in Australia* (Final Report, November 2021)

Independent Medicines and Medical Devices Safety Review (UK), *First Do No Harm: The Report of the Independent Medicines and Medical Devices Safety Review* (Report, 8 July 2020)

McMillan, John, *Review of the Narcotic Drugs Act 1967: Final Report* (Report, July 2019)

Panel to Review the Transparency of the Therapeutic Goods Administration, *Review to Improve the Transparency of the Therapeutic Goods Administration: Final Report* (Report, June 2011)

Royal Commission on Health (Report, 1925)
Royal Commission on Secret Drugs, Cures and Foods (Report, 1907) vol 1
Royal Commission on the Decline of the Birth-Rate and on the Mortality of Infants in New South Wales (Report, 1904)
Sansom, Lloyd, Will Delaat and John Horvath, *Review of Medicines and Medical Devices Regulation: Discussion Paper* (November 2014)
Sansom, Lloyd, Will Delaat and John Horvath, *Review of Medicines and Medical Device Regulation: Report on the Regulatory Framework for Medicines and Medical Devices* (Report, March 2015)
Senate Community Affairs References Committee, Parliament of Australia, *Current Barriers to Patient Access to Medicinal Cannabis in Australia* (Report, March 2020)
Senate Community Affairs References Committee, Parliament of Australia, *Number of Women in Australia Who Have Had Transvaginal Mesh Implants and Related Matters* (Report, March 2018)
Therapeutic Goods Administration, *TGA International Engagement Strategy 2016–2020: Highlights and Achievements Report* (9 September 2021) <https://www.tga.gov.au/resources/publication/publications/tga-international-engagement-strategy-2016-2020-highlights-and-achievements-report>
Victorian Law Reform Commission, *Law of Abortion* (Final Report, March 2008)
Victorian Law Reform Commission, *Medicinal Cannabis* (Issues Paper, March 2015)
Victorian Law Reform Commission, *Medicinal Cannabis* (Report, August 2015)

D Cases

Gill v Ethicon Sàrl (No 5) [2019] FCA 1905
Gill v Ethicon Sàrl (No 6) [2020] FCA 279
Ethicon Sàrl v Gill (2021) 288 FCR 338
Health Care Complaints Commission v Petros [2019] NSWCATOD 83
Jodie Philipsen v American Medical Systems LLC, NSD 35/2018
Kathryn Gill v Ethican Sàrl, NSD 1590/2012
Right to Life Association (NSW) Inc v Secretary, Department of Human Services and Health and Family Planning Inc (Vic) (1995) 128 ALR 238
Transcript of Proceedings, Ethicon Sàrl v Gill [2021] HCATrans 187, 630 (Keane J)

E Legislation

1 Australia

Abortion Law Reform Act 2008 (Vic)
Abortion Law Reform Act 2019 (NSW)
Access to Medicinal Cannabis Act 2016 (Vic)
Acts Amendment (Abortion) Act 1998 (WA)
Australian Constitution
Competition and Consumer Act 2010 (Cth)
Crimes (Abolition of Offence of Abortion Act) 2002 (ACT)
Criminal Code Act Compilation Act 1913 (WA)

Criminal Law Consolidation Act 1935 (SA)
Explanatory Memorandum, Narcotic Drugs Amendment Bill 2016 (Cth)
Explanatory Statement, *Therapeutic Goods (Medical Devices) Amendment (Implantable Medical Devices) Regulations 2017* (Cth)
Health (Improving Abortion Access) Amendment Act 2018 (ACT)
Health (Miscellaneous Provisions) Act 1911 (WA)
Narcotic Drugs Amendment Act 2016 (Cth)
National Health Reform Act 2011 (Cth)
Poisons Act 1927 (Vic)
Poisons Standard February 2016 (Cth)
Poisons Standard June 2024 (Cth)
Regulator of Medicinal Cannabis Bill 2014 (Cth)
Reproductive Health (Access to Terminations) Act 2013 (Tas)
Termination of Pregnancy Act 2018 (Qld)
Therapeutic Goods Amendment (2022 Measures No. 1) Act 2023 (Cth)
Therapeutic Goods (Medical Devices - Specified Articles) Instrument 2020 (Cth)
Therapeutic Goods (Guidelines for Multi-Site Licences) Instrument 2020 (Cth)
Therapeutic Goods (Medical Devices) Regulations 2002 (Cth)
Therapeutic Goods Act 1966 (Cth)
Therapeutic Goods Act 1989 (Cth)
Therapeutic Goods Amendment Act 1996 (Cth)
Therapeutic Goods Amendment (Medical Devices) Act 2002 (Cth)
Therapeutic Goods Amendment (Repeal of Ministerial Responsibility for Approval of RU486) Act 2006 (Cth)
Therapeutic Goods Regulations 1990 (Cth)
Therapeutic Substances Bill 1937 (Cth)
Therapeutic Substances Bill 1938 (Cth)
Therapeutic Substances Act 1953 (Cth)
Therapeutic Substances Regulations 1956 (Cth)
Trade Practices Act 1974 (Cth)

2 United Kingdom

Dangerous Drugs Act 1965
Dangerous Drugs Act 1925 15 & 16 Geo 5, c 74
Misuse of Drugs Act 1971
Misuse of Drugs Regulations 2001
The Misuse of Drugs (Amendments) (Cannabis and Licence Fees) (England, Wales and Scotland) Regulations 2018 SI 2018/1055
3 United States of America
Federal Food, Drug and Cosmetic Act 21 USC (1938)
Federal Food, Drug and Cosmetic Act 21 USC (1938)
Food and Drug Administration 21 CFR 314.80 (2024)
Marijuana Transfer Tax Act 1937 Pub L No 75-238, 50 Stat 551
4 European Union
Regulation (EC) No 726/2004 of the European Parliament and of the Council of 31 March 2004 Laying Down Community Procedures for the Authorisation and

Supervision of Medicinal Products for Human and Veterinary Use and Establishing a European Medicines Agency, [2004] OJ L 136

Regulation (EC) No 726/2004 of the European Parliament and of the Council of 31 March 2004 Laying Down Community Procedures for the Authorisation and Supervision of Medicinal Products for Human and Veterinary Use and Establishing a European Medicines Agency, [2004] OJ L 136

F Treaties

Convention for Limiting the Manufacture and Regulating the Distribution of Narcotic Drugs, opened for signature 13 July 1931, 139 LNTS 303 (entered into force 9 July 1933)

Convention of 1936 for the Suppression of the Illicit Traffic in Dangerous Drugs, opened for signature 26 June 1936, 198 LNTS 301 (entered into force 26 October 1939)

International Opium Convention, signed 19 February 1925, 81 LNTS 319 (entered into force 25 September 1928)

Single Convention on Narcotic Drugs, signed 30 March 1961, 520 UNTS 204 (entered into force 13 December 1964)

G Other

1 *Government Material*

'About Transvaginal Surgical Mesh Devices', Therapeutic Goods Administration (Web Page, 19 December 2023) <https://www.tga.gov.au/products/urogynaecological-transvaginal-surgical-mesh-hub/about-transvaginal-surgical-mesh-devices>

'Accessing Medicinal Cannabis for a Patient', *Therapeutic Goods Administration* (Web Page, 27 March 2024) <https://www.tga.gov.au/accessing-medicinal-cannabis-patient>

'Access to Medicinal Cannabis Products', *Therapeutic Goods Administration* (Web Page, 9 July 2020) <https://www.tga.gov.au/access-medicinal-cannabis-products-1>

'Action Plan for Medical Devices – Progress Report Card: December 2023', *Therapeutic Goods Administration, Department of Health and Aged Care (Cth)* (Web Page, 23 May 2024) <https://www.tga.gov.au/resources/publication/publications/action-plan-medical-devices-progress-report-card-december-2023>

'Adverse Event Monitoring Internationally', *Therapeutic Goods Administration* (Web Page, 30 October 2018) <https://www.tga.gov.au/safety/safety/safety-monitoring-medicines/adverse-event-monitoring-internationally>

'African Medicines Agency (AMA)' AUDA-NEPAD: African Union Development Agency (Web Page, 2022) <https://www.nepad.org/microsite/african-medicines-agency-ama>

'Amendments to Restrictions for Prescribing of MS-2 Step (Mifepristone and Misoprostol)' (Media Release, Therapeutic Good Administration, Department of Health and Aged Care (Cth), 11 July 2023).

'ARTG Search', *Therapeutic Goods Administration, Department of Health (Cth)* (Web Page) https://compliance.health.gov.au/artg/>

'Australia-Canada-Singapore-Switzerland-United Kingdom (Access) Consortium' Therapeutic Goods Administration (Web Page, 2 November 2023) <https://www.tga.gov.au/international-activities/australia-canada-singapore-switzerland-united-kingdom-access-consortium>

'Australian Public Assessment Reports for Prescription Medicines (AusPARs)', *Therapeutic Goods Administration* (Web Page, 25 July 2019) <https://www.tga.gov.au/australian-public-assessment-reports-prescription-medicines-auspars>

'Australian Register of Therapeutic Goods', *Therapeutic Goods Administration* (Web Page, 29 October 2019) <https://www.tga.gov.au/artg>

'Australian Regulatory Actions – About Transvaginal Surgical Mesh', *Therapeutic Goods Administration* (Web Page, 20 December 2023) <https://www.tga.gov.au/products/urogynaecological-transvaginal-surgical-mesh-hub/australian-regulatory-actions-about-transvaginal-surgical-mesh>.

'Australian Regulatory Guidelines for Medical Devices (ARGMD)', *Therapeutic Goods Administration* (Web Page, 18 October 2019) <https://www.tga.gov.au/publication/australian-regulatory-guidelines-medical-devices-argmd>

'Authorisation Procedures – National Authorisation Procedures', *European Commission* (Web Page) <https://health.ec.europa.eu/medicinal-products/legal-framework-governing-medicinal-products-human-use-eu/authorisation-procedures-national-authorisation-procedures_en>

'Authorised Prescriber Established History of Use Lists', *Therapeutic Goods Administration* (Web Page, 15 January 2024) <https://www.tga.gov.au/products/unapproved-therapeutic-goods/prescribe-unapproved-therapeutic-good-health-practitioners/lists-products-established-history-use/authorised-prescriber-established-history-use-lists>

'Brucellosis Laboratory Case Definition (LCD)', *Department of Health (Cth)* (Web Page) <https://www1.health.gov.au/internet/main/publishing.nsf/Content/cda-phlncd-brucellosis.htm>

'Cannabis Re-Scheduling Proposal – Questions and Answers', *Therapeutic Goods Administration* (20 January 2016)

'Conformity Assessment Overview' Therapeutic Goods Administration (Web Page, 19 June 2024) <https://www.tga.gov.au/how-we-regulate/manufacturing/medical-devices/conformity-assessment/conformity-assessment-bodies/tga-conformity-assessment-certification/conformity-assessment-overview>

'Consultations & Reviews', *Therapeutic Goods Administration* (Web Page) <https://www.tga.gov.au/consultations-reviews>

'COVID-19 Medicines', *European Medicines Agency* (Web Page, 2024) <https://www.ema.europa.eu/en/human-regulatory-overview/public-health-threats/coronavirus-disease-covid-19/covid-19-medicines>

'COVID-19 Personal Protective Equipment', *Therapeutic Goods Administration* (Web Page) <https://www.tga.gov.au/products/covid-19/covid-19-personal-protective-equipment-ppe>

'COVID-19 Tests', *Therapeutic Goods Administration* (Web Page, 16 May 2024) <https://www.tga.gov.au/products/covid-19/covid-19-tests>

'COVID-19 Vaccines', *FDA: US Food and Drug Administration* (Web Page, 30 August 2024) https://www.fda.gov/emergency-preparedness-and-response/coronavirus-disease-2019-covid-19/covid-19-vaccines

'COVID-19 Vaccines', *FDA: US Food and Drug Administration* (Web Page, 30 August 2024) https://www.fda.gov/emergency-preparedness-and-response/coronavirus-disease-2019-covid-19/covid-19-vaccines

COVID-19 Vaccine: International Collaboration' *Therapeutic Goods Administration* (Web Page, 16 September 2021) <https://www.tga.gov.au/products/covid-19/covid-19-vaccines/covid-19-vaccine-international-collaboration>

'COVID-19 Vaccines', *Therapeutic Goods Administration* (Web Page) <https://www.tga.gov.au/products/covid-19/covid-19-vaccines>

'Database of Adverse Event Notifications (DAEN)', *Therapeutic Goods Administration* (Web Page, 30 October 2018) < https://www.tga.gov.au/database-adverse-event-notifications-daen>

'Fellowships', *European Medicines Agency* (Web Page, 2024) <https://www.ema.europa.eu/en/partners-networks/international-activities/fellowships>

European Medicines Agency, *Annual Report 2021* (Report, 2022) 133 <https://www.ema.europa.eu/en/documents/annual-report/2021-annual-report-european-medicines-agency_en.pdf>

European Medicines Agency, *Annual Report 2021* (Report, 2022) 133 <https://www.ema.europa.eu/en/documents/annual-report/2021-annual-report-european-medicines-agency_en.pdf>

'Former Senator Brian Harradine', *Parliament of Australia* (Web Page) <https://www.aph.gov.au/Senators_and_Members/Parliamentarian?MPID=6H4>

Health Ministers' Meeting (Web Page, 2024) <https://www.health.gov.au/committees-and-groups/health-ministers-meeting-hmm#members>

'Import', *Therapeutic Goods Administration* (Web Page) <https://www.tga.gov.au/how-we-regulate/import-and-export/import>

'International', *Therapeutic Goods Administration* (Web Page, 2017) <https://www.tga.gov.au/about-tga/international>

'International Activities' *European Medicines Agency* (Web Page, 2024) <https://www.ema.europa.eu/en/partners-networks/international-activities>

'Know Your Treatment Options for COVID-19', *FDA: US Food and Drug Administration* (Web Page, 19 December 2023) <https://www.fda.gov/consumers/consumer-updates/know-your-treatment-options-covid-19>

'International Scientific Guidelines Adopted in Australia', *Therapeutic Goods Administration* (Web Page) <https://www.tga.gov.au/resources/resource/international-scientific-guidelines>.

'Know Your Treatment Options for COVID-19', *FDA: US Food and Drug Administration* (Web Page, 19 December 2023) <https://www.fda.gov/consumers/consumer-updates/know-your-treatment-options-covid-19>

'MBS Online', *MBS Online: Medicare Benefits Schedule* (Web Page) <http://www.mbsonline.gov.au/internet/mbsonline/publishing.nsf/Content/Home>

'Medical Devices', *European Medicines Agency* (Web Page) <https://www.ema.europa.eu/en/human-regulatory-overview/medical-devices>

'Medical Device Incident Reporting & Investigation Scheme (IRIS)', *Therapeutic Goods Administration* (Web Page, 30 October 2019) <https://www.tga.gov.au/medical-device-incident-reporting-investigation-scheme-iris>

'Medicinal Cannabis Authorised Prescriber Scheme Data', *Therapeutic Goods Administration*, (Web Page, 1 May 2024) <https://www.tga.gov.au/products/

unapproved-therapeutic-goods/medicinal-cannabis-hub/medicinal-cannabis-access-pathways-and-usage-data/medicinal-cannabis-authorised-prescriber-scheme-data>

'Medicinal Cannabis Products: Overview of Regulation', *Therapeutic Goods Administration* (Web Page, 17 June 2017) <http://www.tga.gov.au/medicinal-cannabis-products-overview-regulation>

'Medicinal Cannabis Products: Patient Information', *Therapeutic Goods Administration* (Web Page, 29 May 2018) <http://www.tga.gov.au/community-qa/medicinal-cannabis-products-patient-information>

'Medicinal Cannabis Special Access Scheme Data', *Therapeutic Goods Administration* (Web Page, 1 May 2024) <https://www.tga.gov.au/products/unapproved-therapeutic-goods/medicinal-cannabis-hub/medicinal-cannabis-access-pathways-and-usage-data/medicinal-cannabis-special-access-scheme-data>.

'Overview of How TGA Manages Medical Device Adverse Event Reports', *Therapeutic Goods Administration* (Web Page, 19 June 2013) <https://www.tga.gov.au/overview-how-tga-manages-medical-device-adverse-event-reports>

'Overview of Supplying Therapeutic Goods in Australia' *Therapeutic Goods Administration,* (Web Page, 28 August 2020) https://www.tga.gov.au/overview-supplying-therapeutic-goods-australia

'Partnerships and Collaboration', FDA (Web Page, 2023) <https://www.fda.gov/international-programs/partnerships-and-collaboration>

'Pharmaceutical Benefits Scheme', *PBS: The Pharmaceutical Benefits Scheme* (Web Page) <http://www.pbs.gov.au/pbs/home;jsessionid=cr0heafq4if2nwi8rvl1yxad>

'Press Conference – Australian Parliament House, ACT' PM Transcripts: Transcripts from the Prime Ministers of Australia, *Department of the Prime Minister and Cabinet*, 3 December 2020

'Public Meeting Communique: Regulatory Options for Appropriate Access and Safety Controls for Alkyl Nitrites', *Therapeutic Goods Administration* (Web Page, 7 March 2019) <https://www.tga.gov.au/public-meeting-communique-regulatory-options-appropriate-access-and-safety-controls-alkyl-nitrites>

Reform of the EU Pharmaceutical Legislation', *European Commission* (Web Page, 26 April 2023) <https://health.ec.europa.eu/medicinal-products/pharmaceutical-strategy-europe/reform-eu-pharmaceutical-legislation_en>

'Reporting Adverse Events', *Therapeutic Goods Administration* (Web Page, 7 November 2018)

'Responding to Lateline – Accessing Medicinal Cannabis Products', *Therapeutic Goods Administration* (17 August 2017)

'Safely Using Hand Sanitizer', *FDA, US Food and Drug Administration* (Web Page, 12 April 2023) <https://www.fda.gov/consumers/consumer-updates/safely-using-hand-sanitizer>

'Testing of Alkyl Nitrite "Poppers": TGA Laboratory Testing', *Therapeutic Goods Administration* (Web Page, 6 June 2019) <https://www.tga.gov.au/testing-alkyl-nitrite-poppers>

'TGA Stakeholder Surveys', *Therapeutic Goods Administration* (Web Page, 1 December 2023) <https://www.tga.gov.au/resources/publication/publications/tga-stakeholder-surveys>

'TGA Supports MHRA's New International Recognition Framework for Medicines', *Therapeutic Goods Administration* (Web Page, 2 June 2023) <https://www.tga

.gov.au/news/news/tga-supports-mhras-new-international-recognition-framework-medicines>

'TGA Actions after Review into Urogynaecological Surgical Mesh Implants' *Therapeutic Goods Administration* (Web Page, 17 May 2019) <https://www.tga.gov.au/alert/tga-actions-after-review-urogynaecological-surgical-mesh-implants>

Training Opportunities for Non-EU Regulators', *European Medicines Agency* (Web Page, 2024) <https://www.ema.europa.eu/en/partners-networks/international-activities/training-opportunities-non-eu-regulators>

'Transvaginal Mesh', *Australian Commission on Safety and Quality in Healthcare* (Web Page, 2019) <https://www.safetyandquality.gov.au/our-work/health-conditions-and-treatments/transvaginal-mesh>

'Transvaginal Mesh', *Better Health Channel* (Web Page, March 2018) <https://www.betterhralth.vic.gov.au/health/conditionsandtreatments/Transvaginal-mesh>

'UrogynaecologicalSurgical Mesh Complications', *Therapeutic Goods Administration* (Web Page, 1 August 2024) <https://www.tga.gov.au/news/safety-alerts/urogynaecological-surgical-mesh-complications>

'Using Assessments from Comparable Overseas Regulators for Medical Devices, *Therapeutic Goods Administration* (Web Page, 7 October 2022) <https://www.tga.gov.au/resources/guidance/using-assessments-comparable-overseas-regulators-medical-devices>

'What are Therapeutic Goods', *Therapeutic Goods Administration* (Web Page) <http://www.tga.gov.au/what-are-therapeutic-goods>

'What Does FDA Regulate', FDA: US Food & Drug Administration (Web Page, 18 January 2022) <https://www.fda.gov/about-fda/what-we-do/what-does-fda-regulate> .

'What Is Not Regulated by the TGA', *Therapeutic Goods Administration* (Web Page, 2 August 2012) <https://www.tga.gov.au/about-tga/what-we-do/what-not-regulated-tga>

What We Do' *FDA: US Food & Drug Administration* (Web Page, 21 November 2023)

Australian Government, *An Action Plan for Medical Devices* (April 2019) <https://www.tga.gov.au/resources/publication/publications/action-plan-medical-devices>

Australian Government, *Australian Government Response to the Senate Community Affairs References Committee Report: The Number of Women in Australia Who Have Had Transvaginal Mesh Implants and Related Matters* (October 2018)

Australian Health Ministers' Advisory Council, *Scheduling Policy Framework for Medicines and Chemicals* (January 2018)

Australian Health Ministers' Advisory Council, *Scheduling Policy Framework for Medicines and Chemicals* (February 2015)

'Australian State & Territory Variations from Part 4 of the Poisons Standard', *Therapeutic Goods Administration, Department of Health and Aged Care (Cth)* (Web Page, 11 October 2021) <https://www.tga.gov.au/how-we-regulate/ingredients-and-scheduling-medicines-and-chemicals/poisons-standard-and-scheduling-medicines-and-chemicals/scheduling/australian-state-territory-variations-part-4-poisons-standard>

CSIRO Futures, *Medical Technologies and Pharmaceuticals: A Roadmap for Unlocking Future Growth Opportunities for Australia* (April 2017)

Davies, Sally C, Stephen Powis and Keith Ridge, Letter, 31 October 2018 <https://perma.cc/3RJW-CWZA>

Delegate of the Minister for Health (Cth), *Therapeutic Goods (Standard for Medicinal Cannabis) (TGO 93) 2017*

Delegate of the Secretary to the Department of Health (Cth), *Public Consultation on the Proposed Amendments to the Poisons Standard* (March 2016)

Department of Health (Cth), *Medicinal Cannabis* (Fact Sheet) <https://perma.cc/MWP8-STCY>

Department of Health and Ageing, Therapeutic Goods Administration, *Authorised Prescribers* (18 September 2019) <https://www.tga.gov.au/form/authorised-prescribers>

European Medicines Agency, *From Laboratory to Patient: The Journey of a Centrally Authorised Medicine* (2019)

European Medicines Agency, *The European Regulatory System for Medicines: Bringing New Safe and Effective Medicines to Patients Across the European Union* (2023)

Food and Drug Administration (FDA), *A History of the FDA and Drug Regulation in the United States* (2006)

He, Kiki, Medical Devices and Product Quality, Therapeutic Goods Administration, 'Process of Conformity Assessments for Higher Risk Devices: Conformity Assessment Overview' (Conference Paper, Symposium on Regulatory Fundamentals in Medical Devices) 28 August 2018

International Medical Device Regulators Forum, *Final Document: IMDRF Terms of Reference* (18 January 2024) <https://www.imdrf.org/documents/imdrf-terms-reference>

McGrath, Elizabeth, A/g Assistant Secretary, Medical Devices Branch, Therapeutic Goods Administration, 'MMDR Reform – Patient Implant Cards and Information Leaflets' (Conference Presentation, Association of Regulatory and Clinical Scientists (Australia) Annual Conference, 22 August 2018)

National Archives of Australia, B6295, 3652F, *Canberra Brucella Vaccine Testing Laboratory* (7 June 1974)

National Archives of Australia, B6295, 4034A, *Brucella Vaccine Test Laboratories* (18 April 1975)

Smith, Glenn, Director, Scientific Evaluation Branch, Therapeutic Goods Administration, 'Regulation, Ethics and Reimbursement of Novel Biological Therapies in Australia – An Update' (Conference Presentation, Association of Regulatory and Clinical Scientists (Australia) Annual Conference, 6 August 2019)

Skerritt, John, 'Medicinal Cannabis – What's Happening?' (Conference Presentation, Association of Regulatory and Clinical Scientists, August 2016)

Therapeutic Goods Administration, *Access Unapproved Products (Consumers)* (Web Page) <https://www.tga.gov.au/products/unapproved-therapeutic-goods/access-unapproved-products-consumers>

Therapeutic Goods Administration, *Australian Public Assessment Report for Influenza Virus Haemagglutinin* (November 2018)

Therapeutic Goods Administration, *Australian Public Assessment Report for Mifepristone (RU486) (Abortifacient)* (October 2012)

Therapeutic Goods Administration, *Australian Public Assessment Report for Mifepristone/Misoprostol* (October 2014)
Therapeutic Goods Administration, *Australian Public Assessment Report for Misoprostol* (October 2012)
Therapeutic Goods Administration, *Australian Public Assessment Report for Nabiximols* (Report, 27 September 2013)
Therapeutic Goods Administration, *Australian Regulatory Guidelines for Medical Devices* (Version 1.1, May 2011)
Therapeutic Goods Administration, *Clinical Evidence Guidelines forMedical Devices* (*Guidelines*, November 2023)
Therapeutic Goods Administration, Department of Health (Cth) *Comparable Overseas Regulators – Medical Devices: Criteria and Implementation* (May 2017)
Therapeutic Goods Administration, *Conforming with Therapeutic Goods (Standard for Medicinal Cannabis) (TGO 93) Order 2017* (26 September 2022)
Therapeutic Goods Administration, *Consultation: Regulation of Software, Including Software as a Medical Device (SaMD)* (February 2019)
Therapeutic Goods Administration, *Educational Materials: The Regulation of Medicines in Australia*
Therapeutic Goods Administration, *Final Decisions and Reasons for Decisions by a Delegate of the Secretary to the Department of Health* (31 August 2016)
Therapeutic Goods Administration, *Including IVD Medical Devices in the ARTG* (Version 1.1, May 2021)
Therapeutic Goods Administration, *International Engagement Strategy 2021–2025: Advancing Australia's Health through International Regulatory Engagement (2021)*
Therapeutic Goods Administration, *Medical Device Patient Cards and Leaflets: Requirements for New and On-Market Implantable Medical Devices* (October 2018)
Therapeutic Goods Administration, *Public Summary for ARTG Entry 99193* (2018)
Therapeutic Goods Administration, *Reclassification of Surgical Mesh Devices* (November 2018)
Therapeutic Goods Administration, *Scheduling Handbook: Guidance for Amending the Poisons Standard* (Guidance v 1.1, July 2019)
Therapeutic Goods Administration, Department of Health and Aged Care (Cth), *Special Access Scheme (SAS): Guidance for Health Practitioners Accessing Unapproved Therapeutic Goods* (March 2024)
Therapeutic Goods Administration, *Therapeutic Goods Administration: Annual Performance Statistics Report: July 2018 to June 2019* (Report, October 2019)
Therapeutic Goods Administration, *TGA Consumer Survey 2018* (Consumer Survey, 2018)
Therapeutic Goods Administration, *TGA Stakeholder Survey 2016* (Survey, 2016)
Therapeutic Goods Administration, *TGA Stakeholder Survey 2017* (Survey, 2017)
Therapeutic Goods Administration, *TGA Stakeholder Survey 2018* (Survey, 2018)
Therapeutic Goods Administration, *TGA Stakeholder Survey 2019* (Survey, 2020)
Therapeutic Goods Administration, *TGA Stakeholder Survey Report 2023* (Survey, September 2023).

2 Submissions and Evidence

Australian Commission on Safety and Quality in Health Care, Submission No 46 to Senate Community Affairs References Committee, Parliament of Australia, *Number of Women in Australia Who Have Had Transvaginal Mesh Implants and Related Matters*

Australian Medical Association Victoria, Submission No 38 to Victorian Law Reform Commission, *Medicinal Cannabis Issues Paper* (2015)

Australian Nursing and Midwifery Federation (Victorian Branch), Submission No 75 to Victorian Law Reform Commission, *Medicinal Cannabis Issues Paper* (4 June 2015)

Cancer Action Victoria, Submission No 54 to Victorian Law Reform Commission, *Medicinal Cannabis Issues Paper* (2015)

Cannabis Social Club Australia, Submission No 15 to the Victorian Law Reform Commission, *Medicinal Cannabis Issues Paper* (27 March 2015)

Carolyn Chisolm and the Committee on Behalf of the Australian Pelvic Mesh Support Group, Submission No 130 to Senate Community Affairs References Committee, Parliament of Australia, *Number of Women in Australia Who Have Had Transvaginal Mesh Implants and Related Matters* (17 May 2017)

Christopher Maher, Urogynaecologist, Submission No 154 to Senate Community Affairs References Committee, Parliament of Australia, *Number of Women in Australia Who Have Had Transvaginal Mesh Implants and Related Matters* (25 May 2017)

Clinical Oncology Society of Australia and Cancer Council Australia, Submission No 37 to Senate Legal and Constitutional Affairs Legislation Committee, Parliament of Australia, *Regulator of Medicinal Cannabis Bill 2014* (March 2015)

Department of Health (Cth), Submission No 19 to Senate Community Affairs References Committee, Parliament of Australia, *Number of Women in Australia Who Have Had Transvaginal Mesh Implants and Related Matters* (31 May 2017)

Evidence to Senate Community Affairs References Committee, Parliament of Australia, Canberra, 19 September 2017

Evidence to Senate Community Affairs References Committee, Parliament of Australia, Canberra, 6 February 2018

Evidence to Senate Community Affairs References Committee, Parliament of Australia, Melbourne, 3 August 2017

Evidence to Senate Community Affairs References Committee, Parliament of Australia, Perth, 25 August 2017

Evidence to Senate Standing Committee on Community Affairs Legislation, Parliament of Australia, Canberra, 23 November 1995

Evidence to Senate Standing Committee on Community Affairs, Parliament of Australia, Canberra, 15 December 2005

Evidence to Senate Standing Committee on Community Affairs, Parliament of Australia, Melbourne, 3 February 2006

Health Consumers Councils across Australia (Health Issues Centre (Vic), Health Consumers Queensland, Health Consumers' Council (WA), Health Consumers Alliance of SA, Health Care Consumers Assocation (ACT) and Health Consumers New South Wales), Submission No 21 to Senate Community Affairs References

Committee, Parliament of Australia, *Number of Women in Australia Who Have Had Transvaginal Mesh Implants and Related Matters* (31 May 2017)
Health Issues Centre (Vic), Submission No 115 to Senate Community Affairs References Committee, Parliament of Australia, *Number of Women in Australia Who Have Had Transvaginal Mesh Implants and Related Matters* (2017)
Maurice Blackburn Lawyers, Submission No 45 to Senate Community Affairs References Committee, Parliament of Australia, *Number of Women in Australia Who Have Had Transvaginal Mesh Implants and Related Matters* (29 May 2017)
Medical Technology Society of Australia, Submission No 40 to Senate Community Affairs References Committee, Parliament of Australia, *Number of Women in Australia Who Have Had Transvaginal Mesh Implants and Related Matters* (20 July 2017)
Michelle O'Dea and a Working Group of the Cannabis Community of Victoria, Submission No 95 to Victorian Law Reform Commission, *Medicinal Cannabis Issues Paper* (2015)
Penington, David, Submission No 24 to Victorian Law Reform Commission, *Medicinal Cannabis Issues Paper* (14 April 2015) 1
The Australian Lawful Use of Cannabis Alliance, Submission No 35 to Victorian Law Reform Commission, *Medicinal Cannabis Issues Paper* (18 April 2015)
The Royal Australasian College of Physicians, Submission No 52 to the Victorian Law Review [sic] Commission, *Medicinal Cannabis Issues Paper* (April 2015)
Victorian Labor, *Labor: Medical Cannabis Should Be Legal* (Victorian Labor, 2014)
Wendy Bonython and Bruce Baer Arnold, Submission No 12 to Senate Community Affairs References Committee, Parliament of Australia, *Number of Women in Australia Who Have Had Transvaginal Mesh Implants and Related Matters* (2017)

3 Parliamentary Proceedings

Commonwealth, *Parliamentary Debates,* House of Representatives, 16 February 2006
Commonwealth, *Parliamentary Debates,* House of Representatives, 10 February 2016
Commonwealth, *Parliamentary Debates*, House of Representatives, 28 April 1966
Commonwealth, *Parliamentary Debates,* House of Representatives, 29 May 1996
Commonwealth, *Parliamentary Debates*, House of Representatives, 5 October 1989
Commonwealth, *Parliamentary Debates,* Senate, 22 November 2016
Commonwealth, *Parliamentary Debates*, Senate, 6 December 2005
Commonwealth, *Parliamentary Debates,* Senate, 28 November 2005
Commonwealth, *Parliamentary Debates*, Senate, 8 May 1996
Commonwealth, *Parliamentary Debates*, Senate, 9 May 1996
Commonwealth, *Parliamentary Debates*, Senate, 15 May 2003
Commonwealth, *Parliamentary Debates*, Senate, 21 May 1996
Commonwealth, *Parliamentary Debates,* Senate, 23 June 1937
Victoria, *Parliamentary Debates*, Legislative Assembly, 8 December 2015
Victoria, *Parliamentary Debates*, Legislative Assembly, 10 December 2015
Victoria, *Parliamentary Debates*, Legislative Council, 28 September 1927

4 Media Reports, Releases and Podcasts

'Abbott Won't Approve Use of Abortion Pill', *PM* (ABC Radio, 15 November 2005) <https://www.abc.net.au/listen/programs/pm/abbott-wont-approve-use-of-abortion-pill/741434>

'EMA Ought to Approve Coronavirus Vaccine Soon, Says Poland's PM', *Reuters* (11 December 2020) https://www.reuters.com/article/eu-summit-vaccine-poland/ema-ought-to-approve-coronavirus-vaccine-soon-says-polands-pm-idINW8N2ID004/

'France to Suspend AstraZeneca COVID Vaccine Pending EMA Guidance', *Reuters* (16 March 2021) https://www.reuters.com/article/france-spain-vaccine-astrazeneca-idINL8N2LD54D/

'French PM Castex Receives AstraZeneca Shot in Bid to "Restore Public Confidence"', *France24* (19 March 2021) https://www.france24.com/en/france/20210319-french-pm-castex-to-get-astrazeneca-shot-in-bid-to-restore-public-confidence.

'Greg Hunt Says Sorry for Vaginal Mesh Damage', *ABC News* (10 October 2018)

'Implant Files', *International Consortium of Investigative Journalists* (Web Page, 2019) <https://www.icij.org/investigations/implant-files/>

'Pan Founder Wins $55m from Taxpayers', *The World Today* (ABC Local Radio, 14 August 2008) <https://www.abc.net.au/listen/programs/worldtoday/pan-founder-wins-55m-from-taxpayers/477036>

'Medical Devices Harm Patients Worldwide as Governments Fail on Safety', *International Consortium of Investigative Journalists* (25 November 2018) <https://www.icij.org/investigations/implant-files/medical-devices-harm-patients-worldwide-as-governments-fail-on-safety/>

'Medicinal Cannabis "Red-Tape" Pushing Doctors and Patients Back to Illegal Products', *Lateline* (ABC, 2017) <https://www.abc.net.au/news/2017-08-16/medicinal-cannabis-red-tape-government-doctors-black-market/8813962>

'MJA Podcasts 2019 Episode 14: Lifting Restrictions on Medical Abortion, with Prof Caroline de Costa AM', *The Medical Journal of Australia* (Cate Swannell, 1 April 2019) <https://www.mja.com.au/podcast/210/6/mja-podcasts-2019-episode-14-lifting-restrictions-medical-abortion-prof-caroline-de>

'TGA Decision Improving Access to Abortion Care for All Australians Welcomed' (Media Release, MSI Australia, 11 July 2023).

Ainsworth, Michelle, 'Labor to Seek to Overturn "Outdated" Laws Banning Medical Marijana [sic]', *The Herald Sun* (24 August 2014) <http://www.heraldsun.com.au/news/victoria-state-election-2014/labor-to-seek-to-overturn-outdated-laws-banning-medical-marijana/news-story/beed551eb3fa33278061e5e2e9edf8d5>

Allen, Lisa and Emma Connors, 'A Deadly Case of Regulation Gone Bad', *Financial Review* (2 April 2011) <https://www.afr.com/policy/health-and-education/a-deadly-case-of-regulation-gone-bad-20110402-ihyyt>

Andrews, Daniel, 'Medicinal Cannabis to Be Legalised in Victoria' (Media Release, Premier of Victoria, 6 October 2015)

Ault, Alicia, 'FDA Recommends DEA Move Cannabis From Schedule I to III' *Medscape* (19 May 2024) <https://www.medscape.com/viewarticle/fda-recommends-dea-move-cannabis-schedule-iii-2024a100010v?form=fpf>

Australian Medical Association Victoria, 'AMA Victoria's Response to the VLRC's Recommendation to Legalise Medicinal Cannabis' (Media Release, 6 October 2015)

Birnbauer, Bill, 'The Most Influential Man in Politics? Senator Brian Harradine', *The Age* (Melbourne, 16 August 1997) E1(4)

Branley, Alison and Sophie Scott, 'The Rate of Abortion in Australia Is Lower Than You Think', *ABC News* (13 December 2017) <https://www.abc.net.au/news/2017-12-13/the-rate-of-abortion-in-australia-is-lower-than-you-think/9250122>

Casben, Liv, 'Johnson & Johnson to Pay $2.6m to Women with Faulty Pelvic Mesh Implants', *ABC News* (4 March 2020) <https://www.abc.net.au/news/2020-03-03/johnson-and-johnson-damages-for-vaginal-mesh-implants/12021908≥

Clun, Rachel, 'Johnson & Johnson Lose Pelvic Mesh Case to Women in Landmark Judgment', *Sydney Morning Herald* (21 November 2019) <https://www.smh.com.au/national/johnson-and-johnson-lose-pelvic-mesh-case-to-women-in-landmark-judgment-20191121-p53coe.html>

Dart, Tom, 'Independent Committee to Investigate Sandra Bland Death and Traffic Stop', *The Guardian* (28 July 2015) <https://www.theguardian.com/us-news/2015/jul/27/sandra-bland-attorney-committee-death-traffic-stop>

Dart, Tom and Jon Swaine, 'Sandra Bland: Suspicion and Mistrust Flourish Amid Official Inconsistencies', *The Guardian* (26 July 2015) <https://www.theguardian.com/us-news/2015/jul/25/sandra-bland-suspicion-mistrust-official-inconsistencies>

Davey, Melissa, 'Medical Marijuana to Undergo Clinical Trials in Victoria', *The Guardian* (28 August 2014) <https://www.theguardian.com/society/2014/aug/28/medical-marijuana-undergo-clinical-trials-victoria>

de Costa, Caroline, 'RU486 a Safe Option for Abortion: Access Needs to Be Expanded', *Crikey* (9 May 2011) <https://www.crikey.com.au/2011/05/09/ru486-a-safe-option-for-abortion-access-needs-to-be-expanded/>

Deutsch, Jillian and Furlong, Ashleigh, 'Pressure Mounts on EU Regulator to Approve Coronavirus Vaccine – and Fast', *Politico* (12 December 2020) https://www.politico.eu/article/pressure-mounts-on-eu-regulator-to-approve-coronavirus-vaccine-quickly/;

Eban, Katherine, '"A Tsunami of Randoms": How Trump's COVID Chaos Drowned the FDA in Junk Science' *Vanity Fair* (19 January 2021) https://www.vanityfair.com/news/2021/01/how-trumps-covid-chaos-drowned-the-fda-in-junk-science

Editorial, '80,000 Deaths. 2 Million Injuries. It's Time for a Reckoning on Medical Devices', *The New York Times* (4 May 2019) <https://www.nytimes.com/2019/05/04/opinion/sunday/medical-devices.html>

Editorial, 'Time for New Drugs Debate', *Herald Sun* (25 August 2014) <http://www.heraldsun.com.au/news/opinion/time-for-new-drugs-debate/news-story/0b0c20f7dc89ffb535de5cb86db78341>

Gittleson, Ben, Faulders, Katherine and Phelps, Jordyn, 'FDA Chief Summoned to White House Amid Pressure to Authorize Vaccine Emergency Use', *ABC News* (2 December 2020) https://abcnews.go.com/Politics/fda-chief-summoned-white-house-amid-pressure-authorize/story?id=74480021

Gottlieb, Scott and McClellan, Mark, 'You Can trust the FDA's Vaccine Process', *Wall Street Journal* (online, 20 September 2020) <https://www.wsj.com/articles/you-can-trust-the-fdas-vaccine-process-11600633351>

Hamblin, Andrea, 'Parents Face Questions over Marijuana Oil Treatment for Sick Child', *Herald Sun* (18 August 2014) <http://www.heraldsun.com.au/news/victoria/parents-face-questions-over-marijuana-oil-treatment-for-sick-child/news-story/815a8dc2a3075a0885eee16017980648>

Hooton, Amanda and Joanne McCarthy, 'The Nightmare Within', *The Age: Good Weekend Magazine* (Melbourne, 16 June 2019) 19

Houck, Larry K, 'DEA Concurs: Marijuana Meets Schedule III Criteria', *FDA Law Blog* (6 May 2024) <https://www.thefdalawblog.com/2024/05/dea-concurs-marijuana-meets-schedule-iii-criteria/?utm_source=rss&utm_medium=rss&utm_campaign=dea-concurs-marijuana-meets-schedule-iii-criteria>

Hunt, Greg, 'Boosting Australia's Medicinal Cannabis Industry' (Media Release, 2 August 2019) <https://www.health.gov.au/ministers/the-hon-greg-hunt-mp/media/boosting-australias-medicinal-cannabis-industry>

Hunt, Greg, '$2.3 Million to Improve Safety of Pelvic Floor Surgery' (Media Release, 5 April 2019) <https://www.health.gov.au/ministers/the-hon-greg-hunt-mp/media/23-million-to-improve-safety-of-pelvic-floor-surgery>

Keane, Bernard, 'The Lethal Legacy of Brian Harradine: His Long War on Women's Rights', *Crikey* (24 April 2014) <https://www.crikey.com.au/2014/04/24/the-lethal-legacy-of-brian-harradine-his-long-war-on-womens-rights/>

Knaus, Christopher, 'Australian Women Win Landmark Vaginal Mesh Class Action Against Johnson & Johnson', *The Guardian* (21 November 2019) <https://www.theguardian.com/australia-news/2019/nov/21/australian-women-win-landmark-vaginal-mesh-class-action-against-johnson-johnson>

Knott, Matthew, 'Medical Cannabis Closer to Federal Approval', *Sydney Morning Herald* (29 September 2014) <https://www.smh.com.au/politics/federal/medical-cannabis-closer-to-federal-approval-20140928-10n5rd.html>

Landis-Hanley, Justine, 'Doctors Crippled by Religious Backlash', *The Saturday Paper* (29 February – 6 March 2020) <https://www.thesaturdaypaper.com.au/news/health/2020/02/29/doctors-crippled-religious-backlash/15828948009443>

Ley, Sussan, 'Turnbull Govt Delivers Medicinal Cannabis "Missing Piece"' (Media Release, 17 October 2015) <https://perma.cc/7E5D-2EHD>

Ley, Sussan, 'Medicinal Cannabis to Be Cultivated through Single National Scheme' (Media Release, 2 December 2015) < http://sussanley.com/medicinal-cannabis-to-be-cultivated-through-single-national-scheme/>

Long, Claudia, 'Changes To Abortion Regulation Will Come into Effect Next Month in a Bid to Increase Access', *ABC News* (11 July 2023) <https://www.abc.net.au/news/2023-07-11/changes-to-abortion-regulation-in-a-bid-to-increase-access/102584108>

Mallinson, Daniel J and Lee Hannah, 'Marijuana Expands into 3 More States, but Nationwide Legalization Still Unlikely', *The Conversation* (Web Page, 8 November 2018) <https://theconversation.com/marijuana-expands-into-3-more-states-but-nationwide-legalization-still-unlikely-106512>

Marr, David, 'Balancing Acts: How Senator Brian Harradine Straddles Heaven and Earth', *Sydney Morning Herald* (Sydney, 1 February 1997).

Maslen, Kylie, 'I Had One Too: An Online Storytelling Platform Taking the Stigma out of Abortion', *The Adelaide Review* (8 May 2019)

McArthur, Grant, 'The Trip of a Lifetime: Push to Allow Psychedelic Drugs for Medical Use', *Herald Sun* (Melbourne, 14 February 2019) 8

McArthur, Grant and Andrea Hamblin, 'Medical Benefits of Cannabis Must Be Examined, Say Health Experts', *Herald Sun* (25 August 2014) <http://www.heraldsun.com.au/news/victoria/medical-benefits-of-cannabis-must-be-examined-say-health-experts/news-story/a964357a77331b9adfd425578d34c1ab>

McCarthy, Joanne, 'America Has Banned a Group of Problem Pelvic Mesh Devices with Origins in Australia in the 1980s', *The Newcastle Herald* (26 April 2019) <https://www.theherald.com.au/story/6086959/pelvic-mesh-era-ends-as-the-us-bans-devices-18-years-after-fda-approved-them/>

McCarthy, Joanne, 'Australian Medical Association President Confirms AMA Role in Pelvic Mesh Scandal', *The Newcastle Herald* (22 August 2017) <https://www.theherald.com.au/story/4872857/ama-says-pelvic-mesh-support-not-our-proudest-hour/?cs=2452>

McCarthy, Joanne, 'Dr Peter Petros Assured a Colleague He Could "Mollify" Investigators Looking for Answers', *The Newcastle Herald* (2 April 2019) <https://www.theherald.com.au/story/5986291/mesh-doctors-drip-feed-of-misinformation/>

McCarthy, Joanne, 'Pelvic Mesh a Global Medical Scandal with Origins Close to Home', *The Newcastle Herald* (3 August 2017) <https://www.newcastleherald.com.au/story/4493496/scandals-australian-backstory/#slide=1>

McCormack, Ange, 'Should Amyl be Banned? The TGA Wants You to Have Your Say', *Triple J Hack* (Web Page, 17 September 2018) <https://www.abc.net.au/triplej/programs/hack/should-amyl-be-banned/10256338>

McIllroy, Tom, 'Role of Drug Watchdog Questioned', *Financial Review* (Sydney, 31 October 2019) 12

Montgomery, David, 'The Death of Sandra Bland: Is There Anything Left to Investigate?' *The New York Times* (8 May 2019) <https://www.nytimes.com/2019/05/08/us/sandra-bland-texas-death.html?auth=login-google>

Pezenik, Sasha and Thomas, Elizabeth, 'Trump, FDA Tout Covid-19 Convalescent Plasma Treatment, But Some Experts Express Concerns', *ABC News* (24 August 2020) https://abcnews.go.com/Health/fda-issue-emergency-authorization-convalescent-plasma-treatment-hospitalized/story?id=72556828.

Nguyen, Han, 'Site of Former Federal Government IT Provider up for Auction', *The Canberra Times* (2 March 2018) <https://www.canberratimes.com.au/story/6022269/site-of-former-federal-government-it-provider-up-for-auction/>

Scott, Sophie and Alison Branley, 'Mesh Implants: Government Issues National Apology Over "Agony and Pain" Caused by Device', *ABC News* (10 October 2018) <https://www.abc.net.au/news/2018-10-10/mesh-implants-government-issues-apology-to-women/10355546>

Smethurst, Annika, 'Desperate Parents Turn to Medical Marijuana in Last-Ditch Effort to Improve Their Children's Lives', *Herald Sun* (12 January 2014) <http://www.heraldsun.com.au/news/victoria/desperate-parents-turn-to-medical-marijuana-in-lastditch-effort-to-improve-their-childrens-lives/news-story/11d70cfbec24e37668d8dd53378d33eb>

Snape, Jack, 'Pfizer COVID-19 Vaccine Approved for Use by TGA in Australia Ahead of Rollout', *ABC News* (online, 25 January 2021) <https://www.abc.net.au/news/2021-01-25/pfizer-covid-19-vaccine-approved-australia-tga/13087990>

Staff Writers, 'The TGA Has Decided Not to Ban Poppers', *Star Observer* (7 June 2019) <https://www.starobserver.com.au/news/national-news/the-tga-has-decided-not-to-ban-poppers/183671>

Swan, Jonathan, 'Scoop: FDA Chief Called to West Wing', *Axios* (30 November 2020) https://www.axios.com/2020/12/01/fda-chief-called-to-west-wing.mode_comment

Sweet, Melissa, 'New Report: A Damning Indictment of Health System's Failure to Care for Women', *Croakey* (5 April 2018) <https://croakey.org/new-report-a-damning-indictment-of-health-systems-failure-to-care-for-women/>

Valentish, Jenny, 'Opening Minds', *The Saturday Paper* (Melbourne, 23 February–1 March 2019) 8

van Leeuwen, Hans, '"No Corners Have Been Cut" in Pfizer Approval: UK Vaccine Body', *Financial Review* (3 December 2020) https://www.afr.com/world/europe/no-corners-have-been-cut-uk-vaccine-body-reassures-on-pfizer-jab-20201202-p56k2q

'WHO-ICMRA Joint Statement on the Need for Improved Global Regulatory Alignment on COVID-19 Medicines and Vaccines', *ICMRA* (Web Page, 6 November 2020) <https://icmra.info/drupal/covid-19/who_icmra_statement>.

World Health Organization, 'WHO Launches New Initiative to Improve Pandemic Preparedness' (News Release, 26 April 2023) <https://www.who.int/news/item/26-04-2023-who-launches-new-initiative-to-improve-pandemic-preparedness>

Women's Liberation Centre, 'Abortion' (1974) 7 *Vashti's Voice: A Women's Liberation Newspaper* 5

Yun, Jessica, Adhikari, Supratim and Sakkal, Paul, 'Push for "Gold Standard PCR" Leaves Gaping Hole in Rapid Test Supply', *The Sydney Morning Herald* (online, 31 December 2021) <https://www.smh.com.au/business/consumer-affairs/gold-standard-pcr-push-leaves-a-gaping-hole-in-rapid-test-supply-20211229-p59knx.html>

5 Web Sites

'About', *International Consortium of Investigative Journalists* (Web Page, 2020) <https://www.icij.org/about/>

'About the Code', *Medical Technology Association of Australia* (Web Page, 2020) <https://www.mtaa.org.au/about-the-code>

'About Us', *MS Health* (Web Page, 2019) <http://www.mshealth.com.au/about-us>

'About Us', *United in Compassion* (Web Page, 2019) <https://unitedincompassion.com.au/about-uic/>

'History of ICMRA', *ICMRA* (Web Page, 2024) <https://www.icmra.info/drupal/aboutus/history>

History', *ICH* (Web Page) <https://www.ich.org/page/history>

ICMRA, *International Coalition of Medicines Regulatory Authorities: Terms of Reference and Rules of Procedure* (15 November 2023) <https://www.icmra.info/drupal/sites/default/files/2024-01/icmra_terms_of_reference_15november2023.pdf>

'ICMRA Membership Country/Region and Regulatory Authority's Website', ICMRA (Web Page, 2024) <https://www.icmra.info/drupal/en/aboutus/participatingregulatoryauthorities>

'MS-2 Step: User Registration', *MS2Step: Mifepristone, Misoprostol* (Web Page, July 2018) <https://www.ms2step.com.au/register/>

'Introduction', *PIC/S* (Web Page) <https://picscheme.org/en/about>

'Process of Harmonisation', *ICH* (Web Page) <https://www.ich.org/page/process-harmonisation>.

'State Medical Marijuana Laws', *National Conference of State Legislatures* (Web Page, 10 March 2020) <https://www.ncsl.org/research/health/state-medical-marijuana-laws.aspx>

'Unfinished Business: A National Forum on the Impact of Mesh Implants, *Health Consumers Queensland* (Web Page, 2019) <https://www.hcq.org.au/unfinished-business-a-national-forum-on-the-impact-of-mesh-implants/>.

Australian Pelvic Mesh Support Group (Web Page) <https://www.facebook.com/groups/AustralianPelvicMeshSupportGroup/>

Bloom (Web Page, 2019) <https://thebloombrands.com/>

Oil & Gold Los Angeles: The American Dream (Web Page) <http://oilandgold.la/>

Scottish Mesh Survivors: Hear Our Voice (Web Page) <http://www.scottishmeshsurvivors.com/news-media.html>

Sling the Mesh: Raising Awareness of the Life Changing Risks of a 'Simple' Day Case Operation (Web Page) <https://slingthemesh.co.uk/>

'Welcome to the ICH Official Website', *ICH* (Web Page) <https://www.ich.org/>

6 Miscellaneous

Brophy, Catherine Elizabeth, 'The Integration of Complementary and Alternative Medicine into Health Care: Regulating for Consumer Choice, Autonomy and Responsibility' (PhD, The University of Melbourne, 2007)

Chapkis, Wendy, 'Legalization and Medicalization in the Marijuana Reform Movement' (Conference Paper, American Sociological Association Annual Meeting, 2013)

Consumers Health Forum of Australia, *Consumer Guide to Reforms* (12 June 2018)

Featherstone, Lisa, '"The Value of the Victorian Infant": Whiteness and the Emergence of Paediatrics in Late Colonial Australia' (Conference Paper, Historicising Whiteness: Transnational Perspectives on the Construction of an Identity Conference, University of Melbourne, 22–24 November 2006)

Jiggens, John Lawrence, 'Marijuana Australiana: Cannabis Use, Popular Culture, and the Americanisation of Drugs Policy in Australia, 1938–1988' (PhD Thesis, Queensland University of Technology, 2004)

Matthews, Margaret, 'Safe and Subversive: Medication Abortion's Potential to Reshape Patterns of Access and Power' (BA Thesis, Vassar College, 2020)

Sibley, Miles, 'Evidence-Based Practice – A Double Standard?' *The BMJ Opinion* (Blog Post, 24 April 2019) <https://blogs.bmj.com/bmj/2019/04/24/miles-sibley-evidence-based-practice-a-double-standard/>

'UN Commission on Narcotic Drugs Reclassifies Cannabis to Recognize its Therapeutic Uses', *World Health Organization* (Web Page, 4 December 2020)

<https://www.who.int/news/item/04-12-2020-un-commission-on-narcotic-drugs-reclassifies-cannabis-to-recognize-its-therapeutic-uses>

'WHO Endorses Decisions of Expert Committee on Cannabis and Other Substances', *World Health Organization* (Web Page, 2019) <https://www.who.int/medicines/news/2019/ecdd-endorses-decisions-ECDD_cannabis-other-substance/en/>

World Health Organization, *Clinical Practice Handbook for Safe Abortion* (2014)

World Health Organization, *Safe Abortion: Technical and Policy Guidance for Health Systems* (2nd ed, 2012)

Index

Kolibri 360 GmbH
Ferdinand-Jühlke-Straße 7
99095 Erfurt, Deutschland
produktsicherheit@kolibri360.de